A Thread of Years

Books by John Lukacs

THE GREAT POWERS AND EASTERN EUROPE

TOCQUEVILLE: THE EUROPEAN REVOLUTION AND CORRESPONDENCE
WITH GOBINEAU (editor)

A HISTORY OF THE COLD WAR

DECLINE AND RISE OF EUROPE

A NEW HISTORY OF THE COLD WAR

HISTORICAL CONSCIOUSNESS

THE PASSING OF THE MODERN AGE

THE LAST EUROPEAN WAR, 1939–1941

1945: YEAR ZERO

PHILADELPHIA: PATRICIANS AND PHILISTINES, 1900–1950

OUTGROWING DEMOCRACY: A HISTORY OF THE UNITED STATES IN
THE TWENTIETH CENTURY

BUDAPEST 1900: A HISTORICAL PORTRAIT OF A CITY AND ITS
CULTURE

CONFESSIONS OF AN ORIGINAL SINNER

THE DUEL: 10 MAY–31 JULY; THE EIGHTY-DAY STRUGGLE BETWEEN
CHURCHILL AND HITLER

THE END OF THE TWENTIETH CENTURY AND THE END OF THE
MODERN AGE

DESTINATIONS PAST

GEORGE F. KENNAN AND THE ORIGINS OF CONTAINMENT,
1944–1946: THE KENNAN-LUKACS CORRESPONDENCE

THE HITLER OF HISTORY

JOHN LUKACS

A Thread of Years

YALE UNIVERSITY PRESS

NEW HAVEN AND LONDON

Published with assistance from the foundation established in memory of Amasa Stone Mather of the Class of 1907, Yale College.

Designed by James J. Johnson and set in Fournier type by Tseng Information Systems, Durham, North Carolina.

Printed in the United States of America by Vail-Ballou Press, Binghamton, New York.

Library of Congress Cataloging-in-Publication Data

Lukacs, John, 1924–

A thread of years / John Lukacs.

p.   cm.

ISBN 0-300-07188-4 (cloth : alk. paper)

ISBN 0-300-08075-1 (pbk. : alk. paper)

1. History, Modern — 20th century.   I. Title.

D421.L87   1998

909.82 — dc21   97-25045

A catalogue record for this book is available from the British Library.

The paper in this book meets the guidelines for permanence and durability of the Committee on Production Guidelines for Book Longevity of the Council on Library Resources.

10   9   8   7   6   5   4   3   2

To Richard
Amicus fidelis familiæque

Life, like a dome of many-coloured glass,
Stains the white radiance of Eternity.

—SHELLEY

Contents

Introduction   I

Years (1901–1914)   13

   The Ribbon   127

Years (1915–1945)   131

   The Ribbon   325

Years (1946–1969)   330

   The Ribbon   478

Introduction

There is in our historical consciousness an element of great importance
that is best defined by the term historical sensation. One might also call
it historical contact. . . . This contact with the past, a contact which it is
impossible to determine or analyze completely, is like going into another
sphere; it is one of the many ways given to man to reach beyond himself,
to experience truth. . . . If it takes any form at all this remains composite
and vague; a sense of streets, houses, fields as well as sounds, colors or
people moving. . . . There is in this manner of contact with the past the
absolute conviction of reality and truth. . . . The historic sensation is not
the sensation of living the past again but of understanding the world,
perhaps as one does with listening to music. — JOHAN HUIZINGA

I WAS ADVISED TO WRITE an Introduction to this book. For most books
an introduction is not needed, since a book ought to speak for itself.
For this book it is, because of the unusual nature of its form and of its
content.

The contents of this book are suggested by its title: *A Thread of
Years*. It has sixty-nine chapters of a few pages each. Each bears the
title of a calendar year: "1901," "1902," "1903," and so on.

The short chapters consist of two parts. The first part is a description of a particular place and of particular people — their behavior, their
expressions, and the inclinations of their minds at a particular time.
Allow me to call these vignettes. Examples of these vignettes: two men
in Philadelphia in 1901, a foreign visitor in London in 1903, an Englishman in New York in 1907, an American and his wife in Paris in 1911.

The second part of each short chapter is a dialogue. Then and
there a second person challenges the significance of the vignette written by the author, his friend, since that significance is debatable. Why

these people? Why *this* place? Why *that* particular scene? For not only do these places differ, none of the people therein are the same.

That is one peculiarity of this book. Of course the chapters of every book are different, but besides being in sequence, they must cohere because of the story of the book. And *A Thread of Years* does not have a story. But it has a theme.

That theme is the decline of a particular civilization, and the decline of the ideal of the gentleman; two inseparable matters. In 1901 the British and the American empires were the greatest powers in the world. On the map of the globe the British Empire was greatest; but the center of gravity had already shifted across the Atlantic, and was moving westward. The threat to the Atlantic predominance was represented by Germany, with the result of two world wars. All of this is well known. Less well known are the inevitable, and often intangible, relations of power and prestige. The power of the Anglo-American world in 1901 was inseparable from the worldwide prestige of the originally English ideal of the gentleman. That ideal, transformed and qualified by specifically American conditions and ideas, existed in the United States, too, incarnated and represented by a minority of people whose influence still exceeded their numbers. For many reasons: because of some of the inadequacies latent within the ideal itself; because of the shortcomings of many of those who thought, or pretended, to represent it; and finally because of their waning self-confidence — the ideal faded. That this belongs within the history of this century may be the theme of this book.

There is K., a Philadelphian gentleman and a painter with whose birth this book begins and with whose death it also ends. But he is only a pseudo-protagonist in it. Hardly more than one out of every four vignettes describes episodes in his life; moreover, there are no descriptions of his childhood and only one of his adolescence. Still my readers may ask: why have I not simply endeavored to write the life of a latecoming Philadelphian George Apley? (The life and death of the Bostonian gentleman George Apley was the subject of one of John P. Marquand's novels.) The answer is that I am not a novelist but a historian. One ought to do what one does best, and one ought to write about things one knows best. It is thus that about two-fifths of the vignettes deal with Philadelphia and Philadelphians, while other vignettes describe other places and other people in America and in Europe, including a few of my native country and native people. Hence the absence of an immediately apparent coherence. For the main subject of this book is not K. It is *years.*

History has now entered the democratic age, which simply means (the meaning is simple, but its reconstruction is complicated) that the historian must deal with all kinds of people, and with all kinds of events. The first edition of the *Dictionary of the French Academy,* published in 1694, defined history as "the narration of actions and of matters worth remembering." The eighth edition, in 1935, said much the same: "the account of acts, of events, of matters worth remembering." *Dignes de mémoire!* Worth remembering! What nonsense this is! Is the historian the kind of person whose training qualifies him to tell ordinary people what is worth remembering, to label or authenticate persons or events as if they were fossil fish or pieces of rock? Is there such a thing as a person and another such thing as a historical person? Every event is a historical event; every source is a historical source; every person is a historical person. This book does not deal with the Roosevelts, Churchill, Stalin, and so on. They do not figure in it — when they are mentioned at all, it is only in passing, here or there. Its "1917" does not deal with the American declaration of war on Germany — at least not directly. None of its scenes has drumfire in it. They do not consist of great dramatic events. They are period pictures: vignettes. But the underlying theme exists, alluded to here and there: the *petite musique* of a *grande histoire,* the decline of a civilization (civilization, not culture).

This book is not a novel. A novel has a plot, and even a plotless novel (there are such things now) has to have a central character — which is largely missing here, except that K. (and later his wife) reappear in some chapters (only once in the first twenty, though seven times in the last twenty chapters, since a denouement this book does have). The thread of its plot—if plot it is—is thin, and it emerges only as it proceeds toward its end. However, there is "The Ribbon," which the reader will find after the years 1914, 1945, and 1969: a ribbon, within which this thread may fit.

Here enters something that has exercised my mind for a long time, during a now long and wearisome but not entirely unhappy life as a historian. Very early (I was a history student then), I was inspired by the recognition of the inevitable overlapping of history and literature, that not only what a Balzac but what a Jane Austen described—indeed, what they dealt with—belong not only to the history of literature but to the veritable history of a period: that is, of a place and a time. Bath in 1816 differed from Bath in 1803 (Austen felt compelled to state that in her introduction to *Northanger Abbey*), New York in 1920 from New York in 1915, and these are matters for a historian to think about and to research and to describe. Of course we must keep in mind how dramatic changes may obscure the essential human condition, through which continuation exists together with change. I do not mean political conditions but the human atmosphere: the mental, rather than the external, climate of how certain people were inclined, how and what they were wanting and thinking and perhaps believing.

History and the novel have certain things in common. These go well beyond what ought to be obvious: that the fine eye of a novelist may discern much that remains elusive to the research of an academic historian; that "history begins in novel and ends in essay" (Macaulay); or that the aim of the realistic novelist "is not to tell a story; to amuse us or to appeal to our feelings, but to compel us to reflect, and to understand the darker and deeper meaning of events" (Maupassant). A historian could have written that.

There is another common ground. It is fundamental. The instrument of the novelist and of the historian is the same. It is our common, everyday language. History, unlike the sciences, has no language, indeed, no vocabulary of its own. The novelist knows and the historian knows (or at least ought to know) that no "fact" has any meaning apart from our association of it with other facts and—this is important—

from the statement of a fact. History consists of words, because we think, speak, teach, and write with words. Thus Flaubert's celebrated *mot juste* must be a standard not only for the novelist but also for the historian who ought to know (*juste*) that the choice of every word is not only a stylistic but a moral choice. (Whence statements can be made in which the "fact" is precise and yet its suggestion or portent or meaning is false.)

In one sense the task of the novelist is easier. He can invent people and events, which the historian cannot. (I wrote once that therefore it is easier to write a mediocre novel than a mediocre history, while it is probably more difficult to write a great history than a great novel.) And yet there is one more thing in common between the two. It is their necessary recognition of potentiality, together with actuality: of what happened with what could have happened — to certain people, in certain places, at a certain time. Historicity is what makes a novel plausible, and that plausibility *must* be apparent. This is why not only *Old Goriot* or *The Scarlet Letter* but *The Great Gatsby* are essentially historical novels. (Yes: Gatsby & Co. did not exist. But readers of that novel must know that there *were* people and manners and places like that *at that particular time* in American history. The quality of that plausibility is what matters — the understanding that not only Gatsby but what happened to him *could* have happened, *then*.) And the same condition of actuality-cum-potentiality is true of history, too. (And of what Heisenberg discovered of our observations of subatomic matter.) As the great Dutch historian Huizinga wrote: "The historian . . . must always maintain toward his subject an indeterminist point of view. He must constantly put himself at a point in the past at which the known factors still seem to permit different outcomes. If he speaks of Salamis, then it must be as if the Persians might still win."

In the broad sense every novel is a historical novel; and the emergence of the modern novel was part and parcel of the emergence of our modern historical consciousness. This is not the place to argue or even to illustrate this further. But I must say something about the appearance of *the* historical novel, as we are wont to call it, which arose first in the early nineteenth century and which was also inseparable from a then developing historical consciousness. From Walter Scott to Tolstoy and others it occurred that a historical background may make a novel more interesting and perhaps even more telling. Yet that genre of the historical novel belonged largely to the nineteenth century; it is outdated now.

What has happened during the twentieth century is something else. This has been the (not always conscious) recognition that history is more than the recorded past. An appetite for history has spread to people and to mental terrains hitherto untouched, including literature, in many legitimate and also illegitimate forms. One of its marginal evidences is obvious from publishing statistics alone: the decline of the readership of novels, and the increase of readers' interests in all kinds of biographies and autobiographies and histories, including popular and sensationalist ones. What has come about — all contrary conditions and superficial appearances notwithstanding — is an unprecedentedly wide appetite for seeing and reading about things of the past: a mental appetite that is, alas, often fed by many kinds of junk food.

One manifestation of this — one particularly relevant to this Introduction — is not only the so-called documentary or docudrama but the new hybrid thing that has the silly name *faction*. All kinds of writers have been trying this (Upton Sinclair, Dos Passos, Irwin Shaw, Styron, Doctorow, Mailer, Sontag, De Lillo, Vidal, Pynchon in this country, many others abroad, including Solzhenitsyn in *1914*, which is his least valuable book). What is significant is that these novelists are all interested in history. What they have been doing is the reverse of the historical novel, where history was the colorful background. For these twentieth-century novelists history is the foreground, since it attracts them. The appearance of these novelized histories is interesting, because it is a symptom of the continuing evolution of a historical consciousness. But most of these authors don't really know that, which is why their works are flawed: for they illegitimately and sometimes dishonestly mix up history and fiction. So they include and twist and deform and attribute thoughts and words and acts to historical figures —

Lincoln, Wilson, Roosevelt, Kennedy—who actually existed. That is illegitimate, since it produces untruths—no matter that some academic historians may say it serves salutary purposes, as it introduces all kinds of people to history, after all. They are wrong. What they ought to recognize, rather, is the untrammeled spreading of a historical consciousness whereby it is indeed possible that in the future the novel may be entirely absorbed by history, rather than the contrary. But let us not speculate about this further.

In this book I am trying to do something quite different. The very opposite of what these writers have been doing: instead of attributing words, thoughts, and acts to great persons who did exist, I am writing about everyday people whose plausibility exists only because of the historical reality of their places and times. This book may be an attempt at a new genre. Do not take this too seriously. My attempt is imperfect, and I have no interest in inventing new and startling forms. At the end of this century (and indeed of the so-called Modern Age) I am dubious about anything and about anyone who claims to be avant-garde; and as for an Idea Whose Time Has Come (Victor Hugo's hoary nineteenth-century phrase), well, it is almost certain not to be any good. Meanwhile, historical writing still has a long way to go. Max Beerbohm said about the 1880s, "to give an accurate and exhaustive account of that period would need a far less brilliant pen than mine." That was funny and even telling, but in the long run Beerbohm was wrong. History has not yet had its Dante or its Shakespeare. That will come one day, and this book is not that. For, if it is not a novel, it is not history either. In this book I invent people (though not places and times)—yes, I hope plausible and telling types, but who did not actually exist. That is not history. But my purpose—unlike that of most of the above-mentioned writers—is not literary and not political; it is historical. The pictures, the vignettes, of this book are meant to attract the reader's interest to certain people in certain places and in certain times: *couleurs locales* that ought to be good enough to linger in the mind.

If there is beauty in some of these scenes, it is meant to evoke an iridescent mix of sadness and pleasantness in the minds of readers. Yes, *A Thread of Years* is about the sad decline of a civilization, but the colors are not heavy bitumen colors, and the music is not Mahler, while there are a few remnant memories of beautiful things and of decency and goodness. (My original title for this book was *Remnants.*) But the purpose of each vignette is also a sentimental (and historical) education, because inherent in each of these vignettes, *petites histoires,* are reflections of the larger tides of history. And this connection, or meaning, is *debatable,* in the literal sense of that word — hence the ensuing dialogue, a conversation and sometimes a debate with my alter ego, which is meant to explain or, more precisely, justify the vignette.

The question thus arises (as one of my potential publishers posed it): why not restrict this book to the vignettes? My answer is, again, simple: I am a historian, not a novelist. I am more interested in the historicity than in a literary portraiture of a place or of a person, even of my pseudo-protagonist. And it is the suggestion of that historicity that is a subject of debate and that I wish to point out further, together with other related matters, sometimes light, sometimes more profound, through a breezy conversation with myself. For in these discussions, in the second part of each annualized chapterette, I challenge myself. *Myself:* because my interlocutor is my alter ego. He is not an imaginary person; he is not a composite or a confection of someone else. He is more commonsensical, more pragmatic, more direct, more down-to-earth than is the narrator of the vignette, and we argue, add, subtract, agree, disagree.

When the idea (or, rather, the plan) of such a construction first occurred to me I cannot tell. It may be that while the author of my vignettes and their occasional defendant is my European self, my challenger and debater is my American one. "It may be"; perhaps not. But it is no use to discuss this further. This book is not about me, and I am not writing about myself.

Allow me to end this Introduction by expressing what is obvious: that everything that is human is history, including history and, in this case, including this book. Its original title was *Remnants,* not *A Thread of Years;* instead of going on from 1901 to 1991, I chose to end it with 1969; and I changed its original Introduction also. That, too, I wrote in the form of a dialogue. I discarded that version, for more than one practical reason; but I am keeping its end, which read as follows.

"Good luck. Are you on to something that seems to have intrigued you through most of your life? An attempt at a new genre. That's not easy. God only knows why you're doing it. There are so many other books that you can, or ought to do. Well, I guess that whatever I say, you will do it — because, as Bernanos once said, 'le bonheur, c'est un risque.' "

Yes, happiness is a risk (and happiness is a task).

"Well, if you succeed, you will have *done* it."

And if I don't succeed, it will be just another of my books.

"Now you sound like your old friend Owen Barfield, who wrote about one of his friends that he writes, not for a living, not for reputation, but because he can't help it."

Not quite — but I can't help writing *this.*

1992–1996

A Thread of Years

1901

TWO MEN SIT AT THE LARGE WINDOWS of the Philadelphia Club on a Friday evening. The windows are open, it is early September, warm enough for that. The noise of Walnut Street has died down, because Philadelphia is not a crowded city with iron clangor. The men are second cousins, around forty, resembling each other not very much, one taller and leaner, less rubicund than the other, who has just returned from California. The latter has made an important decision. He will move to Pasadena. He is explaining his reasons. They include more than the legendary California weather. He and his wife — as much as himself, he insists, if not more — have sized up the civilities and people in Pasadena: urbane people, most of them Easterners, many of them Bostonians. (That is always a recommendation among proper Philadelphians, who have a sense of respect, because of a sense of intellectual inferiority, for the proper people of Boston.) He talks about some of those men and women, including a few recognizable family names; he speaks of the schools, the club, the theater, and the house they are about to have built, the gardening, the California flowers, the salubrious omnipresence of outdoor life year-round. Of course Pasadena is not Philadelphia, but that "not" carries at least a prospect of "not yet." Already a civilization is developing there that will encompass and typify what is best in America. It amounts to more than a floriferous setting and a healthy climate; it is also a good place for the children to grow up, who will of course go on to their boarding schools and then colleges back in the East, no more than five days away from their parents by train. Yes, California is the West, with all of its pluses and with fewer and fewer of its minuses: civilization there is overcoming the pioneer roughness every day, sometimes incredibly fast, and the evidences of that evolution are all around.

It is a big move for a Philadelphian to leave and go to live in California, from a place where people move less than in any comparable city in the United States, where the web of family connections is as comforting as it is constricting, where respectability is the primary ideal, and not only in public. Queen Victoria has died in January 1901, but Philadelphia is still quite Victorian (all right: Victorian-American). It is not fin de siècle, not belle époque, and will not ever be Edwardian—because in Philadelphia the cult of respectability is inseparable from the cult of safety. That is, at least in part, the Quaker inheritance: the desire for safety, sometimes so rigid as to be uncomfortable. It is thus that his cousin and friend is not going to try to dissuade him, or even to ask more questions than are needed to stitch their conversation along. One of the reasons for this is the Philadelphian custom of refraining from discussing (and, more than often, from thinking about) unpleasant things. That is a habit that sometimes leads to regrettable consequences, when the excessive wish to keep safe is oddly, or perhaps not so oddly, allied to the reluctance to exercise more than customary foresight. But within this habit there resides, too, a modicum of the ingrained respect for privacy; and one of the reasons for his reticence comes from that. He is aware of a certain restiveness in his cousin's temperament, evident in his cousin's few known escapades, usually short-lived to the extent of harmlessness. He, unlike his cousin, is hardly given to enthusiasms— partly out of character, partly out of temperament. His cousin is a Progressive, of sorts; he is not. He has just returned from his summer place in Maine, from Northeast Harbor (Philadelphia on the Rocks, in the epithet to come in the late twenties), that Philadelphian appendage in the cool, rockbound, pale-blue-eyed North (call it Down East, if you wish), with its large and often ungainly gray cedar-shingled houses, where the sharp tinge of the outdoors is complemented by the knowledge of comfort indoors, large brick fireplaces puffing woodsmoke through big chimneys in midsummer, reminiscent of the smell wafting above the gardens of Philadelphia suburbs in the autumn: a comforting sense, as is the knowledge that Philadelphia is but one night away on the Bar Harbor Special of the Pennsylvania Railroad. Yes, for him there is something neither quite safe nor quite respectable about living in California; and his cousin's phrases about the blossoming of civilization in Pasadena do not greatly impress him. He is American enough to believe that life consists of change, but he is also Philadelphian enough to believe not only that change must be tempered by continuity but that change is a kind of continuity in itself—which is why both of them are unable to question the theory of Evolution that they somehow equate with Progress.

There is, however, a difference in their beliefs. One of them is inclined to think (an inclination to think may not be tantamount to a belief, even though it is sometimes more important than a belief) that America is growing ever more able to represent what is best of the civilization of the white race, of England, and of much of Western Europe—and that thus Philadelphia is somewhere in the middle between England and California, and that is how it has been, is, and should be. His cousin believes that the course not only of empire but of all civilization is inevitably westward and without cease; that what is still good in the American East is spreading to the West; and that because of the richness of this country he can partake in that movement with no loss, indeed, with physical and mental profit to himself and to his family. He believes that the future of America may be California, and sooner rather than later. His cousin believes that as America goes so will the world, even though that may not yet be around the corner.

What they talk about are doctors, lawyers, banks, insurance, schools, relatives, railroads, in the Philadelphian manner, restricting the scope of their conversation to what is practical since, again in the Philadelphian manner, what is practical is not only real but safe. They do not know that they are talking about more than that. About the future of America. Of the century. Of the world.

The twentieth century has begun. They espy no trouble in that. Both of them see a world in which the most important portion is being governed by the Anglo-Saxon, the seafaring, the Teutonic, the industrial and industrious races. That seems certain. Like Progress.

I'd like to imagine that their conversation occurs on Friday, September 6, 1901, on the afternoon of the day when President McKinley was shot in Buffalo. The news has not reached the Philadelphia Club. They do not know it yet. Nor do they know that a week later (on Friday the thirteenth) McKinley will be dead, and Theodore Roosevelt will be the president of the United States.

Now you must know that I will return to one of these people — to the California-bound one, in, say, 1912 or 1913.

"When you will, I presume, describe what is happening to his Arcadian illusions out there."

Not Arcadian but Progressive; and ideas even more than illusions.

"All right, except that the idealization of the American West was both Arcadian and Progressive."

And few people, if any, saw the inherent contradiction between these two things. This includes Teddy Roosevelt, who once said to Charles Fletcher Lummis: "I owe everything to the West! It made me! I found it there!" And in 1911 or 1912 he spoke to Lummis again: "California has come mighty close to my governmental ideals." This Lummis, who had been at Harvard at the time of Roosevelt, was a big promoter of Pasadena, a big booster of California, a patron of arts and crafts, a Health and Culture enthusiast, an interminable spokesman for Arcadian Progressivism. He also said that "the ignorant, hopelessly un-American type of foreigner which infests and largely controls Eastern cities is almost unknown here." "Here" was Los Angeles. He was a pompous, insufferable fool, which Roosevelt was not, but both of them were wrong about what would become of California.

"You're telegraphing your punch. What will become of California, what will become of Philadelphia, what will become of America, what will become of civilization. Your Big Questions. But I don't know whether it is sufficiently telling to hang the *Auftakt* of this theme on these two buttoned-up Philadelphia gents, even though they are your friend's relatives, and even though one of them seems to be ready, if not altogether itching, to loosen his high collar. Besides, you have done a little cheating here, using the device of this conversation between two men in the Philadelphia Club. There *was* such a conversation, right there, a small turning point in the history of American literature, and I think you know what I mean."

You mean Owen Wister talking to Walter Furness in September or October 1891 at the Philadelphia Club. The record is there, in Wister's own words. He had just returned from the West. Let me find it. Here it is. Wister: "Why wasn't some Kipling saving the sage-brush for American literature, before the sage-brush and all that it signified went the way of the California forty-niner, went the way of the Mississippi steam-boat, went the way of everything? Roosevelt had seen the sage-brush true, had felt its poetry; and also Remington, who illustrated his articles so well. But what was fiction doing, the only thing that has always outlived the fact? Must it be perpetual tea-cups? The claret had been excellent. 'Walter, I'm going to try it myself! I'm going to start this minute.'" He stood up, bid good night to Furness, and wrote his first Western story, "Hank's Woman," in the library of the Philadelphia Club that night. Then out of "Hank's Woman" came *The Virginian*, the legend of the West for a century to come.

"Which is just about unreadable now."

Which is why it was a milestone less in the history of American literature than in the history of American popular imagination. In any event, Wister was a most peculiar person. His illusions turned into the blackest kind of despair. A few years later Wister wrote a better book than *The Virginian,* a novel about Charleston and the South, *Lady Baltimore;* in 1912 he began a book about Philadelphia, *Monopolis,* which he abandoned; in 1934 he wrote the centennial history of the Philadelphia Club, after insisting that the book written by another member (already printed) be withdrawn and destroyed; and the last thing he was writing before he died in 1938 was to be a book on French wines.

"So he began his writing inspired by the club claret, and his last inspiration returned to claret."

Spare me these paradoxes, though there is something to them. A true and startling biography of Wister is yet to be written, since the revolution of his ideas is more interesting than the man himself. There is an American tragedy of that mind, the tragedy of the insubstantial virility of his American illusions. It is not like Dreiser or even Fitzgerald, since the American tragedy is not about people who want to rise, rather impatiently, in American society. The history of those who attempted to write about the tragedy of American patricians is yet to be done, starting with Fenimore Cooper and perhaps ending with John O'Hara, *alas.*

"Stop right there. You're going on too long."

I know I am, and besides, my California-bound Philadelphian is not at all a Wisterian or Rooseveltian believer in muscular Christianity. He is something of an American hedonist. Like many of those people, including the former Bostonians who are moving to Pasadena, he and those westering Americans are not moved by a bravado nurtured by Kipling or the Bible.

"I presume that our man's wife is charmed by the tinkling of teacups among the ladies formerly of Boston, sitting in the gardens of Pasadena. But, good God, what are they and their husbands talking about, except congratulating themselves frequently for how smart they have been in moving there?"

Well, you may be right about the scope of their conversations and even about their tone. But let's not be too tough on those men and women in Pasadena in 1901. They are still full of an American vitality, and they are not so much hedonists as idealists, which makes almost all their illusions not only understandable but defensible. Let's be honest: it could have been quite pleasant to live in Pasadena in 1901. But there was one thing that few people have noticed, including historians. This is that while California was ahead of Eastern America, and while of course the United States was ahead of Europe, ahead in many things and practices, and I mean not only machines or industry but popular democracy, public education, the secret ballot—at the same time, and in a very important way, America was *behind* Europe, because most of the prevalent American ideas, especially those of the Progressives, were already antiquated and unreal.

"You mean the sempiternal American addiction to Progressive Evolution, including the belief that, through science and education and political and social reform, society and mankind can be made perfect, or at least near perfect. But not far beneath this progressive optimism about the improvability of society lay a deep and hidden but at times sorrily apparent distrust about the improvability of human beings."

That is not my argument here. It is that the moving vision within all those illusions, all that movement toward the West, the advance toward a healthier, open life untrammeled by brittle conventions and by hypocrisy—a vision eagerly taken up by Englishmen and many continental Europeans, too—was the vision of the American West as a *return* to a simpler ideal of manhood, a rebirth of a once lost and legendary but now actually achievable way of life, against the ever paler ideas of the Age of Reason ("the stinking brain" was one of Wister's uglier phrases), which the ever smokier clouds over the cities and the factories of the Old World (and of the American East) had stifled and obscured. Evolution, indeed; but together with Return. In 1895 Wister wrote an article for *Harper's*, "The Evolution of the Cow-Puncher." The West, he wrote, gave the Anglo-Saxon race another chance. "The race was once again subjected to battles and darkness, rain and shine, to the fierceness and the generosity of the desert. Destiny tried her last experiment upon the Saxon, and pluck[ed] him from the library, the haystack and the gutter, . . . [whereupon] his modern guise fell away and showed again the medieval man." This hankering after the Middle Ages was one example of something that not many people recognize: the medieval facet of the American heart. Wister was thinking and writing this around the time when Henry Adams was turning toward Mont-Saint-Michel and Chartres.

"But he wrote this stuff sitting in the Philadelphia Club — after having asserted several times that he did not like to live in Philadelphia, but then he could not shake the Philadelphia dust from his feet, he was to return to it, wearily, and earlier than he had imagined."

Yes, and good-bye to Owen Wister. I repeat: our California-bound Philadelphian is not at all like Wister. What he envisages are pleasantries in the life of an American capitalist in California. Wister would have scorned him. Our man is no amateur cowboy, not at all. Not for a moment does he see himself as the Last Cavalier, except perhaps at some New Year's Eve costume party in Pasadena. For Wister the Last Cavalier was the Anglo-Saxon cowboy that was the drawing with which Frederic Remington illustrated "The Evolution of the Cow-Puncher" for *Harper's,* showing a cowboy, tall and lanky, with a bronzed Anglo-Saxon face, including a drooping mustache, in front of a misty tableau of assembled ancient halberdiers, Templars, Crusaders, Knights of the Roses, and a seventeenth-century cavalier looking wistfully at this American horseman. "There ought to be music for the Last Cavalier," Wister wrote Remington. "The Last Cavalier will haunt me forever. He inhabits a Past into which I withdraw and mourn." But our Pasadena Philadelphian sees nothing of the Past in the West. His vision (if that is what it is) is a blossoming, garlanded near future, here and there braced with a necessary scaffolding of stainless steel, and warmed everywhere by perennial sunshine. He is probably less split-minded than was Wister, who mourned for the past and cheered on the spirit of the future at the same time, to be incarnated by the new American, the Western man. "It won't be a century before the West is simply the true America, with thought, type and life of its own kind" he also wrote. He believed that, too — at least for a while.

"That may be very interesting, but you're not writing a historical thesis. One of the things I miss: you must clarify that scene of those two men sitting at the windows of the Philadelphia Club. Your readers may think that they are those large windows on the ground floor of a majestic club, with Morganatic bankers puffing at their cigars, as drawn by numberless cartoonists of the old *New Yorker*. The dining room and those windows of the Philadelphia Club were, and are, on the second floor, well above the street. More description, please."

All right. The Philadelphia Club is a red brick building, with marble steps and white window ledges and frames. It is handsome rather than elegant, not at all majestic but solid, and noticeable only to those who know what it houses, that is, the most selective of the clubs of that city, its membership made up mostly, though not entirely, of men of the older Philadelphia families. In 1901 it was more exclusive than the Rittenhouse Club with its Beaux Arts building and of course much more exclusive than the Union League (a monumental brownstone building occupying an entire city square, with a big statue up front). That had been erected during the Civil War by Republican nouveaux riches. Well, now, on this Friday evening in September 1901 the rooms of the Philadelphia Club are rather empty, with few diners at the long table, since many of the members live in the leafy suburbs, and the weekending habit is already widespread, even though nearly all of them keep their small town houses for the winter. Agnes Repplier's later acid apothegm ("Suburbanites are traitors to the city") apply to many of them, too. On other Friday nights there are many more diners, with their wives; but in early September the theater season has not yet begun, and in 1901 the Philadelphia Orchestra does not exist. (Philadelphia is habitually about thirty years behind New York: the Philadelphia Orchestra and the art museum came about thirty, even forty, years after the Metropolitan Museum of Art, the Metropolitan Opera, Carnegie Hall, the New York Philharmonic.) I will now add that before their serious talk the two cousins had an excellent and typical dinner at the club: turtle soup or terrapin, or oysters perhaps (September being an *R* month), veal-and-kidney pie, et cetera—no, no Madeiras, though the family bins of the Philadelphia Club still had plenty of those. After that the two men translated themselves to the windows. Some of the parquet flooring and the fine wainscoting were still washed in the evening light, while the gas lamps on Walnut Street below them were being lit.

1902

THE KITCHEN in Larchwood is white. It is all white, pristine white. It has the smell of milk, and the feel of white enamel. The milk is telling because in this house no alcohol is allowed (save for unusual occasions), and it certainly has no place in the kitchen. Milk is sanitary, hygienic, clean, an essential fluid. It symbolizes certain anxieties (and many convictions) of an American Quaker family in 1902 in New Jersey. The look and the feel of white enamel is everywhere, thick and thin: in the thin china cups and the white, blue-rimmed plates piled up in great ordered arrays, resting on the chalk-white wooden shelves of the cupboards and behind the white-framed glass doors of the kitchen cabinets. White porcelain enamel is baked hard on the thick surfaces of the sink and the gas-fired stove; these are new, modern, American, wondrously clean and cleanable and dustless. In the late mornings, until the coming bustle of the afternoons, the kitchen in Larchwood is large, empty, and cool.

Larchwood is white outside too. It is a large and handsome white clapboard house, typical of such spacious houses in South Jersey. Red brick houses are in Philadelphia, across the river, with which the lives of the people in Larchwood are much connected. It was built by their already fairly prosperous Quaker ancestors in 1748, has been enlarged since here and there, but the honest proportions of Larchwood have remained. The women of the house, Kensington's mother and the cook, wear white, too, certainly in the morning and for most of the time in the kitchen. There they walk around in white shoes, white leather shoes. Fifty or more years later their successors will buy white tennis shoes, which are more comfortable for inside wear.

Of course there are the large dark green–leaved trees outside, shading the house, one of them more than a century old.

The house still stands.

"I don't quite understand this. Why hang the beginning of this book on that uninteresting house and people?"

They are not uninteresting to me, and not only because I knew them but because of their meaning.

"You're going to say what you always say, that words are not symbols of things, that they are symbols of meanings. I guess that's true; but now you say that verbal pictures of places, too, are not symbols of things but symbols of meanings. There must be a connection between meanings and things."

At least I did not say *meaningful*—that stupid word of the 1970s.

"But—since I presume that you want to write, or at least suggest, some things about the great changes and declines—a house can be a good symbol of such things. Well, in 1902 there were some very magnificent Beaux Arts private palaces, I don't mean in New York or Newport but perhaps something like the Vanderbilts' Asheville kind of place. The idea and the history of such buildings were not only grander but more telling, yes, of 1902, than was this Larchwood."

I can't write about everything. A thin—a very thin—thread tying this book together is Kensington, who was born there in 1900. You may say that he wasn't interesting either. Well, he was and still is interesting enough for me, again, not only because I knew him, and not even because no human being is uninteresting once you attempt to understand him, by which I mean nothing more than understanding his behavior and some of his conscious thoughts. More important for such a book (which is *not* more important than my affection for him—but that is another matter) is that he was not an untypical American of his age and of his class, of this century and of its American history. "Not untypical" is the best I can say. It is better than "essential" or "average" or "typical." Those are sociological categories. I am a historian.

"Now you sound like Tolstoy, who said that the historian is a frustrated novelist. You don't like Tolstoy, and you once wrote that the reverse is true: that so many novelists, especially in the twentieth century, are frustrated historians. You insist that you're not trying to write a novel."

Yes, Tolstoy was wrong (as he was in that stupid sentence with which *Anna Karenina* begins: "All happy families are alike; only unhappy families are different." Surely in this century the very opposite is true). But let me go on. I am a historian, because I am obsessed not only with the past but with what is real, because the past is the only thing that we know, because the past was not only real *once* but is real now too. And not only in our minds; that is, its reality is not caused by our minds. Also: what happened was inseparable not only from what people thought happened (*that* condition occurred only in the past) but also from what could have happened. Now this is something that the best novelists knew better than do many historians. But I am not a novelist. I do not want to write an American *Buddenbrooks*. Anyhow, a near coincidence: *Buddenbrooks* was published in 1901. But it deals with the nineteenth century.

"And in many ways Thomas Mann is now passé, including *Death in Venice,* which is 1912 to a tee. Though *Buddenbrooks* is more than that."

So back to that Larchwood house. It is pleasant to know that it still exists and that it is kept up by the Historical Society of Haddonfield. But in this book I am interested in what was inside, in the thoughts and the sentiments of its people. Call it the spiritual—all right, the mental—atmosphere. Which is why I wrote a few sentences about that white kitchen.

"There were other American kitchens like that in 1902. You have often said that in thinking and speaking and writing about history what is particular must have primacy over what is general. You just said that those people, or your man, were 'not untypical.' Is that enough?"

The particular means something because it reflects something more general.

"Yes. I know: The Universe in a Grain of Sand. But you are not a poet, and this is not about the universe."

All right: you win. So here are *their* general categories: Americans, Quakers, old family, Philadelphia, Progressives, Anglo-Saxons.

"Go ahead."

They were Americans, American Quakers rather than Quaker Americans. That had been a slow development, a mutation that took at least one hundred years for those people. No one has written about that. There was that tight Quaker web of their relations, connections, habits, customs. But what people nowadays call a subculture was already loosening, one of the results being that some of them would become Episcopalians.

"Well, you once said that if there is any place in America about which a novel of manners ought to have been written, it is Philadelphia, but that didn't come about."

The interior perspective has been missing. Philadelphians lead interior lives, but they — including their Quakers — do not have a taste for mental detachment. Philadelphia has never had a literary culture. Painting, yes. Kensington was a painter. But it is more complicated than that. They know that the Unexamined Life Is Not Worth Living, but they are too cautious, they shy away from that. There is a rigid, a cramped desire for safety in that shyness, but there is a certain charm, perhaps a modest charm in it too. Some of these Quakers who became Episcopalians were socially conscious. But they were not socially ambitious. At the same time they knew that they came from old families, which is exactly why some of them felt safe to loosen those ties and move forward.

"But that is so generically American, too, as you well know: old families in America do not become more conservative; they become more liberal."

Absolutely true for the twentieth century, but not earlier. And of course there was another important element here. Quakers believe in Progress; and Kensington's people, in 1902, were Republicans and Progressives.

"And what was so special about that? So were many other people of the upper middle class. Don't tell me that they admired Theodore Roosevelt."

I don't know about that, but one thing they had in common with him and with most Americans. 1902 was the beginning of the American century, and they knew that America was atop the world. But there was something about their addiction to Progress that was not only an American phenomenon but very Quaker and English, too, at the time. For so were then the great Quaker families in England, the Rowntrees and the Cadburys and the Frys, all of them very progressive, nearly socialist (and philo-Semitic, which is another element). Now *we* know that Progressivism was all wrong, how it led to a vast collapse of illusions, of philadelphian and philanthropic illusions both in the literal and geographical sense of those adjectives. (Even now, at the end of this century, some of their descendants have this bit of queasiness in their stomachs, or should I say minds, when they begin to feel that one might as well rethink the entire meaning of Progress.)

"Well, isn't that true of other WASPs too?"

I dislike that silly word. But you're onto something. I listed the Anglo-Saxon category. And around 1900 that was a relatively new element in their minds: the *conscious* knowledge that they were Anglo-Saxon. That was not as simple as people might think nowadays, as if there had been something easily and instantly recognizable from a name or from a picture, from genealogical facts or from mere physical appearance.

"In 1902 that rise to the surface of their consciousness must have had something to do with the phenomenon of mass immigration."

I think not. For one thing, there were few immigrants visible in Haddonfield. For another, the Quakers were in favor of immigrants — oddly, or not so oddly, the *Illinois,* the first ship bringing Russian Jewish immigrants to Philadelphia, was chartered by the Philadelphia Quakers in 1882.

"But 1902 was not 1882. The immigration of the unshaven must have been all around them. Don't tell me that they had not given that a thought."

As Americans, perhaps. But not as Anglo-Saxons. For two hundred years before 1902 the inhabitants of Larchwood knew that they were of English stock—more precisely, of East Anglian or largely Saxon stock—but they did not think much about that. Their rising recognition of it, after about 1890, had much to do with their newly discovered and soon deeply felt Anglophilia. With the fading away of the old American Anglophobe and anti-imperialist colonial suspicions. Also with the belief, propagated not only by popular xenophobes but by proper whiskered professors at Yale and Princeton, besides T. R. and Kipling and many others, that the present and the future belonged to the North Atlantic Protestant peoples of the globe, people whose freedoms had once originated in the Teutonic forests. Not that they were pro-German (though some Quakers were, and we might meet some of them later). But there was something in them that was surely more Saxon than it was Anglo-Norman. Their women tended to say "melk" for "milk."

"They did not say 'Milch.' You have this weakness for words and sounds and names."

One other thing. Their Philadelphian and English connections. Kensington's name was chosen by his mother. One of their ancestors had been Kensington, an old uncle of her husband's father whom she had hardly known but for whom she maintained a sentimental respect. Kensington's middle name was Richmond, which he never used, not even for an initial. He once told me that he did not know why his parents had chosen that.

Richmond, Kensington, Southwark were neighborhoods and river wards across the Delaware, in Philadelphia. Their names had come with William Penn across an estranging sea. Richmond is a western suburb of London, and there is a Richmond in Yorkshire, too. And Philadelphia is a slow place. It is a red brick city, especially the river wards. Its first settlers were Quaker artisans. And in 1902 Philadelphia was perhaps the only American city where English working-class neighborhoods still existed. I mean working-class, because everywhere else in the United States, including of course Philadelphia, Anglo-Saxon Protestants were the social and governing class, even though they were no longer a majority. In the Oxford neighborhood of Philadelphia, English workers and mill hands still played cricket in 1902. Most of them had come over on the two small oceangoing ships of the American Line, which sailed regularly between Philadelphia and Liverpool and which were named after two Welsh-Quaker Philadelphia suburbs, the *Haverford* and the *Swarthmore*. The Mummers' Parade, a repellent spectacle and a twentieth-century Philadelphia tradition, had English origins; it involved some of those English Midlands working-class people, but then it became a flamboyant whango made up of Italians and Ukrainians. Anyhow, it began on New Year's Day in 1901, in the first year of the new century, the American century, when Kensington was born.

"You've been going on too long. He didn't come from the working class and you spilled some milk at the beginning of this vignette. I guess that meant something, the thing being that by 1902 the blood of these people had thinned, they had become more and more bloodless."

Do you think that I would write a book about bloodlessness? Yes, the blood of his family had been thinning for some time; and now there was their cult of Hygiene, the whiteness and the milk, inseparable from their faith in Progress. But there was, too, a residue of decency whose quality would not deteriorate, an ever smaller remnant but that may have actually improved through this numbing century.

"Good luck. That is *demonstrandum,* and it cannot be easy."

It may not be, because a story has to have shape, but life often doesn't have a shape or even a theme. But history does. Anyway, this book is not about K.'s life. I shall not mention him until fifteen or perhaps even twenty years later in these pages. By that time the American century will be running at full tide.

1903

THE PROMENADE at Earl's Court. In 1903 the London Underground station at Earl's Court already exists, the trains coming out of the tunnel to a deep open cutting, with those smooth, portly, Edwardian-looking locomotives pulling or pushing the coaches. The Underground has a recognizable smell, coal smoke and dusty plush, with a faint whiff of sultana cake. Not long ago Earl's Court was a large exhibition ground, and the Wheel (a very large Ferris wheel) is still visible against the night sky, imprinting on it a dead, circular scaffolding. It is an early summer evening in London. The Promenade is in the open, before the Earl's Court Theatre. The ruling colors are black and white. The whiteness is the illumination of the electric lamps and the marquee of the theater, which casts large, long, black shadows on the ground. All the men wear black; just about all the women wear either white or light pastel colors that seem white because of the glare of the lamps. (Consider how little, in essence, men's clothes have changed through this century, except for the then starched whiteness of their collars and linen, while women's clothes would soon become very different.)

The people, milling in the Promenade at Earl's Court. This Promenade is very middle class. It is different from the Promenade of the Empire Theatre, nearer to Mayfair. That Promenade is inside, not outside, with men and women walking around or occasionally sitting at little tables along a wide, semicircular corridor. The Empire Promenade is at the top of all the promenades of London and indeed of the world. But both promenades are not particularly elegant. That appears from some of the clothes but even more from the posture and the gait of many of the men here. Their eyes are clear but their glancing around is less sure. The Promenade, you see, is a place to pick up girls who have come there to attract men.

1903 is already beyond the century of the greatest extent of urban prostitution, the nineteenth century of gaslight and shadow. Well, here the lights have become electric, harsher and sharper than was gaslight, but the human climate is less harsh, less poisonous than was the commerce of prostitution on the Paris boulevards during the Second Empire and after. This is due to British hypocrisy, which is preferable to cynicism and which, at any rate, is ingrained in most of the people at the Earl's Court Promenade. The girls (there are few women among them) are not at all professional prostitutes, and the men are mostly bachelors, toffs rather than rakes. They have English faces of many kinds, middle-class countenances, knobbly and creased early in their lives. The gray ice of noncommital distance and caution is not on their faces, but the obligatory smile of the pickup is seldom charming; it is rather a grin. Many of the girls are taller than the men. Some are florid and almost monumental. Many of the men have only recently risen to the higher ranks of clerkships, to full membership in the expanding British middle classes. A few of them seem a bit stunted. They do not wear evening clothes but their shoes have been polished carefully. Some of them carry thin canes that they sometimes uneasily stick under their arms as they attempt to approach a girl. The girls know their types very well.

Foreigners do not. At the Empire there is a sprinkling of knowledgeable foreign men. In the crowd at the Earl's Court Promenade there are a number of recent immigrants to England, but I am thinking of a foreign visitor who looks at the scene and the people, perplexed.

The bell tolling in the background is the hum and roar of imperial London, with its traffic and the steam of its great railway stations, a march of time in accord with Elgar's "Pomp and Circumstance," which has a faint melancholy tone, too, unlike the brass-and-cymbal beat of the marches of other military nations.

And this, oddly, also accords with the Promenade at Earl's Court. The Promenade is an imperial charade. It is the converse of, say, an Imperial Durbar of a Viceroy in Delhi; it is a small charade in the center of a great empire, near the center of its imperial city, which in 1903 is still the largest city in the world.

"Surely a period picture, but what is it all about? Let me guess. You are the foreign visitor, and you are perplexed, because you suddenly sense the question: England, the English people, are they really on top of the world?"

You are almost right. Almost, but not quite. What I am interested in are not the first recognitions of seeds of decline but the complicated nature of some of the seeds. There was something particular about the English people, even at that time. They did not want to be on top of the world.

"You mean 'We're Number One,' the trumpeting of such a phrase by Nixon, Reagan, Weinberger—people whom you abhor—would be unheard of in England then: 'We're Number One.' But they surely *thought* that they were Number One. The rest was good manners."

But Goethe was right when he wrote that there are no manners that do not rest on some kind of moral foundation. I see that in Kipling, whose linguistic (linguistic, rather than rhetorical) manners were abominable on occasion, but not always. Think of his "Recessional," in 1897, the year of the Diamond Jubilee, when England surely seemed to be at the top of tops, before the tremor of the Boer War (and the Promenade at Earl's Court is a scene just after the Boer War). Kipling warned his countrymen:

> Far-call'd our navies melt away . . .
> If drunk with sight of power . . .

> For heathen heart that put her trust
> In reeking tube and iron shard
> All valiant dust that builds on dust.

I do not know a German or French or Spanish or Italian imperialist or nationalist poet writing and thinking thus.

"But didn't Kipling write that to be born an Englishman means having won a first prize in God's lottery? You know as well as I do that the English were (and many of them still are) the most racist—all right, race-conscious—people on the face of the earth."

Yes, but their racism is different from, say, that of the Germans, and not only in degree but in kind. Don't forget the burden in "The White Man's Burden"—which, not so incidentally, Kipling wrote for Americans. But there was a side—more, an essence—of Kipling that was not only sensitive but shy.

"That's not very convincing. That might have been true of some of the English (and not necessarily of the best kind among them: weren't some of the Bloomsburyites and the homophile Cambridge Apostles 'sensitive and shy'?). Those people at Earl's Court: many of them were not sensitive but both vulgar and shy. Besides, you're writing about the beginning of the Edwardian age. That was a golden Sunday afternoon—Ascots and Goodwoods, cucumber sandwiches, gauzy frocks on the greensward, the plinking of very thin porcelain teacups—for people on the top. People wrote about how beauteous that time was and what a splendid monarch was Edward the Seventh. At the same time there were intelligent men and women who wrote about the heavy stuffing, the ostentation, the luxury, the arrogance, the monumental floridity, the immoralities, the parvenus and the arrivistes at the court, and the gross side of the portly Edward himself."

I have no nostalgia for the Edwardian age in England, including those superb luxuries (in every sense of the word) of those weekends in those great country houses. (If I have any nostalgia for 1903, it would be for life in a small, neobaroque country house in Hungarian Transylvania, in late September.) Now let me jump back to Kipling for the last time: do you know that he was Stanley Baldwin's cousin?

"And thirty years later Baldwin nearly ran England into the ground."

But he was a nicer man than Chamberlain. Anyway, that's not the point. What is significant is that the British working people were less imperialist than we have been accustomed to think. I recently read a scholarly and compelling study about that. The Conservatives' imperialism and nationalism, which had begun with Disraeli and was then fanned by Churchill's father and Joe Chamberlain, affected them only here and there. Which brings me to the main argument: yes, the British knew that they were the top nation of the world, but they wanted to be left alone. That, incidentally, is one of the reasons — there were other, less attractive reasons — for their untroubled acceptance of the primacy of the United States and of many things American after 1898.

"But people whom you admire, Churchill, first of all, *were* imperialists."

In part because he was Anglo-American; but, no less important, he was Europe-minded, too (as was Edward). He understood that Britain cannot be isolationist: she cannot concentrate everything on the dominions and colonies; she cannot opt out of the European balance of power, first and foremost because of Germany. And in that he was right. You know, the Germans have not forgiven him for that, not to this day — even though he was not at all an addicted Germanophobe.

"Let me get back to that — to me, fairly interesting — Promenade. First: why didn't you pick some other scene? No, not a country house weekend party, that has been done. Say, the Ritz in 1906, or the Admiralty Arch a few years later? Then: you make two cryptic, almost secretive suggestions, one about the physical decline of the race of Englishmen, the other about the perplexity of your foreign observer, *à quoi bon?*"

Ah, the first is a question I cannot really answer, as I probably cannot answer for most of the vignettes in this book, except in this case I will say that I once saw in an Edwardian album a drawing of the Earl's Court scene by Frank Reynolds, who was an excellent and thoughtful illustrator of those times, and it left an impression on my mind.

Incidentally, Churchill's first public—and very brash—appearance involved the Empire Promenade in 1894. There was a Mrs. Ormiston Chant (what a name!), who, in one of those British frenzies of moral indignation (consider that this happened a few months before the Wilde scandal and trial), started a campaign against the immorality of the Empire Promenade, whereupon Churchill, together with some fellow cadets at Sandhurst, attacked the "Prudes on the Prowl" for acting, as he put it, "contrary to the best traditions of British freedom." They tore down some of the lath-and-canvas partitions on the promenade that had been forced upon the managers of the Empire. Churchill was nineteen then.

Now—and I think that this is important—Churchill was no John Bull. (As a matter of fact, some of the letter-writers supporting Mrs. Chant signed themselves "John Bull.") That brutal, stolid and solid, thick-necked and thick-waisted, full-blooded shire-and-yeoman type, John Bull, belonged to the late eighteenth and early nineteenth centuries. By 1865 he was as dead as was Palmerston. He no more represented an English character in 1903 than that spare, gangly, rawboned, thin-goateed Yankee Uncle Sam represents an American character now—or indeed in 1903. Yes, the race—especially the men—had become thinner, and perhaps weaker. And there was another thing, more important, underneath. The Protestant virtues that had helped to make England great were largely gone. Or, more precisely, they were proving to be insufficient.

"That is the subject of a very large book."

Which will never be written. But it does have a bearing on 1903, when two of the strongest spokesmen for an older English nationalism and for some of the older English virtues were the Catholic Belloc and the soon to be Catholic Chesterton. Chesterton is preferable to Belloc, because he was less violent and intellectually more honest. But both of them were exercised, indeed whipped into print, by their sight of the failures, of the hypocrisy, of Edwardian liberalism that was, of course, an outcome of many Protestant strands. They thought—and wrote—that it was decadent and consequently immoral.

"And wrote. That's just the trouble. There was too much of the journalist in both of them."

There is some truth in that, perhaps regarding Belloc especially. But that was the golden age of journalism, which was both good and bad. Bad, because the mass newspapers had arisen, tapping the reservoir of an entirely new kind of potential readership, geared to some of the lowest common denominators of taste and interest. (Wilde once put it: in the Middle Ages there was the rack; now there is the press.) Good, too, because never since have English-language newspapers been as literate as they were then. Harry Cust was a man-about-town and the editor of the *Pall Mall Gazette,* and to the article or editorial about the fall of the French prime minister Casimir-Périer (in 1894, I think) he gave the title "Périer Joué." I think that is wonderful, since it presumed that many of the readers of that newspaper knew French well enough to recognize a pun and that they drank a lot of champagne. At any rate, to paraphrase Henry Adams, the evolution of British journalism from the Custs (and even from the Harmsworths, who were a bad Ulster lot) to the Maxwells and the Murdochs is sufficient to refute all the theories of Darwin.

"You suggested that some of Maxwell's forerunners were already there, milling in the crowd at the Earl's Court Promenade."

Yes, they were recently arrived Leopold Blooms; but remember that I also mention a foreigner who is not an immigrant but a visitor to England, and who is perplexed at the sight of the scene, those people, this England. The reason for that is simple. Our imagined visitor has just arrived from the Continent — and why not from Hungary? — with his mind full of high illusions and expectations about England and the English. He is an Anglophile. In this he is not alone. So were very many men — men, rather than women — in Europe at that time (Anglomania began some time around 1750 and lasted till about 1955, I think) who saw in England, free England, the England that had "saved herself by her exertions and saved Europe by her example," incarnating the best of the modern world precisely because it was conservative and liberal, aristocratic and democratic, at the same time — and, besides, elegant and good-looking. The English word "gentleman" appears, in different ways, in almost all European languages at the time. The English gentleman—his behavior, his clothes, his sports—was an ideal type around 1900. When our foreign visitor comes to London and appears at Earl's Court, he first senses that many of the men there, including the fairly well-dressed ones, somehow do not fit that type. He is perplexed, rather than deeply disturbed, by that. He will return to his homeland from England without being disappointed, but with a few mixed thoughts and ideas.

"Because he is a snob, like most Anglophiles. He thinks of the English aristocracy, whom he may have known hardly at all."

Yes and no. He is not entirely wrong. With all their shortcomings and vices—and there were many—the youth of the English aristocracy (please keep in mind that even their virtues were already non-Victorian, since I am now thinking of people who grew up after the turn of the century) had its fair share of patriotic courage, dying readily and without much thought in and out of the dreadful trenches of the coming world war. Wait a minute: let me find you a passage by C. F. G. Masterman, a good Liberal writer, from *England After the War*, in 1922. Here it is: "In the useless slaughter of the Guards on the Somme, or of the Rifle Brigade in Hooge Wood, half of the great families of England, heirs of large estates and wealth, perished without a cry. These boys, who had been brought up with a prospect before them of every good material thing that life can give, died without complaint, often through the bungling of generals, in a foreign land. And the British aristocracy perished, as they perished in the Wars of the Roses, or in fighting for their king in the great Civil War, or as the Southern aristocracy in America, in courage and high effort, and an epic of heroic sacrifice, which will be remembered as long as England endures."

"That is exaggerated, though the rhetoric is good, and so is his reference to the bungling generals. It could have been written by someone like Waugh, whose thinking had just begun in 1922 and who had his own romantic illusions about, well, some of the aristocracy of England."

Yes, it is exaggerated—in some ways and to some extent. But

where Waugh was wrong, and not only about the Second World War, was his fearful (I mean that word in both of its senses) lack of empathy with the other classes of England. He would have despised those people at the Earl's Court Promenade. But—and this was truer of the first war than of the second—those clerks and accountants and young tradesmen of many kinds were not less patriotic than were most of the English aristocracy. They volunteered in droves. They formed their units and brigades—just think of some of those names that were given them: the Accrington Pals, the Barnsley Pals, the City Battalions—and, obeying those bungling generals (and not a few bungling majors and colonels from the ranks of the aristocracy), they too "perished without a cry." They were less sturdy than John Bull had been, with their thin necks and knobby faces, they knew little of the chivalries of their social betters, but they were patriotic, disciplined, hardly self-indulgent, with sparks of Christ's divine humanity still buried alive somewhere in their hearts. A man like Churchill knew and esteemed them. (One generation later, facing another war, the remnant John Bull types in England were all for Chamberlain, for letting Europe go to the Germans of Hitler, if need be.) The South Kensington Pals, while they knew nothing of being party to "an epic of heroic sacrifice," will also be remembered as long as England endures. Or let me turn this around: memories of them will endure as long as England knows how to remember.

"Now, now. The people of Germany, all kinds of people, were no less patriotic and disciplined, or indeed brave and near-heroic, in that war."

Yes, but the English were said to be a nation of shopkeepers, and some of these men *were* shopkeepers.

"So were some of the Germans. In any event, both they and the English were people of whom Spengler once wrote that they actually believed what was printed in the newspapers. Your Hungarian visitor to London in 1903 had not read Spengler (how could he? that first tome of Spengler would not appear until the end of the great catastrophe, in 1918) but I see that you equip him with an early sense of the decline of the West."

No. The writer of the decline of the West is someone like Saki. Think of *The Unbearable Bassington*. (Incidentally, Bassington and his mother, Francesca, live in Kensington—which by 1912 is Peter Pan country—a little closer to Mayfair than is Earl's Court, though there is a considerable social gap.) *More* than incidentally, *Bassington* is suffused with more than wit. It is suffused with sadness. The sadness is not of the human condition; it is that of a contemplation of a specific place and time, London and its urbane civilization circa 1911, at the end of the Edwardian age.

And there is a Hungarian who was invented by Saki and who plays a small role in an extraordinary book that he wrote the year after *The Unbearable Bassington*. It was published in 1913 with the title *When William Came*. It describes life in London after a sudden and successful German invasion of England. It is an uncanny, absolutely precise description of how people will accept and how they will adjust themselves to a German conquest of their country—not in 1913 but in 1940. The plot is weak, the chapters are a series of morality episodes, but on the level of character descriptions it is superb. The main character is Yeovil, a patriotic Englishman abashed by what he sees all around him (including the thoughtlessness and the mild opportunism of some of his English compatriots, both men and women). Traveling in a train, he meets a Hungarian visitor to England. "A beautiful country," the latter says. "Surely a country worth fighting for." They begin to talk. "The English," the Hungarian says, "grew soft and accommodating in all things. In religion . . . they had come to look on the Christ as a sort of amiable elder brother, whose letters from abroad were worth reading. Then, when they had emptied all the divine mystery and wonder out of their faith, they naturally grew tired of it, oh, but dreadfully tired of it." He adds, "I have always liked the English, but now I am angry with them for being soft."

"That is a good passage but quite implausible. No Hungarians were like that in 1912, they would not talk like that to an Englishman on a train. Besides, you once told me that Hungarians are, alas, not very religious."

You are probably right. Sensitive Englishmen at that time, such as Saki—another was Maurice Baring—had their own illusions about certain foreign people (Baring about the Russians) because of their virility and charm. They were often wrong. But never mind. Their England they knew. And then, after *Bassington* in 1912 and *William* in 1913, came 1914, and Saki, then in his mid-forties, volunteered as a common soldier, dying in a trench two years later. His famous last words ought to be remembered: "Put out that bloody cigarette!" A moment later a German shell hit him.

The Englishmen around him were not soft, but they were thoughtless. That was what killed him.

"Well, this is very fine, but your addiction to Saki may be extreme. First, you are not the kind of writer who will ever be able to equal him. Second, that's not your job. Third, he *was* a period piece."

In one sense—but in one sense only. Mozart was a period piece, too. And history—if it's any good—is all about period pieces.

1904

IT IS THE BEGINNING of the century, and the two youths who talk
excitedly on a June night in Budapest are aware of that. They think they
are on to something that is very new, that is about to change the ideas
of men, and that, they think, will lead to a new order of the world.
That, of course, is not quite the way things happen. However, since I
am interested in *how* rather than *what* they think, I must describe them,
first of all. Their provenance and their ambiance. Both were born in
1886, meaning that they are eighteen years old now. They have just
surmounted the dreadful ordeal of the *érettségi*, or *matura*, or baccalau-
reate, the three-day examination giving account of eight years' work
in the humanistic gymnasium, after which hurdle admission to the university — any university — is automatic. The way to their professional
careers is now clear. Of more moment to them is the prospect of a
golden summer, well earned. They had passed the examination at or
near the top of their class, with full As, High Honors. Their parents
are well-to-do. One of the youths has received the customary cigarette
case, the other the double-lidded pocket-watch, both solid gold. For
the next three months they have no work to do, but plenty of things to
plan, and plenty to talk about.

That is what they do now, often excitedly, breaking into each
other's sentences. They are close friends, often spending time together

on many an evening. Now they are in the room set aside by the parents for their son in the spacious first-floor apartment of a new building (called a villa then) where the family had moved only a year or two before. It is a high-ceilinged room, with stucco decorations running around the ceiling and the small glass chandelier. There is still a faint smell of new paint and plaster in the staircase of the house, which is situated in the Fasor, Alley of Trees, in what is then the rich (or nouveau riche) district on the Pest side of a rapidly burgeoning city. The tall windows are open, the electric light shines out on the dark leaves of the newly planted young trees. On the other side of the street, within a few minutes' walk, is the Evangelical Gymnasium from which they have now been graduated, a school that will acquire a legendary reputation by the end of the twentieth century, having had Nobel Prize winners among its students, many of them sons of the ascendant Jewish bourgeoisie of Budapest, as are these youths.

They are very bright. Their minds are very quick. They talk about their vacation plans, but soon their talk spills over into books, poetry, music, philosophy. I fear that at the end of the twentieth century such intellectual talk has become so rare as to be just about nonexistent, although I have read that some such thing still went on in Moscow or Leningrad in the 1980s—perhaps. But this is not a cramped room thick with cigarette smoke, and their inspiration is not helped along by vodka or cognac. Now they are talking about mathematics and physics, the second being their main intellectual interest. They talk about amazing matters, matters that not too many scientists of the world in 1904 know about and the real meaning of which only a handful of those tend to contemplate, a meaning of which these two callow youths of the Budapest Jewish bourgeoisie are very much aware. One of them had given a paper about the extraordinary qualities of radium to the self-study circle, the *önképzőkör* of the gymnasium, a voluntary association encouraged in the Budapest gymnasiums and chaired by a teacher for those fledgling students who are ready and willing to try their intellectual wings. And now, near midnight on this summer night, their minds take flight, farther and higher. They talk about the meaning of the discovery, of the fact—to them it is already a fact—that this new element, radium, fits but at the same time does not fit into the eternal order of the table of elements that make up the universe, since the properties of the uranium atom are not fixed and constant. That radium and uranium are *changing* elements. And they say to each other that the meaning of this will change the accepted order of physics; indeed, it will change the order of ideas, the thinking of mankind, the entire century. They do not have in mind its practical applications, and they will not return to these philosophic speculations until years later or perhaps not at all. But their talk races ahead for a few minutes, and their eyes glisten. They glimpse (if that is the right word) something a year before Einstein will compress it into his momentous mathematical formula. *Their* talk is not momentous. They will not change the world. But there is a high moment in their mental, perhaps even spiritual, gymnastics that is astonishing.

"You told me once—no, several times—that you did not think that much of Einstein, that Heisenberg had the better mind. If so, these bright kids appearing for a moment as Einstein's forerunners—so what?"

What fascinates me is the climate of their minds.

"You mean the intellectual atmosphere. You wrote about that in *Budapest 1900*. That was believable, probably because you were born and brought up there, although of course two decades later, when things had become different, even though some of those intellectual appetites may have been still extant, here and there. Is that what you are after?"

Not quite. I'm interested in the climate of their particular minds, rather than in the general intellectual atmosphere. But of course these two things are not entirely separable. These youths did not come out of nothing. There was something about Budapest in 1900 that was quite different from Vienna. Or Prague. Or Berlin. No city had grown as fast as Budapest during the previous ten years. More important, there was a vibrant, sometimes coarse, but not necessarily superficial cultural life in Budapest at that time. It featured a kind of virility and optimism that was very different from the neurotic pessimism of the Viennese fin de siècle. That virility and optimism had its shortcomings, but it was the result of an, alas, ephemeral but extraordinary fusion of some of the Hungarian and Jewish (and even German) qualities of mind. You see, while there *was* anti-Semitism in Hungary, in Budapest the assimilation and the integration of Jews, and especially those of a certain class, were probably without precedent in the world at that time. (So were the assimilation and the integration of German families into Magyar culture.) The results were startling and sparkling. Startling, because there was a sudden outburst of creative talent among a cohort of people — though perhaps startling only in retrospect. The sparkling is there in the success of all kinds of quick-minded young Hungarians of that generation, of the Molnár and Koestler type; and while these were intellectual boulevardiers, first-rate among second-raters, there were many truly first-rate minds too — though, alas, most of them unknown outside of Hungary.

But that is not exactly what I had in mind, writing of these two youths as they talk at night in that villa apartment. They will go far. Their parents — rich merchants or lawyers or bankers — will not mind that their sons choose to make their careers in the professions: the title *professor* in 1904 (and for long thereafter) carries a most respectable cachet in Central Europe. But by the time they will have reached the age of their potential professorial appointments, Hungary will have lost the war, the country will be dismembered, and there will be a short-lived Communist regime in which many of the commissars are Jews (though most of them of a different class from that of our two talkative friends), followed by a great deal of official anti-Semitism and the prohibiting of certain professional careers, including university professorships. That will be a dip in their careers, but then in Weimar Germany they will do all right. One of them makes a name for himself, and when Hitler comes to power he comes to America, to the Institute for Advanced Study at Princeton.

"So back to Einstein again?"

No—because the expatriate knows (though will seldom say so) that Einstein is over the hill, that by the time Einstein came to Princeton, struck as he was with his determinism (the "God does not play dice" stuff, which may sound good but is meaningless), he had nothing more to contribute to physics. Our Hungarian will be quite successful, one of the four or five Hungarians who help to figure out the atom bomb, finally an adviser to the Atomic Energy Commission and to Truman and Eisenhower, and so on. The other will give up his physics and mathematics and go into business, though bright as a button till the end. The end comes to both of them, I presume, sometime in the 1950s. They will have drifted apart, but occasionally they will remember their youthful friendship and those great conversations, indeed, sentimentalizing and exaggerating their years at the gymnasium, forgetting what was unpleasant—and there was of course plenty of that, too—during their adolescence.

"I must say that I'm not persuaded by your abiding interest in these two fellows. For two reasons. First, when we once talked about the sparkling success of those Hungarians who made it abroad, it was you who told me that one ought not exaggerate their merits, that every so often their intellectual panache outran their merits, that they were not geniuses, that there was often something Hollywoodish about them, while some of the best Hungarian minds were hardly known abroad. The second matter is something, too, that we once talked about, and it may be connected with the first. You wrote in *Budapest 1900* that there was this extraordinary generation of Hungarians, all of them born between 1875 and 1905. These two protagonists of yours belong to that. But there was another extraordinary cohort of people in the history of the twentieth century: Roosevelt, Stalin, Hitler, Mussolini, Einstein, de Gaulle, all of them born between 1879 and 1890. Well, the ideas of all of them are outdated now (except perhaps for de Gaulle), and isn't that true of your two young intellectuals of 1904?"

Yes, it is largely true—but perhaps that was due to their character (which is why our man, when in Princeton, will keep his judgment of Einstein largely to himself). He and his friend become aware of the holes, not only in the rigid classical physics of the atomic table but also in determinism, positivism, Spencerianism, Marxism, Darwinism (and perhaps — I hope — Freudianism). But as they grow up and life goes on, within and around them, it won't be again as it was in 1904. They are no longer excited or even attracted by the philosophical consequences of those holes. They know that they exist; they nod at them, and then proceed with their work and their careers. I am thinking of our upcoming physicist who will be like many of our historian colleagues, who are not only aware but even willing to aver that of course historical determinism is outdated, but then they go on teaching and writing history as if history were determined.

"And, if that is so, why in the world are these two clever whippersnappers so interesting?"

What is interesting is the moment — how their minds work in that moment, in 1904, and in Hungary.

"The drama of a mental crystallization, the shock of recognition, you mean. But then you just said that that moment of recognition had few, if any, consequences for their lives. Our interest is history, and history is all about consequences. And what was so consequential about their momentous — yes, I know, I'm not trying to be funny — chitchat in 1904?"

Two things. One is that there was, that there *could be,* that particular kind of talk in 1904, which is most probably something (and I am not only referring to the peak subject of their inspiring chitchat, as you call it) that will not happen in 2004 and did not happen in 1804. The other thing is that I know of another such moment in 1904. There was another conversation between two youths that occurred in 1904 (or possibly 1905) and that — indeed, and alas — may have changed the world. Or, rather, it was not exactly a conversation, since only one of them did the talking, in a state of high excitement. That was the young Hitler, then fifteen, as callow a youth as any, speaking to his friend Kubizek. They had seen *Rienzi,* from the peanut gallery in the Linz theater. You know of course that *Rienzi* was Wagner's early opera, the story of the rise and fall of a populist hero, a tribune of the people. After that they walked through the night, through the empty streets, through the suburbs, the fields, and woods, up a hill. The young Hitler was agitated. He began to speak to Kubizek about something that his friend had not expected at all. He had had a vision. He said that his destiny was to help raise the German people to the greatest heights. Thirty-five years later, in August 1939 in Bayreuth, he met Kubizek again and said: "In that hour it has begun." That may have been true—perhaps truer than we are accustomed to think. And it—that terrible *it*—would end, with his suicide, fewer than six years later, at the end of the world war he had brought about.

"Well, that may have led to something. Whereas your two cerebrating adolescent physicists . . ."

I *said* that they did not change the world. But Hitler did. He brought the world to a vast historical tragedy—not just because of his own vision but because one day an entire nation, a great nation, would respond to him. And he came to *know* that could and would happen at some time. His utter loneliness in 1904 grew into a frightful dimension. But what grabs me is the possibility of such visionary moments in the minds of teenagers in 1904. Will there be such in 2004? Allow me to doubt it.

"That is not only arguable but silly. Anyhow, your two Hungarians were luckier than Hitler."

I'd say so, though for most Hungarians the century was far from lucky.

"And eventually—one of your favorite adverbs—they came to America, because of that visionary in Linz. So there is a connection here, though not the one that agitates you."

1905

THERE IS A LARGE CROWD filling both the sidewalks and the street on the rocky slope of the hill, large enough to be visible from the main thoroughfare of the town, half a mile below. Those who do not know what is going on up there might think that there is a large funeral, except that funerals in this western Pennsylvania town do not take place in the afternoons; and it is past three now, on a warm and windy April afternoon.

It is an unusual crowd, not only because of its size but because of its composition, as it congregates in clusters: Irish, Polish, Hungarian people who live in this small town and in its immediate small townships, close to each other but separated by customs that to them seem ancient (they are not, and the customs will not last forever) and by suspicions whose carapaces are hard while their essences are brittle. The men wear dark suits, most of the women wear black kerchiefs (from a distance, but only from a distance, the Irishwomen are more distinguishable from the Eastern European women than are the Irishmen from the Eastern European men). But, as one gets closer, amidst the black clothes and the dark hues there appears a flow of great ceremonial colors: the magenta and the purple of the cloaks and birettas and the white of the albs and soutanes of the clergy, which includes a bishop and his retinue. Their procession has begun.

It is the circumambulation required by canon law for the blessing and the consecration of a newly built Catholic church in this steel town. The bells begin to peal, and soon the mass of people will crowd through its doors, the singing and the organ music will fill its interior. While the bells are audible both below and above that gray, scarred hillside, the singing and the organ remain contained inside. The shape of the church is Irish-Celtic, with a quadrangular, squat church tower, and neo-Celtic rather than neo-Gothic (though with many neo-Gothic elements inside), with an architectural touch that is — oddly, but not unusually — both puritanical and Byzantine. Many years later this church will look older than it is, darker than it looks now, but it will never acquire that sense and smell of spicy darkness that is the inner climate of Catholic churches in southern and eastern Europe.

The bishop of the diocese is in the middle of the procession, throwing sprinkles of holy water from a big silver aspergillum all around. There is a visiting foreign monsignor in the procession, too. Both of them are aware of the spiky problems of this new parish, but I do not assume that they are thinking much about that now. They are immersed in the ceremony of the consecration as it flows on into the High Mass, with which they are more familiar, it being part of their consecrated lives. It will be a long High Mass, so long as to be wearisome, even for those in the congregation (especially women) who, in America and in 1905, remember the rare splendor of high masses from their earlier lives.

It is near twilight when the Mass is ended, and the bells now sound assertive and repetitious. The hard kernels of the crowd, unmeltable except here and there at their edges, disaggregate quickly. The rectory is not yet built; the ecclesiastics and the bishop go on to dine in another rectory, at the main parish of the town. For that sumptuary occasion they will be received by its Irish pastor and his housekeeper and led to a dining room with heavy, factory-made mahogany tables, chairs, and sideboards; with statuettes, including a large bisque one of the Infant Jesus on a corner pedestal, under new but pallid electric lights set overhead in milky Victorian glass fixtures; and with the massive dining table well laid with solid silver. There are sixteen people around the table, including a few immigrant priests from other valleys of the diocese who do not feel especially comfortable, whereas the visiting prothonotary from the Danube valley does. The dinner will be long, but at its end the leave-taking and the departures will be abrupt. By that time a heavy and humid darkness will have settled over the town.

I have known such churches in the mining and steel towns of Pennsylvania, which is one reason why I do not fix the name of this place. It may be Aliquippa or Ligonier or a parish at the edge of Altoona in the west or even Coatesville in the east of the state. Now and then I have been gripped by my sense of their history, together with a sense of sadness, knowing that their history will never be written.

"You mean that you're not going to write it. That is a singular way to generalize."

What I mean is that the history of an American church and of a parish in the twentieth century would be extremely difficult to write.

"I know you well enough to surmise the difficulty, which is, as you once said, that simple people are not simple; as a matter of fact, their ways of thinking may be very complicated. This church in a steel town must be a parish church of working-class people, so that is what you have in mind?"

Partly, but only partly so. To me the great, slow drama of American history—the drama of the mental and spiritual history of a people—may be compressed in scenes such as this one.

"Of 1905? Or, rather, what will come of it, what will become of that church and parish, its evolution—or devolution, if you will—from an Irish to a no longer predominantly Irish parish, if that's what it is today."

Not really. But please do not query me now. For once, pray allow me to pontificate—in the literal sense of that verb. I am trying to make a bridge from what is in my mind to yours: I may fail, but for once, do not interrupt my pontification till I'm done.

To begin with: when you said "church and parish," you were right. This is about America and about the twentieth century. Church history, ecclesiastical history, religious history, Catholic history, what you will, almost always deals with the history of popes, cardinals, bishops, priests, seminaries (or, lately and sometimes lamentably, with the history of church historians). That is too confining. American history is by and large the history of a people rather than that of a state (although the two are never altogether separable), and the history of an American church and of its parish is directly, and surely not secondarily, the history of its people (for which *church membership* is an inadequate term). There are two enormous difficulties here. If it is difficult to find and eventually to reconstruct what people did—especially the so-called simple people, with the poor and scanty documentary residue of their lives—it is more difficult to find what they thought: and even that is less difficult than to know something about what (and how) they believed. The greatest hierarchs as well as the humblest priests have always known this. Cardinal Feltin of Paris said once: "I cannot pretend to penetrate the souls of my fellow countrymen. On the other hand, by their behavior people to some extent reveal their disposition." Note that "to some extent." But the American problem in the twentieth century is even more difficult, because hypocrisy is not the American predicament. That belonged to the nineteenth century, that difference between what people do or say and what they believe. The American predicament is more complicated than that. It is the difference between what people think they believe and what they really believe. The only American Catholic writer who glimpsed something about that was Flannery O'Connor, and then she wrote about Southern Protestants.

The other circumstance is that the church is full, and will remain full. Its Masses will be crowded for many decades. Only God knows all of the reasons why some people turn into regular churchgoers, but I venture to state at least one reason, which is that in the United States, very much including a mill town in 1905, church-going is a mark of or a step toward respectability. Especially among the working class, this desire for respectability was a fundamental matter that Marx entirely missed while toiling away at his vast unreadable opus in the British Museum library. "Has the Immigrant Kept the Faith?" That was the worry of the largely Irish hierarchy in America in 1905, but also long before that and after. (It is the title of a book by a Gerald Shaughnessy, in 1925.) Now the Irish have wonderful insights into human nature but here, I think, they missed — probably because their insight is addressed only to people whom they know, by which I mean mostly themselves. About immigrants they knew, or wanted to know, not much. The churches in America, very much including Catholic churches, were full of people who had acquired rather than "kept" the faith. Many of them acquired the habit of regular churchgoing here, not in the countries they had come from, and for all kinds of reasons, not the least of which were social rather than sacramental. But the melancholy condition in 1905, in Aliquippa or Coatesville, is that the parishioners are badly, very badly, divided. The Irish dislike the Poles, and the Slovaks the Hungarians. The first of these dislikes had been acquired in the New World (there are no Poles in Ireland); the second is largely, though not exclusively, an importation. The American bishops and most of the priests are good enough human beings and Catholics not to dislike immigrants altogether; but they are suspicious of them and of their imported priests. Around 1905 there were American cities and towns where parishes and sometimes entire dioceses broke up, with people marching out to erect their own parishes, their own churches, and in some cases breaking away from the church altogether into national congregations with their own schismatic priests and even bishops. You see, in those neighborhoods of that Pennsylvania town in 1905 there are already more Poles and Hungarians and Slovaks and Italians (when counted all together) than there are Irish. The Poles and the Slovaks had petitioned the bishop for a parish of their own, with a Polish or a Slovak pastor of their own. They would have built the church themselves, they already had enough money for that. But the bishop refused, as so many bishops would refuse such petitions elsewhere in America at that time. The new church and parish is not named Saint Columba or Saint Bridget (Saint Columba is already the name of the large church in the middle of the town, where the pastor gave the dinner to his august guests in his rectory), but it is Saint Aloysius, and the new pastor assigned to it is Irish too. A bitterness between priest and parishioners would not disappear for many years. Even forty years later, when an Irish boy from Saint Columba's would marry a Hungarian girl from Saint Aloysius, his people would speak of a Mixed Marriage. There will be not enough seasoning of charity in the melting pot, and when the differences will begin to melt away, something else than charity will replace them.

Now there are two people involved in this consecration of the church in 1905 who do not see this. One of them is at the dinner in the rectory, the other is not. The first is the ecclesiastical visitor from the Danube valley. He is very favorably impressed with the prosperity of the American Catholic Church. He is impressed, almost to the point of envy, when he learns how much of that building was paid for by the weekly contributions of the people, all the people of the parish, with their preprinted and numbered envelopes dropped into the collection baskets with unfailing regularity. He is impressed by the size of the churchgoing crowd, as they fill all three Sunday Masses: what a faithful, what an obedient congregation! He is a social-minded priest who positively enjoys the absence of those rigid hierarchical distinctions of his own country. The American separation of church and state doesn't bother him in the least. He thinks it is wonderful how many of his former countrymen and countrywomen and their broods have become regular (and contributing) parishioners here. He *has* heard their complaints about the American machinery of the church, of their suffering the imperious predominance of the Irish, of certain odd liturgical and pastoral habits; but he thinks that, on balance, these things do not matter much, the Church and the Faith will not lose these people. He is right and wrong at the same time: right, because this will not be a country whose churches fall into ruins, with Bare Ruined Choirs; wrong, because he does not see that the American populism of American priests and pastors will compromise, if not demean, their spirituality . . .

"But only God knows about that!"

Yes. You are right.

"And the other person, the one who did not come to the dinner?"

He is a wealthy Quaker in Philadelphia, whose Welsh Quaker ancestors owned either the coal mines or the steel mills that made this town, the mills or the mines whence his family's fortune derived. Lately these have become stock companies, corporations, but he still holds some of their shares. The bishop and the pastor don't know that; they think that his family are still owners in entirety or near entirety, and they know how one of the main streets of the town bears the name of the family and that this old Quaker comes to the town once in a great while. So the bishop wrote him to ask for a contribution to the building of this new church; and this man in Philadelphia, usually so cautious with his money (to the extent of a grave stinginess), a near recluse who knows just about nothing about the composition of the new parish, and not much about Roman Catholicism (his forefathers had read George Borrow about "sharking priests who have come to proselytize and plunder"), has been somehow and suddenly moved to send them what in 1904 was an astonishingly large amount of money, asking for God's blessing on their "endeavor." The letter was not dictated or typed, it was handwritten by this crippled old man, with his badly bent back. He then received a flowery thank-you from the bishop, who invited him to the consecration (and, I presume, to the dinner). "Flattery soothes the dull cold ear of age," but the old man's ear had grown dull and cold for many years. So only God knows how he read that letter. In any case, he did not choose to come. He was a recluse of sorts, I repeat.

"Perhaps he talked to God then. 'When a recluse talks with God, how little does he know that such an hour of recollection sums up the aspiration of the world.' That is from the *Diary* of Julien Green."

Oh, there were so many hard-faced men in that parish, some of whom the pastor would appoint to be ushers, foremen of mill or mine, roofing contractors, undertakers, owners of livery stables (and later of used-car lots), who have moved up quickly on the American ladder of success, and whose Americanness was not the willingness of the heart. But some of that willingness of the heart may have been still there, somewhere, perhaps on black November weekday mornings when there are but a handful of people at the early Mass, when the organ is silent, the priest stomps up to the altar, but an Irish wife or mother of one of the foremen sits and kneels next to an old Polish or Hungarian woman in a black kerchief, no longer bothering to sit in the next empty pew, both mumbling something different while they purl their rosaries. But that no longer matters. It is not that they got accustomed to each other, not that their suspicions vanished, but that much of it melted away through the years. But the sad thing is that so did much of the parish itself. Whatever the destiny of its ingredients, the mythical pot itself began to melt.

"Now I heard you out, and I am disappointed in you. I know that you have thought much about Catholics in America, and that you even thought once to write a miniature, the history of one parish that you know. But *this* will not do, and the problem is not merely aesthetical or technical — all right, historical. The heart has reasons that reason knows not, and even if your heart is in the right place, those of its reasons that reason knows not are not to be written or spoken about. The important thing is that those Catholic churches in America have not been there in vain. No terrible beauty was born within their cold walls, and a few dreadfully vulgar phrases have been uttered from some of their pulpits — but someday, at some moment, something just may have happened to someone in each one of them, changing an entire life. Besides, Catholic churches have been less transient than most other places in America. And the Irish dislike of the nether immigrants was transient too: it passed after one or two generations, and not only for pragmatic reasons, such as ward-leaders' politics or that boyo knocking up and then marrying the Hungarian girl. The Irish are good people, except when they are socially ambitious, and there are not many of those among them. You know that, and you know, too, that when a great Hungarian placekicker on the parochial school football team brought the team to the Catholic League finals, that was a decisive matter not only in the minds but in the hearts of the Catholic people of America—which is, I agree, why the history of the Catholic Church and of its people may be difficult to write."

Yours is the last word this time.

1906

LOOKING EAST THROUGH the only Palladian window of Brooklyn College, a professor contemplates the view before his mind begins to wander. It is May and close to noon, but not yet uncomfortably warm, the sun shines strong, the air is not grayed with humidity. He sees a sea of houses, with a few green patches here and there, the randomness of their appearance suggesting the subtropical weediness of so much American vegetation; a few high factory chimneys, a few large red brick warehouses, a few telephone poles with their porcelain insulators, a few white Protestant church steeples picking at the sky, but the sea of houses is mostly unbroken, stretching out in all directions, wide and large enough to deny all impressions of a small town, though it is, almost depressingly, horizontal. There is nothing very urban or urbane about it, either; it is surely not like Manhattan, a few miles away, increasingly perpendicular, with its quickening profile of skyscrapers. Our man lives in Manhattan, not in one of those new skyscrapers, though he hopes to live in one of them one day. He is benumbed by the sight of ubiquitous Brooklyn, with a faintly conscious feeling that those stone towers of Manhattan will not be repeated in Brooklyn, that that striking cityscape will not absorb this lower-middle-class kind of a landscape. He wishes that he were teaching, and not only living, in

Manhattan (which in 1906 he and others still call New York). But one cannot have everything, and his is not the worst of all possible worlds.

It is thus that his mind wanders or, rather, floats across from Brooklyn to Manhattan, from his wide and unconcentrated looking out of the window to a more concentrated kind of thinking about his own prospects. His situation allows him to do that. He sits on a podium, in a large mahogany chair, pretending to listen, in his capacity of chairman, to the eminent professor who reads a lengthy paper in a rather droning voice. To have brought this eminent professor from Columbia to give a lecture at Brooklyn College is a small feather in his cap. Yet the visitor has been a bit too patronizing, and our man is aware, too, that the idea and the content (not to speak of the delivery) of the lecture are not particularly impressive. He is capable of judging that, since both of them are New York professors, professionals and colleagues (though only in the very broad sense of the "academic community").

It is 1906, and they both resemble the Flatiron Building, from their countenances down to their large, narrow, high-buttoned shoes. This in spite of the fact that their racial and national and social origins could not be more different. The Columbia professor is a third- or fourth-generation American. His host in Brooklyn is a first-generation immigrant, with a complex present, past, and future, a condition that involves the present preoccupations of his mind, even though he is, at this moment, not altogether aware how basic that condition is. He is, you see, not a typical immigrant. He knows this, and he knows it more than does his patronizing guest; and he is both right and wrong.

Now, before you say anything and before you tell me that of all the scenes I have till now tried to describe this is the dullest one, let me tell you that once, not so long ago, I gave a lecture at Brooklyn College—which obviously could not be more different in 1989 than it must have been in 1906—and I suddenly thought how it must have been for an imaginary and respectable immigrant professor in 1906. I built an entire imaginary scaffolding around that, including his wishes and problems in the summer of 1906, and here it is.

"You mustn't always tell me what I think. Right now, in this case, I have an idea what you're after. You told me often — and you have made throwaway remarks about this in your books — that the most important thing that has happened to the United States has been immigration, and yet there exists not one really good history, or even not one good novel, about immigration."

Yes, because —

"Let me continue, please. It has not been done because all such novels were written either by Americans who understood Americans well enough but who did not really understand immigrants well enough, so that they idealized them, even such a good writer as Willa Cather in *My Antonia,* or by immigrants who knew their fellow immigrants but who did not know native Americans well enough, as in that otherwise very good book *The Rise of David Levinsky.* You once said that Nabokov didn't really understand Americans well enough either, which is why his best book may be *Pnin.*"

Santayana did.

"Yes, he did, but there are no immigrants in *The Last Puritan.* Anyhow, he said once that the Declaration of Independence was 'a salad of illusions,' while Nabokov in *Lolita* said that his immigrant antihero Hubert or Humbert was 'a salad of racial genes.' America the Lettuce."

Lettuce reason together. First, my Brooklyn professor immigrant is a salad of racial genes, too. Second, 1905–1906 was the peak of immigration to America. For the first time in the history of the United States, more than 1 million immigrants were legally admitted that year alone.

"You told me once that what was needed was someone who understood immigrants as well as older Americans, meaning someone who was fairly at home in both worlds and also fairly equidistant from them, and that there were, and are, very few people like that — which also means that such a person must know and understand and be able to write American English as well as his native language, perfectly or near perfectly. You are that, which does not necessarily mean that you can (or should) write about the great immigration in New York or Brooklyn in 1906."

I am trying to do much less than that. But the mind of my imaginary forerunner interests me, and then *some* things about immigration, about New York, about America in 1906 *may* be reflected in what follows, here and there. You will say that this is trying to do not much less but too much. I shall be brief. Our man, sitting there in his professorial chair in Brooklyn, differs from the vast majority of American immigrants. He is thinking of his coming return to Europe.

"Is that so? You once wrote or told me and proved by some statistics that the vast majority came here with the purpose of returning to their homelands, after having earned some good money here. (Yes, I know: there were exceptions among them, the Jews and most of the Irish.) In any event, that goes straight against Emma Lazarus's nice but smarmy lines."

No — American immigration statistics are inadmissibly imprecise and inadequate. (For a long time they recorded only the number of arrivals but none of the departures from the United States, not to speak of the fact that for a long time they failed to record visitors apart from immigrants — regrettable sloppiness, but perhaps behind that was the old American idea, older than Emma Lazarus, that everyone who comes here wishes to remain here as a matter of course.) But then, while nine out of ten came here with the purpose of going back, sooner rather than later that desire grew faint. Only about three out of ten went back. However, let's drop this matter of immigration statistics. Our man is a special case (or, at least, so he thinks). He would be insulted to hear that Emma's lines about the huddled, the poor, the refuse of the teeming shores, and so on apply to him. He is going to Europe for a visit. Amidst the droning and the rising heat of that room he is absorbed in the details of his coming trip.

"Is he disillusioned about America, with the expectable consequence of being reillusioned about Europe?"

No. He has become mildly successful in America; but you know how vague and misused the word *success* — and, only consequently, the cult of success — is in America.

"You mean that the American cult of Success comes straight from the Jeffersonian phrase of the Pursuit of Happiness. You have criticized that phrase often — I guess, appalled by its present consequences — but you have not considered that that *happiness* meant something else in English in the eighteenth century."

I am not thinking of the relationship — or, rather, of the obvious nonrelationship — of Success and Happiness. I am thinking of the less obvious relationship of success and respect. Most people want to be respected rather than successful, in America as well as everywhere in the world, though many Americans don't know this, since they think that success equals, indeed always produces, respect. But now an important thing. Our man is not one of those who is successful among his own kind, meaning immigrants in his case. He has assimilated himself enough to find himself a place, perhaps an odd place, among native Americans, including some upper-middle-class families who accept him, in their ways, like a round peg in a square hole which nonetheless fits here and there. And that is his main desire: to be an accepted member of the ranks of the American upper middle class, with all the privileges that entails.

"That is why he wishes to be able to have a smart address in Manhattan and, I presume, to be a member of the faculty at Columbia?"

I don't know about his prospects for the former, but he won't achieve the latter, because among the few Americans who will be narrow-minded enough not to let him forget that he is a foreign immigrant are American professors, most of whom carry their own chips on their sloping shoulders, not being upper middle class themselves. (The grandfather of that Columbia professor was a dry-goods peddler in upstate New York.) I'm coming back to his problem with Columbia in a moment. Right now he is vexed about the class of his ship. Not about his class *on* the ship (his passenger contract, which is what ship tickets used to be, is cabin class, *Kajütenklasse* in German) but about the class *of* the ship, the *Kaiserin Augusta*, a German liner.

He is dissatisfied for having let himself be talked into that the day before. This is his second return visit to Europe, in more comfortable circumstances than was his first. This time he wanted to sail on the *Berengaria* or the *Britannic*. Months before he had met at a reception, and briefly, a director of one of Cook's offices in New York. He thought he would arrange his passage with the help of that man. He had not yet learned that in America it is a disadvantage to do business with a social (if that was what it was) acquaintance. In the cool, high-vaulted cavern of Cook's offices, somewhere on lower Fifth Avenue, he sent in his card to this businessman, who came out to greet him rather perfunctorily. He directed him to one of the clerks, who then told him that the Cunarders (then the White Star Line) were booked. That was disappointing—especially since on their passengers' lists (he asked to look at them, for in those days they were available before sailing) he saw the names of two New York families that he knew, or at least pretended to know. He then allowed himself to be persuaded to take a berth on the *Kaiserin Augusta*. Outside there was the bright sunshine streaming through Washington Park, the noise of carriages and carts and cars, a noonday bustle in New York that was not too disagreeable because it was not too frenzied; inside he overheard the talk of a smart couple, wearing and smelling of linen, discussing the location of their cabin on the *Berengaria*. He was disappointed: he felt that the Cook's people had categorized him wrongly because of his accent and his foreign name—his type would fit the German ship. He felt a little better about it next day; after gazing with unfocused eyes beyond Brooklyn, toward the Atlantic. He was daydreaming about the departure, shipboard life, porters carrying his suitcases on to the big German train at Hamburg, bound for Berlin and Budapest.

"Now what is significant about that?"

You must understand that there are tens of thousands of former refugees or immigrants in America who dream—yes, it sometimes figures in their very dreams—about their departure for Europe. In 1992 that has not changed. I have a good friend, a Hungarian lady, who works very hard as a senior executive secretary in New York, saving her money and dreaming of the four weeks she and her husband spend in Europe (not necessarily in their homeland) every August, in good hotels and very comfortable circumstances, every detail of which is planned and anticipated months before. "Those four weeks are what I live for," she once told me.

"Which means that she is unhappy in America. You say that your man is not. But isn't he an insufferable snob? Whether unsure about America or not, he surely seems unsure about himself."

That is true, but he is not insufferable, because he is a romantic, though he never sees himself in that way, and he is not romantic about Europe. He is romantic about American society.

He is not romantic about Europe, and not only because he was not one of the Lazarus people, about whom he is exaggeratedly aware. He did not come through Ellis Island (which was not even there when he landed) or through the dreadful Castle Garden immigration station, because, you see, even then he (or his parents—who knows?) had paid his second-class fare, which meant not steerage, and those who had not come third class did not have to go through the rude processings in Castle Garden or Ellis Island. His stiffness about Europe has something to do with his provenance, about which I prefer not to think much—not because it is particularly disreputable but because I am interested about this man in America and not in Hungary. Why he came to America I do not know. There *were* middle-class people in Central Europe who emigrated to America in the 1890s, but they were few. Life for middle classes at that time was so safe and respectable and at least potentially prosperous that there were few reasons for them to leave it. In ninety-nine out of a hundred cases members of such families emigrated because they had to. There happened something wrong within their family, or, more likely, they had done something wrong themselves and it was deemed best that they go away, and farther than, say, Vienna or Berlin: to New York.

Americans did not and do not know this. Immigrants do not tell them such things. They know what Americans want to hear. Moreover—gradually, slowly, their own recognition of the motives of their emigration changes; it becomes transformed, with new ascriptions of those motives, including clichés in their own minds. All immigrants lie, including to themselves. In this respect our man was no exception. He will enjoy his return visit to some of his relatives and friends, impressing them with his clothes, money, the American side of himself. He will hardly give a thought to the fact that so many things—the taste of the food, of some of the talk, including those cynical jokes in the boulevard coffeehouses, the servility of waiters and servants, and so on—accord with his innermost being. He will think of himself as an American, and he will take some pleasure from the circumstance that some of the people in his native city might also see him that way.

His ambitions, you see, are American. There is some kind of wound in his soul from the past that we do not know (in this respect he is not that different from that great American romantic, Gatsby), but there are all those ambitions of his to belong to the upper middle class in New York. I must say that he has worked hard at this. His English is good. His clothes and his behavior almost always fit a certain pattern. He is not particularly charming, because of his wish to conform. That goes not only for his clothes and his pince-nez, and not only for his ideas and expressions, but also for even his physical countenance. He—at least sometimes—has come to *look* American. Recall what I said about the Flatiron Building.

"Well, besides the great immigration study chaired by Franz Boas, there were certain observant visitors to America around that time who saw something, suggesting the argument that you made elsewhere: not only was Darwin wrong, but Lamarck may have been right, and acquired characteristics *may* be inherited. There was visible and measurable evidence that the physical characteristics of some immigrants changed during their lives in America."

And not only because of a different climate or because of different nutrition.

"But your man is still very uninteresting. Very."

Except for one thing. His mind has not become very American. Let me quickly add that our man had earned an American Ph.D. in political science (though his interest is more historical than theoretical) and then got his respectable job at Brooklyn College, but he is also aware that those Columbia professors snub him.

"That may be lamentable, but there *is* something comic about him."

And tragic too. The tragic element is more complicated than the comic one. Now consider that he is one of a hundred immigrants of his time who has become almost entirely Americanized. As he goes down the street, people who don't hear him speak do not think he is an immigrant. I shan't again describe his clothes and his looks, except to say that he — and I am referring not only to his pince-nez, his barbering, and the American dental work in his mouth — has acquired a face, or rather an expression, that is at least, if not more, as much 1906 New York than it is 1906 Budapest. But what goes on behind that face — though of course not inseparable from it — is something different. Behind this American façade his brain is not a salad of American and Hungarian and German (with a soupçon of French) thoughts; it is a watercourse (I almost said landscape) of different runnels and channels, spilling into each other most of the time. On the conscious level, I mean.

"Yes, I know; but you must spare me your anti-Freudian pontifications, in this instance."

No need for that here, not to speak of the fact that in 1906 Freud has not arrived in America yet — he will make that strange visit to Clark University in 1909, I think. Just to mention another contemporary: in our man's case, Bergson may be more appropriate. "Becoming" is more telling than "being." He so much wanted to become an American that he has almost — well, in many ways — become an American. He not only speaks English better than ninety-eight out of one hundred of his former countrymen; he knows his Emerson, Howells, Jefferson, Lincoln, Hawthorne, Parkman, John Dewey. He knows how to read American newspapers, by which I mean that he knows what to read and what not to read in them and, on occasion, how to read between the lines of their editorials. He is a Republican who admires Theodore Roosevelt. He pays pew rent in a socially respectable Presbyterian church. What he doesn't know is that many people, including his social acquaintances and his few friends, still consider him as a former immigrant. You're right — there is something faintly comic about that. They surely don't hold that against him — except perhaps some of the professors, who are both envious and jealous of him because of his knowledge and his Europeanness, which they, of course, misconstrue. That he doesn't know either.

Now I'm coming to the end, which is the tragicomedy of his intellectual life. Before I go further, one last comic thing. There is, in New York, one group of people who would take him completely as one of their own. They are the bohemians and the intellectuals of Greenwich Village. Wait a minute. I know: Greenwich Village, as such, did not yet exist: In 1906, it was mostly inhabited by Italian immigrants. But American Bohemia already existed, with more bonhomie than now, of course, yet already a bit of a caricature of itself because fitting a pattern, like those red-and-white checked tablecloths or the dripping candles stuck in Chianti bottles at their favorite Italian restaurants. Well, our man wouldn't have anything to do with such people, he regards them as irresponsible, shallow, immoral, unpatriotic, and so on. Sometimes he would stiffly say so. He does not know that some of his upper-middle-class American acquaintances are generous in their indulgence: they do not mind the Art World at all; indeed, they take pleasure from the knowledge that in New York such a thing does exist, composed of artists and bohemians and intellectuals and cultured immigrants. They are all together in his acquaintances' minds, while they are rigidly separated in his.

Now consider that 1906 in America was not only the peak year of mass immigration but also a year near the zenith, if not *the* zenith, of the Progressive intellectual impulse. And that is where our man's troubles rise to the surface of his mind. When he came to America he had convinced himself that America was the future, by which I mean ahead of Europe, not only materially but spiritually too. It is not only that he preferred Lincoln to, say, Bismarck; he preferred Emerson to Goethe. Not that he thought that Goethe was the lesser writer, but because he convinced himself that Emerson was more relevant than Goethe, not only for America but for the present and the future of the world. He believed in the American idea of Improvement, of Progress. Among other things, in Turner's frontier theory —

"Which Turner had cribbed from an Italian."

Yes, but our man does not know that. What he knows (and we know that too) is that in 1906 Progressivism has reached the highest levels of American intellects, that Columbia is the best university in the United States, that the historians there, Robinson and Beard, are top men. Now I come to the essential matter, which is that in 1906 Robinson and Beard are completing their *New History,* a new kind of Progressive, modern, American-type history —

"Wait a minute. *The New History* was not published until 1912. Besides, Beard was then known as a radical, the kind that your great patriot and conformist would shy away from."

Ah, yes, but in 1906 Beard had not yet written *An Economic Interpretation of the Constitution of the United States.* He was not yet known as an iconoclast but as a quintessential Progressive. Robinson and he were completing their *Development of Modern Europe.* They had already written their declaratory preface, from which I will cite only one sentence: "[We] have consistently subordinated the past to the present." Where that (together with all the other shallow ideas of Progressivism) has led you and I know. But our man was enamored with that, it accorded with everything he thought he believed.

Until . . . there came a sharp little shock to him. You see, Robinson and Beard had consulted him. They wanted someone to check the small — very small — portion of their manuscript that dealt with Danubian Europe. They did not know him personally, but they knew of him; they told one of their assistants to contact him for the purpose of checking those few pages, already in proof. And then and there our man found that these great American historians, *Augusti* among the Progressives, were all wrong. There were ten factual mistakes on each proof sheet. More important, there was something wrong with their entire perspective on the history of that portion of Europe. It was shallow, ephemeral, journalistic. The prose smelled of light perspiration (and in some instances light perspiration can be more disagreeable than honest heavy sweat). Well, our man corrected—very, very carefully, explaining his changes in a very long letter—all the factual mistakes. Being the person he was, he did not say anything about their perspective. The smell remained in his nostrils, however, at least for a while. It corresponded with something that flitted into his mind once. Going along a street in New York, looking at a row of new buildings behind which banged the ferrous racket of the Elevated, he suddenly saw that something in that scene of the newest city of the world, with all the steely solidity of their construction and stony richness of their design, was very *old*, perhaps older than Europe. And old in a very different way. Something gripped his heart; they would not last. It was more than a fleeting impression. He understood it, he knew in his bones. But he preferred not to think about it again.

"A tragicomic character. What will happen to him later?"

I don't know what will become of him, and I don't want to think about it very much. I guess that he may marry, late in life, an American woman. He will not have much of a career; he will write a few more articles, perhaps a book. Sometime in the 1960s another Hungarian immigrant, doing research, will run across his name and wonder about this early Hungarian American academic in New York; he will try to find out more about him but in vain. Our man will not be well known. He will not be the kind of Expert who in 1917 would be gathered among the eager beavers making up Woodrow Wilson's "Inquiry." I do not want to speculate about his life except for the numbing democratic destiny. He will disappear with nary a trace (he will have no children), gradually devoured by loneliness and an addled mind. He will be buried in a suburban cemetery outside New York, unmourned and unremembered, somewhere beneath the advancing cement and the thoughtless subtropical burgeoning of American progress. There is an empty sadness in American cemeteries, unvisited as they are—a sadness largely devoid of a sense of the presence of the dead, of that sense which may be inconsolable but still part of living life itself.

"Not much of a remnant, I must say."

Yes, which is perhaps why he doesn't much belong in this book. But one more thing. About those older Americans in New York whom he idealized. They too were remnants. He didn't know that and they didn't know it either. Let me think, for example, of one particular couple, decent, honest, and well-to-do people. He is the president of a small manufacturing company. She is pale, fine-boned, motherly, and slightly artistic, a nice combination. They are not among the one or two socially prominent people whom my man knows, but they are close to him, kind to him: he comes to them almost every Thanksgiving and Christmas. They live in a new graystone apartment house, between Sixth and Seventh Avenues. Their spacious apartment will smell of beeswax. They are not really chic, they are the kind of people who are pleased that they know Oscar of the Waldorf, where they elect to dine sometimes, and who recognizes them (as he does one thousand others). They have their prejudices, some of which they suppress; they believe a goodly amount of what they read in the better newspapers and magazines; their own lives are rather unexamined, they are philistines in some of their ways. They will eventually disappear, too, earlier than they deserve, remembered less than they deserve, even by their children, because they weren't able to cope with what went and came beyond their own time and place. But there was that particular and un-English American kindness in their hearts and minds, and our man—perhaps too late in his life—will realize that he loved them. As someone once said, when we love a person, we see her as God sees her.

"*Non Angli sed angeli?*"

Yes, thirteen hundred years later.

1907

A WEEK BEFORE Christmas an Englishman is braving the extremities of an American winter and the luxuries of Fifth Avenue in New York. He is the headmaster of a school in the Midlands, on a visit to the United States, principally to Philadelphia, where his sister lives, married to the chief engineer of a woolen mill, the purpose of his visit. He has landed in New York two days before. The wintry North Atlantic was fairly civil, getting rough only on the last two days of a ten-day crossing. On the last day snow swirled madly around the ship; little or nothing could be seen; walking on the deck was unadvisable, no matter how bundled up one was. There was snow in the streets of New York but his hotel was comfortable, steam-heated, as were other buildings in New York, to a temperature to which he was unaccustomed but which he did not mind. He minds now the other extreme of temperature: there are savage gusts of an icy wind. A raw sun glares over Fifth Avenue, which he finds amazing.

He is in his early forties, a mild man and a bachelor. Certain ideas and images about America lived in his mind well before he contemplated this journey, gathered from newspapers, a few books, and the sometimes telling letters of his sister (his only sister, and they are rather close; he is looking forward to seeing her again, an anticipation perhaps stronger than his anticipation of seeing another country and another world, but we cannot tell). He has traveled before, on the Continent; he is a learned man. Now, two days after his arrival, he finds himself in the presence of a sensation that differs from the mental and physical sensations he had experienced on his other trips abroad, those compounded sensations of expectation plus recognition plus unexpectedness. Or, rather, the unexpectedness exists: but it is an unexpectedness of size. There is, perhaps, not more to this place than meets the eye, he thinks; but what meets the eye is so much, astonishingly so. Everything is exaggerated — and isn't that typically American? — but the exaggerations are *real*.

What astonishes him is the size of the buildings, of the crowds, of the riches — an opulence driven by energy, massive phenomena different from his encounters with luxury elsewhere. This is 1907, the cusp of the automobile age; already there are more automobiles than horse-drawn vehicles on Fifth Avenue. The shop windows of the great department stores are crimson and silver, one after the other they cascade with luxurious things, and how many of them are larger even than those on Regent or Oxford Street in London. And the crowds of people roiling and milling inside their whirling portals! He has been here for only two days, and those patronizing English ideas and feelings about America and Americans have largely vanished from his mind. He is a book reader, and he is surprised and pleased to see in the bookshops so many fine old crusted English volumes (not to speak of the editions of the Grolier Club). He senses that he is in a country that may be greater and more powerful than Britain, perhaps than the British Empire. But that recognition does not weigh on his mind, which is bereft of anxiety or even of melancholy. One reason for this is the extraordinary amiability and the helpfulness of almost every American he has encountered. Well, they are *not* like other English people — that much confirms his anticipations (anticipations rather than prejudices). As a matter of fact, he finds that they are even less like English people than he had thought before: what a variety of peoples, nations, races! And how friendly they are to an Englishman. ("It is almost as if they were admiring us . . .") Only later does he begin to recognize two different strains of this agreeable American Anglophilia: one among those older Americans who have come to prize their ancestry more and more, beleaguered (though not buffeted) as they are by the waves of newer and newer immigrants coming ashore; the other among these newer people, who wish to identify themselves with his language (rather than with his accent) and with what that language represents.

The cosmopolitanism of New York astonishes him. Its mechanics, and its size. In 1907 the first skyscrapers already exist. And in the evenings when he wends his way in the heartless black shadows of buildings in dark and soulless streets devoid of all human presence, it is those streets that are depressing, not the people; for what he sees and knows of the proletariat of New York suggests not despairing masses but people fearsomely swarming with ambitions.

Two days before Christmas he takes the train to Philadelphia. (More American mechanical marvels: Pennsylvania Station and the great train tunnel under the Hudson were being built, the only railway tunnel in the world beneath an entire bay.) As he sits, not altogether comfortably, in the plush, cinnabar red coach seats of the Pennsylvania Railroad (odd seating, not at all like the railway compartments in England), he sees an Augean spectacle of poison-dead marshes and metallic filth as the train speeds through New Jersey. So he turns to the enormous flopping pages of his New York newspaper, where opulence is recorded again and again, including in a long article about a Mrs. Garfield's reception at 769 Fifth Avenue ("Madame Sembrich and Madame Gadski sang, and Mischa Elman, violinist, played. . . . The vocal selections were chiefly from well-known operas. . . . The apartments [why the plural?] were decorated with palms and flowers. . . . Mrs. Garfield, gowned in a white-tambour-embroidered frock, with blue-turquoise velvet bound about her coiffure, was assisted by . . ." — there follows a string of names of ladies from Boston and Philadelphia, including a strangely named European countess. This may be unthinkable in England, but here it must be thought about — whence such lengthy articles in the American papers.

Philadelphia is a little more like England. A little: not much. Provincial, not cosmopolitan. Domestic pleasures await him. He is pleased, rather than surprised, by how well off his sister and his brother-in-law are. They had met in Leeds or Bradford three years ago. The son of a Midlands foreman, he is an engineer of weaving machines who had gone to work in the huge woolen mills in the Kensington neighborhood of Philadelphia in the 1870s; but how much more American than English he is! He has just bought his first automobile, of which he is very proud. He still plays cricket, and they have an almost English Christmas dinner; but he is full of hard, angular prejudices, talks contemptuously about Irish and foreign peoples, and is, alas, a Methodist teetotaler. But he is good to his wife, who has grown in girth and become quite matronly, in dress and even in some of her preferences. On New Year's Eve they take him downtown to partake in and see that great American spectacle. His brother-in-law is friendly with a councilman and they are invited to ring in the new year in City Hall, a monstrously big building, an exaggeration of something like the Hôtel de Ville of Paris and topped by an enormous tower on which stands a large statue of William Penn. City Hall is ablaze; crowds of people in black suits; men with derbies on their heads even inside; the wife of a politico, under her enormous aigretted hat, sways, perhaps tipsily, along corridors made festive with rows of lilies and potted palms. Now people crowd to the windows: five minutes before midnight, the great yellow clock of the City Hall tower goes dark, and then comes a great roar as it lights up again, and two cannon shots (stationed at the *Philadelphia Inquirer* building) rend the air. Next morning, over tea, he reads the *Inquirer,* which could hardly be more provincial. All the news is local, even that with a connection to the wider world, as, for example, the funeral of the president of the Pennsylvania Railroad, occupying most of the first page with sentences such as these: "Only three great names from the world of finance were missing from the roll of mourners—J. Pierpont Morgan, William H. Vanderbilt and E. H. Harriman." There is another article about Philadelphia police who, during the New Year's Eve festivities, warned juveniles "against the habit of tickling women with feather dusters on the streets." As he reads this to his sister, he laughs, "Well, this must be something American." There is another, rather American headline over a short article: "Police Will Shoot All Mashers in Alton, Ill."

He will visit the headmaster of a Quaker school; he will spend a long day walking across Philadelphia, finding some interesting nooks and side streets reminiscent of an older England, and Leary's emporium of secondhand books. The provinciality and the stolidity of the people, the quietness — except for the hooting of a few horns and the rattle of the streetcars — surprise him. So does, sooner rather than later, the torporific conversation of his brother-in-law. He will receive a farewell present: a new American safety razor of the best manufacture, stainless steel, in a blue velvet–lined holder. His American journey will last three weeks, he will see nothing beyond two cities and only certain portions of those; but he will leave with the impression of a very large country whose presence in the world is larger than people at home in England might think and getting larger and larger, because of all kinds of reasons, perhaps not altogether regrettable ones. Ten years later, in the darkest year of the world war and a very dark year in the Midlands, he will be relieved by the American declaration of war on the side of England; he will somehow think of that as something that has been expectable and just; and he will recall many of his American impressions and souvenirs, including that safety razor on the pockmarked glass shelf in his cold bathroom, still in good working order.

"There are many things in this vignette that are not clear. Your man's amazement at the size and quantity of things and, I presume, of people. 'But the exaggerations are *real*.' Now what do you mean by that?"

That that American bigness and loudness make sense to him. They are authentic —

"Allow me to interrupt. Isn't it true that so many things (and, alas, sometimes people, too) in this mass democracy are caricatures of themselves? That newspaper item about that musicale on upper Fifth Avenue, for example?"

Perhaps. A caricature is, of course, an exaggeration of sorts. And that is an American predicament: things and also people becoming caricatures of themselves because of American standardization; reality and sometimes personality trying to conform entirely to images. The result is utter predictability. Such behavior, including habits of speech, may seem simplistic, though its sources are rather complicated. But it takes more than three weeks here to recognize that, and that is not what my Englishman sees.

"Second question. Why 1907? I can easily imagine an Englishman's reaction to America being like this at almost any time during the first two decades of this century at least."

I'm on more solid ground here. Sometime around 1907 a mutation of the reciprocal sentiments of Americans and Englishmen began to crystallize, in all kinds of ways. Of course 1907 was the three-hundredth anniversary of the settlement at Jamestown—and the history of what was to become the United States of America began in 1607, not in 1492 or in 1776. Well, the British were beginning to butter up the Americans: in 1907 Edward VII gave the parish church in Bruton, Virginia, an old Bible, and then Theodore Roosevelt gave a large and ugly stand for it. An Anglophile and socially ambitious pastor, the Reverend Goodwin Archer, spoke of the Anglo-American symbiosis as if that were becoming more than a tradition. (And the rest is history—or, rather, rehistory—because there Rockefeller's reconstruction of Williamsburg was to take place, twenty years later.) I shouldn't be tough on old Goodwin Archer: he died in 1939 and his son, an American airman in Britain, died in 1943. Still, the most touching part of Williamsburg is the simple stone marking the graves of the Confederate soldiers who fell around the church in the skirmishes of the Peninsula Campaign in 1862—all English names. And there is a novel by Frances Hodgson Burnett, in 1907, that is dedicated to the condition—or, I should say, to the desideratum—of how certain Americans were beginning to cling to their English heritage. The title of her book is *The Shuttle,* meaning that, after all their mutual animosities and suspicions, the English and the American peoples have begun to reknot their ties, to reweave their joint destinies, closer and closer together. On the British side, of course, this inclination to side with the Americans began with Kipling and the Spanish-American War, and it went beyond and beneath strategic and political calculations. But while on one place the shuttle was reweaving, on another plane the threads were unraveling, for the fabric of the American people was becoming less and less Anglo-Saxon or even Anglo-Celtic.

That our visitor sees, but he does not contemplate its long-range consequences. Nor did Churchill, who devoted much of his life to the ideal of bringing the English-speaking peoples closer and closer together, even though it did lead to the American-British alliance in two world wars. During the Second World War my man will be in his late seventies, and his view of the world will not be very different from Churchill's: if the alternative to a German triumph is the gradual transfer of much of the Empire to the Americans, so be it.

"Now, that English willingness to defer to America—was that good or bad? I'm not thinking of its consequences for the history of the world. What I'm asking myself: was that a noble kind of resignation, or a not so noble abdication?"

Neither. Or—perhaps—both.

"One more thing. New Year's Day in Philadelphia. You left out the Mummers' Parade."

I did. Of course the Mummers' Parade was new then; it had begun in 1901, promoted by the mayor of Philadelphia and a newspaperman. I wrote earlier that the mummers were an old English tradition and that some of the first Philadelphia mummers were English mill workers, the same people who still played cricket in Philadelphia together with my English visitor's brother-in-law. And excoriated the Irish. Twenty years later there will be no trace of the English in the Mummers' Parade and not much of the Irish either.

1908

THEY WERE UP ON THE MOUNTAIN for most of the day.

Three men: a Norwegian, an American, and their host, an Austrian: a writer, a scientist, and an engineer. They climbed up to the summit of the Kahlkopf, Bald-Head Mountain, first along a sandy path, then between firs where the path turned gravelly, and then they left the forest behind and walking became more like climbing on a narrow, stony ledge of a track, led with sureness by the engineer. After two hours they reached the humped expanse of the peak, strewn with large bald hummocks of boulders, from where the view was as fine as could be expected, over three valleys and two of the Carinthian mountain lakes glistening in the sun. Their descent took an hour and a half, and then it began to rain. All three felt a healthy tiredness, all three were in fine fettle, good specimens of their race, three men in their late thirties, properly dressed for the chilly weather in heavy tweeds and gray woolen knickers and thick stockings and boots.

And now they sit in a large room of the engineer's house. They talk of the future of the world, of the destiny of mankind, and about these things they largely agree. They see themselves as members of the same band of men, strong possessors of the same beliefs, representative thinkers of the Aryan race. The American, a little older than the other two, is the most "scientific": he is a committed student of racial eugenics. Yet he is a dilettante scientist, as is the Norwegian a dilettante poet, while their host is a professional engineer. The American is less of an Anglophobe than the Norwegian, the youngest of the three, who thinks and says that liberalism and the bourgeois spirit have eaten into the marrow of the English race that is on its way to perdition and decay. The engineer says, yes, "die Engländer werden jetzt auch von den Juden zerfressen" — the English, too, will now be devoured by the Jews. His anti-Semitism is harder and deeper than those of the other two, but then he is Austrian, he says that his country is full of Jews, so he knows what he is talking about, which his two guests think they ought to accept. He is, after all, a cultured and very intelligent man, who has read wider and deeper than his friends, a reader not only of Hamsun and Nietzsche but also of Gobineau and Houston Stewart Chamberlain and so on, the racial thinkers. These three men are their amateur disciples, they belong to a small minority, to conventicles of men nowadays finding each other here and there, with their scientific belief that race is a key to history, *the* key to the history of the peoples of the world. But the essence of their convictions is not hot passion, racial hatred, or even fear. It is their cold belief in the indubitable power of science.

A conspiratorial group they are not. Their acquaintance developed by accident. All three subscribe to a German scholarly periodical, *Die Rassenkunde,* but that is not how they met. The engineer, a devotee of Knut Hamsun, heard of a public lecture in Munich about Hamsun and Scandinavian literature; there he sat next to a Swedish engineering student, a devotee of the racist geographer Rudolf Kjellén. The Swede then introduced him to the Norwegian; they spent two evenings together, became friends; the engineer spent a week with the Norwegian south of Oslo, in the bay, and invited the latter to his house in Carinthia the next summer. The American is a bit of an outsider among these two. He is astonished by the scope of their knowledge; he does not speak much but listens to them most attentively. He is a Bostonian gent, a Harvard graduate, an amateur scholar, working on a book about the primacy of the Saxon-Teutonic races and their endangerment. He is an advocate of stringent American immigration reforms, and since he reads German he admires the thoroughness of German racial studies. He is an addict of the science of eugenics, in his very American, idealistic acceptance of Science. He is a quintessential Progressive: eugenics and hygiene and sex education and so on interest him much more than politics, except for the immigration debates occasionally occurring in America. An article of his in an American periodical — straightforward and somewhat naive — was reprinted and translated in a German one. In this article he mentioned his affection for Germany and Austria and for their mountain people. Then the engineer wrote a letter, inviting him to visit Carinthia on his next journey to Europe.

Because of the American they talk in English, not German. The Norwegian prefers German to English, he prefers everything German to almost everything English, but he speaks English well, and the engineer, too, speaks English well enough — he had once spent six months in the United States with a group studying American long-span bridge construction.

The engineer is a pan-German, convinced of the inevitable decay of the multinational and multicultural Habsburg Empire, sure in his belief that its German-speaking peoples must and will be part of a greater German Reich. The Norwegian is less political, except for his hatred of liberal ideas and of parliamentary twaddling: in a way, toward the poetic though his mind runs, he is the most simpleminded of the three. The American's mind is simple enough because of his commitment to Eugenic Hygiene and Science, and yet he is split-minded, because of the remnant humanitarian essence of his unquestioning and unquestionable belief in Progress. All three men are fond of the music of Wagner, this goes without saying.

However, there is no gramophone in this house. It is a large house, built only ten years before, half surrounded by a forest of large hemlocks and spruces, standing on a knoll, separated by a low ridge from an icy river whose brawling sounds are constant music against the silence of the Alpine night. Inside, the house is partly "modern," that is, modern in 1908, with its bentwood chairs and the *Jugendstil* dressers and tables from the Wiener Werkstätte. While it is *gemütlich* and cozy here and there, there is also a new kind of spartan emptiness. Even though the house stands in the Carinthian mountains, there is no open fire-place, only a large, tile stove in the corner, and the house is often chilly, due to the engineer's conviction of the insalubriousness of overheated rooms. His wife comes into the room where the men sit and talk and listen to each other, still in their woolen clothes (they had been told not to bother to change for dinner), and now it is she, not the maid, who enters. She is a pale woman with an oval face and large round eyes, with a movement and conversation that are restricted and angular. She clutches a shawl around her shoulders and neck and says, "Die Herr-schaften," that is, "Gentlemen," and her husband finishes the sentence in English: "Dinner is served!"

At dinner the topics of their conversation are different, about the countryside and the trees and the Celts who had come here two thou-sand years ago; but when, after dinner, they remain at the table, their hostess having retired, and when their talk about the future of man-kind resumes, it is less energetic and direct than before. Of course they are tired from the long walk, but there is something else, too; the tone of the engineer about what he sees and knows about the coming des-tiny of the world is stronger and clearer than that of the other two. He has something of a personal and political agenda ahead of him; and he is not particularly talkative about that, not at all.

What I want to make clear is that these men, at this time, are fore-runners of the Third Reich—of the Third Reich, rather than of Hitler. At this moment, in 1908, the young Adolf Hitler, suddenly orphaned, a fledgling artist, moves from Linz to Vienna, alone. These three men are of the generation before him, and even though they will live to see the Second World War, they will not be among the men on whom Hitler will depend.

"Well, you said that in 1908 they are still in their late thirties, so that thirty years later they will be rather old."

Except for the engineer, who, I think, will survive the war and the collapse of the Reich rather safely. In 1908 he thinks that a new Hard Age or Ice Age is coming and that men such as he must be among its masters. But thirty years later he is too old for that, even though he may be in very good physical shape. They are Nordics, and Hitler was not a Nordic.

"And so what is the connection then? Three blabbers about racial theories, before the world war, up on an Austrian mountain? That spartan spaciousness, as you put it — a model for *Lebensraum?*"

Now you know that you are only taunting me, you don't believe what you just said. Their ideas issue from their awareness of the coming collapse of liberalism and of a superficially capitalist world. The German and the Norwegian are already nationalist socialists, the American is not. They are Aryan nationalists — except perhaps for the American, who is not a nationalist in the way the others are. He is a racialist rather than a nationalist, while it may be argued that the proportions are the opposite in the case of his host.

"All right — now let's get down to basics. This American: did you have Lothrop Stoddard or Madison Grant in mind?"

No — or only in the sense that this Bostonian gent is in league with them, as their follower and admirer. And in 1940 — that crucial hour of the century, you know my view of that — the pan-German engineer will be happy, or at least hopeful, witnessing the German conquest of Western Europe. The Norwegian (if he is still alive) will rush to join Quisling, while the Bostonian — well, he just *may* be an America Firster, but he will not want Hitler to be victorious. That will be the secret wish of another breed of people.

"Aren't you letting him off lightly? Just because he is one of those Progressives?"

Yes, like Margaret Sanger et al., all believers in Eugenics and Elimination of the Unfit and Euthanasia, and so on, circa 1908 and for a good few decades later.

"You dislike the Progressives so much as to think that all of them were social Darwinists."

No, they weren't. That term has been overused; and this application of Social Darwinism to Americans has been wrong. The Progressives believed in Evolution; the Germans, in the Survival of the Fittest. They are two different things, you know. I admit: my American amateur scholar of race and such in this instance believes in both. But he is American enough to believe in the first even more than in the second. The German Austrian doesn't. There's the rub: you cannot do much to further Evolution, but you can surely do something to ensure the survival of the fittest by eliminating their enemies and the unfit. And there is something in the cold categorical imperatives of his host that sets his American guest aback — a little. Their belief that men, with a cold brutality and will, can and will control much of nature. When he leaves the next day and goes down the valley to the rail station, the road widens, running along the river, in the middle of which a great tree trunk flows downward in the roilng water, turning its large branches like an enormous screw. That view fills him with a bit of satisfaction, though I cannot be sure what it really makes him think.

1909

AN ARTIST AND HIS WIFE are leaving Philadelphia, they are moving to New York. For them Philadelphia has become insufferably bourgeois, with its pervasive cult of mediocrity. He has been saying this, to shock people, at dinner parties, studios, in his club. Now he and his wife are doing something about it. They have taken an apartment in New York, he has found a studio that is perhaps less cozy but as convenient as the one in Philadelphia. The apartment in Manhattan, too, is less cozy than their red brick house on Latimer Street, now emptied out. Tearing themselves away from their native town and their friends and their surroundings (both he and his wife are old Philadelphians) has had its expectable difficulties, but their material prospects are not unsatisfactory. Both of them have money enough not to be principally dependent on his income from his etchings and paintings, while he does have a contract from a big New York publisher for a series of illustrations. They have inherited money, just about sufficient for a fairly comfortable setup in New York, for an existence that is more than bohemian, indeed, nearly upper middle class. Of this condition he and his wife are much aware. He is a (professional) gentleman artist, and she an occasional lady writer, categories stressed by both, with an occasional emphasis on the former.

Now they sit in the club car of the Pennsylvania train, well dressed, giving an impression of self-assuredness. They sit rather stiffly, talk little to each other, and the woman smiles only once during the two hours from Philadelphia to New York, a mechanical smile when she addresses the waiter.

They are not particularly happy, for a variety of reasons. Their departure from Philadelphia was less festive than they had hoped. There had been, a fortnight before the moving date, a large dinner party, including a couple of toasts, but that was predictable, almost routine, and, alas, infested with some of their dulling relatives. When they rose from the table, one of their friends, one of the few Philadelphian patrons of the arts, one of the few with a touch of panache, had said, rather loudly, "We'll see you off at the train, with champagne!" That was inspiring enough for them to look forward to that occasion. But the group seeing them off under the smoky glass-and-iron vaulting of Broad Street Station was smaller than they had expected, and there was nothing like champagne. The wife said, "We will be only ninety miles away, you know!" and there were pecks and kisses on the platform, a current upper-class custom noticed with some amazement by other, more humdrum people around them. Obviously they (especially she) would return to Philadelphia from time to time. They are not burning any bridges. Their Philadelphia background is an asset to be displayed in New York, where people, all kinds of people, ought to know — and to be impressed with the fact — that they are patricians, not provincials.

But now, as the train roars through a blackening New Jersey, in the well-lit train steaming smoke through the dripping darkness, there are moments of premonition about what awaits them in New York. Oh, everything has already been arranged, a man will be waiting for them at the station, there will be an automobile cab to take them to their new flat, and he has a luncheon date the very next day at a club, and she will be going to tea at the Washington Square apartment of a great Philadelphia lady married to a very rich New Yorker (a visit that she had carefully plotted months before their moving). But there is the prospect of their social balancing act. They are leaving behind the philistines, the dullness, the unwillingness to consider anything that is unusual and new — exchanging Philadelphia for the electric crackling air of New

York, where there are ample spaces for anything modern and sophisticated, including vernissages, galleries, European dealers, French restaurants, bohemianism together with coruscating wealth. They will be among artists, intellectuals, members of a class of opinion, partakers of the offerings of Modern Art, Modern Music, Modern Ballet, Female Suffrage, perhaps even of Sex Education and *Les Demoiselles d'Avignon.* Membership in a class of opinion is a relatively new American phenomenon. In Philadelphia it merely separates them from the rest; in New York it elevates them from the common run of people, this possession of opinions that may mark not only superior brains but superior tastes. Yet they are, at times, uneasily aware how in New York they will not only have to associate with motley members of that class of opinion; on some occasions they may even be dependent on some of them and be seen as belonging to their company. Will they be able to impress people with that other essential thing, with their inherited and asseverated membership in another, higher class of Americans? At this moment they do not know. And we might sympathize with them, were it not that there has appeared a gray freeze on their faces, and not only because of the subterranean and subaqueous tunnel twilight: for they are not a nice couple, and love has long since drained away from their hearts.

This mental snapshot—it is less than a portrait, and perhaps even less than a sketch—of this unpleasant couple has one purpose only, and that is to suggest the appearance of a new kind of people in America at the time: the Liberal Snob. People who have caused much harm, almost always, and often despite themselves—

"Circa 1909, as you put it. All right, they may have begun to appear around that time, enough of them to constitute a phenomenon—but didn't they have forerunners? Weren't the mugwumps liberal snobs? Beginning late in the 1880s, all those New England reformers and Progressives?"

Ah yes, but between 1880 and 1910 a new phenomenon had

arisen—or, more concretely, a new set of people had begun to appear. They were the Intellectuals—the first congregation of a class of opinion, a class whose self-ascribed members were exaggerated and acutely aware and whose self-ascription was different from the self-awareness of people of other classes. It is not only that a Bostonian or a New York mugwump or a Progressive or a liberal Republican would not think of himself as An Intellectual until well after the turn of the century, if at all then. Just consider how little Henry James wrote about Intellectuals, though he wrote plenty about Artists.

"And your Philadelphia couple, anno 1909: do they consider themselves to be Intellectuals?"

Yes they do—and I must presume that they would not have thought so ten years before. What is also interesting, if not significant, is that after, say, 1970, their descendants, liberal snobs, will begin to shy away from that term. That of course will be the result of the shortcomings of the intellectuals themselves, but that is another story (the end of which comes around 1990, when there are hardly any intellectuals left who are not academics, while not all academics are intellectuals). But what interests me is the double self-ascription of my couple: they think of themselves as Intellectuals of the Upper Class.

"Well, I agree that that was a period phenomenon, though you sure are subtle about those terms. Perhaps too subtle. You know as well as I that *the intellectual* as a noun, designating a certain kind of person, began to appear, first in England and then in the United States, during and after the 1880s, having been brought to these parts of the world mostly by immigrants from Russia, where the intelligentsia was a special class of people who read much and who were different from the only other class of people in Russia who knew how to read but who read little, that is, the bureaucrats. The transmigration of that term to the English-speaking world from a very different people and society may have been ridiculous but there it was. That very word *intelligentsiya* is one of the few Russian words literally inserted into English, the *ts* itself being a translation of a Russian letter."

That's just it. It is something else than the Russian ballet, or Tolstoyanism, or the *casaque* fashions of, say, Poiret (again circa 1909–1910). And, you see, there is this split-mindedness—horizontal split-mindedness, rather than a vertical schizophrenia—of my couple, early prototypes of Liberal Snobs. They do not like immigrants. And they will say so, though not forever. But there is that small seasoning of their anxiety: in New York it will be difficult for them to stay apart from those other Intellectuals. That was easier in Philadelphia, but there their ascription of membership in a separate class of opinion meant nothing. In New York they think (and hope) that they can have it both ways. And for a time they do. They think that they can keep the Finer Things of Life, Art and Culture and Taste, for themselves, away from the clammy and clamorous hands of up-and-coming eager beavers and, indeed, profitably so; that modern democracy is not only compatible with but must be dependent on a social and cultural upper class restricted to people such as themselves.

"Concrete examples—or results, please."

They will find their place in New York, for one big reason only: their ingrained ability to adjust themselves, including their ideas, to circumstances. There will be moments when that superb ability will be put to difficult tests—the Armory Show in 1913, for instance, when their opinions about modern art will be eagerly solicited by their mundane acquaintances among the New York upper bourgeoisie; but they will wiggle out of it by making a few small remarks which will strike their hearers as both enigmatic and knowledgeable. During the war my man will become a successful and prosperous illustrator, with his commissions dependent on patrons and editors, some of them Jewish, to whom certain remarks and gestures perfected by his wife will suggest that these merchants and middlemen of art are fortunate to commission him; but these men will know the lay of the land—and, to a considerable measure, so will he. Admitting that, of course, to no one, including his wife, including himself. About fifteen years later they will retire to Philadelphia, where they will be well situated not only financially but socially, because the success (or, rather, the publicity) he had acquired in New York will have melted away the last remnants of the unspoken reservations that some of the Philadelphia philistines may have had about their "eccentricity," meaning their professions and their opinions. They will vote for Wilson in 1912 and in 1916, for Cox in 1920, for Coolidge in 1924, for Hoover in 1928, for FDR in 1932; they will choose to favor Matisse by 1920, Mencken by 1924, Clarence Darrow by 1925, Hemingway by 1928, Frank Lloyd Wright by 1932. People will think them opinionated, and opinionated they will remain, but *how* and *why? That* is a complicated question, about which we may glimpse something from the *when,* though only God knows about such things, including why they have remained childless, and why they so coldly and cordially stay together, disliking each other more and more every year.

1910

MADAME DANSKA, A EUROPEAN SOPRANO, is on a tour of the United
States. Her schedule is not her first choice; as she said to her impresario
when he brought her the plan, angrily slapping her chalk-white hand on
a table, "Noch ein faute-de-mieux?" — another second best? The first
faute de mieux included London, where Madame Danska had been very
eager to perform at Covent Garden; instead she was booked for a solo
evening at Albert Hall. (Still, it *was* a gala concert, and the honorarium
was adequate; indeed, the notices contributed to her American invitation, including the Metropolitan, the prospects of whose near fabulous
emoluments gleam before the eye of many a European artist in 1910.)
However, even before arriving in New York they have learned that she
will have but one appearance at the Metropolitan, in *Der Freischütz;* but
there will be a tour of solo concerts of arias and Lieder in Boston and
Philadelphia and Richmond. She was not pleased with this arrangement, even though the money was good. The impresario was cowed,
even though he was accustomed to madame's outbursts of temper.

The Danska is a big woman, and as she comes close to the difficult age of forty, those outbursts come more often, and sometimes
debouch into authentic tears. She *is* a prima donna, though perhaps not
one of the prime sopranos of Europe, but still good enough and rudely
energetic enough to defend and promote and embellish her reputation.

When it comes to money or to publicity she is a tough fighter, a heavy-weight. Her origins are properly obscure; there *was* a Danski, a little Polish nobleman husband in her early life who disappeared soon (did she make him leave? he was an inveterate gambler, the kind whom the croupiers at Monte Carlo knew as a bad sort). One of her main assets, besides her physical and operatic ones, is her quick mind, including the rapidity of her curiosity, which is more intellectual than erotic, surely at this stage of her life and career. (The impresario is her lover.)

Her first appearance is in Boston. She does not like it. There is a late-winter gale, with electric lights swaying, spilling broken shivers of light; the hall is not packed with people; and those she meets before and after her performance she finds to be stiff and dull, with a large sprinkling of professors who interrogate her about the German poetic provenance of some of the Lieder, knowledgeable as some of them and pedantic as most of them are. The notices are good, but the Athens of America is *ganz provinzlerisch*, a provincial town, she says to the impresario, with so many of those men looking *tierärztlich*, "like veteri-narians," a German phrase of slight social contempt. (She is wrong: at worst, those men have the faces of respectable clerks, while the better bred among them have long, naked Yankee faces.) In New York she is nervous, the noisy opulence of much of the city and of the Metropoli-tan weigh on her. She sings well and the notices are again good, but she had hoped against hope that the manager might be impressed enough to invite her to come back; this does not happen, the manager is very powerful, he has her number, and he can have the best in the world, at almost any time. Then she goes to Philadelphia, where she is appalled by the fact that her privacy is being compromised, since the doors of her hotel suite, including that of her bedroom, are louvered ones (the management having noted that Madame Danska and her companion impresario have separate names and passports, they are obviously not married). "Another provincial place," she says, angrily. It does not even have a symphony orchestra. But she is booked not at the ugly, ram-shackle Opera on North Broad Street but at the Academy of Music, the appearance and the accoutrements of which, plus the good acoustics, do not disappoint her; and the accompanist is excellent. Nor is she disappointed by the private dinner offered to her in a very small town house, but one with beautiful furniture, in a dining room smelling of the varnish of recently restored paintings. She also has an interesting conversation with a Philadelphian, discussing the words of some of her songs and arias; both of them are opposed to the current idea of translating some of the arias into English. There is more, after all, than the relation between the meanings of certain words and their sounds. The question arises whether one may talk about things apart from the words in which one not only expresses them but thinks about them. "Without our perceptions of them?" her conversant says. "Without our sentiments," says Madame Danska.

There comes a long and not very pleasant train ride to Richmond, about which she and the impresario know nothing; and she is not much encouraged by what some of the Philadelphia people have told her: that Richmond is a charming place. They arrive late; it is dark, an evening in late March, with a bitter wet wind blowing. But, as far as the audience goes, Richmond is her greatest success. There is a veritable ovation; and two receptions, one in a house to which she is taken in a barouche pulled by two black horses and attended by a white-wigged courtly Negro in black silk breeches. And she is not displeased with her looks as she sees herself in the large gilt-framed mirror in the entrance hall, her hair shining in the golden light cast by a William and Mary, Protestant baroque chandelier; candlelight everywhere, that does wonders for women's faces, whether with fine bone structures or not. An old gimpy gentleman hovers about her, obviously much taken with her art and her sophistication. He is from Charleston, South Carolina, whereto he invites her for a musicale, offering to transport her in a private railroad car (perhaps moved, too, by her complaints about American trains). She could fit this within her remaining few days in America. But she chooses not to do so—better to spend the last three days in New York, where she will see, among others, one of her musician friends from Vienna. It may be that she is foolish not to accept the Charleston offer; but then she does not know that.

In any event, America has turned out to be different from the way she had imagined it. Very provincial; old-fashioned, too, she will say when she gets back to Europe, talking with her acquaintances and friends in Bad Ems, where she is booked for June. "Ganz modern, ja," she will say, "und sehr verschieden, mit verschiedene Leute" — yes, very modern, but very varied, with all kinds of people, and some of them quite interesting.

"Danska at the Metropolitan. Not enough of *that*, I think. You say that the manager has her number. I think I know what you mean: the American tendency to be taken in by second-rate artists from Europe, which this manager knows, but others do not."

You are not quite right. Danska is not quite second rate. And the odd, and sometimes wonderful, thing about America is that some second-raters — incidentally, not only from Europe but also from England, and not only artists but intellectuals and academics and writers — sometimes turn out to be first rate in America, because of their living and working conditions here but also because of some less tangible circumstances.

"Is this why she should have gone on to Charleston?"

Perhaps. Anyway — she would have liked it.

"And become the protégée, or even the mistress, of the rich Southern gentleman?"

No, I didn't think that. Besides, it can work the other way too: first-rate people brought over here, plenty of money and advantages, better positions and working conditions, and their work here is no longer very good. Think of Einstein. Or of Solzhenitsyn. But then I was writing about a singer.

"Is the impresario small, thin, with a pencil-thin moustache, black hair that he dyes?"

Yes, I'm afraid; but then I did not want to do a cliché. One last thing about Danska: a prima donna and a diva are the same thing, but she now prefers to think of herself as the latter rather than the former. But what interests me is the intelligence of this otherwise often crude woman: her recognition that America (of which, of course, she sees very little) is so spacious and that it contains all kinds of different people. In 1910, that is.

1911

THE HOTEL LUTETIA in Paris is a great pile of a building on the Boulevard Raspail, where it crosses the rue de Sèvres and the rue de Babylone. (Why that boulevard was named after Raspail, who was a nonentity of the Left, a *laïc* politician and anticlerical chemist, I do not know; but then much of Paris was built up during the nineteenth century, with the result that many great streets were named after ephemeral figures, and much of the Boulevard Raspail still has something of a Third Republic look. And there is something Babylonian about the size of the Hotel Lutetia. Thus the mysterious workings of cognomology.) In 1910 the Lutetia was completed. It was the first big hotel built on the Left Bank in those years when much of Parisian chic and the great cosmopolitan hotels were on the Right Bank, though there were still the remaining aristocratic houses in the Saint-Germain district and some new and expensive apartment houses going up between the Invalides and the Eiffel Tower. The Lutetia was not in the luxury class of the Crillon or the Meurice or the Ritz, but in 1911 it was perhaps only one rank below them and impressive in its own way, with a few contemporary excrescences of luxury popping out of its carved oak panelings here and there. It has suites, rooms with telephones, big toilets and bidets and baths, a big restaurant with plate-glass windows above the boulevard. Confirming the expectations of its owners and managers, it was soon frequented by foreign tourists but even more often by well-to-do people from the provincial cities of France. During the 1920s, when the adjective *bourgeois* was more pejorative than it is now, the prestige of the Lutetia may have gone down a bit, since it had the measure and the impression of something *bien bourgeois* (rather than *grand-bourgeois*). Its public rooms were (and, I presume, still are) proper places for the wedding receptions of middle-class families. I read somewhere that for one or two nights before June 10, 1940, Charles de Gaulle slept there. A few days before that Reynaud had made him undersecretary of national defense. I suppose he found the Lutetia convenient, since it was close to the ministry of war in the rue Saint-Dominique. On his first night at the Lutetia I think that he had just come back from the front, or what was left of it. Those days in early June 1940 were extraordinarily beautiful, with a relentless sun in the sky. De Gaulle knew what was coming; the prospect of the fall of Paris opened up vastly before him. As he stepped out of the Lutetia he could see the wide boulevard emptying of traffic and the great city emptying of hope and faith.

The Lutetia was the kind of big hotel the Germans customarily liked; yet, for some reason, during the Occupation no Abwehr or Gestapo were lodged in it. During the liberation of Paris in August 1944, the first tanks of General Leclerc's army came down toward the Seine on the Boulevard Raspail, past the Lutetia. Since then it has been refurbished and remade. It is, I think, often frequented by Germans now. It has survived eighty years of this century, indeed, the entire historical twentieth century, which, as we know, began in 1914 and ended in 1989. It has survived two world wars, and, surely on the outside, it looks as it must have looked in 1911, when an American couple would stay there and when a Romanian poet would sit on the sidewalk terrace of a café on the corner of the rue de Babylone, looking up at it.

"An American in Paris. I know, that's the 1920s, and has been written to death. You wanted to avoid that, because you have this phobia about clichés, which is not always an asset, because there are many clichés that are true."

No, you are wrong—I *will* come back to Paris some time in the 1920s. Kensington, then in his twenties, was there studying painting. American artist in Paris in, say, 1925 or 1927—that may be a cliché but I cannot avoid that. But this is not about the twenties and not about K. and not about artists, though there is a connection. The Americans who just arrived at the Lutetia are his uncle and aunt. Their experiences do not, however, fit the customary clichés. He is a Philadelphia lawyer, large, florid, round-faced, a Quaker turned Episcopalian, Yale graduate, sportsman, fisherman, with a summer house in Maine. She is thin, pensive, and somewhat dyspeptic. Of course she is more interested in music and art than is her husband, and she speaks a little French, while he does not. She was prepared—though of course anxiously—to like France more than was her husband. Yet he has a better time in Paris than she has. Their experiences differ from their expectations. The train from Le Havre to Paris was bigger and faster than they had expected. The Lutetia was larger and more modern than they had expected. But she had wilted and feels tired and will, alas, be often tired during their twenty days in Paris. She is overwhelmed by much of it; he isn't. They will see the sights, spend an evening at the Opéra, another one at a concert; they will visit an art dealer who had been recommended by a lawyer friend in Philadelphia, and they will be set back by some of his talk and his prices; another acquaintance of the Philadelphia friend, a Parisian lawyer, will invite them to a good restaurant somewhere near the Parc Monceau, which they will like, I mean the dinner, the Frenchman, and especially his wife, sixtyish but vivacious and self-assured, birdlike, piquant, and witty. But there will be more than one evening when Mrs. elects to stay in their room. A light supper will be brought up to her. He will then go out, and not to the Folies-Bergère. He will walk a lot. He will open his eyes and lungs and begin to breathe in Paris, and enjoy it.

"Knowing you as I do, he will *not* meet a Paris whore while his Madame *s'est retirée.*"

Neither will he be transfixed by the sight of an erotic piece of lingerie in a shop window, as was Mr. Bridge in *Mrs. Bridge*. Anyhow, he is not like Mr. Bridge at all. He is not particularly suspicious, indeed, he has a bit of the bounder in him. Also, their itinerary is not the standard one. For some reason our couple go from Paris to Switzerland, a few days at the Italian lakes, and to England, not at the beginning but at the end of their trip. He will be slightly disappointed in England and in the English, including his connections, since he will be set back a little because of their occasional rudeness and by their indifference to Americans. In 1911 the French were not like that.

"But your ascription of the motives of your man's newly found Francophilia is unconvincing. You're not going to tell me that you write about these people because they prefer French spring lamb to English roast mutton, or the courtesies of a French concierge to the matter-of-factness of an English doorman?"

Those things have something to do with it but not very much. There is something in Paris to which he responds. It goes deeper than the pleasant weather and Parisian things in June. He is a Philadelphia lawyer, a former Quaker, a clubman, a Taft voter, but not without a touch of being a free spirit. (Being a free spirit is not always a virtue: sooner or later he will deceive his wife, on propitious occasions of course, and by 1911 he is, alas, an agnostic, even though during his infrequent attendances he finds himself at home among the people and under the neo-Gothic vaulting of the Church of the Redeemer in Bryn Mawr, Pennsylvania.) The interesting thing is that he has an appetite for freedom in an American sense, which, he feels, the French have too, though in different ways. That feeling is then fortified by all kinds of mundane matters, by his surprised recognition that France, Paris, including the Hotel Lutetia in 1911, are more modern and efficient than he had thought before, so that they are worth being taken seriously, and not only because of their art of living. Consequently he will be strongly pro-Allies four years later. Ten years later he will not only encourage his nephew but contribute financially to K's going to live and study painting in Paris for a year. Another fifteen years later, in 1940, he will be the first among his law partners to join the Committee to Defend America by Aiding the Allies, he will be outspoken against and contemptuous of the Philadelphia isolationists, including some of his Quaker relatives and friends. Whereas the Romanian—

"The Romanian?"

The Romanian poet who sits at the sidewalk café terrace at the corner of the Raspail and the rue Babylone, looking at the Lutetia. (Incidentally, that café and terrace still exist.) He sits with friends, with a broad, black artist's hat on his head (which, in 1911, was called a *Calabrien*). He is a practiced Francophile. He knows infinitely more about France than almost any American in Paris, including of course the newly arrived couple from Philadelphia. He can recite French poetry by the yard. He, in darkest Moldavia, read and felt and adored the renaissance roseate breath of Ronsard and Du Bellay. He knows all the Third Republic prosaists from Victor Hugo to Anatole France, a bit of French philosophy, and the French names of astonishingly many birds and flowers and vegetables and even insects and fish. He lives in an unspeakable room somewhere behind the rue Jacob. He is a remittance man, dependent on money from Bucharest or Jassy. He is a proponent of *Latinitas, vitalisme,* Barrès's *La colline inspirée,* telling French people that Transylvania is Romania's Alsace-Lorraine. Except for the dark mahogany iris and the surrounding yellow of the white of his eyes, his Balkan face may almost pass for that of a Frenchman of the deep Midi. His French is so perfect that not too many detect a foreign accent in it. He knows many French intellectuals, students, girls, while he depends on the fleshy charms and, more important, the occasional (and of course nonrepayable) loans from his thirty-eight-year-old Jewish mistress from Czernowitz, whose husband is in the fur business. At the same time he is an avid reader of Maurras and an anti-Semite. He is a scoundrel. In 1940, after the fall of Paris, when our Philadelphian, four thousand miles away across an ocean, will think that his country, the United States, must engage itself against Hitler and the Germans, our Romanian in Bucharest will be among the intellectuals of the Iron Guard, an admirer not only of Mussolini and Maurras but of Hitler and the Germans, reacting to the fall of Paris by telling his friends in

Bucharest that the French had it coming to them, they were corrupt to the bone, he has known them for more than thirty years.

"Now why this tirade against the Romanian, what does he have to do with 1911?"

Because in 1911 he looks up at the Lutetia with admiration and envy. He thinks that France is on top of the world, and he wishes only that he had plenty of money (preferably from a rich woman) to live in Paris forever. Forget Ronsard and Du Bellay: his imagination is fixed on the luxuries that that Babylonian hotel suggests. And he is not entirely wrong. In 1911 Paris is *in floribus*. And the American senses that too.

"Wait a moment. Why 1911? If I had to pick a year when the love affair of some Americans with France was *in floribus* it would be 1902 or 1904. You know what I am speaking about. Edith Wharton has just ensconced herself in *tout Paris* and bought her first Panhard, and soon Henry James is coming over from Rye for a motoring tour of Normandy and the Loire (the automobile era had arrived in Paris even before New York); Henry Adams has discovered the medieval charms of Chartres and the Virgin; scoundrels like Boni de Castellane (and why must they be Romanian? in 1940 there were plenty of French opportunists and collaborators) are sweeping the daughters of the richest American millionaires off their dainty feet at the Jockey Club and the Pré Catelan; Sargent is flitting around among the parvenus; the best of American painters (so much better than those ragtag intellectuals of the twenties), such as your favorite, Childe Hassam, are inspired by an ineffable atmosphere that will stay with them forever; the greatest of private collectors are already American (except for that Russian sugar millionaire whose name I forget); John G. Johnson and Albert C. Barnes are there from Philadelphia and know the painters; and those slickest and wisest dealers in the world, Vollard and Durand-Ruel, are impressed not only by the size of the American wallets but by the knowingness of such Americans."

That was a bravura performance, and you may be right. But I am speaking not of Americans but of the French. There are, you see, turning points in the histories of nations that are visible only in retrospect, and often not even then. When I say turning points I do not mean mile-stones. You know that. Turning points in life, such as when a woman, dressing for an evening, realizes in front of her mirror that, yes, she is still good-looking, as a matter of fact, more comfortable with her worldiness and self-confidence than she once was, but she suddenly *knows* that she is no longer young, that she is stepping across a thresh-old into another room, into another chapter of her life of which she sees no end.

"This was not a bravura performance because you and I know that even the most beautiful women in the world are never, and I mean never, satisfied when they contemplate themselves in their mirrors."

Because they do not see themselves as God sees them. Women don't love themselves, because they know what love is, meaning always the love of *another*. Well, I was trying to say that my metaphoric woman is both comforted and saddened in that moment. But you are right: my metaphor is not a good one. What I am interested in is that such turning points are cusps, momentary high peaks, the nature of peaks being that they have two sides to them. Such was 1956 in the history of the United States, about which I have thought much; in a very different way, I think that such was 1911 in France. The French had recovered their confi-dence to a point—a transitory point—where they, perhaps for the first and only time, were in balance with the necessities and achievements of this chronological century. And that was visible in Paris in 1911. For the first (and, I fear, the last) time in this century, their technical achieve-ments were impressive. Our American, for example, was surprised by the huge steam locomotive of the Etat (or was it the Ouest?) Railway. A mundane matter, but then so was the worldwide excellence of the French automobiles you mentioned a moment ago. Yes, Blériot was the first to fly over the Channel in 1909, and in 1911 a later mass-produced American car will be named the Chevrolet, but that is not what I have in mind. What I have in mind is this surge of monumentality in French architecture that is there in 1911. I am not thinking of the Eiffel Tower or of the Gare d'Orsay or of that monumental Grand Palais of 1900 on the Champs Elysées but of the years, say, 1909 to 1912, when hundreds of modern apartment houses were built in Paris, with the names of their architects carved into a stone usually to the left of their elegant portals. Their styles, in retrospect, are wonderful balances of Beaux Arts and modern, so much better than the crazy-ugly concrete confections of Gaudí in Barcelona or the secessionist monstrosities in Brussels or Vienna. They are not as clearly modern as some of the Scandinavian and Finnish and, yes, even some British houses around 1912. But these Parisian buildings have proved themselves. They have stood the test of time. They are still there, well kept up, their façades cleaned of grime every twenty years (once De Gaulle insisted on that, starting in 1958). I am referring not only to their façades and styles but to their comfort and luxury and modernity: in 1911 they were as modern as were their contemporaries in New York, except perhaps for the slowness of their electric elevators — tiny cages, all mirror and varnish. The Hotel Lutetia is not the finest example of such buildings, but it fits. (What happened to French architecture and modernity after 1945 is another story — their modern architecture is among the worst in the world.) You see, this 1911 is not the Paris of Proust. It is the Paris of Valéry Larbaud, of *Fermina Marquez* (what a wonderful book that is!). I am also thinking of the fact that in 1911, during the second Moroccan crisis, the French were not panicky, they were more confident facing the kaiser than during the first one in 1905; that the sordidness of the Dreyfus and the Combes business was behind them; that their great writer and seer was someone like Péguy and not Zola. They had accumulated a spiritual capital, and it was enough to carry them through at least 1914 and the Marne.

"What you are trying to do — I know it is not easy — is to tell something about the music of a time. But I think you have spent too much on that ephemeral architecture — architecture, of which some German once said that it is frozen music. But then your friend Jacques Barzun once wrote, 'Is music melted architecture then?' "

No, though my point is that those buildings have not melted. But I am glad that you mention music, because 1911 was the peak of Debussy and especially of Ravel. The French had not only caught up with German and Austrian symphonic music but had indeed overtaken it. (And Russian, too: forget the 1912 Stravinsky éclat, though it took place in Paris.) I hope that when my American couple sat through their concert in Paris they heard something by Ravel, those fantastic and heart-wrenching harmonies whose beauty is everlasting, eternal rather than "modern" (as are, too, the best paintings of the Impressionists). By God! He wrote "Alborada del gracioso" in 1905, "Introduction et Allegro" in 1906, "Rhapsodie Espagnole" in 1908, the Mother Goose Suite in 1908, "Gaspard de la nuit" in 1909, and "Valses nobles et sentimentales" in 1911 (the peak! especially those short twenty bars of the first one), as was "Daphnis et Chloë," which he was finishing that year.

"Wasn't it Diaghilev who ordered that?"

Yes, Ravel may have depended on the presence of that Russian, just as the French depended on their Russian alliance in 1914, but that was not what carried them through the battle of the Marne . . .

"All right. *Fluctuat nec mergitur* — 'She will float but not sink' — the motto on the arms of the city of Paris. *Lutetia Parisiorum* of the Romans. I suspect that the name *Lutetia* may have had something to do with your writing of this."

That never occurred to me. This is not a paean to Paris.

"Last question. Have you ever stayed at the Lutetia?"

Never. It is not my kind of hotel. I prefer smaller ones like, say, the Pont-Royal — built, incidentally, also around 1910–1912, I think. I stayed there often in the 1960s but not lately, because it is very expensive now for an American, with the dollar going down.

1912

LET ME NOW RETURN to K.'s other second cousin (or is he his great-uncle?), the gentleman from Philadelphia who translated himself to Pasadena in 1901. "Everything suffers from translation except a bishop," a Victorian Englishman once wrote. However, this gentleman has prospered in California—except that now, in June 1912, he does suffer a disappointment. He had expected to be a member of the California delegation going to the Republican National Convention in Chicago. But he has just learned that the politicians in Sacramento failed to put him on the list; he was not appointed. He did, you see, become interested and involved in politics. He had gone to California as something of a hedonist, but there he became something of a reformer. He was Philadelphian enough not to be an unadulterated hedonist, but he was, if you remember, attracted to the pleasures of everyday life that the income from his capital would allow him to have in the gardens of California. You may remember, too, that during their conversation eleven years before at the Philadelphia Club, his relative faintly disapproved of that, without saying so; but our man believed that the future, including the future center of American civilization, would be situated in California.

He believed that in 1901, and he believes it still in 1912. But after a few years he found that his leisure in southern California came to be a burden. He became civic-minded—in stages. The local theater, the local arts center, the local hospital—subscriber, contributor, fundraiser, board member. By 1912 he is recognized as one of the leaders of the community, partly because in California his ten years have made him into a well-established resident, partly because his name is one that comes easily to mind (the lazy and safe and routine American habit of appointing or rewarding those whose names have become familiar). In 1912 he is more than a committed civic personality, believing in progress and reform not only in arts, science, medicine but also in education, suffrage, politics. It is in California that he has become serious about politics, a mutation that surprises his relatives in Philadelphia, where he had shown no interest in civic matters at all.

In 1912 he is fifty years old, healthy but a little less rubicund than ten years before, because he controls his drinking habits and also because the prolonged rays of the California sun have affected his skin. His countenance was soft and round when he left Philadelphia; now the first formations of jowls have risen on that face, together with symmetrical fans of wrinkles around his eyes. But he is a nice-looking man, in his light gabardine suit and well-polished shoes. The garageman in Los Angeles tips his cap when he receives a tip after cranking up the engine of our man's car. He drives himself away from his downtown office, where he was told that (as he had already surmised) the list of the delegation was all but filled in Sacramento. He drives alone, somewhat embittered. The road from Los Angeles to Pasadena is mostly paved, though there are a few rutted, dusty miles still. He sheds his coat jacket as he walks through his house to their recently designed Japanese garden. His wife is not yet home, their Filipino houseman tells him. It doesn't much matter: he finds it difficult to talk to her about his ambitions; she has not been enthusiastic about his interest in politics. In that sun-baked garden he suddenly feels lonely and tired.

It would be easy to imagine him as a lightweight, a soft and soapy and spoiled and largely immature male, one of those newer American types who were excrescences of the Gilded Age, men who never had to worry about money, who did not have to throw themselves into the struggle of life (and who perhaps even keep a mistress or two to compensate themselves for the chilly domestic domineering of their wives). There would be some truth in that picture but not enough. After all is said—or imagined—he is a good-natured person who has selected to own his progressive ideas for reasons more complex than a desire to fill the vacant portions of his time and life in California. He and his ideas may be less selfish than those of most Progressives, who keep telling people how they ought to live, which is more selfish than living as one wishes to live. And lately he has begun to sense that this Californian optimism about the improvability of society may be well and good and progressive and American, but that so many of its votaries and advocates do not know much of human nature, perhaps because they don't want to. Lo and behold, he is becoming a conservative—of sorts.

Well—the summer of 1912 was one of those rare moments that are both milestones and turning points in American history and in the history of California. It was a turning point in the history of the Republican Party, as it turned away from and against Teddy Roosevelt, becoming the conservative party from then on.

"Yes and no. Wasn't McKinley the conservative candidate, running against the radical Bryan already in 1896 and 1900? More important: the Republicans eschewed, because they disliked and feared, the adjective *conservative* then and for decades afterward, taking it up only in 1960 and thereafter."

I didn't forget that. But recall what William Allen White, that prototypical Republican Progressive, wrote in 1912, damning the Democratic Party, "the inevitable legatee of all conservatism in this country." But I am not writing about the misuse of political terminology in America. I am writing about California and Progress. Those in the California delegation going to Chicago were all Progressives, ready to cheer and shout and put up Teddy Roosevelt. They were ready to rush the platform in Chicago, but then there were one thousand policemen in their way, and hidden from the sight of the delegates, under the bright bunting of the platform, there was barbed wire.

"Not so fast! I know what's on your mind: had Roosevelt been nominated, he would have been elected, he would have been the president of the United States in 1914, and the world war and the history of the entire world might have been different. But 1912 was *not* a turning point in the history of American Progressivism, and you know that. Wasn't Herbert Hoover a Wilsonian and a Progressive, and even Richard Nixon, who put Wilson's desk into his office? Not until seventy or more years later would Americans—some Americans—begin to feel uneasy about the cult of progress, following their disillusionment with liberalism. 1912 was the high tide, the high-water mark of Progressivism in America, no matter what happened to Roosevelt and his ephemeral 'Progressive' Third Party."

Yes, and it was the high tide of Progressivism in California, too, which interests me. Remember what Roosevelt said to one of his booster Californians: "California has come mighty close to my governmental ideals." Well, ideals or not, the idea that education and legislation, that Progressive reform, can change the world (including human nature) was running so high and fast in California that California (as so often since) seemed almost a caricature, an extreme exemplification ahead of the rest of the country. Wait a moment: let me look up their legislative record from Kevin Starr, that excellent historian of his state. Here it is, a list of the Progressive laws voted and enacted in California in 1911 and 1912: laws suppressing gambling, betting at racetracks, slot machines, red-light districts—and the direct primary, the secret "Australian" ballot, the popular election of senators, the nonpartisan election of judges, the initiative, the referendum, the recall. And some other Progressive measures, too: the promotion of Sexual Hygiene and the establishment of a State Commission on Lunacy (very Californian, that). Starr quotes a California newspaperman as saying that suffrage "became a serious issue when attractive, well-dressed women took it up."

"You wrote that your man's wife—though presumably well dressed—was not interested in politics."

No, she wasn't, though I am inclined to think that she was in favor of women's suffrage, as were almost all her friends in Pasadena, between bridge and tea and gardening. What interests me is her husband's disappointment, his shock of recognition. He was omitted from that delegation by the politicians, even though—or, perhaps, because—he was an idealist, a reformer, who, at that stage of his life, had been working for all kinds of progressive causes in Pasadena and putting a fair amount of his money where his mouth was. In that moment, on that afternoon, a recognition flashed through his mind: that human nature will not change, that politicians will not change, and that there was something wrong with the Progressive movement. That recognition did not amount to an explosion, it did not go deep enough, it did not change his life, but there it was, it left traces—and, by and large, he was right.

Now there was another element, beyond politicians and politics. For ten or eleven years he was a witness to and a participant in the fantastic rise of the prosperity and of the development of California. I read in Starr about an ordinance in 1900 "prohibiting the driving of more than two thousand sheep at any one time down any one Hollywood street." But in 1912 automobiles were moving over white bridges, their fenders lightly coated with golden dust as they drove slowly along roads between orange groves, and then on wide, paved streets between new sidewalks and the courtyards of astonishing Spanish-style mansions. In 1912 these were not yet the mansions of the movie people, but they were beginning to arrive. Our man and his wife and the Pasadena ladies were perplexed by the movie people. Their money and their social situation enabled them to isolate themselves and perhaps even to take some satisfaction in that. They had been used to the California experience of newer and newer people coming. But now they were beginning to witness the signs and symbols of a future that was not exactly what they had anticipated. Of course they were exercised by the vulgarity of some of the Jewish movie people arriving from the East. Yet they would soon make their peace with some of the newcomers and with the entire movie world. But did they know — or at least sense — that they were in the presence of the beginning of a new chapter in the evolution of America, where California was to become a fabricated paradise, with fantastic and luxurious conditions of life going on and on, before, during, and between entire world wars, so utterly different from the rest of the world? That something new was about to be produced there that would transform the history of the world and the imagination of mankind? That it would become part of the packaging and, yes, of the message of the American Century? It is I, not my Pasadenans, who is perplexed; I do not know.

"What you are going to say is that, ten or fifteen years after 1912, Hollywood would be the fifth largest industry in America, producing 90 percent of the films of the world, and by that time there will be millions of people in Europe who know the names of American movie stars but who do not know the name of their own prime minister. I heard that before."

No, I'm rather thinking of what Chesterton wrote around that time: the old tyrants invoked the past, but the new tyrants will invoke the future.

"Come on. That may apply to Lenin or Hitler but not to the movie people. Tyrants?"

Tyrants, no (except, of course, in petty and ephemeral ways). But admit that by the 1920s the movies and the moviemakers were more important — by which I mean consequential — in the life and history of America than were Harding or Coolidge or Hoover. And sixty years later Ronald Reagan was silly enough to hang Calvin Coolidge's portrait on the wall of the Oval Office; he should have hung the portrait of Louis B. Mayer there, not only because Mayer was more consequential than Coolidge but because Reagan could thank Hollywood for his amazing career. But I am not writing about the twenties; I am writing about 1912. You know that I have come to dislike most movies — because I dislike and distrust most of the people who make them. But it takes two to tango, and the movie people had the oddest of part-

ners. By 1912 progressive and populist America was ready for the celluloid dreamworld of the movies, because of some of its own dreams
and illusions. And so it was not only because of the climate and the
scenery that southern California became the seat of a new empire. You
see, Aimée Semple McPherson and D. W. Griffith were really the same
sort. Now please listen to Vachel Lindsay, the Midwestern Barefoot
Boy with Cheek, but a much better poet than Whittier was. He wrote
a book, *The Art of the Moving Picture,* at that time. He did not call
Aimée Semple McPherson a Prophetess-Queen, but he did call Griffith
the King-Figure. "The romance of the photoplay!" he wrote. "A tribe
that has thought in words since the days that it worshipped Thor and
told legends of the cunning of the tongue of Loki, suddenly begins to
think in pictures." Now think of that! He saw nothing wrong in that —
he saw nothing but promise in that — this American poet of the people,
who lived by words, a master of words and of their music.

"Go on."

"Within the next decade," he wrote, "cities akin to the beginnings
of Florence will be born among us, as surely as Chaucer came." He also
wrote that movie theaters will mean the end of saloons (Lindsay was
an ardent Prohibitionist then). "Good citizen, welcome the coming of
the moving picture man as a local social force."

"Well, Erik Satie said in Paris that the movies will cure neuras-
thenia."

Satie was, or was trying to be, funny. Lindsay was deadly serious. Los Angeles, he wrote, "will lay hold of the motion picture as
our national text-book in Art, as Boston appropriated to herself the
guardianship of the national text-books of literature." Moving pictures
"may lead the soul of America, day after to-morrow."

He continued: "America is in the state of mind where she must
visualize herself again. . . . There is in this nation of moving-picture-
goers a hunger for tales of fundamental life that are not yet told." (Poor
Lindsay may have truly been a prophet: he has just foretold the coming
of the present national mania for dinosaurs.)

"Now a light is blazing. . . . Man will not only see visions again, but machines themselves, in the hands of prophets, will see visions." He is seeing the future: the video screen. He ends his book: "Scenario writers, producers, photoplay actors, endowers of exquisite films, sects using special motion pictures for a pre-determined end, all of you who are taking the work as a sacred trust, I bid you God-speed. . . . Pray that you will be delivered from the temptations of cynicism and the timidities of orthodoxy. Pray that the workers in this your glorious new art are to be delivered from the mere lust of the flesh and pride of life. Let your spirits outflame your burning bodies. . . . You will be God's thoroughbreds. . . . It has come then, this new weapon of men, and the face of the whole earth changes. . . . It has come, this new weapon of men, and by faith and a study of the signs we proclaim that it will go on and on in immemorial wonder." He wrote this in Springfield, Illinois, in 1915, fifty years after Lincoln had been buried there. Pulsing through these phrases is another American tragedy, about which our people in Pasadena knew nothing. "In after centuries its beginning will be indeed remembered." It ought to.

"I hope you're not saying that Hollywood meant the rise and the decline of the American Century?"

Not meant. Symbolized. And symbols—

"You have taken old Vachel too seriously."

He was young Vachel, an innocent, but at the same time he *was* an important and very American poet.

"But life is not only stronger than theory, it is also—allow me to say this—stronger than poetry. Or than the prophecies of the naive. Just think of the imbecilic predictions people made thirty years after 1915 about the glorious future, the cultural and educational promise of television."

Allow me to say again and again: my concern is not with culture but with civilization. I am concerned with the civilizational illusions of my ex-Philadelphian in Pasadena, with the condition—or, rather, the unavoidable destiny—of all those progressive ideas that turned out to be futile and counterproductive and that, for a fleeting second, our man understood that—

"Well, you did not make that shock of recognition clear enough. But there is another problem with you, which, again, is your European-ness. You wish that America had become more European and less Californian. But 'European' includes a multitude of sins that you know well enough. Or English? If America were more 'English,' well and good. But allow me to remind you: if America had been more English, you would not be quite what you are. There is (and there surely used to be) a largeness of American spirit that exists in California, too. Not every-thing has become corrupted there, and I am thinking not only of the very good quality — and, more important, the ever greater variety — of its wines. You yourself provide one example: your man did not be-come a worse man in California in 1912 than he was in Philadelphia in 1901. This is a large country, and next to the newcomers and their talons and salons in Beverly Hills, he and his kind of people had a place in Pasadena, just as some of them had their places in the suburbs of Philadelphia. There was — there is — a coexistence of beauty and death in California, as there is almost everywhere. That there is a little too much sun and not enough shadow there I will allow."

1913

As the walkers follow the path in the forest they suddenly come out into the open, to a wide, snow-covered meadow slanting downward, beyond which they can see the red tile roofs of the large, gray Grand Mountain Hotel. Still in the shade of the forest trees, the path now runs along the western edge of the meadow, mildly downhill. Beneath the meadow it disappears from sight but then reappears again after one last turn, where it meets the road, hardly more than a few minutes away from the hotel. They welcome the sight, especially the three women, since it has suddenly become cold. It is about four o'clock in the afternoon on December 31, 1913. They are in Switzerland, in the Engadin.

In about ten minutes they reach the hotel. As they enter the main hall, they can hear from the large dining room on the left a thin clatter of china and a tintinnabulation of silverware and glassware as the staff sets up the tables for the New Year's gala evening, with some of them pinning up the decorations; the "GALA SILVESTERABEND" and the "FRÖHLICHES NEUJAHR" transparencies are already in place. Warmth is all around them, reddening their cheeks and hands after their two-hour walk. The women debate whether today it is worthwhile to come back down for the customary five o'clock tea in the lounge, since at least one of them has a late appointment in the hairdressing salon, and they will be bereft of their cavaliers at the *thé dansant,* since one of the husbands elects to take a nap after the longish walk and before the prospect of a long evening.

The women ride up in the lift to their rooms. The two husbands amble about in the hall for a few minutes, discussing matters with the concierge, looking at the newspapers. The last crystals of snow have melted off their brown English sweaters, woolen knickers, thick stockings and leggings, and sensible, high-laced walking boots. The warmth carries a component of recognizable smells, the faint trace of steam heat from the hotel radiators, together with the thin scent of varnished wood and a light smell of consommé from somewhere in the kitchen. Upstairs there is the pleasant odor of freshly ironed linen on beds already turned down for the night. There is the redness of the sunset sky filtering through the double-paned windows; there are the new electric lamps on the night tables and on the dressing table, with their tulip-shaped, cut-glass shades. The radiators are softly hissing. This being a Grand Hotel, everything is comfortable rather than cozy, with touches of luxury here and there which most of the guests take for granted. Soon the sound of hot water rushing into the large tubs is heard through the walls and in the corridors. It is agreeable to feel pleasantly tired when one has the prospect of being refreshed and, while being somewhat blasé about the routine nature of New Years' Eves at the hotel, to still have a sufficient sense of anticipation. All is not well with the world and probably not within their lives, either, but savagery and destruction are not part of their world; if they exist, they are elsewhere.

These are the last hours of the last afternoon of the last day of the last century of progressive civilization, of the one hundred years' peace between the last great world war and the coming one. Of course, they do not know that.

"This is all like *The World of Yesterday*, which is Stefan Zweig's best book *because* of when and where he wrote it, in exile in 1941; but he idealized the security of that world, and you must not do that."

For us that is now the world of the day before yesterday, and I am not idealizing it.

"But you have just painted a miniature that is not even a period picture. It is a period vignette only because of the date you assigned to it."

I am writing, not painting. It may not really be a period picture of the place. The atmosphere of that hotel may not be so different even now, two world wars and eighty years and a historical century later. (Which speaks well of the Swiss.) But the people in those hotels now are very different, including their American visitors. I *am* interested in the variations of Americans in Europe, but the war of 1914 was a European war that put an end to the primacy of European civilization. My returning walkers are Europeans, civilized men and women. The men may even know that a war may be around the corner, but not the kind of war that will come; and they are, at least in some ways, responsible for that. By this I don't mean their ignorance of the future, their misreading of storm signals or whatnot, but something else — a failure of imagination that is intellectual as well as moral.

Now let me suggest something about the coming of the First World War in 1914 that has interested me for many years. There is a duality in its reconstructions, in the reminiscences of people. On one hand there is this universal memory that the war came out of the blue: the sun shone so very strong in the summer of 1914, the harvests and the vintages were more promising than in many a year; and then, unexpectedly, came the first sudden rumble (the news of the archduke's assassination) and the ensuing windstorm. In sum, a bolt of lightning from a clear sky. On the other hand we have the reconstructions of statesmen and of historians: the sky over Europe was not and could not have been clear or blue at all, because the atmosphere was heavy and laden, because the lineup of the warring powers had been in place for years, and because it was only by accident that a great war came in July 1914 and not earlier or later, on another occasion, out of other calculations or pretexts.

This is very roughly put, as you no doubt know, and there is an

explanation of that duality, of these opposite impressions and memories. The first kind, the memories of the blue and golden summer, comes
from common people, including writers of many languages — or, to put
it exactly, from the governed and not from the governors. The second
kind comes from the accumulated calculations of the governors, of the
emperors and kings and presidents, that is, their ministers and advisers,
of the generals and the admirals and the foreign ministers who in 1914
chose war over peace — or, again more exactly, from those who chose
advance over retreat, increments of prestige over unappealing compro-
mises, and whose miscalculations drove entire nations into catastrophe.
But that explanation is not enough. That extreme contrast between the
governors and the governed is false. The latter were not sheep driven
to mass slaughter. Especially the middle classes, on whom, in more
than one way, the rulers had to depend. So there came — or, rather, fast
developed — a war in which entire peoples rushed at each other. The
result was that enormous bloodletting, the fatal wound of European
civilization. (Whether that wound was truly fatal or whether it led to a
chronic illness we cannot say even now.) Anyhow, call it miscalculation
or myopia: the rulers and the ruled were not that different. They did
not see what kind of war this was to be. *That* was the decisive matter.

"You're saying that what caused the war was less important than
what the war turned out to be? That may be a sophisticated argument,
but isn't it hindsight pushed to an unconscionable extreme?"

But everything we know comes from hindsight, which is also why
the cause-and-effect relationship of the so-called natural sciences does
not really apply to human relations. Because of the intrusion of mind,
cause and effect flow into each other, they are messed up, even in the
sequence of time. Don't worry, I won't go into philosophy. I am about
to return to these people in the Engadin, to suggest what was going on
in their minds.

"It's about time. I suspect what is going on in *your* mind. You may
be thinking of the symptoms that existed before 1914, those symptoms
indicating that the cracks of bourgeois civilization were already there,
in some of the violent social outbreaks in the years before the war

and in the violent new experiments in poetry, architecture, music—Picasso, Stravinsky, the Vorticists, the Imagists. And there is the odd sentence by Virginia Woolf: 'In or about December, 1910, human character changed.' Some of this has been done by people who pretend to be cultural historians, you know."

Not some. Too much. Besides, Virginia Woolf wrote that in 1924. She was a Mistress of Hindsight, a Dodona going backward, and, in my opinion, already outdated in 1924, like all of Bloomsbury. All those artistic symptoms matter, but not much. The breakdown of the liberal illusions, of the bourgeois manners of the nineteenth century, would have come sooner or later, world war or no. Still, it was the war that changed everything—or almost everything that mattered. I am interested not in the Subconscious but in what was conscious in the minds of people, evident as that was in their way of speaking—because speech is not merely the outcome of thought but the completion of it, because thought is affected by speech, and not merely the reverse. What interests me is rhetoric. That is the last piece of homework yet to be done by historians: how the rhetoric of 1914 and before—patriotic rhetoric, newspaper rhetoric, in what was of course the golden age of the press—filled people's minds and made them speak and think in certain ways. Perhaps the only man who wrote about that was Karl Kraus. He knew something that Emerson had not known. Emerson said that "the corruption of man is followed by the corruption of language." The reverse is true. There ought to be a serious study that compares the rhetoric of the German and the French and the Austrian and the British newspapers and of course also the talk of some of the politicians at the beginning of the war. Most of their nationalist rhetoric was dreadful, but some of them were more vulgar and brutal than others. God is in the details, or *ces sont les nuances qui querellent, pas les couleurs.* Such a comparison of responsibilities may be at least as telling as the *Kriegsschuldfrage,* the protracted and perhaps endless discussion among historians: whether *Russia* or *Germany* or *France* were more, or less, responsible in 1914 than were the others—and by those nouns they really mean their governments, which, for 1914, is quite imprecise. What concerns me is the responsibility of the middle classes, including their desire — I must say, not constant, and not necessarily ignoble — for patriotic responsibility; but it was thereby that they were ready and often eager to express themselves, to assert themselves with those phrases and slogans.

"Will you *please* get back to your Magic Mountain?"

It is not the Magic Mountain at all (incidentally, that was published in 1924, too), where the protagonists are an idealistic, thin young German man and a Franco-Russian tubercular femme fatale, talking endlessly about Destiny, Faith, Culture, Philosophy — another outdated book, I fear. My two men are around forty, they are solid businessmen, materialists to a tee. Not bosom friends but close acquaintances. One of them is a Dutchman from Amsterdam, the other is from Vienna, Jewish, the director of a large paper factory. They have done business with each other for years. Having found that both of them had acquired the then relatively novel habit of spending a winter vacation in the Swiss Alps and in the same place, they agreed to meet there this year with their wives, whose backgrounds have more in common than those of their husbands, since the Dutchman is married to a Viennese woman. The man from Amsterdam feels a sense of superiority over the man from Vienna, in accord with the then-accepted level of a social anti-Semitism customary among the Western European middle or upper middle classes. He knows (and lets his business partner know, on occasion) that the Viennese businessman is the first of his forebears to have risen, at least financially, to an upper-middle-class level, while he has perhaps three generations of middle-class ancestors in Holland (though only the first one had a substantial income, thanks to all kinds of new business acquaintances, much including the present Viennese one). The Dutchman is comfortable in the company of the Vienna man (who is a *Kommerzialrat,* a respectable title), one reason being his acceptable manners, another being their common cultural interests, giving them enough to talk about besides their business, which does not preempt most of their conversations, except for their mutual laments about the rising costs of labor.

They are more cultured and well read than are many people of their class, including most of the guests in the Grand Mountain Hotel. They speak German of course. Interestingly enough, the Dutchman is even more of a Germanophile than the Vienna man. They know some of the oddities and rigidities of the German character, but their respectful knowledge of German culture is the foundation of their own culture. These burghers of 1913 are not bad people. They are materialists, but they are not the self-satisfied, pompous, humorless bourgeois excoriated (meaning gutted) by the antibourgeois geniuses of the nineteenth century, from Baudelaire to Ibsen, whom our bourgeois admire. They no longer belong to that century. What they are prone to is not sclerosis but neurosis. They look a little ridiculous in retrospect, a bit potbellied above their knickers and a bit ridiculous in their belief in *Fortschritt*, which, as you know, is German for "progress" (though the German *Fortschritt* and American *progress* are identical only in a dictionary sense).

But they have a hidden problem here. They are pessimistic optimists (which is not preferable to being optimistic pessimists). They cannot think or even imagine that *Kultur* is not international and progressive, spreading each year, touching more and more places of the earth. At the same time, they are anxious about the present rather than about the future. Their purpose is to fix the respectability of their personalities in an advancing world. In the Age of Money the instrument of their materialism exists together with their unquestioning acceptance of certain public ideas. What goes on in the recesses of their private sentiments I cannot know and I am not interested in it. I am concerned with their public opinions about the world, which they keep repeating to each other, for complex reasons that do not do them much good. They read the best newspapers, and they believe much of what is printed in them. (For the Vienna man it is probably the *Neue Freie Presse,* and you know what Karl Kraus thought about that.) The Second Balkan War of 1913 had ended. Both the Dutchman and the Viennese are contemptuous of Serbs, Romanians, Russians. Sooner or later, the Viennese says, we (meaning Austrians) must show that we are not the "sick men of Europe." That was a phrase applied for some time to the decaying

Ottoman Empire, but its potential application to Austria-Hungary is another cliché from about 1913, a phrase from some newspaper article which stuck in the Vienna man's mind and with which the man from Amsterdam agrees. Both think that somehow, somewhere, a war will come again, probably in the Balkans. Not an unthinkable prospect. If it has to come, it will come. They are like the Austrian foreign minister who in July 1914 thought that a small war might be a good thing for Austria after all. And our men repeat the current clichés: the Serbs are "not a *Kulturvolk,*" the French are *revanchists,* the Russians are *prä-potent,* meaning aggressive — yes, the Monarchy must not look as if it were to become the Sick Man of Europe. They were talking about these things during their mountain walk.

That of course is not what the women talk about, but not because they are less intelligent than the men. Rather the contrary. Perhaps somehow, somewhere deep down, they know there is something wrong with a world still largely ruled by men, by men such as their husbands: for there is something missing beneath that woolen solidity. The Dutchman's wife is the restless one, occasionally smoking long cigarettes in paper holders. She is not a model wife, though an Amsterdam *mevrouw* and a Viennese *gnädige Frau,* and she knows very well that there are troubles latent in the marriage of her friend from Vienna, too, who shows signs of growing a little stout. The third woman of the party is the Viennese woman's unmarried sister, the best read and perhaps the least good-looking of the three, saturnine, inclined to pessimism, dark-eyed, interested in the suffragette movement, socialism, and ceramics. Thirty years later she will be transported and gassed to death in Auschwitz, at the age of sixty-three. The two couples will survive both world wars, and her sister and brother-in-law will end up somewhere in New York, with their 1913 personae and beliefs still a remnant part of them, like their few browned photographs of that time. What will not survive is the world of the day before yesterday, except in picture books with cliché-ridden captions written by mediocre historians for a little extra money.

1914

ON JULY 28, 1914, the evening in Paris is violet, the sky is violet, the shadows are violet, men's neckties are violet, their stickpins have a glimmer of violet, the Seine around the Ile de la Cité is striped with violet, and so is Madame Henriette Caillaux, coming out of the Court of Assizes. She gathers her ankle-length skirt as she is being hurried to her automobile. Perhaps the violet reflections on her black dress accord with her mood, for amid the jungle of her confused feelings there is one of great somber relief. She has just been acquitted of the charge of voluntary homicide with criminal intent.

This is what happened that evening: the end of the Caillaux trial. Madame Caillaux is the second wife of Joseph Caillaux, who is one of the main political figures of the Third Republic and who had been assailed and hounded by Gaston Calmette, the editor of *Le Figaro*. Calmette went so far as to print some of Caillaux's private and incriminatory letters to his previous wife (or mistress). The present Mme. Caillaux feared there would be more of these to come. On a spring afternoon she bought a pistol, hid it in her muff, presented herself at Calmette's office, knowing he could not refuse to receive her; she marched up to him and shot him dead. Of course her trial was a great sensation. She was acquitted on a basis reminiscent of *crimes de passion:* involuntary insanity at the time of her deed. There was plenty of politics behind all this: Caillaux was, at the time, a man of the "Left," Calmette of the "Right." But this is not worth considering now.

Worth considering is the date. For this is the twenty-eighth of July in 1914. The outbreak of the Great War is imminent. The awesome chain reaction had begun. Austria-Hungary has just gone to war with Serbia; Germany and Russia have begun to mobilize; the First Lord of the Admiralty (Winston Churchill) orders the First Fleet to leave Portland for Scapa Flow, through the English Channel, "scores of gigantic castles of steel wending their way across the misty, shining sea, like giants bowed in anxious thought." But this day the Paris newspapers are still taken with the Caillaux affair, splashed on their front pages.

I can imagine a young Hungarian, walking along the Seine on that violet evening, perplexed as he suddenly comes upon an agitating crowd outside the Court of Assizes, a near riot between the anti-Caillaux and Caillaux people. His mind is heavy with the prospect of war. Theirs is not. Now he may remember how one of the friendly French girls whom he knows and likes, a modest and clever *midinette,* kept talking and talking about the Caillaux affair, night after night. That is what interested her, not the coming of any war.

My Hungarian admires Paris and France. That is why he came here, assisted by a kind of scholarship: to this enlightened capitol of the world, to a culture and a civilization perhaps light-years ahead of Hungarian provincial towns. What he does not know is that he will miss the last open train to Vienna and Budapest; that, together with other Austrian and Hungarian civilians, he will be interned by the French for more than four years, in a prison on the stark Atlantic coast of France in Noirmoutier (which means Black Monastery), subject to painful and diabolically petty vexations by their French guardians. And this kind of imprisonment will be but another outcome of the nationalism of a war which will become something else than an armed contest between states, because now entire nations will rush at each other.

In 1914 (unlike in 1939) the French were ready and willing, perhaps even eager, to go to war. Even Joseph Caillaux, who was once accused of pro-German tendencies. Three days after Mme. Caillaux's acquittal the pacifist socialist Jean Jaurès will be shot to death in a café: another scandal, but one which, by that day, will be overtaken by the news of the imminence of war.

What sticks in my mind is a dual impression of Paris in late July 1914. It is a very modern city (in 1914 there are almost as many automobiles in Paris as there are in New York). Boulevards and avenues shining with electricity, telephones ringing, chic women and men with a sleek confidence in their up-to-dateness. And the Paris, too, of dark smelly tenements and sewers and so many of its people mired in customs and sentiments—with their beliefs and unbeliefs—of decades past. Proust was *chez soi,* at home, in Paris in 1914; but so would have been Balzac. (Not even the traffic would have discombobulated Balzac: on, say, the rue de Rivoli there were as many horse-drawn carriages in 1847 as there were automobiles in 1914.) And then comes a vast surge of emotions— and, yes, one of relief: like in Berlin and Saint Petersburg and Vienna and Budapest and London, people in Paris cheering on the war, their men going into war. Many of these will be clad in the red trousers of the French infantry, which proved to be excellent targets for German sharpshooters. But then came, too, the taxis of the Marne . . .

Well, I know that this is far from telling enough. You see, the meaning of 1914 is so enormous that I cannot really deal with it in a vignette, unless in a clichéd one (crowds in the big railway stations cheering on the thousands of their young men packed in their trains, or some such). 1914 and 1945—these are the only two chapters that I had to rewrite several times, throwing away my earlier versions for these years.

"Well, if you think it is better than the original one I cannot do much about that. But why this interest in the Caillaux? And why bring in another Hungarian?"

Because to me the Caillaux—in 1914—are as interesting as the figures of Proust. But not because of Madame's crime and the trial. Because they incarnate a compound that is both modern and outdated. There is a contemporary picture of Henriette Caillaux that I recall. She wears a black toque with a black feather during her trial, but there is nothing Victorian about that. Her face is modern, too: there is no shyness in her open-eyed gaze, a face with cheekbones forming asymmetrical planes that people in the second half of the twentieth century find attractive, whereas a century earlier, when the feminine ideal was all roundness and softness, people did not. And there is her husband, a bald mustachioed Don Juan, in his so carefully cut suit and vest, with that stickpin in his cravat. Both of them divorced, they are agnostics, high-bourgeois figures, he with his string of affairs with women, a connoisseur of female undergarments, A Character. But a character of an age that we know was rushing past, and modern only in part.

"If so, then the interesting matter is why Madame Caillaux went so far as to kill the enemy of her adulterous husband, but you let that go."

Their marriage, too, was both modern and old-fashioned. Henriette stuck close to Joseph, who then began to cherish her as he grew old. Her loyalty to her husband amounted to something more than a wish for security, let alone calculation.

"So she was one of those things: a modern-minded but at the same time traditional French bourgeoise. Her husband was what the English used to call A Bounder, though a sleek and talented one. And what was this stuff about his knowledge of women's underclothes?"

Oh, I mention this only because according to gossip he often talked about that. And that is a mix, too: this arrogant, self-confident male, but one who not only feels free to talk about such subjects but feels inclined, perhaps even compelled, to do so. Besides being bad form, that suggests something other than superb self-confidence—

"Well, everything has its history: women's underclothes, and also what is under them. I think that in 1914 women did not shave their armpits (there is a peppermint smell around those), and they did not shave their legs either (which means that some of their hair was repeated on their legs). Is this what you mean (of course among many other matters): that things were not that modern in 1914?"

Don't be silly. (I am inclined to think that Henriette Caillaux did shave her legs.) What I mean is that in July 1914 she and her husband—and, indeed, Paris and the French people—are at the very cusp of an age.

"You did not do this very well. Besides, you and I know that there is no such thing as a moment when an entire era ends. Yes, 1914 was the end of many things. But many marks of the end of an era and the bursting forth of a new one were there before 1914. In forms of art, for one—examples too numerous to mention. Or the tearing tensions among the classes. The old order was fraying, and it would have become torn sooner or later, even without the war coming in 1914."

But my argument is that the war *did* come and that no one recognized what it would mean and that the emotions (and, yes, also the reasonings) that brought about the war were the results of many things, just as the war proved to be the awful beginning of many things. Of the entire twentieth century, which was a short one, lasting seventy-five years, from 1914 to 1989: for the First World War led to the Second World War, and the Second World War to the cold war, which ended in 1989, with the Russians giving up their entire East European empire. That is how it was, contrary to the stupid idea that the Communist revolution in 1917 was the key event of the century, that in 1917 "history changed gears," a phrase by James Burnham or Bill Buckley, I think. The cusp was July 1914, not November 1917. And one other result of the war was that *old-fashioned*, especially in American English, became a pejorative adjective—until about thirty years ago, when it began to slowly rise, perhaps imperceptibly but surely, on the stock exchange of words and ideas. I mention America because in some ways America was on a cusp, too: it was in 1914 that Henry Ford began his mass production of cars, and it was in 1914 that for the first time more than one in one thousand Americans were divorced.

And the war—otherwise always a modernizing factor—oddly, or perhaps not so oddly, kept the French from becoming more modern. Of course there was their exhaustion, with nearly 1.3 million of their men dead in the trenches. But in the 1920s and 1930s France was anti-

quated, not only her institutions but her people. One example: politicians such as Louis Barthou or Yvon Delbos, publicists such as Charles
Maurras or Geneviève Tabouis, were principal figures around the time
of the Caillaux trial (some of them, I think, even testified during it, but
whether for or against Caillaux I cannot tell) — and twenty years later
they were principal figures in French politics (Barthou and Delbos as
foreign ministers) still. I do not know any other country like that. And
Hitler understood this French weakness, this weakness of aged bourgeois: it led to his great successes and then to the Second World War.

"You did not answer me about the Hungarian. What did he have
to do with all this? Did he write about the Caillaux affair?"

No, and I do not know whether he really bumped into the court-
house crowd that evening. But he really existed. His name was Aladár
Kuncz, a first-class writer who wrote an unforgettable book about his
internment in the Black Monastery. One other thing in his favor: in
spite of his dreadful experiences he did not become a Francophobe.
He probably knew more French literature than Joseph Caillaux (who,
however, was not an uncultivated man). Aladár Kuncz was probably
awed by such Baudelairean lines: "L'elixir de ta bouche où l'amour se
pavane" — the nectar of your mouth where love strides up and down.
That was something to be appreciated and savored by a Francophile
seventy years ago, but to how many people does it appeal now? Wasn't
Baudelaire, too, a poet of an age now past? Do kisses mean less now
than they did in 1914? I am afraid so, but I must leave it at that . . .

"You can't just leave. You are ambiguous about French nationalism in 1914. You lament its existence, and yet you suggest something
like respect for it."

Because it was a mixture of nationalism and patriotism. I have, as
you know, made repeated efforts in my writing and teaching to insist on
the fundamental difference between old-fashioned conservative patriotism and modern populist nationalism. But life is more complicated
than that: these categories often overlap and spill into each other, and
so it was in July 1914, soaking even through the verbal and emotional
fabric of the Caillaux trial. And yet we must distinguish between the

two. Few people, alas, have done so. George Orwell was one: patriotism is defensive, nationalism is aggressive. Even more profound, Bernanos: "that collective greed called nationalism, which perverts the notion of 'fatherland' into the idol of a 'people's state.'" Yes, *that* is the deadening cross that mankind bears, a cross fabricated by people themselves, now and in 1914.

"There is something large hidden here. Love of a country and hatred of an enemy; and that, in the long run, hatred weakened entire peoples?"

Yes, but only in the sense that people (and persons) do not get tired of love — they only get weary of sin. Of course they have an infinite capacity to deceive themselves.

"Well. Let's turn back the focus. I think that Bernanos would have despised (since he was in his twenties in 1914, he most probably did despise) Joseph Caillaux more than he disliked Jean Jaurès."

I think so too. But would he have so despised Henriette Caillaux? I am not sure. Amid the confused motives of her act he would have seen a small glimmer of honor. And for Bernanos it was honor that mattered, always and ever.

The Ribbon

I T MAY BE NECESSARY to provide a ligament for this odd book with this ribbon, consisting of an inevitably incomplete and in some ways impressionistic tapestry of elements in the macrohistory of sixty-nine years. (By *tapestry* I do not mean anything grandiloquent. I am thinking of the Bayeux Tapestry, but not of the magnificence of its art, only of its format, which resembles that of a cartoon strip: an unfinished ribbon.)

So **1901**: the first year only in the chronological sense of a century (consider that the application of the word *century* to a period of one hundred years appeared in English in 1606, less than three hundred years earlier). Queen Victoria was still alive and the Hundred Years' Peace still endured (there had been no world wars since 1815) and the British Empire was the largest in the world, but there was now America, the United States having chosen to become a world power in 1898 and the British government and people immediately and instinctively accommodating themselves to that, without talking about it: yes, a proof that the point of gravity of the history of the world was moving across the Atlantic, 150 years after Bishop Berkeley ("Westward the course of empire takes its way"). And, as Bismarck was once supposed to have said, the most important thing in the coming century would be that Americans spoke English. And sea power ruled, and the destinies of England and of the United States were coming closer together. And by **1902** there were Americans, previously untouched or hardly conscious of the Anglo-Saxonness of their heritage, who were thinking about it. Queen Victoria has now passed away, but the era of a certain culture and civilization marked by her name had been passing away even before her death; her son Edward would be a very different king, marking a very different era; and there came then the end of the Boer War, which in the long run proved to be not much more than a Pyrrhic victory for the British. And by 1903 the Americanization of British everyday life had begun, and on many levels. Meanwhile, there were men in Germany, including Kaiser Wilhelm, who were beginning to think that they were now powerful enough to claim at least equality with the British — for many reasons, first among them the superior character of German *Kultur* over their commercial *Zivilisation*. Yes, Edwardian civilization was reaching a very high degree of sophistication, and hypocrisy was still the cement that held civilization together (it does that always and everywhere, which is why we may lament its passing, its displacement by a moral and intellectual sleaziness pretending to be "sincere" or even "honest") — but civilization began to show its cracks. And by 1904 in the middle of the European continent, in the swelling cities of *Mitteleuropa*, something else was fermenting and beginning, with sudden realizations in the minds of very different people; the theory of relativity was among these intellectual recognitions, but perhaps more important was the rising of a new kind of subjectivism, the belief that not only the physical but the spiritual essence, the very minds of men and women, are not just conditioned but inescapably determined by people's racial provenance. This had much to do with the last great migrations of the white race. By 1905 large numbers of Jewish and Slavic peoples had settled in the cities of Germanic Europe, and with the Jews, it was not their outlandish presence as a strange religious group but the opposite, their successful assimilation, that led to a new kind of populist envy and racial resentment among masses of the indigenous inhabitants. In the United States this was different. In Europe the peak of the migrational influx had already passed; in America, 1905 and 1906 were the peak years, when for the first time not hundreds of thousands but more than 1 million immigrants came ashore. And the United States was a very large country with very large spaces, and the rhetorical and political and social conditioning of Americans was different. Not simpler: different. And this is why what America did to those immigrants and what those immigrants did to America involved transformations that were not always visible and were often convoluted, changing both how the immigrants were thinking of themselves and how the native Americans were thinking about their place. And these transformations involved the universal and apostolic Roman (but more and more American) Catholic churches, too. And, unlike Europeans, Americans were not much disturbed by the *successful* immigrant. And of course there were exceptions to that kind of American generosity. But the Successful Immigrants did not always understand that, as indeed they failed to understand the complications of the American mind, thinking that Americans were a simple people, which they were not. And it was otherwise with the English, who by 1907 knew that Americans were not only richer but perhaps as powerful as they were and that there were obvious advantages in accepting that—for their country and for themselves. No Englishman or Englishwoman would any longer reject or shun American friendship, not even the sputtering snobs among them. And by 1908 a new, racially inspired philosophy—less pragmatic but more categorical than the racial prejudices of the British—would soon fuse with thoughts about a new kind of order, in many a German and Austrian mind; and in that year there were arrogant moves chanced by Austrian diplomats and tactless statements uttered by the German kaiser. And by 1909 there was of course a wide scatteration of snobs in America, too, but their prejudices were less racial than social and cultural, often inseparable from a new phenomenon: that of an American liberal elite, the self-conscious forming of a class of opinion—for this was the coming of the high tide of American Progressivism, when publicly stated opinions and preferred judgments and averred cultural tastes were becoming as important as were private prejudices resting on social provenances. And by 1910 the great migration of art and culture, ranging from the transportation of the greatest works of European art to the translation of European artists and performers to America, had become a tide. And by 1911 there was a reverse trans-Atlantic movement, too, when more and more Americans of the upper classes had sensed an affinity with the culture and the civilization of France—at a time when, luckily for France, its own self-confidence had risen and when, at least momentarily, it seemed that its diplomatic as well as artistic talents had overtaken that of the Germans. And on the other edge of the Western world, in California by 1912, something new was beginning. Theodore Roosevelt was cheated out of his nomination at the Republican Convention in Chicago, but Progressivism, the same Progressivism that Roosevelt touted, lived on in California, but now it would lead to something altogether different and on another level: the movie culture, meaning the pictorialization of American imagination. And in 1913 there were Constitutional Amendments and Armory Shows and Little Renaissances in America, but in Europe it was the last year of the One Hundred Years' Peace, though no one thought about it in that way, and why? because all kinds of people, decent people, thought that *some* wars, somewhere (to wit, in the Balkans), were normal, perhaps even necessary things for the preservation and vitalization of civilization, of *their* own civilization. And in 1914 came *The* War.

1915

On a hot July evening there are many people on the boardwalk of Cape May, New Jersey, many youngsters around the amusement and ice-cream booths. Some people, avoiding the throngs, walk the narrow pebbled beach now that the tide is out. Among them is a foreign family who does not look foreign from a distance. This is the family of the Austrian military attaché in Washington, here on their summer vacation: the mustachioed father in a black alpaca coat and ivory trousers; the ample mother in a billowing dress of great dark folds; their boy, perhaps eleven or twelve years old, in a white-and-blue sailor outfit and a sailor cap with a broad band of gilt letters, S.M.S. *Maria Theresa*. Above them and set back from the boardwalk is a Gothic-colonial hotel, a gaunt and assertive edifice, its porches with thin, high, fret-worked arches. People are sitting in white wicker armchairs on their porches or the front lawn, like a spread of black and white cauliflowers.

Many years later, in a darkling apartment in Vienna, the father will look at a sepia photograph of his family in those days, already fading. Printed on the bottom is the name of the American photographer and the caption: "On the Boardwalk. Cape May, New Jersey." Written in now browned ink on the top is "24. Juli 1915," with the goosey pot-hooks of Germanic calligraphy.

"Das war das alte Amerika." This was the old America, the father now says, implying that the old America was washed away by the ocean tide of the war.

July 1915 was three months after the sinking of the *Lusitania*. The slow turning of the course of the American ship of state slightly but perceptibly toward the Allies had begun. The staffs of the Central Powers' embassies and legations in Washington knew that; but they were not yet ready or willing to believe that America and Americans would one day wage war against their countries. They took great comfort in the existence of their American friends and acquaintances, in the presence of American places where they were so agreeably welcome. Cape May was one such place. By 1915 it had become less fashionable than it had been twenty or thirty years before, when presidents spent part of their summers there; but it was still fashionable enough for solid Philadelphians, with its Victorian mansard-roofed houses, pale blue hydrangeas, beach plums. In July 1915 this Austrian military attaché, who has sprung from the small nobility of a backward province and who has been posted to Washington with a barely adequate knowledge of English and an even less adequate knowledge of the structure of American society, thinks that perhaps Cape May is not what it has been (this is the third summer that he has taken his family here); perhaps they should have chosen another place for their vacationing this year, for reasons political and social. He has learned a few things about Americans. One is that *die beste Gesellschaft*, the top people in the society of Washington, were taking their vacations elsewhere. The other is that many of those people had begun to be quite outspoken about their sympathies for the British and the French. There is a duality in his mind: he thinks he knows how to appreciate the value of association with *die beste Gesellschaft*, while he attributes their present political preferences to moral as well as ancestral shortcomings in their characters.

At the same time there are the friendships and sympathies of other Americans, in Washington and Philadelphia and Baltimore — not only people of German ancestry but also Western Progressives who dislike the English, Eastern Republicans of the anti-Roosevelt persuasion, and, lately, a few rich or political Irish Americans whose company the

Central Powers' embassies and legations have not particularly sought before but whose hearty and booming anti-British Americanism is now very welcome. Our man inclines to think that such people are the real Americans, uninfluenced and uncorrupted by the ominous rising wave, the tide pushing American opinions closer and closer to the cause of France and, of course, England. He does not believe that that tide will become strong enough to definitely alter the course of the giant American ship of state; but he is, of course, wrong.

"The German presence in America, German expectations from America, Germanophilia and Germanophobia in America—these things have interested you for some time. Together with their connections to other things. I don't think that this is of any moment now, in 1994, when people of German descent in this country are the largest ancestral group, more numerous than those of English or Scots ancestry. They haven't Germanized America. Just the contrary—an American with a German family name is now considered a WASP."

Two things interested and still interest me. One is the instinctive conformity of society and politics in America. In 1915 American society was turning anti-German. This would have happened even if that U-boat had not sunk the *Lusitania*. A complicated thing, and I do not mean that there was evidence of some British complicity in the *Lusitania* story, and I do not mean only the rising of Anglophilia in such places as Newport or the Anglomania of some American dowagers, but strange things like Francomania not only in Newport but on Beacon Hill in Boston. This is an interesting story, this pale love for France among the descendants of the Puritans. For Catholic and anti-Catholic France: it involved not only Henry Adams's discovery of Mont-Saint-Michel and Chartres but also the attractions of the French eighteenth century, of the Enlightenment, for the descendants of Puritans among whom the last traces of a belief in original sin had evaporated.

"Well, Santayana saw that, even though his main target was the genteel Anglo-Saxon tradition of the New Englanders. But Santayana was no Mencken, and he elected to live in England, he associated himself with England during the war."

During the First World War but not during the second. But that is another story. What interests me is the evolution of American thinking about the war. Notwithstanding Wilson's hesitations and his split-mindedness, the movements of public opinion, of government and society, were nearly synchronized at that time. And I believe there were turning points in that evolution, subterranean but here and there palpable, and that some of them occurred in the summer of 1915.

"You mean symptoms, rather than turning points—such moments as when, in 1918, the dowagers and the directors of the Westminster Kennel Club ordered the dachshund to be omitted from the one hundred or more recognized breeds shown at the great annual dog show in Madison Square Garden. Six years later, in 1924, the favorite dog shown was the German shepherd, which outnumbered the French poodles."

Yes, and in that year for the first time more American investments went to Germany than to any other country in Europe. Such coincidences have often amused and intrigued me.

"But, for God's sake, you are not going to connect that uneasy flicker of recognition, the first moment of uneasiness in the mind of that dopey Austrian in Cape May, with the anti-German mania that would be raging in this country in 1917 and after? Your mania for seeing connections sometimes goes too far."

No: it is only that scene and that moment which interest me. And then there is this other thing, the conviction of these people that there was an older America that was better, more honest, and therefore inclined to like them, their countries, and their cause, too. That would happen again—before, during, and after the next world war, when many Germans and German Americans will idealize Herbert Hoover. But when people get sentimental their knowledge of reality tends to weaken, and dangerously so. After he returns to Washington, this military attaché drafts a long dispatch to Vienna, stating that, in spite of

English and French propaganda, there *is* Old America, standing firm against all insidious machinations. His sentimentality will obscure the increasingly less than subtle evidences that he and his wife are being snubbed by more and more people in Washington. (Soon they will be dropped from certain lists.) They will take consolation from their visits to an old American friend from an old American isolationist family (yes, I know, that adjective was not yet current in 1915), who lives on Eutaw Street (they are intrigued by that spelling) in Baltimore and who likes paradoxes, telling them to keep in mind that precisely because the United States is a dynamic country, nothing that is important ever changes there. He keeps repeating this until March 1917, when they finally have to stop believing him. Soon afterward they are told to close the legation in Washington. There will be a last party, a sort of farewell gathering, in the house of one of their remaining Washington friends (including some people with whom the Austrian diplomatic staff had not previously been inclined to socialize). It will not be a sparkling occasion, but one startling moment came during the unexpected toast pronounced by a German Augustinian priest (startling because of his pronunciation: the good Father expressed his gratitude for the providential help of what sounded like "the vice consul of France," when what he said was "the wise counsel of friends"). Our Austrian family will have few American friends by that time, but those friends will remain faithful, some sending them food packages after the war, others visiting them in their stuffy, dark apartment in Vienna. In the midst of the Second World War the former military attaché, then in his late seventies, will be (as are most Austrians) pro- as well as anti-German at the same time. He will also be pro-American, not only because of his memories but because of his conviction that his people (and indeed the Germans) will have much less to fear from the Americans than from the Russians (or from the British or the French) after the war. And he will be, of course, right.

1916

AT THE YALE CLUB on Vanderbilt Avenue in New York, on the walls facing the elevators on the upper floors, are a few old photographs in plain black frames, mostly of famed Yale football teams of the past. I am not a Yale man, and I have no interest in football, but there is one picture I have gazed at more than once. It is a wide, panoramic photo of Company A, Battalion C — Yale men at the Plattsburg camp in 1916, in uniform, putting themselves into readiness for service to their country. There are matters in that picture that attract my historical imagination — well as I know how that kind of imagination is broad and narrow at the same time. One of these matters is how *modern* those men look. By this I mean their leggings and puttees and excellent boots and especially their wide-brimmed, felt U.S. Army campaign hats, half–Boy Scout, half-Western. Yes, the twentieth century began in 1914, but the only soldiers who looked truly modern then were Americans and Australians — and not only because of their campaign hats but also because of their wide smiles. There are smiles on most of those fifty-odd faces, thin-lipped as they are but by no means grim — perhaps self-conscious but also quite confident. It is a sunny photograph, in more than one way. It must have been taken in midsummer 1916, but the scene is light-years removed from the Somme. It is characteristic of American optimism, meaning that it is vague but strong. The strength matters more than the vagueness, in the short run at least. It reflects the belief of this company of men that their duty to their country and their duty to their class and their duty to themselves are completely and unquestionably in accord. That belief is the source of their confidence, and the Plattsburg camp is a perfect fit for that. Plattsburg embodies the ideals and standards of Athletic Christianity, American Patriotism, and such Teddy Rooseveltian nouns as *Zip* and *Pep*. The Plattsburg experience had much that was Boy Scoutish about it, but there was more to it and more to those campaign hats, too (the style was created for the army in 1912 and called the Montana Peak). That concordance at Plattsburg of camping and soldiering, scout life and army life, came easily at that time, both being preparations, predicates, essential elements for a manly comportment. It was but an extension of the Boy Scout motto "Be prepared" — yes, prepared even for war, if need be. But what kind of war? That is where the vagueness comes in.

There are reasons, many reasons, to ask questions about the ideas of the men of Company A, Battalion C, at Plattsburg in 1916. But intentions must be judged from acts. It is not their ideas, it is their behavior that may have been unexceptionable, by and large. There may be no reason for us to admire them, but there may be reasons enough to respect them. "What's good for us is good for America," they seem to think; "what's good for America is (well, it may be) good for the world." There was a contradiction between these two sets of beliefs, connected as they seem to have been in 1916 and for a long time thereafter; but it has marked much of the twentieth century, and the fading of these beliefs, even when they were wrong, may perhaps be regretted now.

Don't think that what I see in that picture is the high point of American idealism and of American self-discipline — two things that are seldom in accord. It is a picture of a moment in American history, but what interests me is what led to it and what it led to.

"But aren't you idealizing those people in the photograph?"

I'm not idealizing them. I do not envy them. I wonder at them. At times.

"I know that you don't envy them, but why should anyone envy Yalies in 1916 just because they are well-to-do and healthy and ready for some kind of organized adventure, a tight stiff bunch of big boys Outward Bound?"

You don't understand. What I can imagine is people, including myself, having at least a twinge of melancholy envy, not for them but for their situation: for *the United States in 1916*, when it was so solid, so prosperous, so sure of itself, so different from what in 1916 was still the Old World, and I do not mean only the contrast between Plattsburg and the Somme.

"You might have considered that in 1916 many of those boys may have thought not much if anything about the Somme but more about a little adventure on the Mexican border, with Black Jack Pershing. But it is not my job — or my character, I hope — to be cynical. Only in this case I am tempted to do a bit of the devil's advocacies."

Yes, that's not quite like you, but in this case go ahead. Let me repeat: it is the moment that interests me. It reflects a revolution in American attitudes that remains unprecedented in American history. In 1914 not one in a thousand Americans thought that his country would or should involve itself in the European war — indeed, most Americans took a self-righteous pride in thinking and saying that they and their country were unlike the Old World, America being a sinless nation. Two years later many of the same people were itching to go to war against the kaiser, to fix up the Old World, to show what Americans could do "Over There." Of course, a strong strand of sentiment — American exceptionalism — connected these only seemingly contradictory bunch of ideas. But that is not my concern here. What interests me is that among the hundreds of books addressing the origins of the American entry into the world war (incidentally, that term *world war* was an American invention, starting in early 1915, I think), not many have dealt with the revolution of American attitudes by going beneath politics and even beneath what goes by the inadequate term *public opinion,* including, of course, the press. Historians are better at this—or at least they ought to be better—than social scientists, but they are more than often unaware that public opinion and popular sentiment, even though they may overlap, are not the same.

"They are not the same, but they surely overlap and form each other, especially at that time, when people got their ideas almost exclusively from the press. Remember what Robert Louis Stevenson wrote in, I think, *The Amateur Emigrant:* in America 'the business of life is not carried on by words, but in set phrases, each with a special and almost a slang signification.' "

That is largely true. So many of the monumental matters in this country are tinted illusions that often fade the more quickly the more the eye seeks them. I suppose that is what the famous green light at the end of *The Great Gatsby* means—a meaning that, I fear, has been misunderstood and sentimentalized by most of its commentators. But *The Great Gatsby* brings me back to my original argument, which involves both the sources and the consequences of that war, in which America and Americans suffered infinitely less than any of the warring nations of Europe and yet it created the habits and it stayed in the minds of every one of the characters in *The Great Gatsby,* which is supposed to be a book about the Roaring Twenties.

"Including Tom Buchanan, the villain, whom I can very easily imagine—I can see him—in that photograph of those beefy Yalies. They were *not* aristocrats (perhaps precisely because some of them thought that in America they were). The true American aristocrat was someone like John Jay Chapman, who in 1913 went to Coatesville, aghast at a horrible lynching there—worse, the burning alive—of a black man and then the kicking of the remains of his skull through the streets. 'What I have seen,' Chapman wrote, 'is not an illusion. It is the truth. I have seen death in the heart of this people.' "

Now you *are* the devil's advocate. Those Yalies knew nothing of Chapman and Coatesville, and I will say that if they had, some of them wouldn't have cared much, but at least some would have, and that is what matters, though perhaps only in the long run. And that is why I gaze at that photo in the Yale Club—perhaps especially because I'm a European.

"Is it because of your Europeanness that you know that the devil is not the enemy of God but one of His instruments? Will you allow me that?"

Of course; and I think that I may also be American enough to allow that the trouble in this world is not so much with the Devil as with his lawyers.

1917

Three weeks after the American declaration of war on Germany, K. and his mother (he is fatherless now, his father was carried away by bronchial pneumonia when his only son was ten) are visited by a young man whom K. much admires. He will be somewhat perplexed by how their visitor talks, but it will take some time until that will disturb his mind and it will take years before he will comprehend the elements of that perplexity. You see, in April 1917 K. is still a young boy with a Philadelphia Quaker upbringing, naive and innocent (two conditions that are not necessarily identical, perhaps especially among young Americans), meaning that he is not only unwilling but still unable to stare at the complexities of human nature. (He will learn to do this at a future time, but some of his naïveté and innocence will remain throughout his life — one of his charms.)

Admiration and respect mark his relationship to this visitor, who is four years older than he: in sum, a boy's attraction to a young man whom he regards as a model. Well, almost. The visitor is Morris Josiah Williams. He has been a counselor at K.'s summer camp, year after year. The first year he had nothing to do with K.'s "tribe," which consisted of the youngest boys (the boys are divided into groups named after Indians). K. admired him from afar. There was an unusually determined, strong-voiced authority about him that differed from the more tight-lipped (and often soft-spoken) leadership exercised by other counselors. Next summer, upon his arrival, K. was exhilarated to learn that his tribe would be assigned to Morris Josiah Williams — whom his charges are supposed to call Mr. Morris the first year and Morris the second year. At the end of the second and in the third year (K.'s last year in camp), some of this leader's favorites, including K., are allowed to call him Joe.

This was a spartan summer camp in the Poconos, a few miles uphill from Bushkill Falls. It was a Quaker camp, more spartan than military, except for the food, which was more abundant and healthful than in other summer camps. There were no sports on Sundays, though there was ice cream and First Day School (Quaker Sunday school), with camp elders who spoke at Meeting when "moved to" and who, like the Head and his wife, still said "thee" and "thy." But the camp was not emphatically religious or exclusionary. Its patrons and inmates came from the upper strata of Quaker families of Philadelphia and southern New Jersey; most of the boys came from Penn Charter or Germantown Friends or Friends Select, the prime Quaker schools in Philadelphia; and there were Episcopalians among them, too, the sons of erstwhile Quaker families.

Morris J. Williams (this is how he now prefers to sign his name) is a Quaker still, of a Quaker background that by 1917 has become rare in Philadelphia: artisans living in red brick row houses in Frankford or Southwark — Orthodox, narrow-minded and honest, lower-class, strict and modest, but of course not penniless, even in the worst of times. His father is a tool-and-die maker, and he was enrolled in Friends Select on a charity scholarship.

He has an almost bulletlike head, a powerful neck and chest. He could split an inch-thick pine plank with a quick slap from the bottom of his palm. He shows that off. "Our tribe will be made up of Fighting Quakers," he said. One Sunday in 1916, after an English Quaker worthy had visited the camp and said a few words about the sufferings of Belgium and the British people and their purpose in the war, Morris J. Williams said about the British, "They come here to soft-soap us." "The German people are no worse than the British, and as for the French, they are rotten." Stand up for your beliefs, he told the boys gathering around him from their longhouse bunks at night. "I am proud to be an American Quaker, and you ought to be, too."

He liked to have admirers, perhaps especially among the nicer-looking boys, including those with nice-sounding old Philadelphia family names. During their last summer together he wrote twice to K.'s mother (the counselors were told to write a report to the families of their charges). Coming home from the camp one hot August evening in 1916, he helped to carry K.'s camp locker down the many steps of the Reading Terminal, where K.'s mother and uncle were waiting with a cab. They offered to take Williams with them, but his gear would not fit into the cab, and then K. insisted on helping his counselor, the two of them going together to the trolley stop at the corner, where they said their farewells while the mother and the cab were waiting.

Now, about eight months later, Joe Williams calls at K.'s house on Cherry Street (near Twentieth, where the last recognizably Quaker patrician neighborhood in Philadelphia is around the corner from Saint Clement's High Episcopalian church). His neck is stuffed into a white celluloid collar, he wears a tight three-button suit, and he talks about the war. He won't wait until he is drafted, he says. He has volunteered. "You," he says to K., "are still too young to go into the army, and that's a pity." His talk is peppered with many of the current national slogans: this is a fight for democracy, there is no other choice, this is a war to end all wars, the kaiser is the enemy of mankind, the Germans will be taught a lesson. He will go to boot camp next week, and after basic training he hopes to be sent to officers' training school.

He had things to do in downtown Philadelphia and thought to call on K. and his mother. He is the same Joe or Morris Williams he was last year at camp and the year before: he is neither less nor more self-confident than he was then; only his clothes and some of his ideas are different. K. recognizes this; his mother knows it. "He is a fine young man," she says when the door downstairs closes behind him. "I hope that he will get safely through the war." That he does not much sound or even look like a Quaker she doesn't say.

❊   ❊   ❊

K. remembers something about the Fighting Quakers.

"Wasn't that attorney general among them, A. Mitchell Palmer, during that Red Scare, around 1920?"

Yes, and his enemies called him the Quaking Fighter. But it goes back much before that. The Philadelphia Quakers were divided during the Revolutionary War. Most of them were pacifists, some of them Tories, but there were many who went to fight on the American side, calling themselves Fighting Quakers to assert their patriotism. Brigadier General Smedley Butler of the marines, another Philadelphian martinet of the twenties, was just such a Quaker (as were Nixon's parents in California, I think). There was that class element, too, seventy-five years ago: upper- and lower-class Quakers, many of the former sliding away to Episcopalianism, while the latter, like their Baptist and Methodist neighbors, were responsible for the persistence of Blue Laws in Philadelphia for a long time. Remember how in that summer camp there was ice cream on Sundays in 1916? That allowance may have had something to do with the weakening of the Quaker strictness in that camp. The dates mean something, because until 1922 in the city of Philadelphia, the Blue Laws prohibited the vending of ice cream as well as playing baseball and showing movies on Sundays.

"Well, then, why make so much of that unbearable and unattractive Athletic Christian, or Muscular Quaker? You portray him as one of the now-extinct lower-class Quakers. In reality, wasn't he American, rather than Quaker, and I do not necessarily mean his ideas? He is the kind of puerile American for whom the employment of physicality is not only the meaning of manhood, it is the meaning of everything. But that may be found in all times, all places, among all classes. There are Episcopalian stockbrokers whose self-confidence almost collapses at fifty, when someone whom they regard as inferior keeps beating them at tennis or squash. About their employment and status in society they feel secure, while about their physicality and about their status among other males they are not. So this brute of yours is not a special case.

There were all kinds of Americans who turned from pacifists into militarists in 1917."

From *convinced* pacifists to *convinced* militarists? There was a duality there, as there was in Woodrow Wilson's mind.

"We know that. But duality may not be the right word. Inconsistency? Perhaps."

No. Split-mindedness, rather—the ability to hold two essentially contradictory ideas in one's mind. And on the conscious level. But I don't want to be too didactic about that, important though it is. What I was writing about was not the education or the inconsistency or even the split-mindedness of Morris Josiah Williams. The ideas of the Crusade for Democracy were there in 1917, and he adapted his mind to them. That adaptation was effortless, it cost him not a thought. He was not carried away by a wave of sentimental American patriotism. What matters are not ideas as such but what people do with them: how they choose them, how they wear them, how they adjust them to their personalities and circumstances. Some of his ideas may have changed; he did not. He was less an opportunist than a conformist. Not every conformist is a coward. Rather the contrary; and this young man was a bully. It took some years for K. to recognize that, as his mind matured. Then he will have sensed or, rather, recognized something else, too: that Williams may have been a homosexual. He does not want to think about that, really, in part because he had no homosexual experiences with him during those summers in the camp. But then he remembers some things and episodes in that camp about which he had not thought earlier. Such is the mysterious alchemy of the human mind.

1918

A DAY IN THE LIFE of a Scotsman in April 1918. He is thin and bony, with strangely unmoving blue eyes; his eyebrows and eyelids are pale and narrow, as are his lips and his clipped moustache. He is forty-five, self-consciously straight, advancing with a long, loping military stride which he has learned to enforce on his steps, since he is not tall. He is in Paris. "C'est un monsieur anglais," think people who look at him in the street. They would not know that he is in Paris on an official, or at least semiofficial, mission. He is a Scots Liberal of modest parentage (Kirk people), had won a Cambridge scholarship, became a journalist of some repute, is known by members of Parliament and by such people as Masterman and Buchan; he is informed, canny, socially as well as politically ambitious, while those ambitions are carefully calibrated by his native calculation and acquired manners. The previous year Lloyd George created a Ministry of Information, whereof he has become an official. Within a year the duties or, rather, the competence of that ministry has begun gaining acceptance, albeit sometimes a reluctant one, in other departments of the government, including the more august realms of the Foreign Office. "Their reach exceeds their grasp," some people in Whitehall would say, but matters have been largely left at that. This man has few influential critics, in spite of his rapid rise in the governmental hierarchy. He knows that; he is fairly confident; he enjoys the trappings of his position and the authority now entrusted to him. On the day before his arrival in Paris he was in the Foreign Office, talking to an Undersecretary of State about his mission. He was pleased with that, as he was pleased, too, with the respect with which he (with his diplomatic passport, "On H.M. Government Service") was treated by the passport officers on both sides of the channel. He had a surprisingly smooth crossing (longer than usual: because of the advance of the Germans, he had to take the channel boat from Newhaven to Dieppe). He got to Paris late at night, proceeding to a hotel on the rue de Rivoli where a small suite had been reserved for him, and there was an invitation for lunch from the ambassador.

When he calls on the ambassador his spirits brighten further. The ambassador shows him the text of Field Marshal Haig's Special Appeal to the British Army, issued but two days before, on April 11: "With our backs to the wall, and believing in the justice of our cause, each one of us must fight to the end. The safety of our homes and the freedom of mankind alike depend on the conduct of each one of us at this critical moment." The Germans have driven a vast bulge into the Allied lines, and they are closer to Paris than at any time since September 1914. But the ambassador also shows him some of the latest intelligence: the Germans have stopped their push before Amiens, which might be a very good sign. He issues from the majestic portals of the British Embassy into a suddenly bright afternoon sunshine. He has but a five-minute walk down the same rue Saint-Honoré on his way to a meeting at the Cercle Interallié, a new club formed during the war in a fine building. There a *huissier* takes his coat and hat and accompanies him to a room where a motley group of men are waiting for him.

There are nine of them: a Czech, a Slovak, a Romanian, a Pole, a Serb, a Croat, a Slovene, and two Frenchmen, one of them a translator. They will talk in French, which our Scotsman has learned to read and speak, though perhaps not well enough for purposes of diplomacy. What he is supposed to do is to hear the people out, and perhaps assess them, since the British government no longer objects to a possible partition of the Habsburg Austro-Hungarian empire, which is what all of these people, aspiring statesmen of the empire's successor states, want. He knows this from the highest authorities in London. He also knows that these people suspect this and are avid for such British support, which he, at this time, may be permitted to intimate. He is, of course, not a professional diplomat — which is perhaps why he enjoys this assignment. So he is not uncomfortable during three long hours and the sometimes interminable elocutions of some of these people. He enjoys their obsequious phraseology, as he enjoys their consideration of him as the representative of the greatest power and empire in the world. He detects, too, an occasional sense of irritation on the part of the French representative, an impatient reaction to this oily deference to Britain over a France, which, after all, was and still is the main patron of these people. It is past seven o'clock when he rises, thanking the participants with a French sentence that he had carefully rehearsed in his head. It has begun to rain, and the lamps on the rue Royale cast a forlorn light. He goes back to the rue de Rivoli, where he orders a light supper to be served in his room, with tea, after which he sits at a desk, unscrews his American fountain pen, and begins to draft a long telegraphic report to the Undersecretary, a dispatch that will be cabled next day from the embassy to London. He begins to describe the people, and his pen flows with an easy sense of superiority. ("Monsieur X., the representative of the Slovenes, gives the impression of a dealer in secondhand jewelry whose eyes are wide open because of the sudden prospect of a promising purchase from an unimpeachable source. M. Y., the Romanian diplomat, is smooth, sleek, and probably untrustworthy, though that is secondary now because of his determined dependence on our goodwill. M. Z., the Serbian, is a great patriot, whose virtues are fused with some of the tribal loyalties of Balkan banditry.") Then he writes his main paragraph. "I suggested to these people that H.M. Government is not opposed to the application of the principles of national self-determination to the land and the peoples of Austria-Hungary, without stating a definite plan or commitment. They were very pleased with that."

He has been, after all, a supporter of some of these people: as a journalist, he had been a trenchant critic of the Habsburg empire and a proponent of national self-determination for many years. Now much of the world seems to be going his way. Before going to sleep, he allows the images of the day to flit and flow through his mind, foremost among them his lunch with the ambassador, which he had not anticipated, and the ambassador's willingness to share secret intelligence with him. He will be sleeping well. He has had a full day.

❋ ❋ ❋

"You have this nostalgia for the Habsburg empire."

Not at all. Or, rather, not very much. What I have a contempt for is the idea of national self-determination.

"But that was Woodrow Wilson's idea, the bee in his bonnet."

Yes, and I greatly dislike Wilson, whose head, incidentally, was nothing like a bonnet. However, my vignette is not about that. It is about bureaucracy. Inattention. Irresponsibility.

"I thought that your vignettes were supposed to deal with a specific period and place. How do those big things relate to April in Paris, anno 1918?"

They relate to this puny Scot, because he is a bureaucrat and nothing else—an ambitious bureaucrat, I shall add, as behooves an erstwhile journalist. And now he is an instrument in promoting a movement that in a few months will lead to perhaps the most catastrophic consequence of the First World War and the groundwork for the second: the dissolution of the only great power between Germany and Russia. Of course, history is full of examples of what Tocqueville once wrote: a dwarf may rise high simply because he finds himself on the top of a great wave. This is different, because a new kind of bureaucracy in government has by 1918 become entangled and overgrown—which is how this man, from the Ministry of Information, is sent to Paris and allowed to suggest to the dismemberers of an empire that the British may be on their side. Which brings me to *inattention*. Yes—for Britain, which was in dangerous straits in the spring of 1918, Lloyd George and Balfour agreed to go along not only with the Wilsonian slogans but with the French and the Italians, who, for their own selfish reasons, decided to promote the dismembering of Austria-Hungary. That went against some very old traditions of British foreign policy, you know. And one of the reasons for it was inadequate attention. They, clever Lloyd George and languid Balfour, did not give much thought to the consequences of that new policy—which is why they let underlings do things, including dispatching this dyspeptic Scots journalist to Paris. But, as you may remember, this man himself does not have a proper sense of occasion, meaning a comprehension of the consequences of that palaver at the Cercle Interallié. His sense of his self-importance is marked by the agreeableness of his recollection of having been asked by the ambassador to lunch, *à deux*. That is what I mean by irresponsibility. Sometimes the British (yes, I know, this man is a Scot) are rather good at that, because of their sometimes narrow-minded thoughtlessness, especially when it comes to foreigners.

"Come on! You're still exercised by the breakup of the Habsburg empire. Besides, what is this odd vignette all about: a treatise about the history—all right, the structure—of British foreign policy or, as people nowadays use that dreadful term, *decision making?* You are writing about a man, and your description of him is wanting. You do suggest, but only once, that not only is he an ambitious would-be diplomat but he *is* in favor of those Slavs or Romanians. If so, when and why?"

Oh, that is one of the reasons why they sent him to Paris, where that gathering of those East Europeans was taking place, perhaps a bit too much under the wing of the French. Before the war he had written in the liberal press articles and perhaps even a pamphleteering book in favor of southern Slavs and Czechs and Slovaks and Romanians. His Scots nonconformist anti-Catholicism inclined him to that, too; that was in the Liberal strain, you know. And it was not Zeus or Minerva who sprung that spark of the idea of national self-determination into Wilson's head. That idea was Gladstonian, nonconformist, and anti-Catholic. But perhaps *Gladstonian* is too much. The anti-Catholic element may have been deeper and wider. Remember how in 1914 that hard-skulled Tory Edward Carson was crazily sentimental about the Serbs—

"But Carson was an Ulsterman. Let's not entangle ourselves in the bogs of Ireland. You're writing about something else, or trying to."

Yes: about bureaucracy, and inattention, and irresponsibility, and, in the case of this Scotsman, about "the contagion of the world's slow stain," which is how Shelley put it, though Shelley was almost always wrong about politics.

1919

DROOP, DREAR, DESPAIR IN Vienna, where the misery of people in 1919 is existential, being the outcome no longer of Viennese neurosis but of the proletarian state to which the city has fallen, due to war and defeat and the end of an empire. Drooping skies, dreariest sentiments, despairing convictions of a population accustomed to their Austrian egotism, which is now compounded with self-pity, the overlay of charming Viennese insouciance gone, at least temporarily, with so much poverty, sickness, and hunger around. Cold rain, mendicant streets, the November sky the color of sour milk. In the afternoon the rain is abating, the wind hurries some of the clouds away, a thin orange glow spreads in the west, and suddenly the wet pavements glisten under the streetlamps, which, perhaps surprisingly, are as assertive now as they were before the war, and so is the clanging of the trolley cars. There are hard white electric lights under palm-leaf canopy, the wrought iron and glass, of the Hotel Bristol, an island now in a wallowing sea of poverty beating up against its revolving doors. Behind that the Bristol's ephemeral clientele is not what it was but a few years ago.

In one of its small paneled smoking rooms sit three men from Hungary who are related to each other and whose categories are not easy to define, since they overlap, but let me try. One is an emigrant, another is a refugee, the third is a fugitive of sorts. Each of them are temporarily Displaced Persons, though in 1919 this bureaucratic term does not exist; it will be devised by an American or United Nations' bureaucracy after the Second World War. The emigrant has some money; it is he who suggested that they meet at the Bristol that afternoon. He does not stay here, but he knows the place, though he is cautious; he asked the other two to come for a cup of tea, not dinner, though they could surely use a good hotel dinner. The fugitive is stocky, the refugee thin as a rail, the emigrant sleek rather than thin, with the beginnings of a paunch. The fugitive has a short, thick neck and close-cropped frizzy hair; the refugee's long, lanky black hair and lined face make a sorrowful countenance; the emigrant is the only well-dressed (or should I say hotel-dressed?) one among them, in a gray American sack suit and a high collar.

The fugitive fled from Budapest to Vienna four months ago, on July 31, to be exact. He was a vice-commissar in the Budapestian Communist government of Béla Kún, who gave up the ghost that day, after 132 days of a fool's paradise for some (including himself), of hell for some of its victims, and of purgatory for nameless and countless others. There was no fight left in these admirers of Lenin and Trotsky when a plenitude of Romanian troops were advancing on Budapest and when they saw a plenitude of hatred in the faces of those in Budapest who were the Others. The fugitive escaped across the Austrian frontier in disguise and with false papers, hoping for the reluctant hospitality of the socialist authorities of Red Vienna. In reality, they wish to get rid of him and his ilk, which circumscribes his situation now.

The refugee took refuge in Vienna in August. He was not a Communist, only a *marxisant* intellectual. He had nothing to do with the Communists' rule, but soon after that the furious hatreds of the anti-Communists smote socialists and Communists alike, especially if they were Jewish. The janitor of his apartment house denounced him to a group of White Cadets. At the university a burly student threatened him with a cane. He hurried down the wide, cold stone staircase of the main university building. Other students were laughing. "Don't go out on the street," his tremulous mother told him. Soon he sat huddled in a cold, smoky train, taking refuge in Vienna from the White Terror, which, he thought, would have to pass soon. He is the poorest of the three in that smoking room, though he has a smidgeon of pocket money; he writes articles for a Hungarian emigré–produced social democratic weekly now appearing in Vienna.

The emigrant is his cousin, who has escaped to Vienna not from Budapest but from New York. A long-lost cousin who translated himself from the old world of Budapest to the New World in 1910 or 1911, after having embezzled money from his firm and being found out soon thereafter. Emigration to America was his way out, as it was for perhaps a dozen other people on the boat: small-time frauds, cashiered officers in debt, deserters of respectable middle-class girls, that is, the mothers of their illegitimate children, escaping scandal and ire — a small and motley and class-conscious minority among the hordes of poor peasants, the huddled mass of emigrants to America. Sailing across a rough ocean in such company, on a packed ship of the Austrian Lloyd (his parents paid for his berth), he resolved to become rich in America and never to travel in such conditions again. Well, he made money. He started a photographic studio with an Armenian, producing mostly illustrations for advertising. He had dabbled with photography in Budapest, he had artistic ambitions, for a while he was doing amazingly well. Then he got involved with one of their lovely rapacious models, he ran into debt, he quarreled with the Armenian. He was irregularly (and often ineffectively) hounded by creditors, but he still had to give up his prize possession, a large apartment containing a studio at a smart address in a new, red-brick apartment house in the East Fifties; he could no longer pay the postwar rent. So he is now an escapee from New York, where some people told him that with a bit of luck and connections, one could turn a thousand dollars into a small fortune in postwar Vienna. He is an American citizen now, with an American passport and with nine hundred dollars in his wallet.

Now the three of them sit together in Vienna, nervous and uncomfortable. The American cousin steered the others away from the large lounge chairs in the hall of the Bristol and into that little smoking room, where they would be less apparent: for there is no good reason to be seen in the company of a recent Communist commissar (or with another obvious refugee from Budapest) in the hall of that hotel, engaged in serious, if not agitated, conversation. One must be careful, especially now. As a matter of fact, all three of them are in a kind of trough, though only months away from the zeniths of their respective fortunes. Less than half a year ago, only last June, there was a moment when he, the American, thought that radiant Manhattan was his oyster (with that copper-haired and vulgar-tongued — yes, that was among her charms — and long-legged young slut being the pearl within). Then a Russian had come along, offering a rather fabulous plan with a minimum of investments (his): a theatrical photo agency, the first photographic superagency for Broadway. It was then that he broke with his Armenian partner; but three weeks later, when he threatened to sue the Russian, the Armenian threatened to sue him, and he was evicted by the girl as well as by the management of the Lombardy Arms, East Fifty-Third Street. A year ago there were a few weeks when his cousin, the refugee intellectual, thought that he was among the vanguard of the agnostic creators of a new humanity in the republic of Hungary, of a new progressive radical elite replacing the remnants of feudalism and clericalism, decaying fat nobles with wine and sausage in their cheeks. He and his cohorts, partially in charge of the universities, would reform Hungarian culture; but soon it became apparent that the government governed nothing, that the ideas that he and his friends cherished were not only impractical but stale. Ideas aside, the fact remained: he and his kind were now despised by people whom they had thought to lead or represent or serve. The fugitive was fewer than four months ago actually in power, a member of the government of the Hungarian Republic of Councils (that is, Soviets), drafting domestic orders, telegrams, and cables, with a hotel suite, an automobile, and an actress (so to speak) at his disposal to boot. Now he was nearly penniless in Vienna, his name among the first on the list of those whom the Hungarian government sought to arrest (and perhaps even condemn to death in absentia).

He is, however, a survivor. He looks like what he is — a tough little bully devoid of scruples, able to hold his own among others of his kind, whether in Budapest or Moscow or perhaps even New York. His American cousin suspects that he would push for a small (and almost surely unrepayable) loan, but no: he has a little money left from an international Communist fund. He needs his American-citizen relative for something else — for a paper, an affidavit — to facilitate his entry to the United States (he has no passport). "You're not going to Moscow, I see?" The fugitive permits himself to grin: there is work to be done among Hungarian Americans in the United States, he and his comrades see eye to eye about that. "I can give you a paper; but you must not use my name after that." The sorrowful intellectual drinks his tea (with plenty of sugar), he doesn't ask for anything, except for attention when he talks about the reactionary forces in Budapest. There is a constant light pain somewhere in the region of his heart, a feeling of guilt as if it were compounded with a small sense of shame. The bitter taste of defeat in his mouth has gone down into his throat and perhaps to his lungs even.

The atmosphere around this threesome is sour rather than bitter. They are wary of each other. They are of the same background, born and raised in the same district on the Pest side of the Danube, but their lives have taken such different turns that they are not a band of cousins, companions, comrades in defeat. One thing they have in common, besides their provenance. They still believe that what has happened to them is only a temporary retreat in the great progress of the world. And about that they are wrong.

"There is a sarcastic touch in this dreary vignette — and it *is* dreary — which your readers will not like and which I do not like. It is not like you, so please explain."

Is it that sarcastic? They are period people. That is more important than the fact that Vienna in November 1919 was a period place, and

I know that my description of the place in this vignette may be hasty. I am interested in those three, in their characters and in their ideas.

"And why, if I may ask?"

They do have one big idea in common —

"Which is that they are Leftists, each in his own way?"

Only roughly put, in a kind of intellectual shorthand. They, including the erstwhile commissar, believe in the inevitable advance of the Enlightenment, in the coming full fruition of Reason in Internationalism, Socialism, Justice. Their provenance has something to do with that. They belong to a Budapestian generation, born in the 1880s, who revolted against or at least broke away from the middle class and the, yes, often stuffy ideas of their cautious parents. And now it is only two years after 1917, a peak period, with many revolutions around the corner: they believe that the world is lurching toward their ideas, everywhere. They are wrong. The coming prophets and leaders, the real revolutionaries, are Mussolini and Hitler. And others of that new kind. What will soon matter, what already matters in 1919, is not class consciousness but national consciousness, a new populism not at all of the Left, which has been losing its monopoly in evoking The People. These three think that the nationalists and the conservatives are reactionary remnants, nothing else. Wrong again. One more thing. Antireactionary they may be, but they are not honestly populists: in their own ways, all three of them think of themselves as being in the vanguard of progress, being qualified leaders of people in a coming world —

"But they aren't heroes, are they? They are survivors in 1919 — of their personal destinies as much as of their failed ideas. There is a connection between those two matters, you know."

That will catch up with them soon. In different ways, of course. The emigrant will return to New York, having failed to parlay his few hundred dollars into a fortune in Vienna, but then he will resume his career as a director of a photography studio in Manhattan, he will marry one of his models, he will become fairly prosperous and Americanized, buying a summer cottage on a lake in New Jersey by 1929, taking up

fishing, and seeing few Hungarians. He interests me the least. The refugee intellectual will realize, by 1927 at the latest, that his earlier ideas
were full of holes; he will become a conservative and a Catholic, writing
thoughtful essays, working in the Vienna office of a big Berlin publisher,
moving to Italy or Switzerland after Hitler comes to power, and dying
there, alone, after ten or fifteen years of honest ulcers, honest religion,
and an honest marriage. The fugitive will worm his way through Ellis
Island, become a not unimportant member in the American Communist Party U.S.A., evade investigations by the Immigration and Natu-
ralization Service—a success among the comrades in New York, not
only because of his reputation of having once been a real commissar in
a real Communist government but because of his Budapestian worldliness, which his New York comrades take for savoir faire. An almost
legendary figure in those conventicles of the twenties that include a
handful of Communist emigrés from Hungary, among them the owner
of a good bookshop (frequented by the staff of the *New Yorker*) whose
plump young wife (a former Budapest chanteuse) the former commissar
will regularly bed. He will be pleasurably involved with people from the
Village until about 1935, when his job becomes more serious, involves
passing a few papers to and from amateur comrades of the Hiss type—

"Now wait a moment. There *was* such a Hungarian Communist
in New York, by the name of Jozsef Pogany—"

Yes. I was thinking of that man, but only because of his name.
Pogany is "pagan" in Hungarian; and I was also thinking of that little
twenties' arts and lit magazine in New York with the silly name *Pagany*.
Meaning "pagandom." *Pagany:* an Avant-Garde of Art and Thought
and Society. Trotsky might have liked it. (Perhaps someone in the Village sent him a subscription, once he was out of Russia and in Mexico.)
In any event, by the twenties the Village atheists have acquired a new
locus in America. Friends and subscribers of *Pagany;* friends and comrades of Pogany. But that is another topic, even though material for
vignettes about period people.

"Well, this is far from being one of your best vignettes, but let
it go."

1920

MRS. BINGHAM LEAVES Paris for Montreux. She is an extraordinary woman: American and worldly, beautiful and clever. About thirty-five, determined and tall like a young tree, possessor of a knowing smile that is one of her greatest charms because of its suggestion of a mature sophistication. (It can also disconcert and freeze people, especially men who don't know better.) She wears her wondrous clothes splendidly. Some of them are furs and coats made for her in New York; there are her Revillon and Paquin and Worth gowns, too, but she does not really *need* them. All in all, a paragon of New World riches and beauty.

Mrs. Bingham travels alone. She is de facto, though not de jure, separated from her husband, a New York lawyer, with much money of her own. She is a marvel, a slender walking statue of liberty in Paris, speaking French perfectly and with less of an accent than the highbred English ladies she occasionally meets. She is more of a Francophile than an Anglophile, like Edith Wharton or Ellen Glasgow or Willa Cather, whose books she reads. (She just read *The Age of Innocence*, published a few weeks ago and brought from New York by a friend. She hasn't yet read *Youth and the Bright Medusa* — 1920, too — and perhaps she won't: she likes novels better than short stories.) At times she seems alarmingly sure of herself. She had arrived in Paris on a blustery, bright March day in 1920, a year after the Wilsonian Americans had departed and a year before the arts and letters Americans would arrive. But remnants of the first group and forerunners of the second were there, and Mrs. Bingham knows a few people among both of these divergent sets. She strides along the corridors of the Crillon with her lovely ankles and absolutely beautiful dove gray strapped antelope shoes, a Miranda apparition.

As for the Parisians: 1920 is the peak of Americanophilia among them. Their sense of gratitude to the Americans for coming over and helping to win the war has not yet dissolved; then, too, many Parisians are modernists. They have all kinds of sentimental notions about the New World, including ideas about great and miraculous wealth. And Paris in 1920 is largely intact, has bled less than have other towns and villages of France, enjoys (temporarily) the sense that France is again *la grande nation* in Europe and in the world. There is an illuminated brilliance in its streets in the evenings, concentrated mostly on the Right Bank, the presence of the hard-polished continuities of an urban and urbane civilization in what Parisians think is still the capital city of the world. They are wrong, but in 1920 that does not yet matter.

This is the rediscovery of Paris, France, Europe, for Mrs. Bingham (she had been in Paris last in the spring of 1914). It is a recovery from something else, too: from a love that took place not in Paris but in America. There was very little in common between her and her handsome weakling of a husband when, in late 1918, a friend of her family, a young man exactly her age, first pretended to fall and then really fell in love with her. And she with him; their affair was consummated on a bright spring afternoon in a bungalow near Charlottesville, Virginia, during a foxhunting and golfing meet (in 1919 such things were not easy to arrange in New York with adequate discretion, and Mrs. Bingham was most reluctant to imperil discretion). And then it did continue in New York, until her lover — his self-confidence immensely bolstered by his conquest of this superb married woman — plucked an opportunity for another illicit affair, now with a young girl just graduated from Vassar, which Mrs. Bingham found out by chance, and the accidental discovery of which was fairly sordid. That afternoon, and for some weeks thereafter, her well-groomed soul was badly disheveled.

A month later she scored a triumph. Her lover told Caroline Bingham that he had ditched that girl; yes, for her; he asked her forgiveness; for the first time he proposed that she divorce her husband and marry him. Mrs. Bingham said no, and thereafter she fled to Paris.

And now she is leaving Paris, too. She has friends in Paris, she has had pleasant days and evenings in Paris, but she is alone with recent memories that make her somewhat restless; and she decides to leave Paris for Switzerland or perhaps northern Italy, having told her family and husband (including his family) and friends in New York that she intended to spend five months in Europe, traveling. Her first stop will be Montreux and a reunion with a much younger friend of hers, a Spanish marquesa whom she had met in Paris in early 1914, when she was already married and when the marquesa was still a girl. Now she is married to a very good-looking Spaniard. They are spending a fortnight at the Montreux Palace, on the cool, sun-lit shore of Lake Geneva. There will be excursions to Glion, Villars, Les Diablerets. Caroline Bingham will join them for a few days and then move on.

The wagons-lits of the Simplon-Express bring her to Montreux; at the station a rented car with a chauffeur awaits her, as arranged. This is the first time she sees that sparkling lake and the splendid mountains, snow-coned and brilliant against the sky. After the asphalt heat of Paris and the racket of the train, everything is wonderfully cool and quiet. Then there is the soft crunch of the gravel as the automobile rolls up the great curved driveway to the entrance of the hotel, between flowerbeds containing begonias, purple heliotropes, white salvias in full bloom. The marquesa and her husband stand at the door, waiting for her. Kisses and embraces; quickly they go to the dining room to lunch; a few serious heads turn, since the two women are very decorative; and the view of the lake dazzles through the brilliant plate-glass windows of the Montreux Palace's dining room, with the chateau of Crillon clearly visible and even Mont Blanc not far away. Much of the same view from her excellent room, with a balcony and an awning.

Mrs. Bingham is at peace. They will meet after five for a short drive and tea somewhere. But the two siesta hours are not yet over when there is a knock at her double doors; a hotel servant brings a note from her friend: may she come over and see her? Of course. The young marquesa comes; they kiss and embrace again, praising each other's looks; they go out to the balcony to sit. The marquesa talks of her marriage. Her husband: married only two years but the way men are; yet she is still very much in love with him. Mrs. Bingham does not say much; she has sized up the husband, one of those handsome, selfish Latin types, she thinks, a good father perhaps, but sooner or later sticky with mistresses. Now comes the revelation. "Ma chère, mon amie, j'ai tant souhaité de vous raconter ça." Younger woman to older woman friend (though Mrs. Bingham thinks she is not the first recipient of her friend's confidences). Well, her husband had a mistress, a girl, and she found that out not long after the first twelvemonth of their marriage, as a matter of fact when she was about to have their baby. Mrs. Bingham thinks, "I'm not surprised," but what does surprise her is the wistful, almost happy smile on the marquesa's young lacquered face. For she had won; and it was a beautiful victory, beautiful in more than one way. She had confronted him; and he not only gave promises and asked for her forgiveness but caressed and loved her more than before. And he gave her proof that he had sent that girl away, so that she, the wife, felt a surge of true pity for that poor girl (for she was poor, a vendeuse in a Madrid dress shop). "Je me sentais si contente, si heureuse, avec une tristesse douce." Now Mrs. Bingham understands that smile on her friend's face, but more than that she does not understand.

Mrs. Bingham smiles and puts her hand on her young friend's hand for a moment, but that is all. She doesn't sleep very well, and the next day she decides to despise her friend's husband, well mannered though he is. Two days later she drives off with the chauffeur to the Bernese Oberland and to Zermatt, returning after a week or so. It is another brilliant noonday; again the gravel crunches under the wheels of her car; but her spirits are in a moiety, one that she knows is entirely different from the duality of the marquesa's spirit about the drama she had recounted. Mrs. Bingham will tell her nothing about her own love affair in New York, about her lover or about that girl, for whom she felt no pity at all. And now the depressing knowledge seeps into her mind and heart: she *knows* that she could not pity her. What she allows herself during the last day with her Spanish friend is an astringent allure of mature worldliness, a few outspoken remarks about people, statements that Zermatt and the omnipresent Matterhorn are boring, and an at most faint suggestion to the marquesa that all is not well with her own marriage in America. But three things discomfit her. That she is no longer very young; that she is so very different from her friend; and that she cannot be otherwise. And then she returns to Paris and then to New York. A few years later F. Scott Fitzgerald will write his beautiful phrase about America being the willingness of the heart, which is often and largely true, but in this instance—and it is nonetheless a very American instance—it is not.

"And it is you who does not like Henry James."

No, I don't, and I can't improve on how Edward Dahlberg put it: "His irresolute style is canonical gabble." Besides—and this may be secondary—my Mrs. Bingham is not innocent; the young marquesa is the more innocent of the two and—an important *and*—wiser.

"Well, I'll be coming to that in a moment. Meanwhile I have a few questions. In spite of everything, you do like the Mrs. Bingham types, especially when they are around thirty-five. Incidentally, is she a Philadelphian?"

No. There was a very elegant and rich Bingham family in Philadelphia, friends of George Washington (entertaining, among other people, the Duc de Noailles as early as 1792), but, to the best of my knowledge, they all moved away. This Mrs. Bingham was born, I presume, in Cincinnati, coming from fairly old money.

"Now a nasty question. Would it have been better if the good-looking Spaniard had made a pass at her—I mean, better for her?"

Not at all. Your idea for plots is too crude. She would not let her vanity overcome her pride, or at least she seldom did so. But there is a small touch of truth in your nastiness: she was beginning to feel out of place, so much older than this Spanish couple. Her strong dislike of the husband rose after her talk with his wife, and that was decisive. And now I must admit one thing to you: some of this, I mean the marquesa's story, came to me after having read an immortal passage in Galdós's *Fortunata and Jacinta*, which is one of the greatest novels of the nineteenth century and, alas, too little known. I cannot do better than cite it, a passage so profound and beautiful that I copied it out. Here it is. Jacinta, the young wife, "let herself be caressed. She wasn't angry. But in her soul, a phenomenon very new to her was taking place. She felt two different feelings . . . shuffling, superimposing themselves, one, then the other. Since she adored her husband, she was proud that he had scorned the other woman for her. This pride is primordial and will always persist, even in the most perfect of beings. The other feeling stemmed from the virtue underlying her noble soul, and it inspired her to protest against his having abused and pitilessly abandoned the unknown woman."

"Go on."

"The victory of Jacinta's vanity didn't prevent her from seeing that underneath the trophy lay a crushed victim. Perhaps the victim did not deserve it; but whether the woman deserved her fate or not was not Jacinta's concern, and on the altar of her soul there was a tiny flame of compassion burning."

"And your Mrs. Bingham is incapable of that. But Galdós uses the word *virtue*, and doesn't Mrs. Bingham have her virtues?"

Yes. Her virtues are Protestant, and American.

"Is that a shortcoming, and can she help that?"

It may or may not be a shortcoming, but the main thing is that she *knows* that she cannot help it. And this vignette is about her, not about the marquesa. Besides, the marquesa herself is not really very much like Galdós's Jacinta. You will admit, however, that that tiny flame of compassion burning on the altar of Jacinta's soul is admirable (and, perhaps, very Spanish and Catholic).

"One last remark or, rather, question. Your description of Paris in 1920 is fast and flimsy, but perhaps you thought that there was not much place for it in this story — and this is a story as much as a vignette. But then you write almost longingly of 1920 on the Lake of Geneva, and, pray, why this repetitious insistence on the crunch of the gravel?"

That is a weakness of mine, the soft crunching of the gravel under the wheels of large cars in the driveways of places like Montreux or Lausanne, Palace-Hotels or Beaux Rivages — they were exquisitely kept and raked, like those flowerbeds. For me it is a crucial evocation of the atmosphere of rich places in the early twenties in Western Europe. It is not only that I can see that picture; I can hear that sound.

"Well, just don't overdo those things. And one really last question: what will happen to Mrs. Bingham? Don't you care?"

I do care, but I also know where I must stop — in this case, I mean.

1921

BASIL AND CYRIL are English (indeed, Edwardian) names, and I presume that many a Basil and many a Cyril must have walked the long platforms of the Gare Saint-Lazare to board the boat trains to London, via Calais-Dover or Boulogne-Folkestone or Dieppe-Newhaven. And now in September 1921 there is a Basil talking with a Cyril on one of the platforms of that railway station (immortalized by Monet in 1877). But they are not English; they, Vasily and Kyrill, are Russians, and the train stretching out along *Voie 19* is bound not for the channel ports but for Cherbourg, for Kyrill is not going to London. He is on his way to New York.

This is but another stage in the hegira of these two brothers in their early twenties, who stand in the mist and the smoke of that platform, wishing each other good luck. They have been traveling—fleeing—for more than three years already. Beginning in the summer of 1918, from Saint Petersburg to Kiev, from Kiev to the Crimea, from the Crimea to Constantinople, from there to Athens and to Marseille and to Paris—on slow, frozen Russian trains, Turkish freighters bobbing up and down, badly rusted Greek passenger ships.

The night the Bolsheviks took (if that is the word) the Winter Palace, on November 7, 1917 (October 24, Old Style), Basil was at the opera, less than a mile away, hearing Chaliapin in *Don Carlos.*

Don Carlos is a long and boring opera; and when the performance was over, he stood outside in his greatcoat, lit up a long Russian cigarette, and pondered his immediate future. At the same time somewhere in the Caucasus, in a dissolving Russian army, his brother was wending his way home, reaching it finally a month or so later. Their parents' house was still warm, well heated during that chaotic winter, at least two of their domestic servants still with them, Bolshevik regime or no. Their elderly father, a landowner, a onetime member of an elite corps of guardsmen, thought that Lenin and his rabble would not last. Their mother was not such an optimist. Father, mother, the two brothers, and their sister, Kyra, abandoned their house the next summer, making their way to the Crimea, which still seemed to be well outside the reach of the Red bands. Six months later there came chaos again; the Reds were approaching. Some gold coins got them on a dreadful Turkish boat bound for Greece. At the last minute, literally so: everything had been arranged, but the Turkish captain kept spitting on the *napoleons d'or* and rubbing each of them on his sleeve before he would let the family off the gangway and pass through the bulkhead door. Kyra was lucky; in Athens she met and married a Greek count, dubious but moneyed. (There are no Greek counts, the family knew that; but then, this man said that he was a Corfiote.) The father acquired a bad cold when the four of them were sitting up all night (October 1920) in the drafty train lashed by sheets and buckets of rain on the way from Marseille to Paris; he never recovered from his flu and died a month later of pneumonia in their rented rooms in the rue Daru, within sight of the Russian Orthodox cathedral of Paris. His pessimistic widow then had a stroke of luck: old French friends of hers asked her to stay with them in their summer house at Saint Jean-de-Luz (and, then, if she chose, to remain there through the winter, together with their Basque housekeeper, a disagreeable old crone with whom the Russian lady nevertheless learned to get along).

And now it is September 1921, and the two brothers know something that most of the nearly 1 million emigré Russians are only beginning to admit to themselves: that there is no longer much hope that the

White Russians will win the civil war; there will be no more help from the Allies; the Bolshevik regime is going to stay.

Vasily Georgevich is the more intelligent of the two, Kyrill Georgevich the more dashing. They talk nonchalantly on that station platform; they are moderately well-dressed and more than moderately self-assured. Except for their large bony hands and their Russian cheekbones few people would identify them as the impoverished Russian emigrés that they are. Their nonchalance is an outcome not only of their pseudo-noble breeding but also of their knowledgeableness. That is an extraordinary capacity that some Russians possess, together with their extraordinary ability to speak foreign languages so well. These two have learned to know Paris very quickly, to know thoroughly what matters in Paris, including the different strata of the accumulating Russian emigré colony, now rising to tens of thousands, whose circumstances they know only too well and whose illusions they dismiss. Which is why they have decided not to stay here: Vasily will soon leave for Berlin, and Kyrill is going to seek his fortune in America. There is more of a chance for an intellectual career in Berlin than in Paris, and Vasily speaks German as well as he speaks French; Kyrill has a friend in New York, a Georgian prince with whom he served in the army and who has written to him about how, in America, fortune can be coaxed to smile on a man such as himself. This friend writes that White Russians are often welcomed not only in New York but in Palm Beach, Florida, invited by lovely rich women, who may energetically push their husbands to look out for their protégés and try to secure good jobs for them. Which is what has happened to the prince, who has now a fine little apartment in New York ("of course smaller than in Saint Petersburg but larger than what you have in Paris") where Kyrill can stay for a while ("except on certain afternoons — you will understand!"). "Ah, Kyrill," Vasily says. "Get on the train now, it is time. And good luck, gigolo!" "And good luck, scribbler!" Kyrill says. "And keep an eye on Mama." They kiss and embrace each other.

Vasily takes his white handkerchief from his pocket and waves, waves at the train as it moves out into the dark. Kyrill leans out from the corridor window and waves, too, but not for long; he has to secure his seat in that third-class compartment, which is nearly full. His brother stands on the platform for another minute or so. Then he turns and goes out of the station, and he feels suddenly accosted by what had so rapidly become for him one of the many usual scenes of Paris: the arc lights on the square; the garish shining of a brasserie, its awning lettered by the familiar beer advertisements; the long, narrow avenue with its tightly serried houses and high mansard roofs that not so long ago, before the war, looked modern and now look hopelessly middle class. He feels cramped in Paris. He is used to the spaces of Russia. There is the wrought-iron sign of the Metro entrance, and while he crosses the square a dactylic Russian rhyme suddenly blooms and buzzes in his head.

And, for the sake of giving a kind of meaning to this vignette, I think I ought to spin out the story of the two brothers further, for I am not really writing about Russian emigré life in Paris in 1921. I am writing about these Russians in the West, in 1921, at a turning point in their lives, when they know that they will not be able to return to Russia, ever. I have no great affection for Russians, Red or White, but I admire the panache of these two, their ability to find their niches in the West: emigrés, yes, but exiles? Less and less so. Especially for the ones like Kyrill in America, where he will find himself more at home than almost anywhere else, very much including England, where he spent three dreadfully long, gray, and rainy months in 1921, looking in vain for an occupation and for people to feel at home with. (Once he met a solid stout fellow of an Englishman whose first name was Cyril, and Kyrill said that this was his own name, too, and the Englishman said not a word.) The bigness of America will mean more to him than the Puritanism of America, which he will not take seriously at all, and Americans will be amused by that; and there will be moments when, when he looks at North Broad Street in Philadelphia or at an avenue in Indianapolis, their very width and breadth, their hardwood porches, will remind him of the width and breadth of Russian avenues, whether in Saint Petersburg or in Nizhni Novgorod. His brother, in Berlin, will advance from the management of a theatrical agency (at first in charge of such dreadful things as Cossack choruses and Georgian dance troupes and amateur Russian ballets) to a serious desk job in a cosmopolitan German publishing house. Both brothers will marry and divorce and marry again; and in the 1930s, long after their mother has died and been buried in France, Vasily will come to America, too. Both of them will serve in the United States Army in the Second World War, having mixed feelings about the Russians' military successes, and — such are the paradoxes of pilgrims' or, more precisely, of emigrés' progresses — at the end of the war it will be Kyrill who is stationed in Germany, while Vasily will serve as a Russian translator in Japan, on General MacArthur's staff. In the course of their duties both of them will meet Soviet Russian officers who will call them *amerikanskis,* and in Darmstadt or Wiesbaden in 1945 one Soviet colonel will always bow and kiss the hand of Kyrill's American secretary, which she will enjoy. "He's exactly like your Russian friends in New York," she will say. "Not at all," Kyrill will say, but still . . .

"There is something missing here. What I wanted to read about was Russian emigré life in Paris in 1921, that mix of crooks and crazies and charming people, throwing whatever money they lay their hands on to the wind, parties and nightclubs called La Petite Russie or Shéhérazade or whatnot, with Gypsy musicians and White Russian colonels, now taxidrivers, going outside to start their taxis in the cold, with their cages of canaries hung above the front seat."

Sorry about that. All I could do here was to suggest — and not very well indeed — how some of these Russians took to the West, and perhaps especially to the United States. The Russian-American symbiosis, you know.

"Well, then, your vignette should have been about a dashing, and unscrupulous, wasp-waisted former officer of the Russian Guards laying his plans for the conquest of Palm Beach."

Probably. But there were funny misunderstandings, tragicomedies, too — plenty of *Pnin*s in America, which is of course Nabo-kov's best book, even though he (and his commentators) would be loath to admit that.

"You said once that Nabokov did not really understand America."

But Americans admired Nabokov, which was his great luck in the end. Anyhow: what fascinates me is the smartness of my two Russians. They know, well before almost everyone else, that there is no way back to Russia — and not so much because the Reds won as because the Whites lost. They did not think much of the Reds — remember Vasily going to the opera the night of the Bolshevik Revolution (together with hundreds of other Petersburgers) and pensively smoking his ciga-rette before hurrying home? But that was Saint Petersburg. In Paris in 1921, he and his brother laugh at the story of the "Immortal Regiment" of one of the White armies, which was truly immortal, since it took good care to have no casualties. But these two brothers are not cynics; they are realists — realists about what is behind them and even about what is ahead of them. One more thing. It is in 1921, when Kyrill and Vasily leave Paris, that Russia and America, for entirely different rea-sons, both withdraw from Europe. Politically, that is. But twenty years later, they return in full force and meet in the middle of it in 1945.

"And Kyrill will be in Germany, and Vasily in Japan, both in American uniforms. Incidentally, will they Americanize their names, then becoming Cyril and Basil?"

I think so. But only their first names. The rest will not matter, be-cause they will have no children.

Or any successors of their kind.

1922

IN THE RUSSIAN INN, on Locust Street in Philadelphia, a congenial group of men sit at a long table and talk about interesting things. It is an October evening, and the lamps outside are swaying in the wind. The Russian Inn is run by an immigrant couple from Russia, and it has the marks of a Russian restaurant in any provincial American city — checked or folk-embroidered tablecloths, a few bad oil paintings of Russian scenes, two large brass samovars on a corner table, small pink-shaded lamps, and, descending from the ceiling, a very peculiar chandelier. However, the atmosphere is congenial, since the Russian Inn is the only "bohemian" restaurant in Philadelphia at this time. Its owners are respectful of this group of guests, including especially the tallest man of the group, who is a regular patron, which is also the reason why (though the Russian Inn is not a speakeasy) wine and liquor are made available to them during this third year of Prohibition.

Their conversation is about paints, books, prospects of art. They are inspired by the fact that modern art, mostly from Paris, has arrived in their city (they know almost all the paintings that John G. Johnson collected and kept in the strangest places in his house on South Broad Street, and they also know of the new and wondrous purchases made by Albert C. Barnes); that the Philadelphia Museum of Art is about to be built; that they themselves have been able to own small or new masterpieces; that some of them are painters themselves; that, in sum, a renaissance (or is it a "naissance"?) of culture and art, of a growing private and public appreciation of fine things, has become possible here, in Philadelphia. They see the prospect of a coming cultural impasto, an overlay on the dull tastes of philistinism, over the *Blue Boy* taste, the blueberry-pie taste, the cinnamon-bun taste, over the very adjective *tasty*. There are moments when they see themselves somewhere in the vanguard of a renascent society in their city, in a rising new world where the better and finer things will, because they must, matter.

They are not intellectuals, they are not bohemians — even though, in 1922, most of them would not mind these words being applied to them by people whom they like. Three of the men are painters; three are amateur patrons of art; the tall, bony man mentioned earlier is a member of an old and historic Philadelphia family. Almost all are younger than forty-five, older than thirty. Except for K., now twenty-three, for whom this is a memorable event, since he finds himself in the company of men he admires and respects, his artistic and social superiors. Two days before, the leading patron of the arts had met him at the Pennsylvania Academy; they talked for a few minutes about painting, and then he suggested that K. join the group at the Russian Inn.

It is 1922, and among some of these men the old, generous American willingness to recognize talent, independent of publicity or celebrity, still exists. Yes, something like a renaissance may be occurring across America, and here in Philadelphia, too. It is more real than the "Little Renaissance" of 1912 or 1913 that was symbolized by the Armory Show in New York, against which the philistines howled outside (and at the fiftieth anniversary of which, a gala event, their descendants will be inside, making their noises of approval, though not quite sure of what they think they think). That Little Renaissance soon degenerated among the Provincetown dunes. But in 1922, much more than in 1912, the great migration of art from Europe to America is almost at full tide, not only because of the near omnipotence of the American dollar but because of the accomplishments and the knowledgeability of private American collectors — a migration, including not only pictures and sculptures but craftsmen and artists, whose only precedent in history may be the migration of Greeks to Florence and Bologna and Rome after the fall of Constantinople. Entire castles and medieval Spanish convents will soon be transported to California and set up there, stone by numbered stone. Suddenly, within a few years, the collections of American millionaires will bulge with many of the finest paintings of the world. But what I am writing about is a wafting of spirit, extant and now present even in solid, near-somnolent, provincial Philadelphia (and you know that I appreciate some of its virtues). One consequence of that spirit is how some Philadelphians will be inspired when they realize that northern Italian stonemasons now in their city are able to fashion beautiful stuccowork on their new houses and ceilings. In the 1920s the Museum of Art had been long overdue. It will be built finally, about fifty years after New York's and at least thirty after Boston's and even Chicago's. But in 1922 George Woodward, an old Pennsylvanian and an eccentric Progressive, is planning and building his French Village, that cluster of such wonderfully done up small Normandy houses in the green bowers of Mount Airy. That is what inspires me in retrospect. There was a temporary breeze of beauty in the air then, in the houses and gardens, something freshening the vision of even some of the stuffiest of citizens and brightening the eyes of their wives. Nothing like this happened in Europe at that time (or in England).

But now a crude consideration—call it ethnic, national, racial, or social—that I cannot avoid. These men at the Russian Inn are Anglo-Saxon gentlemen. Do they think that they are in the vanguard of art? Not really. Of society perhaps. But they are not snobs. They do not think that they are at the top of their world; they are not Kiplingites, which is to their credit, and they have not filled themselves with self-assurance. They are amateurs, in the true sense of the word. They like (genuinely like, and not only admire) Utrillo, and some of them like Matisse (at the expense of, say, Sargent or Winslow Homer, the latter being a mistake). They also prefer Turgenev to Dickens and Maupassant to O. Henry. What they do not know (and what the remnant Philadelphian Kiplingites do not know either) is that their own breed and the ideals of their race have been weakening. They will not be strong enough to shoulder the accumulating burdens of the century. They will not be leaders for much longer. Do they know what, at that very time — 1922 — is happening on the English-speaking shores across the Atlantic, in Ireland, where the English ascendancy is becoming extinct? Whether in Ireland or in England, youth and income are departing together. Here in America youth and income are still accumulating. Except that youth does not accumulate — just the contrary. For youth and the cult of youth are two very different things. And this is why, soon after America becomes a repository of much that is best in the art of the Old World, these men in the Russian Inn, on Locust Street in Philadelphia, will not attempt to ride the rising tide and perhaps not even be able or willing to construct breakwaters.

Here, during their talk at the Russian Inn, some of them discard their Philadelphian verbal reserve. But they make the somewhat unsure statements of the putative patron of art who is thinking as he speaks, rather than speaking as he thinks, whereby he does not quite think what he thinks he thinks. K., very self-conscious in their company, speaks very little and listens much. What he hears impresses him; the memory of this evening will be important to him. As he leaves he hears someone playing a piano in a house asleep, in the tired darkness of sleeping Locust Street, in the tired darkness.

"In the tired darkness. Your melancholy is getting the better of you."

You may be right. Too much retrospect is not good history, and not good literature either. But that small spiritual wind — I called it a breeze — I wanted to write about it as it was in Philadelphia and in 1922, perhaps not because it inspires me but because I have, I admit, a melancholy respect for it.

"What you suggest throughout is that during this century the Anglo-Saxon race was weakening — and not only in the Dublin Pale or in pale England but here, too. But at the same time you write that, unlike in England, in America youth and income were still accumulating in the twenties; and then you say something rather oblique about the accumulation of youth."

That I can explain, I think (or hope). What I find appealing about these people—at that moment—is of course the American youthfulness of their spirit, their American optimism about what can be done. But more important are their aspirations of maturity—the very opposite of the cult of youth. And this harks back to the American past: the difference between the times of George Washington and those of Warren Harding. There was no cult of youth in America two hundred years ago. To the contrary, there was a perhaps premature, perhaps a bit priggish, but nonetheless admirable cult of maturity. The cult of youth, very much there in the 1920s, is the result of the fear of aging. And in the 1920s that is pervasive—and not only among those bald, sclerotic old codgers bursting their lungs at the Harvard-Princeton game or in their and their wives' habit of occasionally calling themselves "boys" and "girls." It is there, too, in so many young men of that time, in their dread of becoming thirty.

These men at the Russian Inn were different. They would recoil from such phrases as "I'm going out with the boys." That may be trivial, of course. What is not trivial is the mental burden of their Protestantism. By 1922 most of them have abandoned most of that cargo, its obviously outdated Victorian and biblical hypocrisies, its moralism. They still have honesty and energy enough not to retreat to some kind of Unitarian ethics. For me, *ethics* and *ethical* are whitened, sepulchral words, very different from *moral*. But for these men, that difference is not sharp; they recoil from *moral* as much as from *ethical*. Not because they are not moral people. But—at least for a moment, or perhaps a decade—they put Art and the truthfulness of intellectuality over the truthfulness of morality. And this was so for refined minds on both sides of the Atlantic. Harold Nicolson once said about Samuel Johnson: "To Johnson, untruthfulness was not a moral blemish only, but an intellectual defect." *Only?* The opposite is true. Nicolson put *intellectual* above *moral* as a matter of course.

"But that came because of the rhetorical misuse of *morality.*"

It did; but the recovery of the proper use of *morality*—I do not mean its sense, which lived on within most of them, a saving remnant—did not, could not, occur.

"This is too much, and you know it."

I know it, but I know, too, that the consequences were disastrous. An example, again exactly fifty years later: a modern sculpture, a giant clothespin, was erected on City Hall Plaza, in the center of Philadelphia, in 1972. The mayor, Frank Rizzo, a brutal and uneducated man, spoke out against it, calling it a monstrosity. Sturgis Ingersoll, one of the best Old Philadelphians, one of the best private patrons of art, was appalled—he was all for the clothespin. Unfortunately, Rizzo was right and Ingersoll was wrong. He died soon afterward.

"You say Ingersoll, and I suspect that the tall, bony leader of the 1922 group was he. Am I right?"

I admit that you are—I took a small part of this vignette from a few sentences of his unpublished autobiography, but not all of it, not the Russian Inn. That I invented or, rather, added. Here is another little addendum: around 1954, at the height of the McCarthy wave, the owners changed its name to the Inn. Then it was again renamed the Russian Inn, a few years later. It no longer exists. An insignificant note, except that Frank Rizzo would have approved of that eradication of *Russian,* while Ingersoll would have thought it ludicrous.

"But are you talking about culture, or about civilization?"

Civilization, for God's sake. That's the trouble. That *was* the trouble. My men thought that the cause of culture was more impor-. tant than the cause of civilization. And in 1922, and in Philadelphia, it seemed so. But it wasn't. They took civilization—their civilization—for granted. But that must never be so. Seventy years later it is civilization that is falling apart. You know, of course, that for the Greeks the word *culture* did not exist.

1923

I'D LIKE TO describe a sunny scene that for a brief moment attracted people, a sunny moment that was shorter than they thought: I have in mind the French Riviera in 1923. There exists a remnant poster, lately reproduced, advertising (in English) "THE SUMMER ON THE FRENCH RIVIERA — BY THE BLUE TRAIN." On an impossibly high stone viaduct the Blue Train is speeding ahead; underneath the viaduct the colors are blue, sand, orange, and white: the beaches of the Riviera, blue mountains beyond the bay, a scatteration of people in smart bathing costumes, shining little orange points bobbing in the blue water, shining little white flecks of sails. There are many people, but the beach is not crowded. I think that the poster may have been made later than 1923, but both the atmosphere and the design are quite appropriate for 1923. (Train buff that I am, I know that the Train Bleu, the first all-steel wagon-lit train, blue and no longer mahogany, started to run Riviera-ward on the P.L.M. line from Paris to Nice in the last days of 1922.)

It is running in 1923, it is the beginning of the Riviera habit in the summer. The salubrious charms of the Riviera had been discovered by Lord Brougham and his friends ninety years before. They traveled there in the winter and in early spring, away from the cold and rain and fog of England, for the sunshine, the flowers, the warming caress of the air. The French followed them only later; the glamorous phrase *Côte d'*

Azur was coined by a Frenchman around 1890. Then came the Russian princes and the *haute volée* of Europe. Spring in Cannes, Nice, Monte Carlo: an annual gathering of the rich and the famous of Europe, England, the Russias. People who chose the Riviera in the summer were fewer and less remarkable, though there was an estimable number of writers and painters among them. And now, in 1923, after a war which in Western Europe left the impression in living memories of caked blood and dark rain and mud and wire, its survivors, another generation, are coming southward, ex-Protestants avid for the pagan Mediterranean. In the summer they seek an escape forward, not only from the dampness of the North but from an entire civilization ("botched," Ezra Pound wrote) or, rather, from the civilities of an unusable past. The tastes of the Provence, the scents of the Provençal flowers, the dry noise of insects fluttering in the grass, the pipes of shepherds, the chants d'Auvergne, and, far in the southwest, the parched ancient Pyrenees are more than tourist attractions. For a brief moment they inspire a host of men, these ancient sounds and notes create new music, it is there in the hearts of Englishmen, Ulstermen. Listen to Arnold Bax's "Mediterranean," from 1923: Impressionist, as was Ibert's "Escales" of the same time; a short piece shimmering with the charm of the southern slopes of Provence, cascading toward the Mediterranean. Bax was of Ulster ancestry, as was Cyril Connolly, who wrote at that time that the south of France is a "sacred place," "the expression of the complete south, the cradle of my civilization." Has there been such a yearning for such places before? And so a horde of bright young people pour into the Train Bleu at the Gare de Lyon, avid for living in the pour of the sun.

Yes, there was this Mediterranean moment, though only a moment it was. Unlike what would come afterward, when travel, for us, is an escape to some kind of a past. It had much to do with modernity. The twenties were, after all, the only modern decade. Breaking away from all the Victorian standards, from the traditional (and badly encrusted)

visions and artifacts of reality, was authentic then. No matter what the long-range results—and you and I know how disastrous some of those were—this was understandable, not only because history means change but because of the understandable reaction against that horrible war. Its symptoms were seen everywhere, in clothes, other fashions, the relations of men and women. *There* was a revolution, the greatest in perhaps fifteen hundred years. The last time women had showed their uncovered legs was in the fifth century A.D. The "revolutions" of the 1960s, ranging from the miniskirt through pornography to obscene art, were nothing, and I mean nothing, but loud and overly publicized recapitulations and exaggerations of the twenties. So in 1923 women no longer shielded their rosy faces from the sun; for the first time in perhaps fifteen hundred years they stretched out their naked limbs; nudity appeared openly now.

"Yes, it had something to do with sex."

Incidentally, or not so incidentally, that three-letter word became very much current just about that time (though mostly among English-speaking people), as did the then universally approbatory and indeed exclamatory adjective *modern*.

"But you are wrong to force all of that into the 365 days of the year 1923."

Oh, I will tell you why I do this. Also, recall that I am writing about a very short moment. That cult of a new paganism was insubstantial; it degenerated fast. Once the Bright Young Things and the Tender Is the Night people got used to the flesh of those aromatic fruits rioting on the stalls of the Riviera, they could not avoid the taste of bitter kernels, kernels of human deceit (including self-deceit) and, yes, even of death.

"You mean the Hemingway, rather than the Fitzgerald, shortcoming, the idea of the penis being mightier than the sword."

No, I mean what Anna de Noailles writes at the same time about love, *amour:* "Le seul combat contre la mort." It is a discovery for northern people, not entirely untrue but not quite true enough. In any event, easily miscast and misinterpreted. Around ten years before 1923,

Saki had written about "a moderately safe flirtation with a woman who has just got husband enough to give her the flavour of forbidden fruit." Around 1923 many men and women begin to think that there is no such thing as forbidden fruit, and all kinds of disasters, personal and social, therefore ensue. Besides dismissing moral traditions, they fail to realize that the world of Jane Austen, too, was laden with *amour* — and, yes, to use an unpleasant modern term, with sexual intrigues — but that governing element in *amour* is almost always more than sex.

"Be careful. You are all buttoned up. Don't sound like a Victorian who doesn't want to know much about sex."

That wasn't the trouble; the trouble was when they didn't know enough about women. Not all of them, by no means. Think of Thackeray. Listen to Trollope. Captain Batsby asks Lady Albury, "Don't you consider her divine?" Lady Albury replies, "My dear Ben, one lady never considers another to be divine. Among ourselves we are terribly human, if not worse." That is very good.

"Stop right there. You're again going too far. This entire 1923 vignette goes too far. Come now, is this the way to write history? Yes, yes, I know: not *history* but *about* history. But history, as you and I know, must be concrete and precise. You write about Bax and Ibert, for example. They wrote Impressionist music, but music must not be used to describe history. It may give a tone to a certain time, but it is not a picture. And Bax was inspired by the Mediterranean, too, but the Impressionist music he wrote — and I'm only referring to English music, since you are mostly taken by the English flight to the shores of the Mediterranean — was there already: Delius and Holst."

Not born Englishmen, or half-English —

"That is a quibble, and not my argument. My argument is that you have squeezed too much into 1923 and the Riviera. I know your conviction, that history must describe what people think and believe, including perhaps even what they don't think and no longer believe. Call it the sensitivities of a period or, more definitely, of a time and of a place."

And what that meant, and what that means.

"Ah, yes, but that is not easy. You may have a point, one point, about 1923, but history does not consist of single points, isolated sparks, alone."

How right you are, alas. But my point was a simple one: to suggest that moment in the sun. And then will come a time when that sea would no longer be invested with that spirit—and by "spirit" I mean not something mythical or pagan but the conscious aspirations of people, of some people.

1924

A YOUNG AMERICAN COUPLE have left the French Riviera for the Italian city of Brescia, in Lombardy. Late in May the almond trees are in flower everywhere, and their scents sometimes mix with the cloud of steam and the smell of warm metal when their train, moving slowly eastward on the Lombardy plain, stops at this or that station. Out of Bergamo an Italian gentleman points out to them a small baroque cone of a city, very beautiful from the distance: the Alta Città! The High Town of Bergamo! The young Americans lean out from the corridor window, in high spirits. Soon their train clatters into Brescia, on time.

In the graceful center of Brescia is the Piazza della Loggia, parts of it built by Bramante and Sansovino and Palladio; there is also a museum of medieval Christianity and an imposing castle. A traveler in the sixteenth century wrote that in Brescia "there are so many beautiful fountains that it is a real Paradise." But they are not coming to Brescia to see the fountains; they are in Brescia to get a car. An O M, which is the abbreviation for Officine Meccaniche, Brescia.

They had wanted to buy a Hispano-Suiza, which they had heard about in New York; they had seen one in Oyster Bay, Long Island, and a few more on the Croisette in Cannes. There they found that the Hispanos were very expensive, even though in 1924 dollars in Europe stretched far and even though they *were* looking for an elegant touring car, having chosen to live in Europe for two, three years at least, members of the first generation of rich young American expatriates on the Riviera. An automobile dealer in Nice showed them a picture of O Ms and estimated their prices, which were significantly less than those of the Hispanos. Since they were sufficiently interested, he found an O M to show them, a beautiful model, all lacquer blue and brass. Telegrams passed between Nice and Brescia. They would get their automobile at the factory and drive it back to the Riviera themselves. They left their three-year-old daughter with the Belgian nanny and took the train to Milan, where they spent a comfortable night, and then on to Brescia.

Now it is a heavenly morning, green and gold and pink under a cumulus-flecked azure sky, very warm in the sun but with long cool shadows everywhere cast by the stone buildings in the narrow streets. An Italian gentleman in a black suit, resembling the man who pointed out Bergamo to them in the train, awaits them at the station; now he drives them through the city to the factory to pick up their car, after which, he tells them, it will be the director's pleasure to invite them for lunch. Around the bright piazzas they are driven; all the fountains are in working order, either splashing seriously or splashing joyously in the sunlight. It is the kind of day, or the kind of hour, when expectations and the appetite for living are sharp. When they come to the factory, their car is there, ready, standing in front of the office building, a solitary elegant automobile on the sweep of a stone-paved driveway. It looks almost exactly the way they had imagined it. It is a deep magenta, and the lacquered metal is magnificently resplendent, mirroring the sun, with brass fittings, including a wide brass band around the headlights, maroon leather, a teak dashboard, and a mahogany *volant*. "It is really smart," the young woman says. "Sportier than a Hispano, don't you think?" says the young husband. And large. And impressive. Now they are driven around, first on the circle around the factory, then on an empty road between Lombardy poplars; and then they are shown all the workings of the car, the young husband takes the wheel, while the Italian driver in a white linen cap sits next to him up front. Then they go back to the office and sign a sheaf of papers. Then they are driven to the best restaurant in Brescia, accompanied by the director of the firm and his assistant, in two cars.

By that time it is past two o'clock in the afternoon. The lunch is excellent, even though the conversation is halting here and there, since they talk in French, with a few English phrases thrown in by the director. They talk about cars, Brescia, America, Italy, and a new order of things here. It is a time of optimism. There are promises and thanks. And hopes. About the Italy that is now very modern, also about Mussolini. In northern Italy the first autostradas are being built, the world's first superhighways, radiating out of Milan (the director shows the plan on the map). Northern Italy shines in the sun.

On their way back, in Milan they see men in black shirts, Fascisti — masculine, narrow-waisted, and youngish (though not all of them). They see them on some of the best streets and in some of the best restaurants. Understand that Fascism was a northern Italian phenomenon. Mussolini started it in Milan.

"You seem to have this weakness for Mussolini, which people will misunderstand."

I am glad you said "seem," because you know very well that this is not so. Of course, I prefer him to Hitler or to Stalin. But he had enormous weaknesses — character failures, really — which did him in at the end.

"Keep in mind that you are not writing an essay in comparative political theory."

No, I'm not — except for one thing. I've always been dissatisfied with the sloppy and, yes, dishonest employment of the word *Fascism* to cover every dictatorship or every authoritarian movement of the non-Communist variety. There were great differences between Fascism and National Socialism, especially in 1924 and then for some years. Hitler was not a Fascist. Of course, there were similarities, too. That had much to do with the fact that Hitler was the stronger of the two and that, as time went on, Mussolini let himself be influenced by Hitler, thought he had to emulate Hitler—which, I repeat, was due to his weakness.

Anyhow, Fascism was an Italian creation, whereas National Socialism was (and still is) much more universal. And, alas, lasting. But let's not go into that—except to say that Italian Fascism was a passing phase, which has something to do with this vignette about 1924. The beauty of that automobile, the building of the autostradas, the optimism—yes, you may have noted that I stooped low enough to make a quick reference about that train running on time—well, there was that moment in the sun, and it was a *modern* moment, which is why I am writing this. D'Annunzio, Marinetti, Respighi, Pareto, Gentile—they were all Fascists in 1924. Poets, composers, musicians, philosophers, the Futurists. Even the engineers and the designers of modern Italy, inspired by automobiles and airplanes, were Fascists, and for a time Italy led the world in their design. Add to this the order that Mussolini established in Italy, a kind of order that did not (yet) come at the expense of too many freedoms. It seemed as if it were the wave of the present, of a new kind of present, leading to a new kind of future. That is why so many people beyond Italy admired Mussolini and Fascism, and not only because he was supposed to have made those Italian trains run on time. There was that semblance of a new Mediterranean order, nonpuritanical and antihypocritical, a clear rather than a repressive twentieth-century breaking away from the sclerotic and the corrupt inefficacies of the parliamentarianism and liberalism and philistinism left over from the nineteenth century. And my young American couple were impressed by that—at least by its externals, by what they saw and by what they heard (from those black-suited gentlemen and also from the white-capped chauffeur). Not because they were enamored of order. Not because they were afraid of Communism, which was why many other people liked Mussolini. Because what they saw was *modern*. The attraction of Italy lay not only in such things as Venice or the Arch of Titus. They had come to Europe, to the Mediterranean, to remove themselves from Prohibition, from the Babbitts. Brescia was preferable to Detroit, and I mean not only the old fountains but the new automobiles. Riviera scandals were preferable to Harding's scandals, and Mussolini to Coolidge.

"There was plenty for them to read in the newspapers about some ugly things done by the Blackshirts to their opponents, about prisons and so on. You're making your American couple into Innocents Abroad."

Remember, please, that what I am writing about is what certain people *thought* at a certain time and at a certain place. About what they thought was happening, rather than what *was* happening. Yes, what happens is inseparable from what people think happens (though not forever, and the two things are not identical); but these Americans were outsiders, not participants. And in 1924 Mussolini was not yet a full-fledged dictator; there was still a parliament in Rome, and his real dictatorship came about only in 1926 or even later. But that is not my argument here, even though for many years afterward a great variety of people admired Mussolini, including Churchill, who said (even after Mussolini had become his enemy and after Mussolini was dead) that while he, Churchill, surely did not prefer Fascism to democracy, he preferred it to Bolshevism. But I am not thinking of Churchill. I am not even thinking of those many Americans, including American ambassadors to Italy and Will Rogers, who admired Mussolini and who should have known better. I am thinking of Cole Porter, who as late as 1934 — ten years after 1924 — wrote his two lines about Mussolini in those sunny ditties of his in "You're the Top!" They go: "You're the top! / You're the great Houdini! / You're the top! / You're Mussolini!" Two lines which have been excised from *The Complete Cole Porter*, published decades later in New York and supposed to include all of his lyrics.

"And your young American couple are Cole Porter people, meaning modern and antipuritan and antiphilistine and irreverent — is this what you mean? Don't spin that out further, because soon you will say that the Riviera was Cole Porter country and that Cole Porter was the Fitzgerald of American popular music."

No, I won't say that. Besides, the Cole Porters discovered the Lido in Venice, which drew many rich and chic Americans in the 1930s, not the 1920s.

"I read somewhere about Harry's Bar having been started by one of the Ciprianis in 1932."

Yes, that was still the golden age of Mussolini. Do you know that when Ezra Pound was received by Mussolini in 1933, he called that day the starriest day of his life? (Incidentally, it was January 30, the day Hitler became the chancellor of Germany.)

"Well, innocent or not, weren't your American couple a bit light-headed, taken in easily by many things, such as Mussolini & Co.?"

"Perhaps. But not forever. And I shan't speculate about them further. Their future troubles, if any, may come from alcohol or adultery or eventually the drying up of their inherited money, including what American dollars bring in France. But, yes, in 1924 they are still innocent, at least in their ways, and in that merry month of May the world, they think, is still opening up before them. That is, of course, an illusion, but it involves something more than their private lives. They believe what they see, and some of what they see seems authentic and promising. It is a semblance, and while semblances are often misleading, they are not altogether devoid of a certain reality. The proof of any semblance is its endurance, and that 1924 semblance, though real and palpable for a moment, did not and could not last. Like the world of *The Green Hat,* also published in 1924, in London. It is a book about disenchantment, written by a sophisticated Armenian, Dikran Kouyumjian, *id est* Michael Arlen. But my Americans are not disenchanted — yet.

1925

ENGLAND, in 1925, is gray. Sixty years later people in England are tired
of fog, rain, wind—of damp winter darkness and of chilly spring mists
and of grayness. "A sky of bad milk," one of their writers puts it. In
1925 English grayness still had something light in it. One can sense
this even in that bounder Priestley, who wrote about coming to London then: "There is a certain kind of smoky autumn morning, coolish
but with the sun somewhere not far away, with a railway station smell
about it, that brings back to mind those first days in London, when I
would hurry out of King Edward's Mansions to catch an 11 bus to Fleet
Street." And Waugh in *Brideshead Revisited* called the 1920s the "last
decade of Englishmen's grandeur." He was half right.

Historians will say, and not without reason, that he was wrong—
that by the midtwenties the decline of Britain and the decay of the empire were evident in many tangible ways. There were physical, material
facts all around. A generation of Englishmen and Englishwomen saw
the facts—I mean those who had lived through the war, even those
"hard-faced men" (the famous words spoken to George V by his secretary) "who made out well from the war." Before the war there had
loomed before them the agreeable future "of sinking into the thick, de-
licious syrup of Edwardian society by sheer weight of income if [they]
wanted it," as someone else put it. After the war their youth and their

income were going together. There were Americans who saw this. It was after all an American Englishman who wrote *The Wasteland*.

Looking at England from the east, from the Continent, it did not seem so. To most Europeans, England was still the greatest, the most admired power in the world. To many of them, English gray was English cloth, reliable and long-lasting, light gray flannel, decorous like the English monarchy. Aristocratic and liberal England, that unique combination. "My father was in love with England," an older Hungarian friend once told me. They had visited England in 1925, "and he taught me what was to be loved there." They may have been exotic guests in England. Whether they were treated like poor relatives in certain country houses I do not know. But I think that they were like the young Cyril Connolly in the houses of his mother's favorite sister, who had married a rich man: "Aunt Mab was very beautiful but she also had special smells, smells of furs and Edwardian luxe. Bishopscourt, Loughananna, Rochestown, Marlay, the names of her houses . . . held a poetry for me." (Some of those houses were in Ireland, but never mind.) Such names may have held a poetry for my old Hungarian friend. They hold it for me, too, even though I am a prose writer. To me Compton Wynyates is more elegant than Choisy-le-Roy, not because of the shape of its sound but because of its form on paper. Anglophilia is not musical, it is verbal.

Well, the history of Anglophilia, of Anglomania, is yet to be written, and I am afraid that it never will be. (Or at least not well.) I am only writing about one moment in history, in 1925. About England with the coal smoke and the brittleness of certain convictions and the weakening of the Latinate English prose and the far-flung navies melting away, but also with the prevalence of certain manners, of the soft cement of hypocrisy, of those stiff upper lips which were more than parts of a rigid mask. Yes, the hard-faced men who made out well in the war were there (not only businessmen but members of the Royal Yacht Squadron, in their white duck trousers and navy blue blazers, grinning at the bearded George V at the wheel of the *Britannia*). But there was still that inclination of Englishmen and Englishwomen not to take themselves (and their ideas, which almost amounts to the same thing) too seriously. There was their compulsive sense of social self-consciousness, sufficiently cruel at times but sometimes tempered by humor. "These people have character," my old friend's father had said. Of course, character may exist together with a lack of imagination—and sometimes even with a weakening of convictions.

But the aroma of an old flowering and the soft flannel, the wet grass and the gardeners at their mild work, were still there. And the beauty of youngish English matrons draped in gray peau-de-soie frocks and approaching the Ritz on Piccadilly on, say, November afternoons in 1925: momentary scenes more elegant than those to be found in Paris or New York then. But I must watch lest I give the impression of trying to be another Dikran.

You will think, I'm afraid—and with plenty of reason—that I have given in to my penchant for impressionism, and to an extent that is unsuitable for a historian. So my only excuse is this: history must be, indeed it is, descriptive and not definitive, whence there must be some place for a historical impressionism on occasion.

"I am your closest friend, which is why I will warn you only when you're courting serious trouble. That will sometimes work, because you are not incurable. You are a curable romantic. My curative amendments this time will not be addressed to what you fear—to the amplitude of evidences that exist in the writings and the memories of many Englishmen to the effect that there was little majesty, or even much elegance, in the English grayness in the twenties. Think of those interminable choir practices in their dreadful schools, those unbroken, pealing voices of 'unhappy cherubim behind stained glass, evilly lit.' That is in the memoirs of Peter Ustinov, but something similar is in what that most English and most honest of writers, George Orwell, remembered. Much of England was insensitive and unimaginative, with its window sashes stuck and hardened by old thick paint."

Yes, what was still stained glass *was* often evilly lit, and those dreadful English sash windows *are* what the French call them — *fenêtres à la guillotine* —

"Please don't interrupt me now when I am quite indulgent. Just consider that I refrained from mentioning Forster's *Passage to India* having been published in 1924. Its very reception was ample evidence of how tired thinking Englishmen had become of empire."

A Passage to India is a bad book, and not only because of its effects. I interrupted you again because of Orwell: when it comes to the decay of empire, *Burmese Days* is a better book.

"I'm not thinking mainly of the weakening of their imperial convictions but of the weakening of their appetite for life. That was only covered up by the antipuritan puritanism of the English twenties, including Bloomsbury as much as the fretful social-sexual whirl of the Bright Young Things (not very bright, but let that go). Chesterton once wrote that despair does not consist in being weary of suffering but in being weary of joy."

Oh, *despair* is too much. Too strong for England in 1925, not a mot juste.

"I allow that. Good point. And you are writing about nostalgia in two ways at least. One is the nostalgia that foreigners, continentals, had about England in 1925. That sounds true, and it is acceptable, except for one main thing. I'm coming to that in a moment. The other, more dubious one is the nostalgia that Englishmen like Waugh felt for the early twenties. *Brideshead Revisited* could have been written only by someone like Waugh, in the drab, democratic-socialist, for him near-proletarian midforties, reminiscing about the champagne-and-strawberry Oxford of the early twenties, standing in 1944 in that empty, half-ruined, near-abandoned hall in Brideshead. You are right when you say that historians will deny it when he called the 1920s the last decade of Englishmen's grandeur; perhaps you are right, too, when you say that, well, he was half right. But was he honest with himself? His own life, certainly by 1925, was a dreadful mess. Those were the most miserable years of his life.

"But you — and your readers — must keep one main thing in mind.

You have now written about England in 1925, but underneath it all, you have written about . . . well, love. Among other things, about the English masculine ideal that was fading, though not yet in the eyes of other beholders, including some people on the Continent. Much of the old English virility was gone. But a kind of feminine sensitivity was coming to the fore, and you have been sensitive enough to recognize it. Don't laugh—you may be right. For once. There was a mutation in the very image of Britannia circa 1925. She still held her trident and her shield, but she was now something of an older, though still handsome, figure—a governess."

Do you mean someone like that woman in one of Trollope's novels, I think? Let me find the passage. Here it is: "She was very much wrinkled—but as there are wrinkles which seem to come from the decay of the muscles which should uphold the skin, so there are others which seem to denote that the owner has simply got rid of the watery weaknesses of juvenility. Mrs. Morton's wrinkles were strong wrinkles."

"No. England may have been wrinkled in 1925, but Britannia had had none of the watery weaknesses of juvenility. The operative noun is *governess*."

Do you know that one man who felt this—and how strongly!—was Hitler? After Munich, in November 1938, he made a speech at Saarbrücken. That was the first time that he attacked Churchill specifically. He said: "It would be a good thing if people in Great Britain would gradually drop certain airs. . . . We cannot tolerate any longer the tutelage of governesses." And Churchill alone saw the significance of that phrase; he even italicized it in his memoirs.

Now let me go back for the last time to my Hungarian friend and his father, who were in England in 1925. Fifteen years later, in that dramatic, hot summer of 1940, many men and women across Europe were willing to stand up for England. Or, more precisely, for what England stood for. There were, you know, foreigners in 1940 and later who were ready to die—and some did die—for that. Their love for England had something to do with the image, imprecise or not, of an earlier England. But it was also the love for an older and superior civilization.

It was different from the Anglophilia of the nineteenth century, when England seemed to be ahead of the rest of the world. This love was a defense of a still beautiful, middle-aged woman who was being attacked and maligned and whose honor was being besmirched by pockmarked youths in crew cuts. And England was not conquered, which—as we know now, but which people did not know then—was a miracle.

"Yes, the miracle was Churchill."

1926

In 1926 K. is in Paris, learning French and studying painting. There is enough material here for vignettes: the American in Paris, in his garretlike room, at the Flore or the Select, in the large and dirty studio of the private academy of Monsieur Y., who is called *Maître,* with his black silk skullcap (or a large Basque beret, worn indoors and out) and a goatee (as late as 1926). And concierges and their monumental wives, French girls, other Americans pretending to be exiles, and Suze, baguettes, and *pinard;* perhaps one visit to the famous or, rather, infamous house in the rue Chabanais (but only perhaps); a cycling trip to the Provence . . . That is the trouble. Not the trouble of too much or too little, but all these clichés. K's life in Paris is predictable, recognizable, conforming to a pattern, with all of his inspirations and disappointments. And since what matters is memory, the disappointments do not matter much, because they are soon forgotten, while the hyaline wash of his inspirations (or are they aspirations?) remains in his mind, gradually turning into a light cerulean watercolor picture for the rest of his life. K. is not an ignicolist, a fire-worshiper; he is a respectful lover of art and of a few of the finer things in life, which, being young, he can identify rather than distinguish, though no great harm is done, since he is not at all like Hemingway; but then, neither is he a reincarnation of *Roderick Hudson,* this being 1926, not 1875.

For sixteen months he stays in Paris, save for a few excursions, including that sunny, though accident-ridden, cycling journey to the south. There is, however, one other, unusual excursion. On a wintry day he sets out for Berlin, somewhat reluctantly, having been dragged along by a companion. That companion is at least temporarily his closest acquaintance in Paris. He is a Hungarian artist. They struck up a conversation when they were literally rubbing corduroy elbows on a crowded café terrace (yes, the Select or the Flore). K. is pleased to find that his accidental acquaintance is a painter, too, voluble and outspoken about many matters on which they agree. Neither of them speaks perfect French, which also cements their developing friendship. The Hungarian paints in the Expressionist style, not at all current, a style that K. does not really like but which impresses him, at least for a while. This new friendship assuages K.'s occasional loneliness. During the next weeks they meet often. His painter-companion is knowledgeable about Paris. He is also poor and not penny-wise. He takes advantage of K's easier circumstances, though only within limits; he does repay the small sums borrowed from his new American friend — well, most of the time. He is less loyal when it comes to a girl whom he thinks is attractive as well as available and whom K. has found more than attractive; but that is another story, and K. does not find out about that until much later, if at all. On a wet and cold October afternoon, when even the glass-enclosed terraces of the cafés are gloomy, their windows streaked with rain, the Hungarian advances the plan of a joint ten-day trip to Berlin. A cosmopolitan city; a very interesting city, with its avant-garde people, Expressionists; and a very rich patron of the arts, a Hungarian doctor, who would be delighted to see him again, together with his American friend. Besides, Berlin is not expensive. All he asks of K. is to advance his train fare, which he will pay back soon. At first K. is cautious and reluctant, but after a few days he decides to go.

They meet at the Gare du Nord. Bundled in their coats, they sit up all night in the second-class coach; in the morning, K., drowsy and half-sick in the smelly warm fug of the compartment, looks out at an iron morning in Germany, empty stations and brick chimneys and steel cranes rushing by, wreathed in fog, a different world. In Berlin there is snow on the ground and an electric smell in the air that he senses, in spite of his tiredness. The Hungarian has a place to stay, but first he takes K. to a pension in the bowels of a large, dark, fortresslike Wilhelmian apartment house. K. is very unsure at first, but those anxieties melt away: first in the pension, where his room is larger, his bed better, and the bathroom and its water much warmer and more reliable than those at his place in Paris; and later in the streets, in the museums, and especially and unexpectedly in the company of the Hungarian's German and other Central European friends. They welcome this American into their midst and ask him many questions about American life and art, something that K.'s French acquaintances rarely do. Then there comes a near-magical evening in the rich Hungarian doctor's Dahlem villa, which is opulent rather than elegant (*Stilmöbel*, portières, Chinese figurines, including obscene ones, and all kinds of paintings). In Paris K. had no entrée to a dwelling such as this. The talk is all about art, much of it about Berlin theaters, which he does not understand, but enough people talk to him in French and some even in English. They like his tall American frame, his American countenance, his American youthfulness, his American naïveté. And there in a black velvet dress is a quiet girl, with reddish blond hair and the loveliest of freckles on her roseate face. After dinner people sit in the music room and listen to new records on a huge modern gramophone, among them a piano concerto by the Irish composer Hamilton Harty, and when it comes to a particular passage of that romantic rainy music, this girl turns to the young German at her left, asking him for an expression in English, and then turns quickly to K., nodding her beautiful head toward the gramophone. "This grips my heart," she says, in English. This girl, this moment, and these words K. will not soon forget.

"Did you like Berlin?" his wife, Anne, will ask him, six or seven years later. "Oh, yes," K. says. "But it wasn't like Paris."

And it wasn't.

✳   ✳   ✳

"Well. You *could* have found something telling about your friend's April in Paris. But you have this fear of clichés, so you take him to Berlin. And isn't that so because you find Berlin in 1926 more interesting than Paris?"

Not really. During those wintry ten days K. does find Berlin more interesting than Paris, but what interests me is how (and why) that fades so soon. He has no wish to return to Berlin, though he thinks long, and perhaps much, about that attractive Renoir-colored girl. There are several things at work here. One, of course, is his Philadelphian cautiousness. Berlin has an atmosphere of dangerous electricity, which, in spite of its American-like speed and dynamism, is alien — alien, rather than exotic — to him. For K. life and civilization in France are less so, and because of rather than in spite of their differences from Philadelphia and America. So K. will remain a Francophile throughout his life, even when modern French art turns to the worse, even in 1940 when the French collapse, even after the war when, during a trip to France with his wife, he encounters a new kind of French sullenness.

"But isn't there a personal element in this, due to his character? For at least a week he likes Berlin, he is more comfortable there than in Paris, he meets interesting people there, but then he tells himself that he really shouldn't, because it is Paris that he is supposed to like. Isn't that a Philadelphian puritanism of sorts?"

Perhaps, but not predominantly so. There is an honest and decent element in K.'s Francophilia, more honest and decent than the Francophilia of the celebrated exiles of the twenties who, with all their emphatic bohemianism, including their relentless immorality, are seldom more than chatterboxes taking a self-conscious and ridiculously exaggerated pride in their so-called avant-gardism, a coterie roiled by little more than fevered undercurrents of social strivings and snubbings. Of course, they did not have a monopoly on American Francophilia, with all its generosities. That American Francophilia, 1777–1950 (which, in

K.'s case, lingers on even longer), is a complex story. It has not much to do with Lafayette and Rochambeau. But that American liking for France and for the French Enlightenment will begin to fade in the 1930s, except for such things as fashions, and twenty years later that will be gone, too, while the French will have begun to imitate the worst of American things. But back to 1926, a time when the French are still discovering Americans. Before that, Americans to them were exotic, interesting noble savages, *grands enfants* of a new civilization. That was the Crèvecoeur, the Chateaubriand, the Paul-et-Virginie tradition, there even in Baudelaire's discovery of Poe. But what the French failed and still fail to realize is that a *grand enfant* is more complicated than an old man. So they took to, and they still take to, the Hemingway types, because of their sense of inferiority in what they think is virility. The results are that culture minister of the 1980s who calls himself Jack Lang and that glass pyramid, designed by a Chinese American architect and chosen by the French president, plunked down in the great courtyard of the royal history of France.

I've been going too far. I am writing of 1926, not of 1982. "Paris–New York" (a sign at the platform gate leading to the boat train at the Gare Saint-Lazare) still strikes a responsive chord in the imagination of Frenchmen and Frenchwomen. And in 1926 *tout Paris* responded not only to Josephine Baker but to those chromatic American tendencies and music; and there was the new *Ile-de-France*, scintillating across the Atlantic with Ravel aboard in a suite, approaching New-York (which the French, until lately, always wrote with a hyphen) with its over-heated hotels and marvelous elevators and bathrooms and long silver automobiles and trains. There was this thin, silky thread of romantic elegance on the crest of the otherwise complicated Franco-American relationship which has not disappeared entirely. That very word, *américain*, suggests something in France and in French that is different, no matter how slightly, from its meaning in other languages — something that is not only modern but romantic, with a soupçon of dash. And K. was a beneficiary of this, even though he had no connections with *tout*

Paris, not once at the Paris Ritz, while he would have no such hesitation at meeting someone at the Plaza in New York.

"He was an art student in Paris, without much money."

That made a difference, but not much. His affection for Paris was dutiful and respectful. That says something about him, and it says something about the subject of his affection, too.

1927

IN THE HOFBRAUHAUS in Munich, three Catholic priests sit at the end of a long, crowded table. Two are Americans, which is evident by their clerical suits and, at their necks, the narrow white bands, dog collars. One is a German priest in a long and wide rust-black soutane. A German layman, a round little man in heavy German tweeds, sits with them. Amidst the noise, the beer, and the smoke, the arm-in-arm swaying and singing of people at the tables, the monumental women servers in their Bavarian dresses, and the clanging down of the big steins, the Americans seem to enjoy themselves, perhaps more than the German priest but not less than their civilian German companion and guide, who keeps insisting on good cheer all around. It is the end of a long day that had started out under the brightest of early June skies, with the linden trees in full bloom, with many flower stalls in the streets and squares of Munich. After dinner came a sudden downpour, which is why they are inside the famous beer hall and not in its garden. It is a summery rain, they hear the swishing of it but it does not beat against the large windows of the Hofbrauhaus, and the air carries thousands of white and pink blossoms, flying aslant in the wind.

The American priests have come to Munich to buy a painting. Father Sheehan (probably to become a monsignor soon, favorably regarded as he is by Cardinal Dougherty of Philadelphia) became pastor of Holy Savior, a parish in one of the Philadelphia suburbs, the year before. There had been water damage to the far side of the wall behind the altar; the wall has now been repainted, but even with a semi-Palladian arch of stuccowork half-encircling it (and out of keeping with the rest of that neo-Gothic church), it looks rather bare. Father Sheehan has long admired the large painting behind the altar of another church, Saint Teresa, a Descent from the Cross bought in Germany in 1923 by his friend (and sometime rival) Father Dunphy. He has been thinking about and planning for such a reredos picture for more than a year. He has heard about the market for religious pictures in Munich, information emphatically confirmed by a German-American fellow pastor whose brother is the German priest sitting with them in the Hofbrauhaus this evening and whose cousin is the jolly layman, Dr. Kern, a dentist from Regensburg. The other American priest, the younger one, is Father James (Riordan), Father Sheehan's curate in his former parish and an agreeable traveling companion.

They have not yet met with success in Munich. They have gone from art dealer to art dealer, from Sedlmayer to Hanfstaengl and, after lunch, to Bernheim (most expensive, most elegant). They have been led by Dr. Kern, who had called at their hotel at breakfast, volunteering his services as their translator (he knows some English) and art expert and negotiator. There was the problem of size: none of the canvases came close to the dimensions of Holy Savior's wall. There was the problem of price: Father Sheehan, knowing about German inflation and the high European esteem for the American dollar, has come to Germany too late — unlike Father Dunphy (whose worldly knowledge Father Sheehan sometimes remarks upon, *invidia clericalis*). In 1927 the German reichsmark is solid, four to the dollar, and though German prices are still lower than prices in the United States — and though Father Sheehan's purse is large enough for their traveling expenses as well as for their proposed purchase (given his personal savings, the resources of the well-heeled parish of Holy Savior, and a significant donation by one of its parishioners, a brick manufacturer) — the price of the only canvas he instantly liked, a Crucifixion by a minor Italian baroque master of the seventeenth century, an authenticated painting brought out in the Bernheim showroom against a black velvet–draped stand, was far beyond what Father Sheehan can offer. When they stepped out into the blinding sun, Dr. Kern said, "Of course too much, that is what Bernheim is like."

But it was not an unpleasant day altogether. The air was brilliant and dry in the sun; the snowy crests of the Bavarian Alps were pointed out to them; they enjoyed walking around in the cool darkness of some of the churches, especially in the Frauenkirche, whose two round-capped towers reminded Father Sheehan of birettas. For dinner at their hotel the German priest joined them. He is almost skeletal, saturnine, with a prognathous jaw and protruding teeth: a German *Pfaffe*. He does not know English; the dentist translated. After dinner he and Dr. Kern withdrew a few steps from the table, talking rapidly. "Wonderful!" The dentist turned to the two American priests, with a large smile. There is a fine artist, a religious painter, a relative of the *Vater* (he points at the latter with a big flat finger), who just might have a painting for the American parish, or who would do one on command, and whose price will be very reasonable. Nothing is really lost. His name is Zwickau, and he lives in Pirna, south of Dresden on the Elbe river. There is a direct train, a Schnellzug, from Munich to Dresden, three hours. "But the Dschentlmen must be careful!" Dr. Kern said. There is a *town* named Zwickau, near Pirna. But this artist is not in Zwickau. He is in Pirna. His *name* is Zwickau. "Now the Dschentlmen must be careful! It is Zwickau in Pirna! Not Pirna in Zwickau! Zwickau is the artist!" Then they went to the Hofbrauhaus, which the Americans have heard about before, having seen its picture in magazines and travel folders.

Four days later they are in Pirna, where the artist and his family have been well advised of their coming by the dentist's two lengthy telegrams, the first instructing the painter, who has no telephone (this is 1927), to repair to the Postamt and have Dr. Kern called at his home in Regensburg. There the two Americans stop for a day — Regensburg happens to be on the train line from Munich to Dresden and Pirna — and Dr. Kern gives them an enormous midday dinner, when he and some of his friends toast German-American friendship. After that his cousin, the German priest, leaves them at Regensburg, returning to his community, an abbey at the outskirts of the city. The American priests take the Schnellzug to Dresden (passing through Zwickau), arriving at dusk, lodging in a hotel near the river, admiring the baroque and rococo buildings and the lights of the city slowly brightening in the blue evening. They are advised that they can travel to Pirna by streetcar. Next morning they are in Pirna, the trolley winding itself through big cobblestoned streets in the shadows of enormous chimneys. There is no rococo in Pirna, where there are many factories. They have no trouble finding Herr Zwickau, who took the day off to welcome them. He teaches art in a public high school and lives with his wife and mother. There is one more large German midday meal, and there *is* a large painting, whose size alone appeals to Father Sheehan, not to speak of the fact that it is a Descent from the Cross.

Zwickau has brought the painting home from his studio in the school. The ceiling of the Zwickaus' apartment is not high enough for the canvas, which is on two large easels nailed together and stands in the hallway. There the light is not very clear, but then it is a somber painting. There is one problem: it is as yet unfinished. The Christ is still missing, though the outlines of his figure in a shroud are visible, lightly limned in. Completed are the mourning women, both shrouded in somber black, looking like Central European nuns. Completed, too, is the full figure and face of Joseph of Arimathea, dominating, nay, entirely filling up the lower right of the canvas. The trouble—if it is trouble—is that Joseph of Arimathea is Zwickau. He stares up at the cross like an actor mired in pathos. He has a lined, very German, Silesian face, expressing something like a disciplined, near-militaristic purpose, a determined German idealism steeped in lament. He has used it as an exercise of self-portraiture for the students at school. He does not avow that, though it is rather obvious. Altogether, the painting, except perhaps for Zwickau-Joseph, whose face, I repeat, has a German early-twentieth-century look, is very nineteenth-century, realistic and monumental with plenty of dark colors and one strong shaft of light breaking through the dark bitumen paint; and, as Father Sheehan sees with relief, liturgically correct. He likes it better than does his companion. That evening, back in the Dresden hotel at dinner, they talk about it at some length. "Don't you think it's a bit too German?" Father James asks. "I don't know, Jim. I like it. The size is just about OK, and I suspect the price will be, too." Father Joe is right. Dr. Kern arrives in Pirna, and the next day the purchase is made. The painter will complete the canvas, and arrangements are made to ship it to Philadelphia within three months, arrangements expedited by the dentist of Regensburg.

Once the painting is installed in the Church of Holy Savior—Father Sheehan wants this done on a Friday and a Saturday, for there is some crimping and a hardly visible crack on the canvas, and of course some of the top, with all those blackish clouds, has to be cut here and there, to fit the curve of the Palladian arch—it will be there, behind the altar, for the parishioners to see, at the early Sunday Mass. One of the well-to-do parishioners, a German-American maker of brazing and welding equipment who had been invited by Father Sheehan to see it when it was unrolled, says, among other things, "Wonderful, Father! It is just like an altar [he means altarpiece] in Germany!" That will not be repeated by Father Sheehan to Father Jim, who comes to dinner at the rectory later on Sunday.

"I was pleased to see that you did not put in Nazis singing and drinking beer in the Hofbrauhaus."

Of course not. There were not too many Nazis around in 1927, though there were some in Munich. But let me insist: my principal interest is in these Irish-American priests, not in the Germans.

"Do you suggest something about that dreadful German dentist being a Nazi?"

No. He votes *Deutschnational* or, more probably, for the Bavarian People's Party—though in 1933 he as well as his cousin, the priest, will approve the decision of that party to vote full powers to Hitler. But I'm interested in that other matter, in the revolution of American sentiments about Germany and Germans and things German, which may have reached its peak around 1927. In many ways it was a reaction against the anti-German hysteria of a decade before. And it was more than political, though it was a reaction against Wilson, internationalism, the wartime alliance with the British and the French. 1927 is in the middle of the Coolidge presidency and a Republican and isolationist era —

"Don't forget that most American Irish were Democrats."

Yes, so are my two priests, even though they are from Philadelphia, which is solidly Republican. But there *is* a national element at work here. Father Sheehan, like many Irish Americans at the time, does not like the English, to say the least. This is not merely attributable to the sufferings that the English had visited on his ancestors in past centuries; there were many smaller but perhaps no less painful indignities visited on the Irish in America by the Protestant English or Welsh or Scots or Scotch Irish. He was pleased to think, after the war, that the American alliance with Britain may have been wrong, that British anti-German propaganda had had much to do with that, not to speak of the profits of the munition makers. To this bundle of beliefs came to be added the recognition that the Germans were not bad people, that Germans liked Americans, that Germany was not such a Protestant country, that German Catholics were preferable to Polish or Italian Catholics, an estimate tallying with Father Sheehan's experience with immigrant parishes in Pennsylvania, in Scranton or in South Philadelphia. Besides, by 1927 there was something like an emerging Germanic facet to the United States. Such different people as Babe Ruth, Mencken, and Hoover were all of German-American origin. They even *looked* German: roundheaded and round-faced, heavier, stockier. They marked some of the decade. In 1928 Hoover will be elected president, the first American president of German — that is, not British, not Celtic — ancestry.

"Hoover said that his ancestry was Swiss."

Perhaps. But he was rather anti-English as late as 1940. And so were some of the Irish Americans, a political condition of which FDR was perhaps exaggeratedly aware. But notice that I say "some." An

Anglophobe Irish American is not necessarily a Germanophile, though some people, such as Father Coughlin, were. You will recall that the younger of the two priests, Father Jim, is not charmed by the Germans. There was this shift between two generations: in 1941 the American Irish are less Anglophobe than in, say, 1915. Yes, in 1941 Father Sheehan still maintains some of his earlier respect for Father Coughlin, and he reads every word of the *Brooklyn Tablet;* Father Jim does not. I can think of only one, slightly lamentable episode in Father Sheehan's public life. By 1939 he is a monsignor, indeed, an auxiliary bishop of some place like Wilkes-Barre. Hitler had invaded Poland. The Polish pastors of his diocese call on Father Sheehan, asking him to make a public statement or at least say something in one of his sermons, condemning the German oppression of Poland. He does not make such a statement, though in his Sunday sermon he delivers a thundering attack against . . . atheists and Communists.

"The Irish are not simple people."

No, they are not. Let me return, for the last time, to the American priests' grand tour of Germany in 1927. The night before the purchase of the painting, Father Riordan said to Father Sheehan: "Joe, I don't like this German dentist. He is up to something." Father Sheehan to Father Riordan: "I know that, Jim. It takes all kinds. The price may be right, but I don't like him myself."

1928

ON A WEEKEND IN September K. and his mother receive an overnight visitor at Cherry Street, a rare event in that household, even though there are now two empty bedrooms on the second floor. For some years now K. has had digs of his own, two slapdash rooms on Camac Street, on a city block in Philadelphia inhabited here and there by a sparse grouping of artists and other bohemians. But he customarily spends every Sunday and at least every second weekend with his mother, who is now ailing with a slowly progressing plague of multiple sclerosis, soon to be dependent on a wheelchair, and bereft each Saturday of an ancient Quaker housekeeper, her veritable factotum. And K. is a dutiful son, loyal to his mother—even as he has an exaggerated awareness of the difference of his generation from hers, by which I mean their valuations of the world and their spiritual aspirations.

Arriving will be Ruth, a poor relative of the family. They have not seen her in something like a decade, though they hear from her, Ruth being a faithful correspondent, twice or at least once a year by means of many closely handwritten lines on a large Christmas card. She is K.'s mother's grandniece, K.'s second cousin, the daughter of the only half-educated and ne'er-do-well among a number of uncles (a poor Quaker, a rarity by 1928). Ruth is strong-minded and plain. (They have not seen her or a photograph of her in many a year.) She did not marry

well. Her husband was an Irishman at least ten years older and less edu-
cated than Ruth, who was a top student in Girls' High (a model school
in Philadelphia) and who was supposed to be a whiz at stenography.
After—indeed, perhaps already before—her marriage fell apart (there
was something, too, about a baby lost), Ruth maintained herself as a
secretary in the editorial department of a newspaper in St. Louis, where
she and her husband had lived since their marriage and where the husband was from. Now she has written that she is leaving St. Louis and is
looking for a job in the East, perhaps in Philadelphia, perhaps in New
York. She says she will be coming from New York, where she will stay
for a few days with a friend. Her parents are dead, she has few relatives,
and she has always had an affection for the white-haired kindness of
K.'s mother, who has answered her with an earnest suggestion that she
spend a few days with them in Cherry Street upon her arrival in Philadelphia, which is happening now.

They do not know the exact time of her arrival, but she is very
punctual; she told them around noon, Saturday, and it is almost exactly
noon when she knocks at their door. K.'s mother need not look at the
busybody (that is the name of those small, street-slanted mirrors outside the second-floor windows of some old Philadelphia houses); she
expects no other visitors; she knows it must be Ruth. Both she and K.,
who is puttering on the first floor, are somewhat taken aback by the
sight of Ruth carrying and slightly panting under the weight of two
enormous suitcases. It appears that she did not take a taxi from Broad
Street Station; she took one of the Market Street trolley cars to Twentieth and walked the remaining four or five blocks. She is a poor relative,
after all. But she makes a pleasant, perhaps even surprisingly pleasant, appearance. She is apple-cheeked, big-boned, cheerful, womanly
rather than matronly, with large brown eyes and an agreeable voice.
She is without makeup, she has fairly thick ankles, she wears simple
woolen clothes, almost though not quite to the degree of unfashion-
ableness, but not because she is a Quaker. She is sensible, as are her
shoes; her attire is that of a professional working woman, without too
much of a touch of provinciality. She is thirty-seven years old.

She likes the house on Cherry Street, which she knew before. It is an old-fashioned house (remember that in 1928 *old-fashioned* is not a positive adjective in America, though it will be that forty years later, at most): narrow, red brick, white-marble front stoop, Philadelphian. Solid, modest, proper, and clean, but there is more to it than that, and Ruth knows it; she instantly feels the still presence of its interior well-being, and not only because of the strong, almost pervasive smell of furniture polish. There are antimacassars on the sitting room (called sitting room, not parlor, but not drawing room either) armchairs, pieces of yellowed lace, a Turkey carpet, a Victorian rosewood piano, and a heavy sideboard, but also two fine ancestral portraits (one of a Quaker ancestress with a white cap and fichu against a black background), a gleaming cherrywood highboy, a long gilt mirror: a climate of coziness with some overstuffing here and there. Only the bedrooms upstairs, smelling of tooth-powder and Lysol, are somewhat forbidding, with their dark mahogany bureaus and beds, but she hasn't seen them yet, K. having lugged her suitcases upstairs. Now there is a light lunch preceded by a glass of cider (this is the decade of Prohibition). "I wish such had been my home once," Ruth thinks, but perhaps only for a moment.

And then the afternoon advances, and there are revelations. Overall, it is most pleasant and unusual, for all three of them. To begin with, Ruth is not so plain at all. She has a full figure, without being heavy; she has a round face, but her brown eyes and brown hair are nice, and her perhaps once plain features are animated as she talks. And she is capable of talking about many things, surprisingly so, including music and many books, which is a revelation of what this young woman has made of herself, as K.'s mother will later say. It was her employers who suggested that she try her luck in the East; they said that she was too good to remain in her position as a secretary and that in St. Louis there was no chance for her to advance any further, whereas there are publishing houses in New York and Boston and Philadelphia. She is modest when recounting this but also full of spirit, as when she says that she had for some time thought of leaving St. Louis for good. What follows is the most surprising of the revelations. She has become a Roman

Catholic. (And this, K. and his mother think, despite the fact that her low and alcoholic husband, the Irishman, was a Catholic, too.)

Dinner has been prepared by the housekeeper, whose day off this is; but the table is nicely set, and the mother has to do not much more than warm and bring in the dishes. The mother took some special care in planning the dinner tonight; and Ruth has a healthy appetite, she finds it enjoyable indeed. Her hands are stubby, she has almost no wrists, her nails are unpolished; K. sees that, but she holds her fork and knife easily, almost delicately. Soon after dinner K.'s mother retires; dishes are customarily left for the housekeeper to wash and dry and put away; she will be back before long. And indeed she comes in by the front door before ten o'clock, a heavy presence shuffling toward the kitchen, forbidding, surprised, and even vexed (old servants do not like overnight guests, especially not poor relatives) when she finds K. and Ruth deep in conversation.

For there is now a bond between them. Simply (or perhaps complicatedly?) because K. finds many things that she and he can talk about — politics, books, magazines, and, yes, art and painting, too — with quick conversational spurts revealing that they have many opinions in common. K. had thought (if he had thought about it at all) that he was in for a dutiful and probably dreary evening; and now he finds the company of this relative more than pleasant, for she is intellectual as well as earthy, with a hearty fertility of common sense. For the first time in his life K. feels the sexual attraction of a woman because of her mind, because of her opinions, a sexual attraction that might not exist without that intellectual element. It is compounded, too, with his sensual discovery of the attraction of an older woman. She says one or two things about her newly found religion, too, not because K. asks her (he is too shy and well mannered for that), but it comes up when she queries him about the household routine on Sunday mornings, because she will go to Mass. "You know," she says a minute or two later, "I've been thinking that I have always been a Catholic at heart. Because it is the Catholic view of human nature that alone makes sense to me. And if people say that they believe in Christ they might as well believe in him in real." "In real," she says. And then she says that there were many things wrong with her husband, including the hard and narrow tribal customs of his Irishness, but when she lost her baby he asked *her* to forgive *him;* and before he died in the hospital (they were already divorced), he thanked her for having brought the priest; "perhaps that was the only time in his life that I saw him content."

It is near midnight when each of them go to bed. That night K. has a very erotic dream about himself and Ruth, which disturbs him and fills him with a strong sense of shame (for he remembers much of the dream next morning, when he is exceptionally shy, as if he had had a guilty sexual encounter with Ruth the night before, which of course he hadn't). But that will pass soon, and Ruth is unaware of what K. feels and thinks. She slips out of the house early, returns from Mass in the cathedral for a few more hours of that now familiar pleasantness in Cherry Street. It is near twilight when she says a heartfelt good-bye to K. and his mother; they have urged her to stay longer, but she had made plans to stay with another, to them distant, relative across the river, in Camden. K. insists on sending for a taxi, and his mother on her coming to see them again, surely for Thanksgiving.

Two months will pass until Thanksgiving, during which many things will happen. Ruth will be hired as a typist-secretary at a Philadelphia (and Quaker) publishing firm, Lippincott's. She will cross from Camden every day on the ferry. K., whose mind will be filled with his infatuation for a prospective fiancée (Anne), will still be thinking of Ruth, suggesting to his mother that they ask Ruth "to have pot luck with us" some weekday after her work at Lippincott's. His mother, who likes Ruth and who is impressed with her instant acquisition of a position with a firm such as Lippincott's, of course agrees. But then — it is now late October — comes a telephone call from Ruth: she has to go to New York. She is giving up her job in Philadelphia. "There is a prospect for me in New York," she says, and she will stay with an Irish woman friend. "But you must come for Thanksgiving!" the mother says, and Ruth thanks her and agrees. And three weeks later, at an unexpected time — at ten in the morning — there is another telephone call, a toll call from New York, with an unexpected voice. It is Ruth's Irish friend in New York. Ruth has asked her to call, for she won't be able to come "down" for Thanksgiving; she is in a hospital and may have to stay there for a couple of weeks at least. K.'s mother calls him with this news. "I wonder why she didn't write us," K. says, and suddenly he feels very stupid, hearing his mother say, "She may be too weak; she probably can't." And now K. — bless him — goes to see her in New York. He finds her wan and dying. But her face broadens and glows with sudden pleasure when she sees him, and she grasps his hand and holds it. "I have cancer of the liver, you know," she says. "It came so sudden. And I know I haven't got long. I didn't want to burden all those Philadelphia relatives. And your mother, give her a big kiss. I am very tired. But nothing really hurts. Now you must go. The priest is coming soon. God has blessed me, and He is blessing you, too."

What *is* blessing? K. thinks, as he leaves her. What is *her* blessing? he thinks during those dreary two hours in the train roaring past the landscapes of metallic filth in New Jersey and the satanic (well, almost) mills of North Philadelphia. And what is *our* blessing? he thinks, on this darkening November evening, as he walks out of Broad Street Station to Market Street, which, in 1928, looks like an ungainly forlorn, poor relative of Broadway, with a new monumental movie palace (the Mastbaum) in the urban wilderness. There should have been a better place for someone like Ruth in this world, and this should be a better world, he thinks. He is not hounded by heaven, he is only haunted by that strange deep smile on Ruth's face and by her words. Of course. He only thinks that he has an unbelieving heart, but "in real" he doesn't. He will think of Ruth often for a while, and then less and less, but the essence of that smaller and smaller memory of hers will never entirely vanish, because I think that such essences are immortal gold, whereas the period pieces — 1928, Philadelphia, Cherry Street, poor Quaker relatives — are but alloys.

"Keep in mind what Edmund Wilson wrote about *Brideshead Revisited*—that it was 'a Catholic tract.' "

Wilson was wrong, and this is not anything like *Brideshead*—

"But it has traces of a Catholic tract. And it is the 1928 that I question. Could this not have taken place in 1908? Or in 1948?"

Now wait a minute. The more *Catholic* a tract, the more *timeless* it must be. Whatever is wrong with this vignette, it is not timeless. All right, the essence—or, say, the quality—of Ruth's faith may be timeless. But the main theme of this vignette is not Ruth's religion; it is, rather, her unexpectedness. This is a vignette and not a short story, you know.

"And would her revelation—if that is what it is—not be unexpected by her relatives in 1908 or in 1948?"

Perhaps—but not quite. Cherry Street and the family, and their relationships, and K.'s own personality, his sensitivity, his ideas, they would have been different in 1908. Or in 1948. One or two years up or down, I may admit. But 1928 is clear enough in my mind. Do credit me for not having said anything more about that year: that, for example, K.'s mother in November would vote for Hoover, whereas Ruth and K. would vote for Al Smith.

"Well, I hope it will be clear enough for your readers. I worry about that sometimes, you know, and you should, too."

I worry about it plenty. Besides, there is something I haven't done well in this vignette: the great loneliness of someone like Ruth, who happens to be a sensible and practical and perhaps even gregarious modern American woman. I should have painted in more great loneliness on Market Street, Philadelphia, 1928. This can be a very lonely country, where people can and sometimes will freeze to death not in a forest or on a mountain but on broad avenues in the giant shades of enormous buildings with many of their lights on but all doors locked tight at night and no one approaching . . .

"One more thing about religion. Conversion is always an individual drama, and you and I know now of Quakers who suddenly become profound and even zealous Catholics. But what happens when

Quakers become Episcopalians? I cannot quite imagine flashes of inspiration, a drama there."

No, you are quite right. It is, rather, a gradual slide — though *slide* is not the mot juste; it is a movement forward and up, not down. It is not devoid of social consciousness. But it is not opportunistic. It may even have something to do with American Quakers rediscovering the Englishness of their roots. It happened with Logan Pearsall Smith, who went on from Philadelphia to London and wrote wonderful little books about the English language.

"And what does that have to do with Ruth?"

Nothing. But she is a small American saint. The way of Christ goes from God to this world, you know, not the other way around.

"So this *is* a Catholic tract, after all. Don't bristle at this. All right, a vignette about a Catholic. An *American* Catholic. Granted."

1929

LATE IN THE VELVETY NIGHT a pianist is playing. He is a little man, nearly gnomelike as he hunches low over the keyboard of a large piano, which is black, as are his tuxedo and his big horn-rimmed glasses. He plays many of the black keys.

This is in New York, in one of the private rooms of a grand hotel, where a party is dissolving. Some of the men and women have left. Some are still sitting on the cushiony small sofas around the cocktail tables. A few stand around the piano, admiring the player, listening to his playing.

He plays the sophisticated late-twenties' tunes of Gershwin, Kern, Rodgers and Hart: "Manhattan," "Thou Swell," "Maybe," "I've Got a Crush on You," "How Long Has This Been Going On?" How long has this been going on? Not very long. None of these tunes were written before the midtwenties, and none of them were played the way this pianist is playing them now, in early 1929. There are the soft dissonances in his left-hand chords, the now drawn-out and nonchalant syncopation, the ascent of three- or sometimes even four-finger chords into the melodies played by the right hand—that is, the increasing presence of harmonic texture, softening his embroidery of those simple melodies, together with the decreasing insistence of their beat. In sum, the impressionist essence of what otherwise is still called the music of jazz.

This is something new in the spring of 1929; it attracts the people who gather around the piano, not because it is modern but because it strikes them as melancholy and beautiful. ("Jazz" was not really melancholy, perhaps not even the blues were.)

Their ears have lately become accustomed to these harmonies.

1929 is only a decade away from ragtime, only a few years after the Charleston and of "Swanee" and the Irving Berlin ditties, with their simplistic, insistent rhythms. But this kind of playing, this kind of music, is different, even though the tunes were produced for Broadway musicals, even though they consist of the routine thirty-two bars; they are different, too, from what their composers had written but a few years before, such as "Lady Be Good" or "They Didn't Believe Me" or "Look for the Silver Lining."

American music has now sprung to the zenith of the world, having moved swiftly from Tin Pan Alley to something complex and smart. Its glitter is not superficial, it is suffused with certain interior riches that float high above the opulent productions of Broadway, tainted as they are with some vulgarity even when their orchestrations are at their best. It touches, on occasion, the heartstrings of some of its listeners, through some of those new, finely dissonant harmonies. The color is the essence; it is not added to the drawing, it is the drawing.

Some of it accords with the time and place. On that late winter evening the atmosphere, too, reflects the ascent from the Wurlitzer New York of, say, 1910 to this room: much black and silver, the women smart and modern, with their long fingers and long single-strand pearls. Outside are the pearly double strands of lights all along Park Avenue and the big-wheeled automobiles gliding by on the wet street — or on a thin white layer of snow. But whether it is cold or warm, windy or still, overcast or starry outside does not matter. Late in the velvety night this pianist is playing, and the velvet of the night is inside.

Again I think of the chords that this pianist touches, because he is making them up as he plays. They are improvised. Improvisation is essential for this work. It is dependent on the composers' scores, which already have their share of novel harmonies, but he adds to them, creating them anew, enriching them with something that is more than a superimposition. They flow to this gnomic pianist's fingers not so much from his brain as from his heart. These melancholy harmonies have something to do with a yearning, including the yearning of a second-generation American immigrant for an American and urbane elegance, for an elegance also incarnated in certain women; but it is less physical than it is social and spiritual. This kind of yearning has existed and exists elsewhere in the world, too. But here, in America, it created much of this music. And this kind of music became very American, not only because it was produced by newfangled Americans but because so many Americans responded to it. It was melting-pot music no longer. It became something else.

Of course it didn't last. That harmonic moment did not last. The high bourgeois climate in New York did not last. There is a book about New York written in 1929 by Paul Morand, a fine *haut-bourgeois* French writer who spoke English and wore bespoke English clothes impeccably, who admired London at first and then wrote about towering New York. But on his last page of *New-York* Morand asks, how long will these magnificent buildings, how long will that monumental civilization that they represent, prevail? He foresaw the crumbling of American urbanity, of the civilization of New York, in 1929, not in 1969 or 1989, not after the devolution of much of New York into a northern Calcutta. He saw the steel and the stone and the luxuries institutionalized, but he thought, and in the end wrote, that there was not enough substance there, they would not suffice. An "ephemeral renaissance," a "magnificent purgatory" was New York. "Will it explode and sink one day?" Whether he understood something about the music I now write about I do not know.

"I hope that this is the last time you write about music."
Yes, this is it.
"Seeking some historical significance in it, I mean. Your talent

must be exercised on grounds that are more solid than that. You try to paint with words, but a painter makes up not only his colors but his canvas, and this kind of canvas is too squishy and soft."

Yes. Only here I have been spinning out something that I wrote for *American Heritage* ten or so years ago. I answered an editor's circular query addressed to historians: "What is the one scene or incident in American history you would like to have witnessed—and why?" Others wrote about the moment that Columbus landed or of Fort Sumter or of Lexington. To my mind came New York in 1924, Aeolian Hall, and the first performance of "Rhapsody in Blue." The editors liked it so much that they printed it in a box and in larger type than the rest. Well, it was not that good, and 1924 is not 1929, and what I've been trying now is surely more *nuancé*.

"It is *nuancé*, all right. For one thing, I don't understand what you mean by a yearning that is social and spiritual."

That should be simple. It is the aspiration to rise in society, but one propelled by idealization: the pervasive malady of people who are more romantics than they are snobs.

"Are you thinking of Proust or someone like him? You are writing about music, for God's sake."

No, I may be thinking of Stendhal, who once wrote that no duchess is more than thirty years old to a snob. But there is more to the inspirations of music in this one instance. Think of the listeners whose spirits are lifted, if only for moments, by this kind of music; they therefore admire this pianist. Some of them may think or say, "I wish I could play the kind of piano you play." Think of the pianist who admires the handsomeness of some of his listeners. He may think, though surely not say, "I wish I could look like you." This reminds me of the conversation between a priest and the late-medieval German mystic Meister Eckhart. The priest said, "I wish I had your soul in my body." Eckhart said: "That would be useless. A soul can save itself only in its own appointed body."

"That is impressive—even as you have jumped from 'Lady Be Good' to Meister Eckhart. But now to a small point. In 1940 Paul Morand was a Pétainist, if not a pro-German collaborationist."

I know that, and I think I understand his reasons. By the late thirties Morand had become convinced that the Anglo-Saxon virtues which he had once admired had become outdated and weak. He was not the only former French or European Anglophile who thought that. One example is Drieu la Rochelle, who then became a National Socialist of sorts. But while some of the French Naziphiles — Bardèche, for instance — liked American movies, they did not like American music. And this brings me to a last and for me very important observation, about which I have been thinking often, and in this instance I presume to think that the ground is not too soft. This is that everybody — note that I do not even say "nearly everybody" — who responded to that kind of American music, whether in the Americas or in Europe, including in Germany (and there are Gestapo reports about that), hated the Nazis. Because of the Nazis' vulgarity. Whereas the new Nazis and the skinheads not only like rock, their very get-togethers are thumping with rock, they sing and dance and often march to rock. Of course rock — *all* rock — is brutal music.

"Well, Bill Clinton and George Bush like rock, too."

There may be some significance to that.

"Brutality? Come on!"

No. Puerility. And while much in America in 1929 may have been puerile, American music — that kind of music — was not.

1930

K. AND ANNE ARE MARRIED in Wilmington. It is a beautiful, though hot, Saturday in late June. The small Episcopal church is packed with flowers, the heavy damp odors of which swirl around and around, stirred and lifted by the whirring fans. Anne's family comes from Wilmington; indeed, one of her granduncles was a founder of this church seventy-five years before, which is why her parents wanted the wedding to take place there, a wish to which she consented, at first reluctantly and then unwillingly no longer. She was born and brought up in the green suburbs of Wilmington, in reality more country than suburb, but she never cared much for the young horsey crowd there; she was interested in ballet, books, and art, one after the other, in an ascending sequence of emphasis. She left Wilmington early, going from a finishing school straight to the Pennsylvania Academy of Fine Arts in Philadelphia, where she met K., and that was three years ago. She lived with a maiden cousin and then in an apartment with another student and then they went to Paris for six months and then she saw K. in Philadelphia again, first suspecting and then more and more confident that he was in love with her, which indeed was the case. He was one of the most promising students at the Academy, while she was no slouch (especially in her carriage, lithe and always beautifully straight, which complemented her interesting, asymmetrical face and glorious, oceanic red hair). Now in her ivory-and-cream wedding gown, she is an apparition.

Her bridegroom is nervous. He customarily feels out of place in Delaware because of its Southern touch, which Anne has learned to appreciate anew, of course with some reservations. The church is full, with many more people from the bride's than from the groom's family, though Anne insisted against a big wedding, and she assured K. that there won't be too many Foofads, meaning First Families of Delaware. This made him feel better, for many reasons, assuaging, too, his worries about his mother, who is in a wheelchair now; besides, he does not quite know how his mother would feel about all that drinking at the reception, not that she is a teetotaler, but then she is law-abiding, and the law of the country is Prohibition still. But of course all goes well in the end, including the reception on the lawn of Anne's parents' house: not more than seventy people, and K. drinks a lot of champagne.

I am no Joseph Hergesheimer (or F. Scott Fitzgerald, who lived in Wilmington with Zelda for a year or so in the late twenties). There is no reason for me to write more about the atmosphere in Wilmington or about Delaware society circa 1930, though that could be interesting enough—the Southern touch, the flowers and the bourbon old-fashioneds and juleps, the cambric gowns of some of the women and the odd, slow courtesies of some of the men. I am interested in something else—in the gradual sea change of some of K.'s views, which has begun several months ago and which has been influenced at least indirectly by Anne. She is the stronger of the two, but in this marriage, unlike in so many other American ones, this will do no harm. Something started to appear, if not crystallize, in K.'s mind on the Friday before the previous Christmas Eve, when he and Anne had tickets to an especially well-produced *Nutcracker* at the Academy of Music in Philadelphia. She had convinced him to come with her (their tickets were donated by her aunt, a Friday-afternoon orchestra subscriber). K. had thought that the *Nutcracker* before Christmas was for children, but this was not really so: there were plenty of well-dressed and sometimes fidgety children in the audience, but this was a very grown-up performance, rather sumptuously done, with the lovely ballet and with the excellent Philadelphia orchestra in the pit. And the nineteenth-century music and the nineteenth-century setting on the stage and the nineteenth-century costumes and movements, perhaps especially the courtly solicitude of the white-wigged old gent in black, dancing and swirling protection and guidance over the young girl, touched K.—he had lost his father early in life, you know, he had hardly a memory of him. Hearing that music and watching the stage, he felt a taste of sugar, of candied fruits, and a sense of pale, profound, fragrant colors, of bergamot and tangerine. "It was really beautiful," he said to his fiancée. There was a movement of his heart (and mind) toward the past, more an attraction than a necessary respect for a certain kind of tradition, the first movement of his mind away from his rigidly unquestioning convictions about the conventions of modernity—in art, that was. And I think that Anne had, gently, already moved him that way.

The newlyweds have not much money. The wedding had to take place in late June, to enable K. to finish the academic year (he is teaching painting in a suburban girls' school). They will have no more than a four-day honeymoon; some of Anne's relatives have offered their house on the North Shore of Long Island. Next summer, they hope, they will have enough money to spend a month or so in France, which will be their real honeymoon. Coming out of the church, K.'s mother beckons to K. and gives him an envelope, a wedding gift from one of his uncles. It contains five one-hundred-dollar notes. He opens the envelope as they sit in his Ford, before driving away. "By God," he says, "let's not go to Clinton Street. Let's go and spend the night at the Bellevue. Or perhaps drive on to New York." "No," Anne says. "We'll save that money, and, besides, I am too tired to sit in a hot car for hours." Their apartment on Clinton Street (across from the house where Agnes Repplier lives) was made ready by Anne before the wedding; they will spend their wedding night there and drive to Long Island the next day. She even made the breakfast things ready for them, and she is slightly irritated with him when he admits that he failed to bring his two suit-cases over to Clinton Street the previous day; now they have to stop at his dingy, emptied rooms to pick them up.

On Route 1 the drive from Wilmington to Philadelphia takes an hour. The warm, damp air flows in the open windows of the car, and Anne no longer cares what happens to her hair in the wind. Some-where on Baltimore Avenue they have a flat tire. When K. climbs out to change it, he is abashed to see that he had not wiped off one of the JUST MARRIEDs chalked on by their friends in Wilmington. It is an Ital-ian neighborhood, and a woman steps down from the hardwood porch of a house, saying, with the widest of smiles, "What a beautiful bride you have! Joe and Tony! Come help this gentleman! It's hot, lady, I give you a drink!" All is well in the heat and the dust when they start again and ascend the bumpy evening avenue while their hearts descend into a valley of happiness.

"Well, you have filched this last sentence from Valéry Larbaud—one of your favorites—from his 'Beauté, mon beau souci,' about two English lovers, Reginald and Queenie, at Combesbury: 'Ils descendi-rent pour s'asseoir un moment au bord de la rivière Yeo, où il trempè-rent leurs mains. Et vers le commencement de l'après-midi ils entrèrent dans la vallée bienheureuse.' But that is about England, was written during the world war, is a small, nostalgic canvas."

Well, isn't that a beautiful sentence? It has haunted me for de-cades. But I haven't filched it because of its sound. Also, it is but the first part of Larbaud's *Amants, heureux amants* (published in 1920). It is appropriate, because K. and Anne are *amants, heureux amants,* at that moment, not in the Yeo Valley but on Baltimore Avenue in Philadelphia, but there is much more to it than that. In some ways America in 1930 is older than England and Europe, by which I mean some places and some people and some mental conditions and feelings and sentiments. This is 1930 and is quite different from Larbaud's nostalgia in 1920 for

an idyllic 1906 in the west of England. In plain English: after the earth-
quake of that most catastrophic of wars, some things in America were
still spared in 1930. But only here and there, of course. There is that flat
tire, you know.

"Well, you gave plenty of vent to the idyllic. And that bergamot
and tangerine—are they colors, or are they tastes? They are too much.
Or too little: your description of K.'s 'conversion' is not very convincing. Or clear."

It wasn't clear in K.'s mind, either, but it was a flash of insight, a
move away from the Ezra Poundish exclamation "Make It New!" It was:
see and imagine what is human—and then make it so. And eventually
it will govern his art, as it has begun to govern his life. Thanks to Anne.

1931

See 1957.

1932

"*Tout Berlin!*" A MAN EXCLAIMS. "*Tout Berlin* is here!" He stands in the middle of a small group, part of a large crowd of people in the large drawing room (*Salon* in German) of the first-floor apartment of a villa in Dahlem, in the West-End of Berlin, which is now the residence of a Hungarian Jewish operetta composer. It is a starry occasion, celebrating the great success of the Berlin production of his latest musical. Unlike in New York, here such parties gather one full day and night after the premiere, after the theater reviews in the big newspapers have been printed, read, and digested. After-dinner parties are another Central European custom, called soirées, beginning about nine o'clock and often going on to the early morning. The party has now begun: droves of people are still arriving, the doorbell keeps ringing, a maid clothed in black bombazine and a starched white cap struggles with the fur coats heaped on her muscular arms, there is a pervasive cloud of perfume and of much, much cigarette smoke. The lights are bright, nearly garish, since they are overhead: all the rooms have chandeliers, whence the dark shadows in the corners. The furniture is all plush and fruitwood, except for the man's study, the *Herrenzimmer,* with two bookcases that rise to the ceiling and much paneling. There are heavy portières in every doorway. The pieces are comfortable rather than valuable, most of them being *Stilmöbel,* that is, good reproductions (though, as Saki would say, trying to be Louis Quinze while often lapsing into William the Second). The host is not responsible for all that. He is a recent renter, not the owner, of this apartment in this large, graystone, bulbous villa, built around 1910. The night outside is misty and rainy, with a few arc lights illuminating the residential streets of Dahlem; the wet wrought-iron gate glistens, while the narrow flowerbeds and the grass in the small courtyard in front of the house are damp and dark. The atmosphere inside is both ponderous and nervous. *Tout Berlin* is not *tout Paris:* indeed, *tout Berlin* is an exaggeration, though not entirely false. What makes for the combination are the people: bankers and actors, journalists and actresses, doctors and filmmakers, photographers and caricaturists, non-Jews and Jews—the upper Bohemia of Berlin now, in 1932. But then, this party is really *Mitteleuropa* as much as it is Berlin: at least one-third of the guests are men and women from Budapest, Vienna, and Prague, even though most of them live in Berlin now.

Berlin and Germany—but Berlin more than any other city in Germany—has been attracting such people since about 1919. Journalistic Berlin, photographic Berlin, cinematic Berlin, literary Berlin, intellectual Berlin, artistic Berlin, musical Berlin: they flock to this cosmopolitan city to make their careers and fortunes, and many of them stay. There are many factors in their movements: there is the fact that the main language (and much of the culture) of their Central Europe is, after all, German; there is the fact that the audiences of theaters and films and the readership in Berlin repeat, in many ways, those in Budapest, Vienna, and Prague, and on a larger and more profitable scale. So there is, among many other things, the presence of Hungarian spice in Berlin, superficial but also sensibly pungent, lightening the taste of the heavier German dough, which is heavy even in that cosmopolitan and in some ways Americanized Berlin of the Weimar years. That, too, is a main factor in the present success of this *Mitteleuropa* operetta, with its silly-schmaltzy libretto but its music suffused with a few Hungarian rhythms and melodies that are both sentimental and modern, half-Danubian and half-Broadway, with semisophisticated harmonies, with touches of late Lehár and early Gershwin. This is 1932, after all, a good long distance from *The Student Prince* et al. The production itself is a glitzy confection, a mix of Budapest and New York (or, more precisely, of what *Mitteleuropa* thinks and imagines is New York), rather modern, with strenuous efforts to create an atmosphere suitable to the tone of the music: plenty of Grand Hotel and gold lamé, harshly lit scenery, and unambiguous Sex Appeal.

That is why the play is a success, and its composer knows it. This is a new pinnacle of his career. He is a little man, with a long pale face and enormous ears. Unlike most of the people at his party, he is rather shy. No, he does not disbelieve his success or even the prospect of his play being taken up by New York or Hollywood, the gossipy talk being bandied around him that night. He takes pleasure in his surroundings, in his residence in Dahlem, in the rich villa-apartment, in the measure of his guest list, and perhaps especially in his being cosseted by the German lovelies around him, towering blondes or thin Berlin girls with a determined piquancy in their dresses and faces: actresses, starlets, perhaps one of them his temporary mistress now, promising to stay with him after the party will be over. I do not know. What interests me is his melancholy. He knows something: what is happening to him now, this short brilliant chapter of his career, will not last; it is but a way station of his life. But the prospects of Paris? New York? Hollywood? Perhaps. But there is something in the Jewish heart of this man, a nervous rather than fundamental awareness of the tragic essence of life, caught in glimpses of his awareness of himself when he climbs out of bed in the morning, whether next to a deeply breathing German girl or not, padding in his slippers to the bathroom: "This is where I now am, and this is where I am not, and this is—perhaps—where I should not be." Like George Gershwin's, that melancholy face is a mirror of a melancholy soul, and what beauty there is in the harmonies of his compositions arose from momentarily synchronized fusions of his melancholy with his aspirations to a sophisticated world.

For Gershwin, in New York, to wit. But this is Berlin, in November 1932. In fewer than three months Hitler will be the chancellor of Germany, and the Third Reich is around the corner.

* * *

"You are not very clear about the premonitions of your Jewish composer. Is he worried about his career, or about what is around the corner in Germany? If he is anxious about the first, that has nothing to do with the second; and you say nothing about the second condition, even though you repeat that it is November 1932. A party before the catastrophe. But not a single word about it. These people could not be oblivious of the situation, they could not have been that self-centered and dumb."

They are self-centered but not dumb. But the odd thing is that no one at that party, indeed, no one in *tout Berlin* thinks of what is about to come. It is not at all like the cinematic script of *Cabaret*. There is no Nazi gang of toughs lurking around that street in Dahlem. There are no Nazis or secret Nazis or Nazi sympathizers at the party, not even among the servants or chauffeurs. As a matter of fact, the Nazis just lost votes and seats in the reichstag elections. Some of the people do talk about politics. They think that the Hitler wave has peaked, that the Nazis have started going downhill. There are others who may be less optimistic. But none of them can even imagine what is going to happen. And if you cannot imagine something, you cannot think about it; you will think and talk about other things.

What I am writing about is not really a party before the crash or about pirouetting on a volcano. Something exists within the mind of my man, alive within that melancholy of his, a vein deeper and thicker than pessimism—hence his sense of disbelief at this very time of his winnings. He may be aware, at certain moments, of his personal condition. Of the historical situation he is not. He somehow knows that his fortune will not last, because it cannot.

"Because it *cannot?* What is he—a prophet? Or merely a self-doubting Jew?"

No, he is no Weininger.

"Otto Weininger?"

Yes, the Weininger who wrote *Sex and Character,* in 1901, I think, and then killed himself. He foresaw the rise of a tremendous wave of anti-Semitism which he attributed to the sins of many of the Jews themselves. The Weininger about whom Hitler once said that he had been one of the few honest Jews in the world. Of course, Weininger was wrong, for more than one reason. Here is what he wrote: "Humanity thirsts for a founder of a new religion, and the struggle moves toward a decision as in the Year One. Between Jewry and Christianity, between commerce and culture, between woman and man, between earthbound life and a higher life, between nothingness and Godhead mankind will again have to choose. These are the two opposite kingdoms: *there is no Third Reich*." Well, there was to be a Third Reich, and it was to be ruled not by the religion of Christianity but by the religion of the Folk. That is ahead of my man in Berlin, who does not fear a coming wave of anti-Semitism, yet he is deeply uneasy about . . . well, about *something.*

"The dark wings of dark angels, flapping, reverberating, in his soul? Weininger's vision was grandeur and guff, and you better watch out lest it becomes yours, too."

You're probably right. But one last thing about Weininger. He was not only wrong in that he could not foresee a Third Reich. There was a third alternative, and a real one, besides his Jewry and Christianity. Weininger was wrong, too, in his bloody damnable Germanic obsession with a Higher Life. Earthbound life is troublesome enough, and whatever we know of a higher life we know right here and now — which is one of God's greatest gifts to us. That was one of the things that Simone Weil knew and Weininger did not know.

"I thought that you were writing about Berlin 1932, and not about cosmic theology."

Well . . . yes.

"You are a historian, you are writing about human nature. You have no great opinion of the people at that party. I know that. So why not a word about what happens to them later — I mean, soon afterward?"

That is easy. Many of them will leave Germany for points farther west, most of them for the United States. Among the non-Jewish men and women present (the majority of the guests), some will elect to become Nazi party members, many will be famous actors and film stars during the Third Reich, but, especially after the war, most will cook up sentimental memories of how wonderful artistic life was in Berlin before Hitler. I can see opportunists and cheaters and chiselers among them, but no more and no less than in most groups of people, including the opportunists and cheaters and chiselers among those who have made their way to London or New York or Hollywood.

"And your protagonist, the composer?"

I fear that his life will be tragic. His international pilgrimage will go on, after Budapest and Vienna and Berlin, to Paris and New York. He will escape with his life, but he will not be among the successful ones; he will not make it in America, his mind will darken, he will suffer much and die a miserable death. He, too, will remember November 1932 as a wonderful memory, gilded by contrast and by time, probably forgetting all his private forebodings then. I only hope that a German chorus girl will accompany him on that pilgrimage, eventually becoming his faithful wife, a quiet heroine with *Hausfrau* talents and virtues, on whom the mercy of God will perpetually shine because of the merciful faith with which she clung to her sad little husband till the end.

1933

AN OLD WOMAN IN AN OLD GREEN TWEED COAT clambers off the train in Aiken, South Carolina. She tugs at her coat angrily because she is uncomfortable: it is mid-March, very warm suddenly, and she finds herself in a great coil of humid air, with a cloud of marsh midges swarming around her unkempt gray head. The Pullman porter puts down her two bags gently: one is a very old cracked leather grip, the other a commodious new one, given to her by American friends. She forgets to tip the porter, and she speaks with a curious Irish voice, but the porter knows that she is not one of the Irish biddy housekeepers or nurses catching up with their employers on their spring vacations in Aiken, that she is some kind of a lady, which he saw when her American friends showed her to the Pullman and put her in her compartment at Pennsylvania Station and which he saw from other things, too; he was attentive and respectful to her during the day and a half from New York down. Yes, and as he takes up the little stool at the Pullman step and the train starts moving, he sees his passenger being welcomed and fussed over by some quality people, who take her to a wood-paneled station wagon with a chauffeur.

She will be the house guest of one of these people. In the winter, until about late April or early May, Aiken is a place for rich horsey people from New York and Long Island, with a few other families from the hunting country in the middle reaches of New Jersey and a sprinkling of Charlestonians. The sumptuosity of the United States has made this place into what it is: a healthful sporting resort for wealthy men and women. The American Depression is at its depth in March 1933, but not many evidences of that are visible here. The visitor from Ireland does not think much about the Depression, and not only because she has seen few of its evidences. She is accustomed to the good fortunes and to the wealth of Americans, from which she has been capable of drawing some profit for herself lately. She is an Anglo-Irish woman of two considerable accomplishments, of which some Americans have become aware and the recognition of which has matured through the years to respect and friendship. Widowed young during the First World War, she turned to writing amusing and terse stories of Irish country life, replete with hunting and horses, a practice that she kept up even during the worst years of the twenties, meaning the Irish guerrilla war against the English. Some of her stories were reprinted in the *Atlantic* and in other American magazines, read mostly by the wives of American horsemen but then amusing enough to capture the interest of at least some of their husbands. After 1925 American visitors to Ireland, seeking hunting and fishing and the Dublin Horse Show, began to appear again, and this aging Irishwoman had sense enough to respond to their inquiries, inviting some of them to visit (in July and August, of course) the large freezing mansion south of Cork where she lived with her brother and sister-in-law. She impressed them with her acid wit and with her seemingly inimitable knowledge of the Irish trade in high-grade horses. Beyond sixty now, she still rode to hounds. She rode, too, in the big cars of these American visitors, from place to place, from Punchestown to Aussolas, where she made (rather than helped) the transatlantic visitors find thoroughbreds and superb Irish mares for half what they would cost in the United States. She helped to choose and sell some of these animals, drawing agreeable commissions from both sides. Now she was invited to visit her erstwhile customers, friends, purchasers, and charges in America.

She is well bred enough to be at ease with the rich, whether in Ireland or America or England; and she has friends, or at least old acquaintances, not only among the American financial aristocracies but among a few of the English hereditary ones. This means that she expects and receives the help and the courtesies and the occasional gifts offered to her, with minimal expressions of gratitude. In this their American offerers detect a modest reserve rather than arrogance. They are not altogether wrong, except that her reserve is not modest; it simply seems so when this otherwise outspoken old woman feels that it is not only more comfortable but also more propitious for her to say not much. She wears an air of independence that is not an affectation. She knows that she is old, that her people are old, that Anglo-Ireland is old, that the entire Empire is old, that she is a remnant—and that these munificent and well-behaved Anglophile Americans may know some of these things but not enough. There is a fierce intelligence burning behind those deep-set eyes of hers; and when she clutches her rather ugly shawl with her bony, brown-speckled hands, as is her habit, her friends know that she is about to say something interesting or amusing.

In the fields and in the stables of South Carolina she is not talking fetlocks and withers but crop and blood. When a young and rich and aspiring debutante from New York swoons over her and asks about her life in Ireland, "What do you do when you aren't writing?" she answers, "I inspect my barnyard, and I take a turn amongst my poultry, which is a large inquiry." When they ask her about a common acquaintance, a rich and talkative old American who keeps a big house in London, she says that he now has long periods of silence or talks into his beard, which makes conversation with him perfectly delightful. Such repartees are more than often twists of what she remembers from having read Lady Mary Wortley Montagu or Sydney Smith; but she is not a plagiarist, they surge up naturally in her nervous brain. When someone asks her serious and concerned questions about the Troubles in Ireland, she recounts the story about a letter that an English absentee landlord wrote to his Irish agent: "Don't let the tenants imagine that by shooting you they will at all intimidate me." Her audience is relieved and laughs, but she knows that it is not quite like that.

But she likes her comforts, the attention paid to her, and the prospect of people buying horses and eventually a full pack of Irish hounds while depending on her advisory ministrations. She likes the determined excellence of this place: the partition of the tackrooms and the stables, the daily drag hunts, the small racetrack, the polo, the Aiken fences (they look a little like Northern Irish fences, with brush packed between the crossbars). She is amused to learn that the children of many of the families are enrolled in two prep schools in Aiken, one for boys, one for girls, and that the headmasters, all the masters, and even the matrons are English; the only Americans besides the students are the black cooks and maids and other help. In an American way, the youngest boys play bicycle polo on small-wheeled bikes on the soccer field. Unlike in England, here these rather rich Americans live in houses that are comfortable but not opulent, though their food and drink are sumptuous enough. They travel a lot, coming down here late in November, returning in their Pullman drawing rooms to New York and Long Island for Christmas and New Year's and then coming down here again until the invasion of the heat in early May. It is a pleasant life, and these are fortunate people—by and large, she thinks.

On her last night in Aiken she sleeps in the village inn. Her solicitous hosts had arranged that, it will be more comfortable for her, since their house, including the small guest wing, is about to be cleaned and closed up for the summer; and the chauffeur will take her to the early train to New York, which is what she prefers, in order for her to meet an American publishing lady for tea in New York the day after and then to directly board the *Caronia* that night. Her bags are packed with many gifts, and her mind, with the pleasantest impressions and memories of her six weeks among the best of circumstances in the New World. It would be a sentimental exaggeration to compose a verbal picture in which she is homesick enough to long for straggling Irish villages with their smoky pubs and miry, manure-strewn yards. She does miss the spare talk and the small gestures of her relatives, and she knows that she will tell them many things about her American visit, but not everything. She may even tell them that some of her American friends were boring, especially in the evenings. She will not tell them that the Americans' great fortunate prosperity, their unique situation in the world, may last for a while but perhaps not too long, because they are not immune to the fate of those, on her side of the ocean, whose standards of behavior they emulate. That is not an intellectual opinion; it is a racial and a historical feeling, lodged, with other truths, in her aging bones.

"Your old Irishwoman sounds like Edith Somerville."

In parts, perhaps; but she is not Edith Somerville.

"Now let me tell you something. I think you write too much about rich Americans, the American upper class. They are not interesting enough, except for some snobbish and nostalgic — or ignorant — readers. Why are they so interesting to you? You don't know that many of them, you don't share their social lives, you have never been to Aiken — yes, I know, you were once down in South Carolina for a January riding and shooting week."

And I did rather poorly, not even behaving very well, I think. But that is irrelevant. I am not — certainly not now, at this stage of my life — a snob. My interest in the upper classes is not very acute, especially not in this country, where they are so predictable. At the same time, I think I know and understand them, and I am writing about a time when what mattered was not their ways of life but their ideas and illusions about the world, which in the 1930s — Depression and Communism and Hitler notwithstanding — were not altogether out of sync with those of the majority of Americans.

"Come on. How many of these people voted for Roosevelt? What did they think of the New Deal? The strongest illusions of many of these people involved money."

I'm glad you said "illusions," because the belief in the supreme reality of money is an American illusion, one not restricted to moneybags. What is amazing is how big this country is and was in 1933, when the Depression, dreadful as it was for so many millions of people, affected others hardly at all — and not because they were unconcerned or selfish, though some of them surely were. For a foreigner in America during the Depression, especially (but not only) when he or she was a guest of the well-to-do, the Depression was hardly visible, while the abundance of America was. And how far away was this country from a social revolution! There was, too, this paradox: it was the patrician Roosevelt who not only coaxed the people out of the Depression but saved much of American capitalism and the ways of life of the American rich. But that is not my point. My point in this vignette is that in 1933 the rich in Aiken were remnants and they didn't know that, but the lady from Northern Ireland did. And they were remnants not because of the inevitable erosion of capitalism—or, say, of old and stable money—but because of the inevitable erosion of their illusions. Illusions about the superior character of the Anglo-Saxon—all right, of the Anglo-Saxon-Celtic—race. Of its power, and of its virtues.

"You mean the worldwide *appeal* of its power, and the *appeal* of its virtues, don't you?"

Yes. And a woman may sense this better than a man.

"But their women and, more probably, their daughters will know this. Ten years later, in the middle of the war, they will let themselves to be aroused and will go to bed wih slick brilliantined South Americans, including of course Argentinean polo players, at the Plaza, for a *cinque-à-sept*."

Please. Some women from Long Island, perhaps. That doesn't belong to this vignette, if it belongs anywhere at all outside a story by John O'Hara. El Morocco and the Stork Club, 1943—they have little to do with Aiken, South Carolina, and of course nothing to do with Anglo-Irishness or with the Empire, 1933.

1934

THE TERRACE OF THE Golden Hind (Hotel Goldener Hirsch) on the main street of Rothenburg-ob-der-Tauber is bright and warm on a golden July day. The lunch is good, the hock is excellent, and so is the service. Rothenburg is a seventeenth-century city in Upper Bavaria, wonderfully preserved and kept up, a tourist attraction; but its streets, while full, are not unduly crowded in July 1934, containing perhaps fewer foreign visitors than a few years earlier or in the years that will follow.

It is now after two o'clock, and an English couple are about to leave the terrace. They are standing and talking to their neighbor at the next table, an American with whom they had begun to chat across their tables toward the end of their long luncheon. Now their conversation stretches out enough to suggest that they should take a demitasse together in the lounge of the hotel. They will leave next morning, taking different directions.

They talk about their impressions of the town, spilling over into their impressions of Germany at large. That morning they saw most of Rothenburg, walking its streets, contenting themselves with one museum. They suddenly heard from around a corner the shrilling of fifes and then the cadences of a German song: they came upon a platoon of

Hitler Youth, young boys in their early teens looking healthy and happy as they marched in their short trousers, some of them carrying small flags and fanions, and with a drummer boy at the end of the platoon. They were disciplined and yet not rigid or tight-lipped; their singing was military but not unpleasant, because of the high timber of their adolescent voices. The three visitors agree about the atmosphere of Germany and its people now: cheery, confident, with prosperity rising all around. All in all, Hitler's Germany does not seem to be what so many people and newspapers in England and in the United States say, or at least imply. It is efficient and prosperous, not dark but sunlit, not morbid but sane, with its friendly people looking liberated and not oppressed. All of this strikes them this day in Rothenburg, though they had seen much of this before they came to Rothenburg, the American from Cologne and the Rhine towns, the English couple from Trier and along the Moselle. They may have expected some of this—which is perhaps why they had decided to travel this summer to Germany.

Now my purpose in this sketch is not to suggest that these visitors are blind or stupid. This is what they see, and their impressions are not altogether deceiving. In the evening they sit together again and drink an extra bottle of a fine green-gold Rhine wine, as the westering sun gilds the towers of Rothenburg, and the pleasantness of the last twilight hour gilds their newly found appreciation of Germans and of Germany. "Well, they [meaning the Germans] seem to be happy," the American says (he is in his forties, naive and cheerful and comfortably stout, a well-to-do bachelor from a large American city). The Englishman says, "They seem to be jolly enough," and his wife (about thirty-five, with a reedy slenderness; fairly smart, and more voluble than the men) says, "Yes. It is enough. And I am happier here than in Le Touquet, where you play golf and I play tennis and bridge, with some dreadful people, if I must. I don't know that I don't prefer the Germans to the French. Our chambermaid—you know, the red-cheeked one—told us this morning how she and everyone here are so much better off with Hitler." Her husband (a lawyer: careful with his words and therefore with his thoughts) may not go quite that far; nor does the American, who is perplexed rather than carried away by his impressions. But they approve of the Germans and the new Germany, surely now.

"Now tell me, why this vignette at all? Is it to praise the Third Reich before Hitler went really bad? I know you better than that, so please explain."

I want to tell one thing and suggest another. The first is the extraordinary nature of Hitler's achievement. *Extraordinary* is not necessarily an adjective of praise. Genghis Khan and Ivan the Terrible and Jack the Ripper were all extraordinary. But unlike any other revolutionary or dictator—surpassing even his friend Mussolini—Hitler within a few months tore Germany out of its darkest social and economic and financial and political depression (putting an end to unemployment, for example, something that took his contemporary Franklin Roosevelt many more years to accomplish, and then incompletely). And he did this not simply with his autobahn and armament projects, which in 1934 had only begun. He gave his people an enormous charge of confidence. Now German confidence is dangerous because it so easily drifts into superiority and arrogance; but this is not what these visitors saw in the summer of 1934. They saw a cheerful, clean, and, yes, well-meaning people—a climate of prosperity and a salubrious kind of society in contrast to the gray and depressed and corrupted worlds of parliaments, politicians, and press lords, with their vulgarities and lies, in the great capital cities, over which hung clouds of untruths. It was around that time that Huizinga—perhaps the greatest historian in the twentieth century and a very antithesis of Hitler—wrote: "Like smoke and petrol fumes over the cities, there hangs over the world a haze of empty words." These visitors in Rothenburg did not know much about Hitler. I cannot blame them for that in July 1934. They did not see a concentration camp (they were not that numerous in 1934), and they did not see a Jew beaten up in the streets, where, incidentally, there were still many shops with the Jewish names of their owners, though perhaps few or none in Rothenburg.

"Didn't they have a single unpleasant experience or sight in Germany?"

Oh, probably a few, including one even in Rothenburg, where an elderly German attempted to lay hold of them and propagandize them: a corpulent man with a stiff collar reddening his neck. He looked like Hindenburg or Ludendorff or Hjalmar Schacht, in that high celluloid collar of his—not at all like the younger Germans in the streets. "I can see him in one of those spiked German helmets," the Englishwoman said. But by 1934 the spiked helmets were gone. The Third Reich was very modern, you know.

"But was it for modernity that these English and the American came to Germany? When people travel, they travel not only in space but in time. They seemed to be impressed by the presence of an old and yet very alive Germany. Didn't they think they were seeing a positive experiment, perhaps one not quite applicable to their own countries, but there it was—a new compound of the best in the old and in the new?"

Perhaps they sensed this, but they did not think that far—although, I repeat, they were neither blind nor stupid. But let me come now to my second point. They did not know much about Hitler and probably didn't even much like him, but they liked the German people. It was the German people whom they credited with health and honesty. Hitler might be right or wrong, but these people were all right, they think, and say—and this is what I am concerned with here. Note that this is July 1934, only a week or so after Hitler and his minions made their purge, the Night of the Long Knives, when they not only killed hundreds of their own storm troopers but took the opportunity of murdering many respectable and conservative national figures, including General Schleicher, the previous chancellor, and his wife. Now everything we know from evidences of public opinion and of popular sentiment indicate that the German people were not repelled or even shocked by those events. To the contrary, in July 1934 Hitler's popularity had risen higher than before, reaching one of its highest peaks.

Of course, one should never condemn an entire people. There were Germans who understood the presence of evil portents, and there were many others who at least sensed them. But the vast majority, Germans of all classes, were full of cheer, willing to be led or at least to accept Hitler and what Hitler was saying. In July 1934 the German people were not all right.

"And when would these three innocent Anglo-Saxons recognize that? Or perhaps they were not that innocent?"

They would recognize it in 1939 or at the latest in 1940, when they would be patriotic enough and when even their memories of that sunny German summer in 1934 might change as well as fade. *Innocent* may or may not be the right word for them, simply because innocence seldom means much more than a genuine inability to imagine or to see certain things. But in 1934 the Germans were unwilling, rather than unable, to think about certain things — and while their unwillingness may have contained some modicum of innocence, the quality of that innocence was different from that of these well-meaning visitors. And that was the trouble — a deep trouble — latent in July 1934.

1935

IN THE MARSHES of the lower Delaware, Philadelphia gentlemen are
out for reed birds. At eleven on a late October forenoon, the sun has
disappeared and the air is unseasonably raw, but they are warm enough
in their weatherproof shooting jackets, whipcord trousers, and boots.
Three hours earlier they had assembled in the courtyard of one of
their houses, paved with Belgian blocks, their automobiles driving up
punctually (at least two of them wood-sided station wagons), extract-
ing their excellent guns (at least one Purdey among them) and leather
cartridge cases and leather-covered silver flasks, with the wife of their
temporary host bidding them good-bye after having issued from that
big suburban house with her maid, who was passing hot coffee around,
while the windows of the house were crimsoned with the morning sun.
Now the sky is universally overcast, but it is a big sky, an endless gray
canopy almost Western in its expanse; for the far shore of Delaware Bay
is not visible at all, and the low marshes stretch out in every direction.

The season for pheasants and doves has opened this day, and
all around Philadelphia and in the Pennsylvania country shotguns are
crumping and popping. But these gentlemen are in search of reed birds,
a tradition among them, one shared only by the marshes' native inhabitants, who trap and fish and bag birds for their living. There is an agreeable relationship between these Philadelphians and their guides, who,

expecting them, come out from weatherbeaten, brown-gray shingled shacks and clapboard houses. They have been advised of the day of their guests' coming by a customary letter, since they have no telephones (and in 1935 some of them have no electricity yet, either). Then they walk down a narrow, rutted sandy lane to where it becomes engaged with the water below a rough dock, at the edge of which sandpipers, gulls, and other birds pick at the shells of dead or putrefying crabs. They clamber over the low gunwales of five rowboats, and then they push into the small channels of the marshes, rowed and sometimes poled along by their guides among the tall reeds and the canes and the cattails and the jewelweed and the water lilies. There are squishy sounds as the skiffs slide ahead, eventually fanning out across a mile. Then they stop. This is not like duck shooting; in the bows of each boat two men stand erect, watchful, with their guns at the ready. From a distance, their heads can hardly be seen, hidden as they are by the tall grasses of the marsh. Up close, the scene is a nineteenth-century one with the sportsmen standing in the boats, their hired guides sitting in the back. Now a pale sun appears, and the marshland is beginning to glisten.

I have chosen this vignette because of my fascination with Old America, by which I mean something that has impressed me ever since I came to this country: that in so many ways America was not ahead but behind the Old World, not only in its ideas (and also in some of its remnant freedoms) but in the ways of life of so many of its people and, of course, in its natural habitats and bounties. It is 1935, a year of Technocracy, Broadway Melody, Streamlined Design, the Hudson Terraplane, the CIO, Pan-American Airways, "Anything Goes" and "Begin the Beguine," Dorothy Parker and Peter Arno, and neon and fluorescence. And here, hardly more than a hundred miles from New York, is the Thousand-Acre Marsh and rivulets with such names as Blackbird Creek and Augustine Creek and King's Hammock, inhabited by people who have lived here for a very long time and who make their living by fishing for shad and even for sturgeon, by oystering and turtling, and by trapping muskrats by the thousands. Across from the reed-bird shooting there was a hamlet by the name of Caviar, New Jersey, because as late as 1900 the Delaware was one of the biggest bays for sturgeon in the world. Some of these sturgeon weighed two hundred pounds. The roe of the females was extracted and salted and packed in hundred-pound kegs that were then taken to Philadelphia and sold at ridiculously low prices. In 1935 most, though not all, of the sturgeon are gone; but there is still plenty of riparian and riverine and paludine fauna around. (There is also a town called Bivalve, across the river.) The reed birds are particularly desirable because of the nutty gaminess of their flesh. They taste like ortolans. These Philadelphians come down here each fall because this is exactly what their fathers and grandfathers had done forty, fifty, or even more years before, except that then they went out for reed birds more than once a year, and not only down the Delaware but in the Neck, among the roughneck people in the tidal marshland at the southern end of Philadelphia and still within the city limits. But the scene must have been much the same.

In 1935 some of these Philadelphia gentlemen have seen and enjoyed (and presumably danced to) "Anything Goes," and they have driven Chrysler Airflows and flown Pan-American, and they (or at least some of their wives) have read and enjoyed the Peter Arno cartoons in the *New Yorker;* but this day in the marsh is as much a part of their Philadelphian lives as are all these features of a modern world, which is how their minds can be not only a hundred miles south of New York but light-years away from the Soviet Union and the Popular Front and Hitler's Third Reich and Mussolini's Abyssinian War, which they can read about in the newspapers. Their ideas about war and peace may be almost entirely outdated. One of the reasons for this is their satisfaction in knowing well enough what and whom they should know: a philistine knowledgeability, with its want of interest and imagination about much else. Another is the American benevolence of their decency, which makes them hold on to what in 1935 are antiquated ideas about human progress and the destiny of the world. At times they have uncomfortable thoughts about the way the world, including the United States, is going. But their minds are still unaffected — well, almost — by matters so far from their accustomed lives.

They are philistines as much as they are patricians, but they are good sportsmen. They are good shots, most of them, and they return, with a bag of at least half a dozen birds each, to the clapboard shack of the chief guide. In its low-beamed rooms hang perhaps one hundred pelts of muskrats and red foxes and also a magazine photograph of Franklin Roosevelt (at which some of the gentlemen wink among themselves, all of them being Republicans in 1935), hung between two fishing gaffs and an old barrel-loading musket, which the men examine and discuss in what is perhaps an unduly extensive conversation. Behind the shack they unpack a large hamper on a trestle table with the help of the guide's wife (who also keeps spinning out a goodly string of hunting and trapping stories). Beer is provided by the marshland host, and after his receipt of a rather munificent fee for this day, he, as is customary, brings out a large, meaty terrapin to be stuffed into another canvas bag. One of the sportsmen, who has a small town house in downtown Philadelphia, may deliver the fowl and the turtle to the kitchen of the Philadelphia or of the Rittenhouse Club, or perhaps an adventurous wife may be in charge of their festive game dinner this year.

"I presume that K. is not in this group."

No, he is not a hunter.

"But, being Philadelphian, he probably knows many of these people. I suppose that he likes nature but not killing."

Not only that. In 1935 he is thirty-five years old, and despite his family connections, he has little money; he does not go shootin' and fishin' with these sporting gentlemen.

"Well, your scene is interesting, though about your conclusions I'm not so sure. However—Lady Mary Wortley Montagu once wrote, 'danger gives a *haut goût* to everything.' I doubt whether there is any danger in that kind of shooting, but do reed birds have a *haut goût?*"

Cannot tell you, not having had any.

"You told me once that you do not particularly like small birds, that ortolans, quail, squabs, are lost on you. Be that as it may, your depiction of an Arcadian day in the marshes may be too idyllic. Wasn't there any discomfort?"

There was some, I guess. There was some shooting across (and hence one joke about a miscarriage of justice—one of them is a lawyer), and the smelly fifteen minutes with the one hundred dead muskrats were too long, with their marsh host puffing at cheap tobacco and the smoke floating in coils and smears in that low-ceilinged room. One of the Philadelphians had incipient emphysema, but he did not mention it; he stepped out of the room, which then became the signal to break up for lunch. There was also a little strain in their laughter at the woman's stories when they ran on a touch too long. But all in all, their guide and his wife are good people, and their annual patrons appreciate not only their services but their characters.

"And what is so different here from the way English grouse shooters or salmon fishers treat their beaters or gillies? Or German barons their gamekeepers?"

It is different because they are Americans, which means that lordly gestures of temporary friendliness are not natural to them. They are not patronizing; they respect the skill and the craft of the watermen. But there is more to it than that: it is almost camaraderie. Suppose the trapper from Delaware is compelled to come up to Philadelphia because he has, say, a legal or a tax or a land problem, and he calls at the office of one of these gents, a lawyer. The lawyer will receive him with pleasure and give him all of his attention—perhaps more attention than would be given to certain other people among his clients. That would not be the case in England or Germany or France.

"In England too?"

Yes—I think that Amiel was right when he wrote of the English: "Between gentlemen, courtesy, equality, social proprieties; below that level, haughtiness, disdain, coldness, indifference. . . . The politeness of a gentleman is not human and general, but quite individual and personal." Of course that was circa 1882. It may even have been true of Boston in 1882. But the politeness of an American gentleman in 1935 is human and general, which says at least one good thing about American democracy.

"You have said that you do not particularly admire these Philadelphian sporting gentlemen, but now you project something that suggests a respect close to admiration."

If so, I have been wrong. I respect them . . . a little. What I have is a nostalgic respect for so much of Old America surviving in 1935.

1936

A RENOWNED ENGLISH LIBERAL historian is giving a lecture at Bryn Mawr College, in that leafy suburb of Philadelphia, on the Main Line. The lecture, endowed by and named after a wealthy descendant of one of the college's founders, is an annual occasion, paying an honorarium sufficient to have enticed this Englishman to come across the Atlantic, especially when he found it profitable and propitious to combine the lecture with a visit to Yale (where he spoke for less money but was put up for five days in the guest suite of one of the colleges) and with a week in New York (where his American publishers treated him). *Summa summarum*, by the time he descended to Philadelphia, he knew that he would return to Cambridge with a substantial increment of dollars. And now in Bryn Mawr, too, he is treated with a respect that borders on obsequiousness (chauffeur at the station; high tea with the college's president and eminent visitors, including historians from the University of Pennsylvania and the American Philosophical Society; the faculty capped and gowned for the occasion; and a fawning female assistant professor who teaches Tudor history). His lecture, "The Early Whigs and English Patriotism," is a temperate success, for a number of reasons. The considerable honorarium notwithstanding, he has given this paper before, although he is more than reasonably sure that this fact is not known to any of his American hearers. Consequently he is bored with this text: moreover, he is not a good speaker, here and there he wheezes and mumbles through some of his lines, while he deedily fiddles with his spectacles. Yet he thinks that he is compensating for this, *anglice,* with a few well-placed and well-paused brief intrusions of wit (old wit, but then his subject is Old Whigs).

All in all, he is well received by the audience. He, in turn, is pleasantly taken, at least to some degree, by the surroundings in Bryn Mawr: the spaciousness of those Englished stone buildings; the fine courtyard; beyond the college, the lawns and the impressive houses, Georgian and Jacobean and Tudor in their styles; and, then, the wide-eyed and open-hearted American feminine generosity of his reception. But I must write "to some degree," because while the mind of this man still keenly calculates and his memory is a well-ordered labyrinth, his heart and his imagination (and he is not much over fifty) have stiffened and desiccated long ago, and hence his response to new places, new people, new ideas, new experiences is carefully (and selfishly) limited. That is an old habit which his respectful admirers may mistake for English reserve and wisdom.

For two nights he is the guest of wealthy Philadelphia Quakers in their impressive graystone house not far from the college. There is some fine furniture in this house, including eighteenth-century Philadelphia-made tall-case clocks and sideboards that impress this English worthy less than they should. Some of the glasses in the cupboards vibrate when the clocks metallically titter and chime. Next day is one of those pre-ternaturally hot April days in eastern America, with its odor of damp, warm upholstery in the automobiles, to which he is exposed for some time; but then it is agreeably cool in the afternoon within the thick stone walls of the house where another tea party is offered in his honor. "Under certain circumstances there are few hours in life more agreeable than the hour dedicated to the ceremony known as afternoon tea." That is the first sentence of Henry James's *Portrait of a Lady,* which for me is one of his better books, though I do not like Henry James much, one reason being his beginning a book with such a sentence. Why do I stick this cranky opinion of mine into this vignette, here? Because of a connection that this visiting English scholar has with his hosts . . . and with James. He comes from a Cornish family, and his hosts' ancestors were Quakers from Cornwall. Cornwall, like most of Celtic Britain, was and is Liberal. He is an English Liberal, a Cambridge Liberal, an Edwardian Liberal—the period connection with James—and his hosts are American liberals. They do not know how stupefying and blood-less English liberalism has become by 1936, for decades having been driven by necessity further and further away from individualism be-cause of democracy itself. They like his trimmed yellow moustache, his tweed waistcoat, taking them for English and scholarly eccentricities, unaware that this man has for many years now lived at some distance from his body, though considering that body more carefully than the habitations of his mind.

Conversation during this private tea party is not as smooth as that of the previous day at the Deanery of the college, since from time to time it turns to politics. There is a refugee German Quaker (there were a few such specimens), a professor, among the guests who is anxious to ask the visiting Englishman about how England sees Hitler, about what England will do now that Hitler has marched into the Rhine-land, an event that has taken place six or seven weeks before. Well, he should have known, or at least sensed, what this renowned English historian thinks from his lecture the day before, because there was a suggestion about the present in "The Early Whigs and English Patrio-tism." The early eighteenth-century Whigs were the true English patri-ots, the early champions of the rights of Englishmen, he said, since their Englishness was not compromised by cosmopolitan or Jacobite or European special interests. The German Quaker professor's accent and some of his mannerisms and some of his English usages may be heavy, but he is a learned man and not really an insistent or an intrusive one. But this Englishman either ignores him or dismisses him rudely, though not with the habitual English rudeness to unfamiliar people and those encountered in unaccustomed situations—that is merely a racial defense mechanism of people who are naturally shy. This English scholar is not shy. He says that the Rhineland is a German province, after all; that fairness behooves (he says "behoves") us to recognize that the Germans have as much of a right to national self-determination as other people; that Germany ought to be brought back into the League of Nations; that no one should expect England to enter into continental alliances; that only special interests contemplate a war; that England is committed to peace, not to war.

His American Quaker hosts like to hear this. They are decent people, though they are narrow-minded, especially when they think they are being broad-minded. They are not devoid of generosity: they and their kind of people helped this German refugee to come to Pendle Hill in Swarthmore, and soon they will be helping more German refugees. But it is 1936, and their minds are very slow. Four years after this April day they will still be pacifists and isolationists, though by October 1940 their minds will begin to slowly turn. They are generous in their estimation of their English guest, too: when, in 1940, they will read one of his articles signifying that his public conversion to Churchillian militancy has been completed, they will see in that no conversion, only Englishness. During and after the war they will send him large parcels of coffee and chocolate and tobacco and rather expensive woolen vests. His thank-you letters will be belated and perfunctory—but then, so was he in 1936.

"Your dislike of this man is too obvious. Also, were you thinking of someone like Trevelyan or Rowse?"

No, although they were Cornishmen and Liberals. Anyhow, Trevelyan and Rowse are quite different, in temperament and socially too. My dislike is for that whitened, almost sepulchral type of English liberal, who caused much harm to England through much of this century, including in the thirties.

"Now don't be like those American conservatives about whom you once wrote that they hate liberals more than they love liberty."

No, I am not writing about American liberals. And I am not like

Knut Hamsun, whose admiration for Hitler sprouted from his contempt for Gladstone and liberalism and the English. He had a special hatred for Gladstone, for what he saw as Gladstone's carefulness, his hypocrisy: "How he avoids taking a false step!" Hamsun wrote in the same book, *Mysteries* — let me haul it down, there are phrases in it that sound like Hitler, fifty years before the 1930s — "the logic in my blood expressing itself." Now here is an interesting line: "A girl would get tired of an ugly intellectual sooner than she would of a handsome dunce." *That* is why Hamsun, with all of his great talents, is a period piece, because I don't think that this sentence any longer holds true.

"Don't switch the topic, please. You did not make strongly enough what to me is a main point. Your Englishman is *lazy*."

Yes, he is lazy, but remember what I suggested: his heart is desiccated, his spirit sluggish, but his brain still quick enough to adjust all kinds of things to his circumstances.

"Now let me defend him, though I dislike him too. Doesn't his slowness have something to do with a deep Anglo-Saxon — all right, Anglo-Celtic — sense of scruples? I think it was Christopher Sykes who once said that scruples and sloth make happy bedfellows."

Yes, but not in his case. This man is a calculating animal, an opportunist. Which has something to do with his being an academic. His carefulness is both more and less than English carefulness. You know what Chesterton wrote: "I believe in getting into hot water. I think it keeps you clean." Churchill would have liked that. But this man is the kind who hated Chesterton, who would have regarded him as vulgar. (And so would he regard Churchill, at least for a long time.)

"Your Jamesian connection is not convincing either. James was a Tory — of sorts. You know the joke about him: James the First, James the Second, and the Old Pretender."

James had more in common with this man than with someone like Churchill, let alone Chesterton.

"One last thing. Was your man a good historian?"

Earlier in his life, yes — he had a good classical education, he read much, and because of his English literary sense, he was dubious of the scientific pretensions of some historians. But his doubts were merely instinctive, he never thought them through. I guess scruples and sloth again. Or, rather, Sloth patting Scruples on the head. Good English minds are wiser than they are clever, but the wisdom of this man was sham wisdom. His Philadelphian hosts may have missed that, perhaps also because of their generosity. The avarice of some of their Quaker ancestors was gradually bred out of them. Of course, generosity does neither wisdom nor magnanimity make.

"Well, there is not much magnanimity in this vignette of yours, either; but you have this saving grace of liking to get into hot water."

That is nice of you to say, but my reason is not mental cleanliness. It is comfort.

1937

THE GREAT GERMAN liner *Europa* is leaving New York, standing out to sea. The tugs have pulled her to the middle of the Hudson, and now the great ship makes her turn, and as her powerful propellers churn and make a small maelstrom, the sight of the *Europa* from the Manhattan shores and windows is majestic, as she begins to tread the waters, with only a thin sliver of steam rising from her massive funnel. The tugs cast off, and their men stand on their sun-washed decks, waving a cheerful good-bye. They like this German ship and its crew. Some of the farewell crowd at the end of the pier still wave their handkerchiefs, but they are now diminishing by the minute, and so is the noise and the hubbub in the giant shed, which is quickly emptying, including the New York policemen whose presence is considerable at the North German Lloyd pier because of the occasional appearance of picketers at the berthing of German ships flying the swastika flag. On this beautiful September noon there are no demonstrators.

Now the German liner's farewell salute to New York, a deep bourdon bass horn, travels and trembles over the river; and high up on a Wall Street skyscraper a young secretary goes to the window. She espies the *Europa* moving ahead on the sun-stroked waters of the bay. Two of the firm's lawyers come into the room. "The Germans are leaving," she says. They know this; they have ordered that a large farewell basket with champagne and whisky and a card reading *Auf Wiedersehen!* be sent to the stateroom of the leading man of the group of industrialists and financiers whom they had seen several times during the Germans' visit to New York and for whom they had given a luncheon two days before.

The Germans are pleased. They are leaning on the railing of the upper deck, watching the fabulous sight of towering New York sliding by, while the strengthening breeze reduces the heat of the sun, though not enough to keep the heads of some of them from perspiring. Soon they leave the deck and descend to the first-class dining room. The sunlight streaming in makes the white tablecloths and napkins glisten, and the captain himself appears to greet them before they sit down, for they are important passengers. The lunch is excellent. They talk about their American experiences, which were very good, surpassing their expectations.

There are five of them, two industrialists, two financiers, one lawyer, all of them middle-aged, rather German-looking: solid, corpulent, with blue blinking eyes behind gold-rimmed spectacles, most of them bald, one of them, a Swabian, has thick dark hair. They had been anxious about their journey to America, which was arranged and partly financed by the German Association of Manufacturers with the principal aim of securing more goodwill and business for Germany among reputable American manufacturing and banking and legal circles (in addition to which two of the German *Herren* had some business for their own companies, whence their contribution to the costs of this rather expensive journey). They knew that the reputation of the new Germany, of the Third Reich, has been compromised in America (as they say in German, *betroffen,* "damaged") because of the propaganda of all kinds of people, including of course Jews. That was why their travel was supported by the Reich Ministry of Industry itself: to impress the better kind of Americans (*erstklassige Leute*) with the solidity, the reliability, the positive features, of the new Germany, represented by these conservative German gentlemen, some of whom have had long-standing American business connections. Only two of them are party members, but here of course they do not wear their party badges in their buttonholes, except one of them at the reception at the German consulate in New York.

They need not have worried. That has gradually come to them, careful and cautious as they have been, threading their way through New York and Boston and Washington, until now, sitting at lunch, with ample napkins in their ample laps, they beam at each other with satisfaction: "Es war ein Triumphzug," one of them says, a triumphal tour. Well, an exaggeration, but perhaps not much. All the Americans they have met were friendly; some of them were forthcoming. It was not only that they have faced no troublesome conversations, but they feel that at least some of their American hosts were suggesting, with a word here or there or with a gesture, that they did not believe all the propaganda directed against the Third Reich, "und sie wussten woher es kommt" —they knew where that was coming from. One of the five *Herren*, the oldest among them, went so far as to meet a former acquaintance, if not a friend, in New York, a Jewish banker who had left Germany with his family two years before. They needed to discuss some business involving the latter's assets left in Germany, their transfer quite legally and properly arranged, but their main purpose was to renew, if only once, their acquaintance; and while there was some unspoken tension during their meeting, the older German kept saying to his erstwhile colleague that, yes, some things in Germany were regrettable but also unavoidable and they are bound to become better in the long run, "es wird nicht so heiss gegessen," things will be cooling down. However, he had found it judicious and necessary (and perhaps patriotic), to mention to the commercial attaché of the German embassy in Washington that he was about to have a meeting with a Jewish gentleman, formerly of Berlin, in New York. The attaché simply acknowledged this, but when the group was at another reception at the German consulate in New York, the vice-consul (a young man with a party badge in his buttonhole) came up to him and said, with a certain emphasis, "Sie sollen nicht viel mit Juden verkehren" —please avoid having business with Jews. But then this man was not particularly un-friendly, either, and the older German thinks that he has done the right thing (including his cautionary self-protection of course).

So, as the lunch proceeds, they congratulate themselves and their country and, perhaps indirectly, its government: American friendship and goodwill for the Reich is extant, more than people may think or read about in the papers. They see, too, tables and tables of well-dressed, friendly Americans around them, sailing on this splendid modern Ger-man ship (winner of the Atlantic blue ribbon but a few years ago), ex-uding American goodwill and understanding. The Germans think, and say, They are not against us. "Nie wird man Amerika in einen Krieg gegen uns entwickeln." "They" (the French? the English? the Jews?) will never be able to involve America in a war against Germany. And this is not very different from what many of their American acquain-tances seem to think and perhaps even say: "we should never again have to fight these people, no matter what happens."

Now, this is September 1937, which is the high tide of American isolationism: not of American-German friendship, but of the American reaction against the memories and the propaganda of the First World War. That reaction began among American intellectuals in the early twenties. But the movement of ideas in this country is very slow. That "revisionism" has reached its high tide in 1937, when the idea (An Idea Whose Time Has Come?) that the American entry into the war in 1917 was wrong, that the entire war was wrong, has filtered down to pub-lic and popular opinion, including textbooks, magazine articles, comic strips, scholarly works, the findings of congressional committees, Neu-trality Acts, and proposals to amend the Constitution. And not only in the Republican Midwest: works describing the evils of American inter-vention in the war in 1917 are now selections of the Book-of-the-Month Club. Some of them are bestsellers. They are praised in the *Atlantic* and in the *Yale Review,* by Nevins and Commager, the most eminent liberal historians, and they are read with interest by many people, including some whom this German delegation has met.

"And meanwhile Hitler is rising. But what is your purpose here? Another illustration of the condition that an idea whose time has come cannot be much good? Or of the slow momentum, of how slowly ideas move, how slowly—and wrongly—they become popular? All very interesting and telling, but in 1937 that was only *one* strand in the thick, bushy bundle of American sentiments, while Roosevelt's inclinations, for instance, were turning in a very different direction."

Yes, of course; but here I am interested in the Germans, not in the Americans. They were not altogether wrong in what they saw here in 1937, and neither were their American acquaintances; and yet they were wrong, in the long run, of course because of forces beyond their control. These Germans even remind me—physically, too—of some-one like Helmut Kohl in the 1980s or 1990s, who is not and would not have been a Nazi in the 1930s but who is the kind of German Rhine-land Catholic who in 1933 may have voted to give Hitler his Enabling Act (as indeed the Catholic Center Party in Germany did). Now keep in mind that the thirties were for many Germans a golden age of pros-perity, of order, of national greatness, of Germany's rising reputation in the world—indeed, perhaps the sunniest six years in the history of Germany in this century for all but the unhappy few. And there were entire German generations, including my group of industrialists, who remembered it that way.

"Now is it your argument that these Germans are bad people be-cause they made their peace with evil? They surely do not think that Hitler is evil, though they do worry about him, here and there, a little. Or are you saying that they know how Nazism consists of half-truths but that they prefer half-truths not only to lies but to ideas that are not respectable enough?"

Let me tell you: these Germans of my vignette are not altogether bad people. They are businessmen. Yes, they may be unwilling to recog-nize certain things that are evil when it is in their interest to do so. But is that special to the Germans? What may be special, and lamentable, is their German idea of respectable nationalism, their acceptance of the authority of a nationalist — any nationalist — government. Yet while they are not better, they are individually probably not worse than are other people, including anti-Germans, anti-Nazis, anti-Fascists, democrats, liberals. What matters is what they will go on to do. Who knows? Perhaps the least Nazified among them will come to abhor Hitler and Hitler's regime — while he will hope that his awful wife will die (in one of those bombing raids, if must) so that he can then marry his big floozy mistress and retire with her to Bavaria. Perhaps the one with the Nazi badge will protect, hide, and feed Polish or Jewish prisoners — and will do so long before the last weeks of the war, too. Not impossible; I knew of such people. What I fear is that on another bright day, say, in 1953, some of these same Germans will be debarking from the first-class cabin of the Lufthansa *Senator* flight in New York, blinking in the American sun, older, perhaps somewhat chastened, but again prospering, well fed, and well suited, ready to meet some of their old American acquaintances but also new ones, Republican industrialists from the Midwest — ready to remember the happy days of 1937 and knowing that now, in 1953, happy days in German-American relations are here again, when the great enemy of both is Soviet Russian Communism and Germany is of course a bulwark against that.

1938

THE EIGHTH OF MARCH is a cold day in Berlin. An eminent American has arrived there to meet Hitler. Around noon he and the American ambassador, who will accompany him to the chancellery, walk out from one of those big Berlin luxury hotels (it is either the Adlon or the Esplanade), through the gloomy magnificence of its great halls, the dark wood panels gleaming under a hundred lights coruscating in the high cut-glass chandeliers. As they step outside there is the sudden relief of the northern light, with some sunshine breaking through.

The Reich chancellery is only a few minutes away by car. The new Reich chancellery, designed by Albert Speer, is now being built, but even the old chancellery has the marks of the new era. Above the marble jambs and the lintel framing the huge door leading to the chancellor's office, the initials A. H. are carved into the marble transom.

The American has arrived in Germany the day before, traveling in a car across central Germany from Prague. He is impressed with what he has seen: the highways and the prosperity and the new housing in the towns and villages. He begins his conversation with Hitler by expressing his admiration for the many evidences of German prosperity and order, which is only the proper way to begin a conversation with a foreign head of state. His admiration is sincere and goes a touch beyond the customary courtesies. Hitler talks well, not at all like a dictator or a fanatic. He is confident, his arguments are well calculated in advance. His American visitor is at some disadvantage with Hitler. There is a duality in the American's mind. He sincerely admires many things in the new Germany, but he is also aware that the regimentation producing such achievements is not applicable to America, and he feels it necessary to say so; he introduces such a remark, briefly, in their conversation as if that were a caveat.

There is no duality in Hitler's mind. He knows how to appeal to the inclinations of his American guest. He speaks at length about the dangers of Communism, the infection that threatens Europe and from which his Germany is now protected. His American visitor agrees with that. It is Russia and Communism, not Germany and Hitlerism, that threaten the peace and order of the world.

Upon their return from the chancellery, the American ambassador gives a luncheon in the visitor's honor. That evening the Carl Schurz Society (which had arranged the invitation to Berlin) gives a dinner where the main speaker is Dr. Hjalmar Schacht, the economic wizard of the Reich, whose round, creased face above his high, round collar somewhat resembles that of the American visitor. He praises the political record of the latter effusively: it was a tragedy that this American "had not been able to fulfill all his great plans" because of the economic depression, while it is Schacht's personal belief that the political career of his guest will continue. The next day, Hermann Goering gives a fabulous lunch at his opulent country estate, where heralds in medieval German costumes sound fanfares; among the enormous host of servants, a silk-stockinged and bewigged footman stands behind each guest. The American is somewhat startled, though he is not unimpressed with the great Hermann. He is more at home with the German industrialists and financiers who keep calling at his hotel suite later that afternoon. The next morning, he leaves for Warsaw, another stop on his European journey. It is a comfortable hour of departure, a pleasant morning. There are many German well-wishers, bouquets of flowers on the platform, while the smoke is rising to the iron vaulting and the glass dome of a large Berlin railway station. It is the tenth of March.

✳   ✳   ✳

And now, for once, I have departed from my self-imposed standards in this book. The above describes a real historical episode, real historical personages, people who really existed, and it summarizes a conversation recorded in certain German and American archives. The difficult thing will be to explain why I have done this. Anyhow, do you know who the eminent American is? He is Herbert Hoover.

"That round crabapple face and the high celluloid collar ought to have told me something. But now two questions. First, where did you get all these details? Second, as usual, why does this matter? Or, rather, why does this matter so much to you that you would break your custom?"

I'll answer your second question first. All of this inspired my imagination because I found here some details that may be significant both in the short and in the long run. The short run—if that is what it is—involves the Germans. It is the matter of the time, among other things. These events in Berlin took place—I am thinking especially of Goering's *wunderbar* luncheon—forty-eight hours before Hitler's move into Austria, the Anschluss.

"I don't see the connection. The Anschluss—all right, it was the first of Hitler's conquests of other countries, the chain Austria-Czechoslovakia-Poland leading to the outbreak of the war—but wasn't Hoover's visit a mere coincidence? I say to you often, you must watch yourself, because coincidences may be interesting, but they are not necessarily meaningful. And why the emphasis on Goering's feast, which seems to have been nothing but another of his *kolossal* productions? I must admit that I would have liked to have been there—no, not for the heralds and their goddamn trumpets and tabards but to see that fabulous electric-train layout of his, not to speak of the food, which must have been rather good, surely no *cuisine minceur*."

Because—and not many people outside specialists of the Anschluss know this—Goering was the architect of the Anschluss. A mere forty-eight hours after the Hoover banquet, Goering took over an entire country by telephone. As a matter of fact, Hitler was somewhat hesitant — Goering kept pushing him ahead. Goering's telephone calls to Vienna on Friday, March 11, threatening an invasion (in reality, the first German troops did not cross the Austrian frontier until the day after), made the Austrian government resign, with the Austrian chancellor canceling the plebiscite that he had hoped would confirm Austria's independence. Schuschnigg had announced the plebiscite on the evening of the ninth, to steal a march on Hitler. But by noon on the ninth Goering and Hitler knew from their Austrian Nazi agents and spies that Schuschnigg planned to spring the plebiscite on them and to announce it later that day. Yet all during that Hooverfeast, not only no word of that, but Goering's composure was perfect, he the genial host of hosts: fat, charming, making jokes. I can imagine him slapping some of his friends on their backs, when all the while he had plenty to do, plenty to worry about. His self-control was impressive, as was Hitler's during the Hoovertalk. But then, 1938 was their greatest, their most successful year; a few months later, after Munich, Hitler would be the potential master of much of Europe, and the Third Reich was perhaps the greatest power in the world.

"But that did not last; and after Munich, even the American government, not to speak of public opinion, began to turn against Hitler and Germany."

Yes, and that is why the Hoover visit to Germany came at a turning point in American-German relations. Before 1938, many Americans (or perhaps I should say, not a few Americans) were favorably inclined to the new Germany, in spite of (or, in some ways, because of) the barrage of news propagated about the brutalities of the Hitler regime, thinking that that kind of propaganda was either untrue or greatly exaggerated, the product of special interests. There were important people who were convinced of that, for example, Truman Smith, the American military attaché in Berlin, a very intelligent officer, and of course Lindbergh, who would visit Germany after Munich and to whom Goering would give the Hoover treatment *plus*. Four days after the Anschluss, Lindbergh wrote in his diary: "I cannot help liking the Germans. They are like our own people. We should be working with them and not constantly crossing swords."

"Well, that was not what Roosevelt was thinking, and Lindbergh was a special case, you must admit that."

I admit that, and I also admit that by that time Roosevelt had Lindbergh's number — forgive that phrase applied to Lindbergh, who had many good qualities, despite his ideological and political preferences — and Lindbergh was no match for Roosevelt then or afterward. But what I find significant is Hoover's response to what Hitler said to him about Communism. It deserves more than the odd little footnote in the history of American-German relations.

"*Footnote* — because Hoover put his foot into it? Why does it deserve more than a footnote?"

Because of what it meant in the history of the United States, during fifty years at least. It is a live matter even now. I saw and heard it when I watched the Republican convention in Houston and heard Buchanan's and Reagan's speeches. It is their belief that the history of the entire twentieth century was dominated by the danger of the worldwide conspiracy of Communism and by the struggle against it. That ideology — for that is what it is, an ideal picture of the world — was believed by millions of Americans before the war and by the majority of Americans after the war (for more than one reason, of course), and it was adopted by some of the strangest people as late as the 1970s and 1980s. It has sometimes suggested — implicitly — that Germany and Hitler and Nazism were less of a danger to the world than were Russia and Communism. But in 1938 that belief was more than implicit. Also, men like Lindbergh and, yes, Hoover believed that not only in 1938 but till the end of their lives; and so did Joe McCarthy ten and fifteen years later and Pat Buchanan even now (sometimes, though carefully, implying that to have fought Germany in the Second World War was a mistake). In a memorandum about his trip written after his return to America, not only did Hoover repeat that many things in Germany were admirable; he also said that the Germans were "not prepared for offensive warfare," which of course was a vast misjudgment. He then added that

Germany had no desire for a war, that they would move not west but east and south, and Hoover felt that this would do no harm for general peace, since Germans "would give better government than now obtains in Rumania, Bulgaria, Hungary and parts of Czechoslovakia."

"That *may* sound like a German sympathizer, but really it sounds more like an American isolationist."

Ah, yes — but there the dog is buried. What Hoover did not realize — or, rather, what he refused to think about — is that once the Germans ruled Central and Eastern Europe, general peace and the independence of Western Europe would not amount to much. Neither would England. And that came to the fore in 1940 — do you know that in 1940 Hoover was still a candidate for the Republican nomination? — when he and Taft and the isolationists and the America Firsters were convinced that it was not in American interests to help the British against what by then had become German rule all over Europe. I am intrigued — intrigued? no, appalled — by the isolationists' and the America Firsters' inconsistency, meaning that they were really neither isolationists nor America Firsters at all. Because the same people who in 1940–1941 were bitterly against an American policy opposing the German domination of the *entire* Continent after 1945 preached the cause of an American crusade against Russia that was subjugating the eastern part of the Continent. The important matter is that Hoover and Taft and the America Firsters in 1940 stood not only against Communism but against all American help to Churchill's Britain. Of course Hoover did not like the English, and he despised the French, but that is not the point. Nor was he particularly sympathetic toward dictatorships. This is evident, at least here and there, in the record relating to his German visit. But Hitler was very clever in appealing to Hoover's anti-Communism, a ploy that he used most successfully during his entire career, both within Germany and without. He knew how his insistence on the dangers of Communism helped him; that was perhaps the main factor why Hindenburg and the German conservatives allowed him to come to power in 1933. And in the United States, too, that ideological worldview led to the Republicans' ascendancy, to their winning election after election, with few exceptions, ever since 1952, when their anti-Communism, even more than Eisenhower's popularity, was a decisive factor. There were other Republicans who prevailed in the 1940 convention—with the help of considerable preparation and some trickery—in overcoming the so-called isolationists and nominating Willkie. By now those Eastern Republicans are about entirely gone—look only at Bush's surrender to the radical nationalists of his party at their convention in 1992. (Incidentally, that is what Hitler, rather accurately, called them in 1940, in a well-prepared interview he gave to an isolationist Hearst reporter.)

"Well, you may make too much of this, but about one thing I agree. Some of the old Republicans called Franklin Roosevelt a traitor to his class. That was not Roosevelt. That is Bush."

Perhaps. But enough of this. Now back to your first question: How do I know these things about Hoover's visit with Hitler? There is something about it in the extensive volumes of the published German diplomatic documents, but I know a nice man, Hoover's biographer, and I asked him about this once, and then he sent me from the Hoover library (the presidential one, in West Branch, Iowa) a sheaf of four documents about the visit, including the detailed record of the Hoover-Hitler talk and a memo of Hoover's account of his trip, recorded by his close friend and assistant. I say, reading and working with archives and documents is easier than writing *this* book.

1939

THE GENTLEMAN FROM Indiana is an isolationist. In September 1939 he is fifty years old, having just celebrated his birthday with friends at his house on Martha's Vineyard. He is an Eastern Midwesterner, by which I mean that he had gone to college at Yale, had and has many friends and acquaintances in New York, and married a girl from Boston, spending their honeymoon in Nantucket (and discovering soon, alas, that his wife's fits of depression, alternating between an extreme nervousness and the sullenest of torpors, was incurable; eventually she had to be put in a mental institution. After many years of most anxious and saddest trepidations—he is a most decent man—he set in motion the legal instruments to divorce her). He has inherited money. He is on the board of directors of a bank in Indiana that allows him to take long summer vacations on Martha's Vineyard, and travels elsewhere at home and abroad. For he is a man of culture, with his interests in art and in literature. Many years ago he wrote a short story dependent on his poignant memories of an Indiana friend who died in France on the last day of the war in 1918; he sent it to the managing editor of the *Saturday Evening Post,* whom he knew and who published it in that magazine. From his European travels he brought back some things, including two Hellenistic bases and some Roman coins, which he had begun to collect and with which he adorned the mantels of his house on Martha's Vineyard and his big house in Indianapolis.

He likes his French wines. But he is an isolationist. He does not particularly like that term, but there it is. He wasn't an isolationist always—not even when that term had become current in America, around 1920. He had been enthusiastic for the crusade against the kaiser, to make The World Safe for Democracy; he was a captain in the army by 1918, though the war ended before he was to be sent to France; he believed in the League of Nations, though he was a Republican. But the national hangover that followed the heady enthusiasms of the War To End All Wars affected him, too. Gradually, as the twenties progressed, his maturing ideas about the world congealed into convictions. The peace treaties were deplorable, the British and especially the French were as selfish and mean as ever, Europe was in a mess, the new Europe was even worse than the old, and there was the new menace of international Communism. America's entangling alliances in the war had been a disastrous departure from its history. There were American national interests, and to secure them was more than enough. He thought that this realization was but part and parcel of growing up, a sober kind of self-knowledge appearing during the passage from youth to maturity, from illusions to realism. And now, in 1939, in view of a new European war, that is endangered again by the cloudy emotional tides of internationalism, by all kinds of people who are tending to propagate the belief that it may be America's destiny to defend freedom across the world, especially in Europe. And there is a president who is inclined that way. Not only is Franklin not Theodore; unfortunately, 1939 is not 1914. In 1914 (and he remembers this) not one among one thousand Americans believed that they would or *should* be involved in a European war. But now, in 1939, with all the disturbing memories about that erstwhile American enthusiasm for getting in Over There, the minds of many Americans are uneasy: perhaps, perhaps, we might be involved again, whether we like it or not. Hadn't the president himself said a few days ago that of course the United States would remain neutral but that he could not ask his fellow Americans to be neutral in their sentiments?

And so, among his friends on Martha's Vineyard, this gentleman from Indiana evinces a feeling of insecurity or, rather, a premonition.

It does not dominate his mind: there are fishing and tennis and contract bridge, which have occupied the day and much of the conversation during this convivial evening; there is some talk about politics, but not much. Yet he feels something that he had only sensed here and there before and that had not disturbed him then, but somehow it disturbs him now: that some of his friends, New Yorkers and Bostonians, see the world not as he sees it, and that they see him not as he sees himself. They may not be committed internationalists or interventionists (his preferred term) — at any rate, not yet — but they are inclined that way. He has his convictions, they have only inclinations; but somehow they seem to think that they are the realists and that he is an idealist. That his midwestern provenance will show through, though he is a cultured man and not a provincial, an American gentleman and not a hayseed. Their affection for him is genuine, but somehow some of them may think that there are things that restrict the largesse of his mind. They will not argue bitterly, not on this September evening in 1939 and not afterward, either; and when, later, the tides of their lives will drift some of them apart, they will remember each other with more than civilized warmth. And when he will die suddenly, and preternaturally, after the war, some of them will say to each other that he was an old-fashioned American and will remember his kindness, his hospitality, his quirks on the golf course, how he looked (always properly dressed, his large feet in his white summer shoes, his long bony wrists mixing the cocktails, shooing his Filipino servant in the white jacket away), the occasional twang in his voice. "He was straight out of Booth Tarkington," one of his women friends will say. "One of the 'Magnificent Ambersons'" (she had seen the movie made of that book, circa 1948). "Perhaps. He was our Amberson," her friend says.

"Let's get down to brass tacks. You are describing an isolationist. But this man was not a typical isolationist, was he?"

Let me try to disentangle this. So many of the isolationists in 1939 were Anglophobes—Irish Americans, German Americans, Swedish Americans, especially in the Midwest (which does not mean that they were Germanophiles, though some of them were). This man was not. Other isolationists were old socialists of the Norman Thomas kind, idealists, or American pacifists, which he also was not. But now don't forget that America First was founded in June 1940 by Yalies, white Anglo-Saxon Protestants. There *were* others of his kind who, with all their cultural baggage—remember that this man was not a provincial—were uneasy (to say the least) about what they saw as a rising cloud of internationalist propaganda abetted by people about whose patriotism and even about whose Americanness they were doubtful. Internationalists included, of course, New Dealers and Rooseveltians, but he was also uneasy about the opinions of some of his Eastern friends, many of them Republicans, readers not of the *Chicago Tribune* but of the *New York Herald Tribune,* whose Anglophile and Francophile inclinations were cultural as well as political. He and his kind were less anxious about what was to happen in Europe than what would happen to America if FDR and the liberals and the interventionists were to have their way. He was suspicious of them—and indeed his suspicions were to be confirmed, step by step, from 1939 all the way to Pearl Harbor. Of course he did not like Hitler. Not many of the isolationists did. But he also did not like the people who were clamoring against Hitler.

"Well, Hitler was not like the kaiser. But, remembering that feverishness and the excesses of all that propaganda against the kaiser and the Germans, he thought that this must not happen again. And wasn't that shortsighted?"

Yes, it was, but there was more to it than shortsightedness. My man—and his kind—feared Communism and Communists. Like Taft (another Yale graduate), who kept saying in 1940 and 1941 that a victory by Hitler posed no threat to the United States and that "the victory of Communism in the world would be far more dangerous to the United States than the victory of Fascism," because Fascists were few and Communists many. Whether my Indiana gentleman would be an America Firster in 1940, whether he would think the same things as that dyspeptic Taft, I do not know; my vignette is about 1939, not 1940 or 1941. One thing, however, they had in common: their preoccupation with Communism. That preoccupation went deeper than their concern about their money or their possessions or even their social status. It was an ideology — one running counter to his conviction that it was he, and not his internationalist friends, who was a realist.

"Aren't you overdoing this? You have been writing about September 1939. Only a few days before that, Hitler made his pact with Stalin. Wouldn't that have turned him against Hitler?"

Ah, you have just hit upon something that has intrigued and even preoccupied me for some time. And that something was not only an American but a worldwide phenomenon: except for a few pro-Communist intellectuals, Hitler's pact with Stalin did not change the minds of many people, because by 1939 what an English wag supposedly said was true: that all the Isms were Wasms.

"I guess you are thinking of that wondrous scene in the Kremlin when Stalin surprised the German delegation by inviting them to a last get-together, which turned out to be a celebratory banquet, and when he lifted his glass of Caucasian champagne, he smiled and looked straight at Ribbentrop: 'I know how the German people love their führer. I want to raise my glass to that great man.' At the same time thousands of German Communists revere Stalin's name while they haul stones in Hitler's concentration camps."

Among other things, yes. There were, of course, a few Communists who deserted the party (some of them reverting to Trotskyism, no big deal). But much more interesting and telling is the fact that not a single Nazi — or German sympathizer — left his party, that avatar of anti-Communism, because of his disillusionment with the Hitler-Stalin pact. To the contrary: they were exhilarated by this smashing news of the Führer's success, by the statecraft of the Reich. This was so because brutal success is always more impressive than ideology, consistency in the use of power is more compelling than a consistency of ideas. *That*, to me, is even more telling than Stalin's statesmanship. And there were many people, intelligent people, who did not and do not understand

what that meant and still means. And not only left-leaning intellectuals but conservatives. In England, too. In 1938 Nevile Henderson, the
British ambassador to Germany, wrote to Halifax: "Right for right's
sake doesn't count for anything anymore, everything depends on the
Isms and the Ology." Wrong, as so often, Henderson. But then so was
Evelyn Waugh. Unlike Henderson, Waugh was exhilarated by the news
of the pact. It is there in his diaries and his letters and in the first sentences of his Second World War trilogy, considered by many as the best
English novel about the war. (I admire some of his other books more.)
Waugh's hero, Guy Crouchback, upon hearing the news of the pact,
says, "The enemy at last was plain in view, huge and hateful. . . . It
was the Modern Age in arms." That was exactly what Waugh himself
thought, for he, too, was an ideologue. For him, the main enemy of
civilization was Communism and leftism. He gave much less thought
to Hitler and Nazism, mostly because he disliked the kind of people
who were agitating against them. Now that the Soviets had made up
with the Nazis, the true colors of the enemy showed and glared. When
a few weeks later the Soviets entered eastern Poland, Waugh was dismayed that Britain did not declare war on Russia. He disliked Churchill
and came to dislike him even more when Churchill supported Russia
after Hitler's invasion of it. After the war Waugh wrote to Diana Duff
Cooper that Churchill's "frightful mistake" was to think that "Stalin
was just old Tsar writ large." But Stalin *was* a Tsar writ large — only not
that shuffling, bumbling kindly Nicholas the Second, but Ivan the Terrible. Of course, both Hitler and Stalin were statesmen; Stalin never had
any compunction about allying himself with anti-Communists (Kemal
or Laval or Hitler or Churchill or Roosevelt or Chiang Kai-shek) when
he thought it would be advantageous for the interests of his Russia.
And there were many instances when Hitler's decisions were not governed by his ideology, either.

But I want to go further than that. When the Isms become Wasms,
that is not a regression to the past. It is something else than Realpolitik.
It is not a return to old statecraft, which occasionally allowed a few
crimes to be committed for the sake of the state. It is, rather, a symp-

tom of the birth of the new barbarism. For instance, Stalin and Hitler will respect and even admire each other to the end — even during the war, when their armies and peoples will kill and burn and starve each other's peoples by the millions. And a new hierarchy will emerge in the German death camps and the Russian prison camps: their commanders and guards will rely more and more on the criminals among the prisoners to help run the camps, since the criminals can govern and rule the other inmates even more cruelly and unscrupulously and efficiently than the guards themselves. Fifty years later there will be entire governments in alliance with and dependent upon criminals, whose power the highest authorities of their states can no longer control or restrict.

"Will you please stop succumbing to your temptation to use this book as a receptacle of historical cerebrations that you are too lazy to write up elsewhere?"

My only excuse is that I couldn't think of something more telling for my chapter on 1939. I found the thoughts of my American isolationist more interesting (and perhaps more complex) than the agonizings of leftist intellectuals in New York. Perhaps my point was that isolationists and indeed internationalists were ideologues, too, though they did not know that.

"All the Isms are Wasms. Good. But haven't you always insisted that ideas do matter, that the most important thing is what people think and believe, and that even the material conditions in this world are but the consequences of that?"

You ought to know better what I mean. Of course ideas matter, but only when men and women incarnate them. That is where not only ideologies but German categorical idealism, including Hegel and his Zeitgeist, are wrong. In so many circumstances people think what they want to think.

"True enough. But what does that have to do with barbarism? Your gentleman from Indiana was not a barbarian. He may have been surprised by the news of Hitler's pact with Stalin, but it did not affect his isolationist convictions, did it? Were Nixon's supporters, including American conservatives, with all their anti-Communist global ideology, disillusioned or shocked when he announced his opening to China? Not at all."

Good point, but not good enough, because I read somewhere — was it in Ehrlichman's or Haldeman's memoirs? — that when they got to the Kremlin, in 1972, I think, they found themselves very much at home with their Soviet counterparts: state security men, law-and-order men, not ideologues. These Californians were agreeably surprised (as Ribbentrop had been in 1939). But I should not have projected that far; I wrote about 1939 and should have kept to that, no more and no less.

"No more, please. Except that you got rid of your Indiana gentleman too fast. You have not really answered my question about whether he was a typical isolationist. Well, I think that he wasn't. You wrote that he was an Eastern Midwesterner — yes, yes, I know there were plenty of Easterners of his class who were still isolationists in 1939 — but he seems to have been as much if not sometimes more at home on Martha's Vineyard as in Indianapolis. And so let me imagine him in, say, 1944 on his way from Indiana to New England. Midway, he has stopped to visit friends who have a country place in northern Virginia or southwestern Pennsylvania, near one of those American villages whose name ends with -anna and carries an old melancholy sound, like Ruthanna, Pennsylvania, or Fluveanna, Virginia. That evening he walks alone and looks out on a lake and woods, a very American scene, solitary and unencumbered by any sign of human habitation, with a touch of wilderness and yet a landscape because of some ineffable sense of past human presences. There settles on him that rare and deep benison of feeling, which is a sense of concordance of place and time at a certain moment of one's life. Of place: because he is now, in 1944, not too comfortable with some of the people in Indianapolis — isolationist Republicans, hardened Babbitts without Babbitt's original naïveté, self-satisfied with their sense of Americanness and chuckling with their perhaps increasingly popular reactions against the president, the government, and the war. And he is uncomfortable, too, with some of the opinions of people in Boston or on the Vineyard, with their notions of how the world after the war will be. Of time: D-Day has already happened, and millions of Americans are sent to Europe, again. He was too old to be drafted in this war; and the mechanical destiny of American has been roaring past him, ahead. This evening stillness (not a leaf is moving), this dark green landscape are his time and place, he thinks. It is a moment when he finds himself at home in a mystic symbiosis with what is still his country; and he may feel, too, that he won't live long."

Well, it is you who departed from 1939 now. All right, because every movement depends on its departure, I think.

1940

THIS YEAR THE FIRST SNOW falls on Hungary on a late November afternoon. It is not much of a snowfall, but it coats the streets and the pavements enough to bring the muted sounds of winter traffic, the squishy movements of automobiles and the padded footsteps of people. Since it is not very cold, the roofs of houses on the Pest side of the Danube remain wet and dark, but higher up in Buda, on Castle Hill, the roofs have turned white, suggesting a peaceable wintriness here in this small country in the midst of the Second World War. Hungary is already an ally of its dominant neighbor, the Third Reich; a few uniformed German officers and more Germans in civilian clothes may be seen in the streets. But there is still a British Legation in Budapest, where the Minister and his pleasant wife are giving a small dinner party.

The Legation is in Werböczy-utca on Castle Hill, in one of the provincial baroque town houses built by the Hungarian nobility in the late eighteenth and early nineteenth centuries. Except for a few stationary automobiles and the street lights, much of that portion of Castle Hill still looks as it must have one hundred years before. A solitary policeman stands outside the house.

The guests walk through a small gate into a cold, stone-arched interior passage and then up a few steps to a large solid fruitwood door, beyond which are instant warmth and the exquisite silent attentiveness of a male servant and a maid: a hush suggesting that they are in the presence of something that is old and comfortable and, to them, familiar. The guests are few. Besides the first secretary of the Legation are two Hungarian aristocratic couples and one younger Hungarian woman, she too from one of the great historic families of Hungary, more vivacious and a little more crimson-lipped than the other women. All of them speak English, of course, but that has not much to do with their dinner invitation. By November 1940 the list of potential guests at the Legation has diminished considerably. No high official of the Hungarian government wishes to be seen as a guest of the British now. (There are some who would still wish to receive an invitation from the British Minister but who also know that they cannot afford the risk of accepting one.) There remains a reservoir of Anglophiles and Germanophobes in 1940: Jews, industrialists, intellectuals, artists, and many among the aristocracy. When it comes to aristocrats of money, of intellect, or of birth, the British, being British, are most comfortable with the last.

His Majesty's Minister to Hungary is an excellent man whose qualities have been appreciated in the Foreign Office well before his present posting. The fact that he is a Catholic with an Irish name is not a handicap in his diplomatic career and perhaps even an advantage in his position in Hungary. But there is little that a British envoy can do in a country whose geographic situation (and not only that situation) binds it more and more closely to Hitler's Third Reich, beyond the limited significance of a still extant British Legation in Budapest and his discreet maintaining of contacts with a handful of respectable Hungarians who sympathize with England. His wife, an Englishwoman of literary interests and talents, is charmed by their life in Hungary and especially by the Hungarians she knows. I am inclined to think that her husband is more aware of the limitations of their remaining social circle in Budapest. Their Hungarian acquaintances are no longer important or particularly influential people. Yet there remain some things that are not emptied of meaning: uneradicated remnants of a past that are palpable in that house and around that dinner table in Budapest in November 1940.

In the entire world England now represents that past. The Minister's Hungarian guests believe that. Their being Hungarian is a condition more decisive than the reserved manners bred into them. They are less temperamental than most of their countrymen, but they can be moody enough to hold to certain illusions. This means that they are more ebullient about the prospects of Britain and the war than are their British hosts. It is, after all, November 1940: the British have withstood the German onslaught from the air, Hitler has not dared to invade England, his ally Mussolini is tasting his first defeats, America is affirming its support of the British side. Of course they talk of many other things besides politics. Traditional Anglophiles that they are, they are different from the bearded, handsome, slightly exotic, warm-blooded, Anglophile, liberal Hungarian nobles of the nineteenth century, partly because of inheritance, partly because of environment. Because their families intermarried with the Austrian nobility, those now present have eyes that are still dark and deep-set but faces that I can only describe as Transdanubian: smooth, long-eared, and long-lipped, partisans of an old monarchical and legitimate order of things. That order of things is still part of their lives, of their houses, and of the Castle Hill house of the British Legation, with gilt arrows of light reflected in the old varnish of a table, with tiny red flames in the small grate of the white porcelain tile stove in the corner, and in the perfection of the respectful attentiveness of the servants. The evening is pleasant. But when they leave, the clear metallic touch and smell of the cold sharpens their senses, and at least one of them — allow me to think that it is the younger woman with the crimson lipstick, trying to gather the clasp of her fur coat with her long, nervous fingers — says something that is more sobering than the midnight air: "I don't know. This will be a long war. And it is a different world from what we think. And there are so few of us."

I do not wish to suggest that the British Minister's view of the world was very different. I can surmise that because he really existed. His name was Owen O'Malley. His wife, under the pseudonym Ann Bridge, later wrote novels in Portugal and England, fair novels about Hungary during the war, fictions inspired by the history she had seen and by the characters of the men and the women she recalled. I did not know them, of course; I was not yet seventeen in November 1940, and my parents were not on the guest list of the British Legation. The matter of the Hungarians there is somewhat different. I knew some of those people, though I think not at the time. I can see the faces of at least two of them, and I can very clearly see the man and the woman opening the door for them. The rest is a composite image in my mind. I invented that dinner party—because it was plausible, then. (The comma is crucial.) All I can say is that this is how these people and their host could have been that night, by which I mean how they *would* have been, which includes something about the kind of people that they *were*.

"And isn't that fiction?"

Yes, of course. But then history too is fiction, though only in the broadest (but sometimes deepest) sense of *fictio,* meaning a mental construction—but a construction that is not only dependent on but strictly, very strictly, circumscribed by what we actually and honestly know. I would call this necessity "fact" except that "fact," *factum,* carries with it a sense of definitiveness, whereas all actuality, we must remember, in the past as well as in the present, must at least be considered together with its potentiality then. I am writing about certain moments in history, and these are not altogether inventions.

What was significant about that particular moment, that dinner in the half-empty and perhaps already somewhat gloomy British Legation in Budapest in November 1940, was the sense, among at least some of those eight people, that this world, their world, will be irrevocably gone—even if, or when, the Germans lose the war and the English prevail. And connected with that was something that has interested me for a long time. It involves Russia, even though they do not talk about Russia during that dinner. Now keep in mind that in November 1940

Stalin's Russia was not in the war and was much closer to Germany than to England; this British Minister, who was a principled Conservative, and his Hungarian guests, who were Catholics from noble families with large estates, had nothing good to expect from Soviets and Communism. Yet they knew that what the Germans and the mass of their followers stood for was more evil and dangerous — because potentially more popular — than the Russians and Communism. That these people thought so, as members of a class that would be deported if not altogether liquidated by Communism, whereas Hitler would let them be (as long as they did not conspire against him), can be ascribed to their revulsion at what they knew of the vulgar brutalities of the Nazis and their sympathizers. But it had at least something to do, too, with a more deeply set reaction, with their very old-fashioned sense of decency. And honor. And to an old civilization to which they belonged.

"Well, you could say that of Churchill, too. Do we need to dine in Budapest to learn that?"

Yes, because in Churchill's case that view of the world corresponded to a stark and simple perspective, to his perspective from the highest and coldest peak of British interests. He saw only two alternatives: either Hitler's Germany would rule all of Europe, or Soviet Russia would come into the eastern half of Europe, and half of Europe was better than none. For the British and for Western Europe, that was. But Hungary was not in western Europe. That, among many other things, shaded the sense of the "different world" that the young woman had in mind that night.

1941

If I were to write a novel, I think I would write one about Philadelphia in 1941 — more precisely, about Philadelphia from June 1940 to December 1941, that is, from the fall of France to the attack on Pearl Harbor. From this you may see that the main thread of the story would be how the thoughts — thoughts, rather than ideas — of some people changed: not from isolationism to interventionism or to international-ism (imprecise and sometimes even misleading terms, those) but from their sense of separation from Europe to their acceptance of the proba-bility of their involvement in the war. But politics would not be the main content of my narrative. It would describe certain people, certain things, certain changes of the atmosphere, including the interior one, by which I mean their moving around some of the furniture of their minds. If such a narrative would illustrate anything beyond a carefully drawn period picture, it would describe how (rather than why) people adjust their ideas to circumstances — a favorite theme or even a convic-tion of mine.

Here are some of the possible ingredients: the hot, lazy summer of 1940 in Philadelphia, so remote from the great drama played out on the eastern edge of the Atlantic. It is June. A young boy, perhaps K.'s nephew, straight out of Princeton, going to debutante dances in the middle of that month, the coming-out parties that blossom like peonies in June (very hothouse garden, very florescent, but with a beauty that is neutral at best and that has a faintly common scent). The manners of these young people, which are careful rather than very good. Once in a while a moment of atavistic American wildness breaks through (like the green, thorny-spiky jungle of vegetation in the subtropical Philadelphia heat, creeping forward here and there over the remote edges of the beautifully tended Main Line or Chestnut Hill gardens), usually around two in the morning, at one of those parties where the band (Meyer Davis's band, of course) breaks into a last Dixieland rag and the girls kick off their shoes and dance wildly on the grass. The great war in France and, later that summer, even the war above England are remote from their lives and their minds and their concerns, less because of the geographic distance or isolationism than because of their incuriousness. The war is almost as remote from them as are the lives and the minds and the characters of people in the Irish or Italian Philadelphia neighborhoods sometimes not more than a mile away from where they live—as remote as, say, Villanova is from Bryn Mawr, half a mile and two stops away on the Main Line of the Pennsylvania Railroad.

In 1940 K. is thirty-nine. He likes his nephew. For the first time in his life he feels a touch of avuncular affection, including a touch of melancholy and perhaps even respectful envy, since the lives of such young men seem freer and happier (and surely more "modern") than the years of his own youth. But across the unavoidable chasm of generations is the still prevalent safety of Philadelphia, with its American-Victorian, provincial, Saxon, Protestant ingredients. And with the unquestioned stability of its institutions. One thing that binds them together is the psychic substance of Philadelphian conventions. At the same time, K. is a Democrat, his nephew a Republican. No great distance between them there, however: in June 1940 both are indecisive. But during the early winter there comes a change. The Germans' bombing of England awakens latent racial and cultural inclinations. Among certain people, such as K. and his nephew, I mean. They no longer differ much about the need and about the propriety of America standing by Britain. Yet during all of 1941, the slow, at times somnolent adagio rhythm of their Philadelphia prevails: a dense soup of customs and sentiments, nutritious, whitish, thickened with flour. And so it remains throughout the war, even though after the night of December 7 no difficult questions remain.

I know that I can't write a novel (for one thing, is there any kind of plot in the foregoing, except for the war coming closer?), but at least there should be sufficient space in a novel to describe some things of that period: how in June 1940 the galleries of Convention Hall were packed with young people (some of them brought down from New York) who chanted "We want Willkie!" and who impressed some of their Philadelphian cousins with their political sophistication; how in July certain members of the Merion Cricket Club and the Philadelphia Country Club went around to their friends and acquaintances to collect shotguns to be packed and sent to England; how in August Bill Bullitt, secretly encouraged by FDR, made a great interventionist speech on the steps of Independence Hall, though few people listened; how in July some Philadelphia Quakers tried to bring together German and English diplomats in Washington, while other Quakers were pro-English; how sailors of a British cruiser, putting in at the Navy Yard, were told in October to avoid taverns in South Philadelphia, where Italian Americans might attack them; how in February 1941 Lord Halifax, the British ambassador, chose to grace a fox hunt with the solidly Republican Plunket Stewarts in Unionville, transported thereto in the private Pullman of the president of the Pennsylvania Railroad; how Bullitt gave the most splendid of debutante parties for his daughter in Pennlyn in July 1941; how Herbert Hoover came to Philadelphia to stay with his friends the Hamiltons, old Republicans, the night before Pearl Harbor (and how I wish I knew what he thought and said at the news of Pearl Harbor—what he said about FDR, I mean); how most of the Catholics in Philadelphia voted for Roosevelt while they adamantly opposed any American intervention in the war; how the enormous brick factories on the edge of the city were being cranked up and beginning to hum;

and how, the day after Pearl Harbor, young people all over Philadelphia rushed to the colors.

"Well, here is proof again that you cannot write a novel and that you shouldn't try. I'm glad that you admit that, but, then, why this recurrent urge toward it, why this need to say, 'If I were to write a novel, this is what I'd write about' "?

You ought to know the answer to that. It has nothing — well, almost nothing — to do with my literary inclinations or aspirations. What I want to do is to write about things and to tell about things that did exist, that did happen, but that cannot be found in any of the history books. Or articles.

"You mean in the books and articles researched and written by other historians."

Well, . . . yes.

"And you take a certain pride in knowing things that they did or do not know."

I think that *pride* is not the right word.

"But that is irrelevant. It is not enough to know things. You and I have agreed on that often enough. Knowing something and expressing it are two different actions, and of course I do not only mean the skill of expression, of writing, of style. Besides, there are things that one knows but that one need not or ought not or must not talk about. Whether one thing or another is stated in a narrative partly depends on the proportions called for by a certain style of expression. That is the artistic question. But it depends perhaps even more on the writer's — on the historian's — purpose."

I absolutely agree. That is the moral question. But is there any moral problem involving the ingredients of such a putative Philadelphia novel? I think not.

"Probably not, but the artistic problem is big enough. This is so because you are too much of a historian, and not only by training or profession or practice or whatnot. The main thing that interests you is what really happened — yes, I know, including also what could have happened — which is probably why you cannot invent a plot, any plot. In the beginning of sketching this idea for a novel, you write that politics would not be the main content of it. But your entire plan is about politics, or political history. It is the history of Philadelphia from the fall of France to Pearl Harbor — nothing more."

Of certain Philadelphians — how they reacted to these events, how these events affected them. Haven't we agreed, at least once, that every novel is a historical novel?

"Yes, we did. But, for God's sake, there is still a difference between a history and a novel. Suppose you write such a novel. What you will be mostly writing about is what interests you: the general history of that period, even when it is reflected in little things, *petites histoires.* I know that you can, at times, do that rather well. But precisely because of your main interest, in this instance your portraits of your characters will be one-sided and incomplete. Your plan is to write about their caution and their courage, their conformism and their self-discipline, their narrow-mindedness and their broad-mindedness, their manners and their thinking, only inasmuch as these are reflected in their tendencies and expressions regarding the politics of that period. You know as well as I that this is not enough. What about the private life (including sex) — the inclinations and the practices — of that young lad you would be writing about? Forgive me for being direct or vulgar, but there it is."

Oh, well, you can write a very good novel without much of that, and I mean a novel that *does* also deal with the profounder relations of men and women. But I know what you mean, and you are, of course, right. But one more thing. You of all people know how much I am interested in 1940 and 1941. Those were my formative years, though I lived them five thousand miles east of Philadelphia. And something else has haunted me through many years, and that is the question, or the problem, Why has no really great novel about Philadelphia ever been written? Philadelphia being a near-perfect scene for a novel of manners, the materials are (or, rather, were) here.

"Well, you may one day write a very good essay about *why* that did not happen, but I doubt whether it is your business to show *how* it should be done."

You are probably right. And so this chapter, this 1941, is not really a vignette but an excursus.

1942

UNKNOWN TO EACH OTHER, two travelers from Hungary land in New York on a September day in 1942. They are appalled by the New York heat. It is one of those mid- or even late-September days when the last heat wave—or, rather, the last heat tide—of the year sits on top of the Eastern seaboard, with everything beneath it feeling breathless and oppressed. The ninety-plus temperature is made worse because expectations of autumnal relief have been thwarted and because the summer-long heat is still packed within the buildings and the dwellings and the streets and the subway and train tunnels of the city. It is their first disappointment on a journey across a sharky Atlantic from a German-ruled Europe in the middle of the greatest of world wars, with nervous expectations about America. But already early in the morning the hot wind of this American September has washed around them as they stood on the decks of their ships, peering toward the Long Island shore in the steamy and pearly haze, hoping to espy the magic towers of Manhattan.

One man comes ashore in Manhattan from an American Export Line ship, having embarked on it ten days before in Lisbon. The other lands in Weehawken on a Panamanian freighter that he had boarded in French Morocco, in Rabat. Leaving Europe behind, he had taken the Casablanca route.

Now they are here, in America. Both of them have important

missions, the eventual performances of which do not exist apart from their personal opportunities, having accomplished their amazing journeys. In history, in life, unlike in science, it is often the exceptions that count. Much of the same is true of travel. What a journey! To have traveled from the middle of a German-occupied continent to the United States, across the Atlantic in 1942 — moreover, not as clandestine escapees or refugees but equipped with proper passports and visas — across German-ruled territories and Fascist Italy and Vichy France and Franco Spain. Even more exceptional is the condition that the traveler from Casablanca is Jewish. I shall not describe them physically, except to say that both are fairly distinguished-looking, even as they pant and perspire while standing by their suitcases in the steam-bathed caverns of the docks. Both are around forty. I repeat that they do not know each other and they do not know of each other, though they will eventually become aware of each other's presence in the United States.

Having cabled radio telegrams (via Mackay–RCA Radio) from the ship to different addresses in New York, they do not step on American shores unexpected; but for the Weehawken arrival there has been a mix-up, there is no one to meet him, though there comes a belated message directing him to a hotel on West Fifty-Eighth Street, where a room has been reserved for him. At Dock Fifty-Six the other man is welcomed by two gentlemen in summer suits; they drive him to an apartment in Beekman Place.

It would be interesting and perhaps pleasant to record the sensations of these two Hungarians, each of whom is urbane in his own way: their experiences during the next few days, their reactions to the fabulous and tangible wealth of this city and country in the midst of a world war, to midtown Fifth Avenue or Madison Avenue; their amazement at the rich shopwindows of the big department stores; but also their unexpected encounter with such names as Cartier and Sulka and Knize, those most elegant of establishments washed under the Nazi flood in Vienna or Karlsbad or Paris and, lo and behold, washed ashore and gleaming here again in New York — truly the New World having become the rescuer and the repository of much of what was best in the

Old. But my task, here, is less to describe these men than to sum up their respective missions.

Let me at least invent (or, more precisely, apply) their names — first names will do. The man in Beekman Place is Iván. The one at West 58th Street is László.

Iván is bringing (among other things, including confidential monies, a substantial draft on an American bank) a secret message from the Hungarian government to the government of the United States, who are officially at war with each other. The message exists on paper, but it has none of the marks of an official document: it has no letterhead; it is typed on a plain sheet, on both sides; it carries neither a stamp nor a signature nor designation of its addressee. The reasons behind the unimpressive format of this paper are, of course, cautionary. The message it contains is not properly addressed from one government to another. It has been drafted by a high-ranking member of the Hungarian Foreign Ministry, revised and vetted by two important personages close to the Regent, and approved (of course indirectly and anonymously) by the Prime Minister. Other ministers of the Hungarian government have not been informed of the existence either of the document or of its bearer and the extraordinary arrangements (wartime passport, wartime visas, and transit permissions, including German and Italian ones) facilitating his journey from Budapest through Zagreb and Venice and Milan and the south of Vichy France and Franco's Spain and Portugal to Lisbon (where his passport is stamped with an American visitor's visa). That is the reason for the noncommittal form of the document: were the Germans to search his luggage and find it en route, it must not contain proof of the complicity of anyone in the Hungarian government.

Immediately after his arrival in the Beekman Place apartment, Iván asks for a typewriter and a sheet of paper on which he types, "Aide-mémoire [an aide-mémoire, in diplomatic practice, is one notch below a memorandum] to the Department of State, Washington, D.C., in care of Professor Archibald Pierson." Pierson is a member of State's European Planning and Research Division. He knows Hungary, where in the twenties he spent two years as a representative of the Rockefeller Foundation. Now a Harvard professor and a Hungarophile, in 1933 he published an article in *Foreign Affairs* about the unreasonable features of the Treaty of Trianon affecting Hungary. Now this cover sheet and the already slightly crumpled paper are clipped together.

What does the aide-mémoire contain? Allow me to sum it up as briefly as possible. The government of Hungary requests the government of the United States to understand Hungary's difficult geographical and political situation; Hungary wishes to detach itself from the German alliance when this will become possible; it will refuse any German request for any kind of military collaboration against the United States and the British Commonwealth; it desires a confidential acknowledgment of the understanding of the American government regarding the above. (That will, among other things, strengthen the hand of those in the Hungarian cabinet who are inclined to affirm their unwillingness to conform to certain German demands, including those concerning the treatment of Hungarian Jews.) Much of this is stated somewhat obliquely in the aide-mémoire, that aid to memory; for, when the occasion arises, its carrier, Iván, must both clarify and expand its contents verbally, with some illustrations of detail.

And, at least in the beginning, all seems to be going well. In Washington he meets Archibald Pierson, who is cautious and noncommittal but not unsympathetic, making copies of the document and taking it with him. In New York Iván meets the former Hungarian minister, whose American wife comes from an old New England family and who had resigned when the Germans made Hungary join their alliance system. He also meets Archduke Otto Habsburg, who has good personal relations with President Roosevelt. A high point of his spirits comes at a dinner party, again somewhere on the East Side of New York, a fortnight or so after his landing. Usually a reserved and somewhat saturnine man, he is momentarily dazzled by the riches of the furnishings, the riches of the table, the crystal riches on the necks and arms of some of the women, the well-bred faces and the well-bred manners of some of the men, the conversation of these people who know Europe so well from traveling and living abroad—all this in October 1942! The triumph of American civilization, America invincible.

But no American response to his mission will be forthcoming (except for a later posting of an agent from the Office of Strategic Services to Lisbon, where he is told to acquaint himself with Hungarian affairs). What Iván does not know is that Pierson is but one, not particularly influential, member of the Planning and Research Board of State; that the analyses and the suggestions of the board are read neither by the secretary of state nor by the president; that the decisions or the nondecisions of the White House or of state regarding Hungary will be very different from what Iván and his friends, whether in America or in Hungary, had hoped. What he gradually learns is that his contacts may count socially, but they do not matter politically. His mission in America will fail for many reasons, including opposition to the Hungary that he represents.

And now to László, the other Hungarian emigré (for, in the literal sense of that word, that is what both of them are). He, too, comes on a mission, one connected with his own refuge in America. His mission was entrusted to him not by the government in Hungary (though there is at least one government official who knows about it) but by certain leaders of the Jewish community in Budapest. He is one of the first to bring a report of the German's murdering of Jews in Poland. Three Jews from Slovakia escaped from Poland in April. They made their way to Hungary. Their report of the horrors was sent abroad: to Switzerland, to Sweden, to the Vatican, and indirectly to the United States, via American diplomatic officials still stationed in neutral capitals in Europe. But now there is a direct route, through László, a most reputable lawyer who is in possession of an extremely valuable document: an American visa issued to him in December 1941, just a few days before the American Legation and Consulate in Budapest were closed, and valid for a year from the date of its issuance. He, too, needed some official help (if necessary, at the cost of some bribery) to travel across German-occupied Europe, including a valid passport (where, unlike in other Hungarian passports, his religion is unlisted). His continental traverse was more difficult than Iván's, but he, too, made his way through Croatia and Italy to what is still unoccupied, though Vichy-ruled, France, where there was a bourse of commotions and rumors and opportunities around the American consulate at Marseille and where he learned that the safest of routes was the Casablanca one, through Spain to French Morocco and from there to America. He, unlike Iván, carries no papers. All of his information is in his head (and in his heart) or a thick address book containing the addresses of Hungarian Jews and names and addresses of Jewish agencies and authorities in New York. But his task amounts to more than being the bearer of the terrible news from Poland. He should also exact some kind of official acknowl-edgment that the American government does not unconditionally con-demn the existing government of Hungary. This desideratum comes not from the Hungarian government, as in Iván's case, but from Jewish leaders in Hungary, who know that such an American commitment, clandestinely given or not, would help the threatened Jews of Hungary by making the government more and more reluctant to accede to Ger-man demands to ghettoize them or, worse, to deport them to Poland.

After a few days in New York László too is hopeful. He dines and lunches with Hungarians, many of whom he knows from Budapest. They are eminent Hungarian Jews who had been both prudent and able to leave with their families and with plenty of their monies in 1938 or in 1939. Three or four years later they are well ensconced in New York. They have reestablished some of their Budapestian living standards, of course adjusted to American practices and settings, some of them living in expensive apartment houses on upper Park Avenue or Central Park West. Intelligent men, with their bejeweled and expensively dressed wives, knowledgeable about politics and people in Hungary, and, per-haps surprisingly (not to László but to us), knowledgeable about Ameri-can conditions, including politics. One of them, a wise, older man, says to László: "In this country everything is possible, and the contrary of everything is possible, too." On another occasion: "At home [mean-ing Hungary] the bankers were Jews, and the criminals were Gentiles. Here the bankers are Gentiles, and there are criminals who are Jews." A throwaway remark, one meant to be funny. These men listen to László's account and to the purpose of his mission with much acute interest. Without exception they declare their willingness to help. Of course, there is more involved here than Jewish philanthropy or Hungarian patriotism: all these people have families and friends left in Hungary whose very lives are at stake. There is, however, a difficulty. They have few connections with important American Jewish organizations. László has addresses for some of them, but that is not quite sufficient.

His necessary contacts are eventually arranged. But his mission also fails. The men from the American Jewish organizations that he meets — and he fails to meet the most important men among them — are of course much interested in what he has to report, but somehow they are unable to grasp the entire meaning of the news he has brought to them. It is horrible, all right; but is it really new? And his news is one thing, but his mission is another. For him, his report and his mission are closely, perhaps inseparably, connected; for his hearers, they are not. They are uninterested in the inclinations, let alone the desiderata, of the Hungarian government, anti-Semitic as that government undoubtedly is. On at least one occasion, László perceives some suspicion on the countenance and in the tone of one of the American Jews: whose agent is this Jew from Hungary? On another occasion, an important Jewish personage asks him about Zionism. László knows something about Zionists in Hungary but not much. That does not work in his favor, which becomes obvious to him when the other man somewhat patronizingly suggests that, for American Jews, the cause of Zionism, of Jewish Palestine, may have priority over the destiny of the Jewish remnant in anti-Semitic Europe.

"Well, this is some vignette. As a matter of fact, it is hardly a vignette at all."

I know that.

"This has obviously been in you for some time, and you just had to express it in writing. I have a feeling that you did not invent this story."

No, I invented it. Except for its potentiality, for its plausibility. In late 1942 there were a few such missions permitted by certain high government officials in Hungary at the time, with the same limitations and purposes that I have tried to describe—except that most (not all) of these attempts at contacts with the Americans and the British were made by diplomats or former diplomats in neutral countries. And their results were by and large the same. One more thing: that surely exceptional, indeed almost incredible, travel from Budapest to New York across the war in 1942 is not my invention. A handful of such journeys were made.

"So: what is the purpose of all this?"

A dual purpose, perhaps. To suggest the misunderstandings of Europeans and Americans (including Jews); but to suggest, too, that such misunderstandings existed at a certain time, at a certain place, among certain people, and that therefore they should not be entirely forgotten. These misunderstandings—I am afraid that I must use a somewhat pompous term for it—involve the texture of history and the structure of society, of American society, by which I mean not something sociological but something that is both subtle and important: how ideas move (or, perhaps, how they are being moved) and how decisions are made. The first part of Iván's mission is successful. It goes as expected. He has an introduction to certain influential Americans, he indeed meets them, they receive him, they listen to him, many of them sympathetically (in part because of his good manners). Most of these people rank (not a proper verb, I know) at the top of American society (this, remember, even includes the Harvard professor who happens to be an old Bostonian). But what Iván does not understand, and what will take him a long time to comprehend, is that these people are not influential enough for the purposes of his mission. He—this is a frequent mistake of Europeans—believes that the functions of society in America are the same, by and large, as those in Europe. That is no doubt true in some ways, but by no means all. Yes, of course in 1942 there are Harrimans and Biddles and Drexels who have important government positions, because Franklin Roosevelt not only grew up with some of them but because he trusts them and their worldly knowledge, which is why he employs them at high diplomatic posts. But there is a duality in Roosevelt's politic character and in his view of the world, too, and by 1942 some of these people are no longer his principal advisers. Now Iván — and there is a duality in his purposes, too, for he is both emissary and refugee, eventually an unsuccessful emissary but a successful refugee — does not know this.

The other emissary, László, is hampered by a misunderstanding, too. He does not know how American Jews and European Jews are different.

"Whoa! Aren't French Jews and Russian Jews different? Or do you mean that American Jewishness and European Jewishness are different?"

Not quite — though in 1942 there was still a difference (and not merely a social one) between some of the mostly older and often German-American Jews and those American Jews who were mostly second-generation Jews from the Russias. Among other things, the former were assimilationists rather than Zionists and liberals rather than left-wingers. I am leaving aside the then newly arrived refugees from Hitler's Europe, who were assimilationists, too. What I am thinking about — and there is evidence for it — is the oddly wanting view of what later became known as the Holocaust among many American Jews at the time. Decades later their views and concerns will change. But not in 1942. Of course, there were many exceptions to that, and that there was a real concern among American Jews and their organizations to help Jews in Europe is obvious; it came to the fore and was able to influence some governmental moves on the highest levels in 1944. But there are two episodes that stick in my mind. One is recorded in Irving Kristol's reminiscences in an article published in the *New York Times Magazine* — in 1976. Here it is. It shocked me to the core. What he remembered, with great relish, was that in September 1940 he and his friends at City College, New York, were divided in camps, the devotees of Stalin and the devotees of Trotsky. "The elite was us — the happy few," he wrote. "What I now recollect most vividly is our incredible vivacity. . . . It *was* an authentic educational milieu [his italics]. Our presentations were intellectually rigorous. . . . It was between these two groups that the war of the worlds was being fought." This about September 1940, when the war of the worlds was being fought in the sky over England, and when everyone who was Jewish in Europe hoped and prayed for Churchill, whom these young American Jewish whippersnappers regarded as a reactionary imperialist. The other episode was told to me by a Jewish friend. Having survived Auschwitz (his parents didn't), he found himself at the end of the war in Germany; from there his recently Americanized Hungarian relatives were able to bring him straight to the United States. He told me that he then met Jewish people in New York who were not very much interested in his story. Their attitude was something like this: "It must have been terrible, but you assimilated Jews in anti-Semitic Europe had it coming to you." Next winter his relatives took him to Miami, where he talked to an American Jew ("a Russian," according to my friend), telling him where he had been — in Auschwitz — a year ago. The other man said, "I was here, in Miami," and laughed. I know that this brute was not typical of most American Jews, but there it was.

"Well, that doesn't belong here. Your entire thesis is implausible — the 'oddly wanting,' as you put it, reaction of some of those American Jews to the first news of the death camps."

Oh, no. That was a widespread reaction, and the American Jews' reaction was not unique. It existed in Hungary, too. It involved a psychic impossibility in comprehending the extent of that particular horror. You see, the Nazis' brutal treatment of Jews was so well known, so obvious, and so persistent in a myriad of awful instances — recall that I lived through these years in Hungary myself — that if someone were to bring news that the Germans were actually killing Jews, one would have thought, well, what else would one expect from them? what else is new? Let me tell you that the full horror of what happened there did not strike me until many years after the war, here in Pennsylvania, when I read a descriptive account of the gassings written by a German witness and published in a German scholarly journal, the *Vierteljahrs-hefte für Zeitgeschichte.*

You may be right about the vignette (or nonvignette); only, my purpose was to say something about the spirit of a certain period that ought to be recorded. And there is another thing that annoys me. It is that stupid movie *Casablanca,* a movie false from beginning to end. One detail: in that movie the chief resistance hero, Victor Laszlo (played by Paul Henreid, I think), is a Czech. Well, Laszlo is not a surname, and it is not a Czech name. It is a Hungarian name. And, only think, if this Laszlo is the heroic leader of a European underground network fighting the Nazis, what is the purpose of his passage through Casablanca to escape to America? Will he run the European underground from New York? Incidentally, my László was one of the last ones to be able to sail to New York in 1942 from Casablanca, as was Simone Weil. My God! Simone Weil and Humphrey Bogart! Well, I can imagine my László going to the West Coast and meeting those Hungarian screenwriters basking in sunny California, their parasitic and hedonist life in Beverly Hills so incredibly different from what's going on in Hungary in 1942 — and that may depress him more than the inadequate comprehension shown by some of his American coreligionists in New York.

"You said that Iván — and I presume László, too — were successful refugees. Have they not built various castles in the air, coming here? You are suggesting something that goes beyond their having escaped from the Nazis in Europe, and in the nick of time."

Yes, their missions in America will fail, but they will not. Their brains and their connections are such as to enable them to build successful careers in America. They may even meet each other once and twice in New York, toward the end of the war, though they move in different circles. Some time around 1948, Iván will find himself at another dinner party in an East Side town house, reminiscent of that first dinner in 1942 in Beekman Place, with the same kind of people hearing him out about the political situation in Central Europe and the awfulness of the Russian imposition of Communism. His and László's families will survive the war in Hungary and will come to America in 1947. Iván and László will have problems with their Budapestian wives, but their children will become professors at Harvard, advisers to the government, presidents of American corporations. Later.

1943

THE FIRST PUBLIC MEETING of the United Nations Council of Philadelphia takes place at the University of Pennsylvania on the first Friday afternoon of December 1943. At half past three it is still light, but the lamps outside and inside Franklin Hall are already lit. There is an estimable congregation of people on that otherwise somewhat sparsely populated campus in wartime. An auditorium is filled by about two hundred students, thirty professors, and a respectable number of patrons of art, of learning, and of internationalism: lawyers, doctors, newspapermen, and Proper Philadelphians, some of whom may have a sense of occasion about this convocation dedicated to the preparation of Americans for their participation in a new order of the world, for which the providing of information and education about world affairs has become unavoidable as well as desirable. The name of the United Nations Council of Philadelphia reflects this. The council was recently refashioned from the former Philadelphia Council of International Relations, and the list of its board members has been expanded.

"One World: A United Nations Roundtable Conference" is the title of this meeting. The auditorium is bright, the steam radiators are softly hissing, and there is a pale wash of benevolent expectations rising to the stage.

But the roundtable is not a success. One of its participants, indeed its star attraction, had regretfully declined two days before. He is the young Republican governor of a midwestern state who recently acquired national attention and approval in the press because of his public disavowal of an "outdated isolationism." An unexpected and instantly appealing invitation to be featured at another place led to his canceling his appearance in Philadelphia, for reasons both financial and politic. Thus the roundtable has been reduced to the chairman and two speakers, one of whom is largely unknown, a last-minute substitution for a foreign scholar from Princeton who has come down with the flu.

The chairman is L. P. Applebach, among the best-regarded of the university historians, who holds the best-endowed chair in British and Modern History and is a Philadelphia fixture. His round pink apple cheeks reflect his name, his twinkling clean gold-rimmed glasses above the benison of his smile reflect both his name and his career. Coming from a middle-class Pennsylvania German family, Professor Applebach achieved a Philadelphia status, being recognizably learned, perfectly safe, and appropriately respectful of the trustees of the university — having also made sure, early in his career, that his Anglophile and Republican convictions were sufficiently known so that whatever origins he may have sprung from there should be no recoil. He introduces the first speaker, who for all practical purposes has now become the main speaker at this occasion.

This man is the professor of international relations. That is a relatively novel discipline in the university in 1943, but he has been making a name for himself lately. His appearance is reassuring: he is lanky, with a well-clipped, small, pale moustache, his voice punctuated with equally well-clipped, short (rather than plummy) half-Episcopalian accents. He wears a button-down shirt; his very properly shined shoes reflect the bright lights above the platform. While L. P. Applebach (whose protegé the present speaker was, and in some measure still is) sits at a golden plateau, at the still unshaded early afternoon of his life, close to the zenith of his career, his younger colleague has been moving steadily toward his own peak — especially because in his field the prestige of his relationship is not separable from his public and published opinions. His occasional and lately more and more frequent column on world affairs is printed in the *Philadelphia Inquirer*. (In 1943 few Philadelphians read the daily *New York Times*.) He has a particular talent for adjusting his opinions to what seem to be the greater movements of the world, a talent that stands him in good stead, beyond faculty politics. It assures the reputation of his intellect and the willingness of people to regard his opinions as being reasonable and timely. In October 1938 he spoke in favor of peace and appeasement, he praised Chamberlain and the Munich settlement. In the late summer of 1940 he was a Willkie Republican. By October he supported the cause of Churchill and the destroyer deal. In 1941 he declared for Lend-Lease. In 1942 *Foreign Affairs* published his article on geopolitics.

In his present lecture he states that the globe is becoming one world. A United Nations' trusteeship of many former colonies may become as inevitable as it is desirable. Small states belong to the past. There ought to be no more place for balance-of-power politics and for spheres of interest. The partnership of the United States and the Soviet Union in this war is especially promising, since they are allied against the reactionary forces of the world. (This man is still a registered and public Republican; but in 1944 he will vote for Roosevelt, a fact that he would reveal to select people. To others he states that he is a progressive Republican, one who is convinced that Woodrow Wilson, with his League of Nations, was right, while probably ahead of his time. That this time has now come is implicit in his well-prepared and judicious lecture.)

But now the smoothness of the proceedings is disturbed, as the other scholar is beginning to speak. He is Polish, now an adjunct professor at Georgetown, a refugee from war-torn France and then from England, an almost skeletal man with a deeply creased face and small, high, knobbly cheekbones. His English is fairly good, much accented but easily comprehensible and properly grammatical. He is both courtly and pessimistic, a combination beyond the accustomed boundaries of American academic as well as Philadelphian discourse. Instead of a constructive discussion, there is an unpleasant presence of disagreements and of ties left untied. This foreign guest speaker is controversial — which in twentieth-century American parlance means someone or something about which people must not engage in controversy. The chairman and the other speaker have given their solid, pragmatic, and well-sounding reasons why Americans ought to trust the United Nations' charter and their alliance with the Soviet Union. This man says that while he of course agrees with the ideals of the United Nations and also with the preservation of the wartime alliances, there are ominous evidences of Russian ambitions and Communist purposes, especially in regard to his native country. The American speaker's reply suggests his disdain and an increasing impatience with that kind of argument: does the Polish guest realize that his distrust of Russia may be akin to the propaganda of Hitler and Goebbels? No, it is not a problem of distrust: the problem is that the Western Allies ought to define the limits of the Russians' sphere of interest, the Polish professor says — or tries to say. Whereupon, the American: "I fear that you do not trust either the statements or the resolve of our own people and their leaders." (Scattered applause.) He trusts them, he says; but how will they be enforced, and when? The chairman, who previously was smiling and patronizing, now enters the discussion: "I think, sir, that you must have a sufficient trust in the American ideals of an international order on one hand, and on the other a much-needed trust in human nature itself." (His malignity is cloaked by a benevolent smile.) But I know human nature, the Polish scholar says. (His smile is small and sad.) That is, alas, misinterpreted by some of the audience, including some of the students, one of whom says, "The guy is a cynic."

Not everyone in the audience thinks that; but there is a feeling (though perhaps not more than a feeling) that more unpleasantness lies ahead in the world. As people leave, the low hum of the city surrounds them. There are wisps of low-lying coal smoke and the sparks and screechy whoosh of the swaying trolley cars on Walnut Street. In a black overcoat and in the company of two or three Polish friends, our guest professor boards one of them for a short ride to Thirtieth Street station, from where he will continue to Washington on a crowded train. I must leave him there.

"And where, may I ask, do the other great scholars repair to?"

I don't know, and I don't much care. Perhaps back to L. P. Applebach's office, where some of them left their overcoats; perhaps to the faculty club; perhaps to their homes. (Applebach lives, very properly, in a nice little Philadelphia town house on Smedley or Panama Street — in reality an alley or mews — close to the Rittenhouse Club, where he is a member, having acquired his house and his membership judiciously, at a socially appropriate time. The other fellow resides in one of the better suburbs, again exactly befitting his status and his ambitions, at a time when in Philadelphia the very name of a particular suburb is immediately telling. He is a member of the Franklin Inn, which is a shade below the Rittenhouse Club, though perhaps his membership in the latter is coming.) In any event, they are in complete and contemptuous agreement about the inappropriateness and the angularity of that foreign professor's remarks. It is possible, too, that after the session they are sought out by — or they seek out — certain members of the audience whose social acquaintance they esteem. In the case of such postmortem conversations, their language will of course be slightly different. It will be tut-tutting instead of being sharp, with appropriate care taken to impugn, however subtly, the quality of the scholarship rather than the inappropriateness of the remarks of their now departing Polish colleague (if that is what he is). That will make an impression on at least some of their hearers, alas.

You will now notice that I have, at the risk of undue repetition, kept using, and perhaps overusing, that word *appropriateness*. You and I know very well that appropriateness (perhaps especially in Philadelphia) is often mistaken for good manners. But that is not as bad as the other matter that I tried to suggest, which is the kind of unwritten rule for such a roundtable or conference or whatnot: the avoidance of un-pleasant or untimely things in favor of a tepid consensus. And a small dagger in my heart is the imputation that the Polish professor is a *cynic*. There is a wound that made me write this 1943 vignette.

"I'm coming back to this in a moment. But before that I must ask you a question. Haven't you yourself criticized Eastern Europeans—and others—who did not want to admit that Germany could not have been defeated except for the British and American alliance with Stalin?"

Yes. But my Polish man was—not only excusably but understand-ably, and rightly so—concerned with the fate of his own country, over whose prospects black clouds were visibly gathering at that time. I can-not blame him for that. And I have criticized, too, Americans' unwill-ingness to think about the prospect of a Russian domination of Eastern Europe at a time—yes, 1943—when certain limits of that domination could have been defined and perhaps still arranged with Stalin. But here I was writing about something that is less rational and more deep-seated: my habitual concern with people's unwillingness to think about certain things, rather than with their inability to do so. And in this case the origins of the cold war were somehow latent in a microcosm, on that otherwise so indifferent December afternoon.

"Perhaps. But the universe in a grain of sand is one thing, in a speck of dust another. And isn't it reasonable to think that the cold war or whatever it was, the conflict between the two supervictors, would have developed anyhow, as the nearly inevitable outcome of the Second World War? Well, I shan't press that point. Now back to your dagger and your wound. You imputed that word *cynic* to a student in the audi-ence, but I think what pains you is that there must have been others who thought in somewhat the same way about your Polish hero—or antihero."

Yes. For example, a man in the question-and-answer period at-tacked the Pole—who, I repeat, was a rather courtly middle-aged gentleman—for being a detractor of the cause of the United Nations, a skeptic, a reactionary, a misanthrope. The man's name was Drabkin; he was a journalist, a Philadelphia correspondent of the *Nation* or of

the *New Republic,* a most unpleasant schemer, and not only because of the succession of his political opinions. My point is that the real cynics were Drabkin and his ilk, because they were neither innocent nor naive, knowing how to drape their suspicions and animosities in what to them seemed the seamless and comfortably spacious cloak of American idealism. Now, many men and women in that audience, including the two prime professors, did not particularly like Drabkin, but the sad thing is that they felt—or rather, thought it best to feel—closer to him than to the scholar-emigré from Poland.

"But at least one reason for that must have been that Drabkin really meant what he said. Didn't he?"

Probably—though Americans are often unable to distinguish sincerity from honesty. But the issue is not that. The issue is that so many people there were more suspicious of the Pole than of Drabkin or someone like him. You see, the problem is not now, and was not in 1943, American innocence or naïveté. People who are truly innocent or naive are not suspicious. The problem with American idealism goes deeper than that. It is an idealism resting on comfortable—and, at best, acceptable—illusions. On noncontroversial illusions. But idealism and realism are not at all contradictory. Only idealism and materialism are.

"And now what about American materialism?"

You know that answer, if answer it is. Americans are merely idealistic materialists, which is not the same as being materialist idealists. That is how the world sees them, and the world is wrong. To be an idealistic materialist may not be the best of worldviews, but it is the American saving grace.

"Even now?"

Ah, if I only knew! But not so long ago it was still so.

"Enough of this for now."

I agree.

1944

THE NIGHT OF July 20 is brilliant in Paris, velvety-soft after a sun-laden day, brilliant because of the canopy of stars and the light of the moon, even as the man-made lights in the windows and streets of the great city are dark because of the wartime blackout.

The streets are silent, but there is a rumble, not in the courtyards but in the minds of many of the people. They have heard the news: the attempt to kill Hitler, one thousand miles away in his forest headquarters on the sandy East Prussian plain. Radio Paris speaks: the attempt failed, Hitler lives. No matter: many Parisians know that their liberation is coming near.

And there is a moment of rumor and rumble in a small black-market restaurant somewhere in the rue Mouffetard or in the rue Solferino — no, not at Maxim's or at the Coq Hardi, which are favored and patronized by the German elite in Paris. The habitués of this little restaurant — whose *patron* has some connection with the Germans, but that is not the point — are a group of French intellectuals. There they sit and talk, with their rather typical intellectuals' faces, in that proto-typical setting with the dark wainscoting, the zinc bar at the far end of the room, with a faint smell of fowl and brandy seething together. They may or may not clink their glasses, but they breathe with relief. *Qu'il vive!* He lives. They are saved — by which they mean that France is saved, Europe is saved, their world is saved, thank God (in whom they do not believe, but that is not the point, either).

The attempt to kill Hitler on July 20, 1944, has been described often, mainly by German historians reconstructing the terrible drama of that day, hour by hour. The sun poured on the pine forests of East Prussia, where Hitler had his headquarters. Because of the sun he would live. His noon meeting with his officers had been moved to a wooden barrack cooler than the cement building — which is why the explosive force of the bomb that Count Stauffenberg slid under the table was dissipated.

The attempt failed.

The attempt had to fail.

It had to fail, not because of the weakened burst of the bomb or because of other failures of the conspiracy.

Had the bomb exploded in full force, had Hitler been killed, had the conspiracy succeeded, there would have been civil war in Germany: murder and mayhem in some of the cities, murderous firefights in some of the garrisons. The SS and the Waffen-SS and the party leaders and the *Gauleiters* would not have obeyed the small group of officers and civilians mostly unknown to them, the new pretenders to the supremacy of the German state, of the government of the Reich. The pretenders would have had to face hard, cynical, resolute men, men faithful to Hitler — and to Goebbels and Goering and Himmler.

And even if — which is very doubtful — the SS and the party leaders could have been successfully sequestered and disarmed, the minds of the vast majority of the German people, of German men and women and perhaps especially their children, would have been dark with bitterness.

On July 20, 1944, the German armies were standing and fighting many hundreds of miles beyond the frontiers of the Reich. Many German cities were already half-burned and half-ruined by the bombs of the Allies; but vast regions of German hills, fields, mountains, towns,

and villages were still untouched by the war. In 1918 the very commanders of the German army impressed upon the kaiser that they were
defeated. In 1944 there was no kaiser, but there was Hitler; after him,
nothing. After 1918 many Germans partook in the national wish to
believe that Germany had not really lost the war, that they had been
stabbed in the back by socialists, cosmopolitans, defeatists, pacifists,
slackers, profiteers, Jews. Had the bomb killed Hitler, what would they
have thought in 1944, and for many years thereafter? The stab-in-
the-back legend would have been more powerful than ever, because it
would have contained the bitter herbs and the baked meats of truth . . .
of a certain kind of truth.

The best the conspirators could hope for was a rapid ending of the
war—meaning an immediate agreement with Germany's enemies to
stop it, meaning the admission of the defeat of the Reich. And that hope
was forlorn: even (or, perhaps, especially?) with Hitler killed, none of
the Allies would have been ready or willing to abandon or perhaps even
to modify their claim for an unconditional German surrender.

Hitler said on the twentieth of July that he was saved by God's
will. Those of us who believe in the existence of God's will must also
know that this does not entitle us to assert how and when it occurs
in our lives. Yet there is more to this knowledge than unreasoning and
unhistorical faith. It may on occasion illuminate our self-knowledge,
which in the twentieth century includes a historical consciousness.
Simone Weil once wrote: "The object of our search should not be the
supernatural, but the world. The supernatural is light itself; if we make
an object of it we lower it." I am inclined to believe, as Hitler believed,
that the failure to kill him in 1944 may have been ordained by God. But
I am also inclined to believe (and not merely because I prefer to believe
it) that the Third Reich had to be (well, it was, wasn't it?) conquered in
its entirety in 1945, because the German people *had* to know that they,
their state and army and cause, were defeated; for them there must be
no doubt about their having lost this war.

On and after the twentieth of July perished the flower of the German, including the Prussian, aristocracy. (Yes, there were other barons,

counts, and princes fighting for Hitler and his Reich, including some even in the SS.) But there was a tragedy implicit in these conspirators' attempt. The best of them knew that even if they were to succeed, many of their people would regard them as traitors. They knew that *this* Germany had to lose the war. For their purpose was not to save the Reich but to save German honor, or what was left of it. German and European and Christian honor. Many of them were descendants of an older world where elements of nobility and of honor existed within a military tradition. Most of them went bravely to the gallows. It is meet and just that they have been commemorated in Germany after the war.

But there were few of them. And they were no match for the modern, popular, democratic soldiery that Hitler had brought forth: miners, mechanics, metalworkers, and meatpackers who became majors, colonels, and even generals in the Waffen-SS, the great soldiers of the Reich, the toughest fighters of the Second World War. There were multitudes of *them*. They were not blind. They were not fanatics. They were clear-sighted. They were cunning. In 1944 they knew, even if they would not openly admit it, that the war was no longer winnable, as it had been or seemed to be earlier. But they thought that the Reich was still preservable, saveable, by their fighting tough, by their keeping faith with the Führer. They would drive a hard wedge between their enemies, they would split their enemies, who did not deserve to win the war against them. In this there was a usually unspoken though at times expressed accord between Hitler and the SS and the majority of the German people in 1944 — indeed, almost till the last days of the war.

Hitler and Goebbels and German propaganda were insisting, without cease, on the unnatural — and, according to them, cynical and immoral — alliance of capitalists and Communists, of Anglo-Saxons and Russians. They used this argument for domestic as well as foreign purposes, not always unsuccessfully. Officially, in public, Hitler refrained till the end from telling the German people what the ultimate purpose of driving a wedge between his enemies, of splitting them, would mean: that is, to arrive at a settlement with one side or the other. But by July 1944 his entire strategy, political as well as military, included attempts to play West against East (and perhaps also the obverse). These attempts amounted to more than propaganda portraying Germany and Germans as the sole remaining bulwarks against the advance of Soviet Bolshevism. In June 1944 Hitler told the field marshal Kesselring to engage in negotiations with American generals about the Germans' evacuation of Rome. He tacitly allowed Himmler to establish contacts with American agents and officials about the fate of the remaining Jews in Hungary. Hitler's aim in his last, desperate counteroffensive in the West, in December 1944, was not to drive the Americans back toward Paris but to drive for Antwerp, splitting the British from the American armies and forcing Montgomery to retreat or surrender, and to make the Americans rethink the war. He was not ignorant of American politics and of currents of American popular sentiment: that, for one thing, the war against Japan was more popular among the American people than the war against Germany, and that some American congressmen and senators were beginning to voice their anxieties about the prospect of a Germany destroyed while Soviet power rose in its stead. Until the end of his life Hitler refused to tell the German people that they should prefer American to Soviet occupation. But in what were the last hours of his life, his appointment of his successors — Admiral Doenitz as president, Goebbels as chancellor — suggests his calculated wish to drive a last wedge between the Allies: Doenitz, the head of the German "conservative" navy and an admiral with a "Western" orientation, perhaps acceptable to the Americans; Goebbels the radical, perhaps acceptable to the Russians.

Now, these thoughts and wishes accorded with the thinking and instinctive inclinations of his followers and also of the German people at large. The German people had more and worse to fear from the avenging Russian hordes than from the Americans. (Their fear of the British was a more complex issue, which I must let pass.) Millions of Germans were fleeing from the advancing Russians in the east (a movement that Hitler tacitly allowed), while the civilian population stayed put in the west. In terms of German public opinion and popular sentiment — that is, of both German thinking and feeling — most believed not only that they had less to fear from Americans than from Russians (which was true) but that the Americans were regrettably misled and shortsighted, not willing or, more precisely, *not yet* ready to recognize that it was an enormous mistake to destroy the German Reich, which was, after all, the bulwark of European civilization against Asiatic Bolshevism; that during the Second World War Germany was fighting two different wars, one against the Western opponents of German greatness, the other against the Communist Soviet enemy of Germany *and* the West; and that the second war was justifiable, something that the Americans would do well to recognize, and soon. Fifty years after 1944, that belief is still widely current among Germans, expatiated upon even by some of their historians. But I am writing about 1944, not about 1954 or 1994. The tendency to impress Americans with evidences of German consideration and goodwill was evident in many instances in 1944. It was often instinctive and not always the result of confidential instructions handed down from above. One evidence of this was that the Germans often treated American prisoners of war much better than they treated the other prisoners. Other evidences were the frequent attempts (often by SS leaders) to enter into all kinds of possible negotiations with Americans. Yet another evidence was the insistence of the Germans in the West, and especially in France, that all anti-German resistance, whether by partisans, *franc-tireurs, maquis,* or Gaullists, was "Communist." That was the essential purpose of German politics, of police and military and propaganda politics: to impress Americans and certain Europeans (with the exception of the British, whom the Germans knew would remain unimpressed) that the Germans were fighting Communism, not only in the Baltics or the Balkans but also in the defense of "European civilization" in France.

The Germans believed that. But so believed, too, many of their subject peoples, even in France. What was going on in France in 1944 was more than the campaign for her liberation. There was a civil war in France, with mass executions on both sides, at least in part because of the many thousands of Frenchmen and Frenchwomen who believed that the defeat of Germany would be a catastrophe.

There is a drama, a psychic drama, latent in the histories of the men and women who were not Germans but who had committed themselves to Hitler's cause, because they saw his Germany as a great historic force against the insidious menaces of Communism and Judaism and the corrupt institutions of liberalism and capitalism, all of them instruments of decay. This was a new phenomenon in the history of Europe. Were these people opportunists? German agents? Traitors of their country? Some of them were; to some extent perhaps all of them were all of those things. But these categories are somehow insufficient. Especially in France. For an Austrian or Croatian or Ukrainian nationalist to throw his lot in with Hitler was lamentable but understandable. For a French criminal to throw in his lot with the Gestapo, to assist in its awesome cruelties and to profit therefrom (there were such men and women), was of course damnable but also plausible. But now consider such a man as Robert Brasillach. I admit that I can imagine him sitting at that table in that restaurant in Paris on the evening of July 20. He was a brilliant intellectual, a poet with a wide knowledge of many things, including the history of films. He was perhaps the most vivid, the most acute among the collaborationist intellectuals. His mind, even before the war, arrived at a stage where he admired Hitler and the new Germany, and he exhorted the French to heed his words. After the defeat of 1940 he called relentlessly for the destruction and indeed for the killing of Communists, Jews, Gaullists, Anglophiles, and resisters, for whom he had nothing but contempt and hatred. His voice was strong and clear. After the liberation of Paris he was imprisoned and tried. In prison and during his trial he was brave. He wrote poems and other things in prison. Among these he wrote one terrible thing. It was read during his trial: "I have allied myself with the genius of Germany. I shall never forget that. And, whether we want it or not, we have lain together with them. During these years all thinking French, in one way or another, slept with the Germans. And the memory of that will remain sweet." A terrible Parthian shot, because not devoid of a certain element of truth (perhaps feminine, rather than masculine) latent in his choice of metaphor.

Brasillach was executed in February 1945. During the winter of 1944–1945 De Gaulle commuted the death sentences of more than half of the collaborationists in prison. He refused to commute Brasillach's. Since that time De Gaulle has been criticized for that, and Brasillach's writings have been republished — often. Many French intellectuals, including resisters and Gaullists, had asked De Gaulle to spare Brasillach's life. He was an intellectual, after all. But: Are not people responsible not only for what they do but for what they say and for what they write? Isn't a word a deed? Or, at least, inseparable from a deed? Wasn't his hatred of his enemies so much stronger than his love of his country? A man ought not be brought to justice because he hates. But every expression of his hate — through deed or word — is justiciable, because of its consequences.

In December 1944, in the cold, dank, damp cells in the prison of Fresnes, there penetrated a surge of hope. Tight-lipped smiles appeared on the prisoners' faces. The rain poured outside, the trees rioted, and their branches bent in the wind. The Germans had broken through the American army in Belgium; they were approaching France again; the fortunes of the war may have changed. For a few days, perhaps for a week or so, the prisoners took heart. *La libération:* what a joke! De Gaulle, the Americans, the British — they may be fleeing soon. Again! The true liberators were Hitler and the Germans. They would return. They would arrive in France, again. Justice would triumph, in the end. Of course the very lives of these prisoners were at stake. But let us not forget: what they hoped for was more than their lives, it was a German reconquest of their country, of their people, of France. So — what kind of patriots were they?

"Well, I didn't interrupt this long fugue — perhaps it is a historical fugue, rather than a historical essay — even though I, and I presume you, too, know that it doesn't fit into this book of yours very well, or at all. I know why you were compelled to write this. First, you *are* a historian. Second, 1944 was a most formative year of your life; and that is second in order, not in importance. But you might have kept this for a separate historical essay."

I know that.

"All right, but why, then, that long disquisition about Hitler and the Germans? You could abbreviate it drastically and write about those French collaborationist intellectuals. Yes, you know a great deal about 1944 and all that, and I will allow you that you know and perhaps see things about that time and those people that others have not written or perhaps not even thought about. But does all that belong *here?* Isn't there an element of your self-indulgence at work here?"

Perhaps.

"And coming back to the 'self.' You need to explain what you mean when you write that our self-knowledge in the twentieth century includes a consciousness of history."

What I mean is that while Socrates was right—all knowledge must depend on or perhaps issue from self-knowledge—his immortal "Know thyself" and even Pope's "The proper study of Mankind is Man," must be complemented and deepened two thousand years later by our recognition that "Know thyself" now means "Know your history." Know your own history and the history of your times, which are not the same things, but they are inseparable. Such is the evolution of our consciousness.

"Which is the subject not of an essay but of an entire book."

1945

In 1945 THE WIND carries centuries in its mane.

In April 1945 the European war—the last European world war—
is near its end. On Saturday the twenty-first, American troops are deep
in the middle of Germany. Now they are entering the city of Leipzig.
There are small clouds of smoke and the crump and the rattle and the
sizzle of battle, but unlike in Berlin to the north, here it is intermittent
and not constant, with long minutes of an unearthly quiet. The April
weather is unseasonably cold, but the sky is bright and the linden trees
in the streets have begun to green and bud and the telephone still functions and so does most of the electricity.

At eleven in the morning Herr A., the city treasurer (*Schatzmeister*), lifts the receiver on his desk. He listens to the dial tone buzzing
for a long moment. Then he puts it down. He sits straight in his office
chair. Then he puts two pills in his mouth, bites down on one of them,
and in less than a minute he is dead.

It is a clean and orderly desk. Perhaps the leather-bordered pad
on the top will be slightly stained by the dead *Schatzmeister*'s saliva, but
it is still a clean desk, not cleared for a last stand but typical of this city
treasurer, unencumbered except for the telephone, an inkstand, a small
reading lamp, that large pad with its green blotting paper, and three or
four thick reference volumes standing stiff at its far left end: an orderly

desktop of an orderly man, this large bald German. This is how the American army photographers will find him, three hours later. They will be startled. It is a frozen scene, a still life of death, because across from that desk, a few feet away, two women, his wife and his daughter, are dead, too. Their skirts are properly pulled down, their eyes closed (did their husband and father close them?), their faces not distorted, though the daughter has slid halfway down from the sofa to the floor.

The treasurer was a party member, but he does not have the small round enamel party badge in the buttonhole of his stiff dark suit now. He is no last-ditch Nazi but a German civil servant who drew the consequences. His world, his German world, had collapsed. Beyond that he would not think or wish to live. He took his family with him. Had his wife and daughter ever talked to him, did they question his resolution? I doubt it. What was going on in their inner selves he of course did not know, and neither do I. I am inclined to think that *I* wish I knew, but he did not.

That Saturday afternoon, on April 21, 1945, in a hospital in Los Angeles, B., a German emigré musician, kills himself. He is a sick man with a cancerous bladder. His illness is not yet terminal; his pain grows and fades, it is endurable, perhaps particularly this afternoon. But he hopes for nothing, and he is in the depths of despair. He has no appetite for life left — or, rather, that is what he thinks, and for him thinking amounts to knowledge. He does not understand that some feelings are best ignored, which is what courage amounts to. But then courage also amounts to the numbing of fear, and his last act of courage is to reach for the strychnine pills. They are in one of the recesses of his wallet in the drawer of the night table. He swallows them, and in a few minutes he suffers a horrible death.

Now please consider that what I want to write about is not death but despair. What I am interested in are not motives but purposes. All modern psychology and even the present-day use of the language confuse the meanings of motives and purposes, more than often illegitimately so. But there is a profound difference between mechanical and human causality. Life amounts to the wish for more life, and when that wish flickers out and dies, we die. Every human action or thought is more than a reaction, because we are not merely pushed by the past but pulled by the future, by our own vision of the future. And when that wish for the future — any future — is extinct . . . Pirandello had a nice phrase: The dead are "les retraités de la mémoire." They have retired from memory, they are the pensioners of memory. True, but not true enough. Yes, everything — every human thought — depends on memory. But what made A. and B. kill themselves on a cruel April day? Was it some unbearable memory? No, not in their cases. It was their despair of the future, of their future.

There were many Germans who chose suicide at the end of the Third Reich. (This in itself was a significant phenomenon: few Communists chose to kill themselves when their rule collapsed.) It is at least interesting that many of these suicides were not committed Nazis, most of whom were or had become cynics and survivors with a sense of cruel humor. (I find it difficult to imagine a resolution to suicide coexisting with any spark of humor.) Our city treasurer was a humorless German — unfortunately not untypical of his generation. His very countenance reflected that: a big bald head and thick neck, small eyes, small nose, the thinnest of lips, a rigid mask that moved up into the officious rigidity of his eyes when looking at papers, people, the world. He was a nationalist, a Lutheran, a veteran of the First World War, *Deutschnational* in the twenties, and not a National Socialist but a believer in duty and in German greatness; in 1933 came Hitler, who was not entirely his favorite, but what a national leader Hitler turned out to be, and what a Reich he built and achieved! So he joined the party, at least partly because of conviction and not merely because of opportunism; his position in the city government was secure. And he followed all the orders and the regulations with utmost strictness. He was responsible, perhaps a bit old-fashioned; as the local Nazi *Gauleiter* remarked about him, "verantwortlich durch und durch." This was the fatal tragedy of Germany, then: the unquestioning and unquestionable obedience of such people as this superbureaucrat to the state, to the *Vaterland* — and now, as Hitler pronounced, to the *Volk*. And now the end of the Reich was at his doorstep.

He should have at least considered that the Americans were coming, not the Russians. He didn't: they were enemies of the Reich. He should have considered that his party membership did not condemn him to be executed: yes, at worst imprisoned for a while, but weren't there untold millions of party members in Germany? No: he could not imagine any life, and least of all a respectable life, in a city and a Reich occupied by the enemies of Germany. He could not, because he did not want to. The future for him and for his wife and for his daughter was not merely bleak: it did not exist. When he first spoke of the suicide plan to his family, he repeated a famous German saw: "Better an end with horror than horror without end." That sounds good, but it is very German. It seems to make sense, but really it doesn't.

There were not many Americans—certainly no refugees among them—who chose to kill themselves around the time of V-E Day. B., this refugee from Europe, did. Yes, he was ill with cancer. Yes, for him too, "better an end with horror" and so on. He thought that he had nothing to look forward to but pain, shame, and loneliness. He was fifty years old. His manhood was gone. If he was to live, the doctors said, there were chances but not the best ones, and he would have to live with a colostomy bag attached to him, day and night. He had no family here, and his last woman had left him. But above and beneath all this there coursed an intellectual feeling now hardened into a conviction, an acrid and black conviction that, his life aside, his world had arrived at its end. This, I believe, even more than the bladder cancer, made him decide on the strychnine pills. Perhaps I should describe this man in a little more detail. He had been a cellist in the Leipzig Philharmonic. He was gaunt, dark-haired, large-eyed and large-eared, large-lipped but talkative not at all, devoted not only to Bach and Haydn but to Rembrandt and Rilke, to Biedermeier cabinetry and the drawings of ships, to fish dishes and Sobranie cigarettes. He was a lonely man, an only child; his parents died young, he hardly recalled them at all. He was one of the Good Germans. One of those who chose to leave the Germany of Hitler, even though his existence was not threatened there, either for racial or for political reasons. He went at first to Switzerland, then to France; he was an excellent cellist, but refugee musicians were a dime a dozen. He played here and there in provincial orchestras and survived in his great loneliness. In 1940 he got his American visa — late, even though his name had been inscribed on the quota lists years before, but others pressed and elbowed their way before him. He arrived in New York, where he did not have the right connections, and then to Los Angeles and Hollywood, where he had a few jobs, though eventually he had to accept a fixed post in a movie orchestra.

There was a large refugee colony around Los Angeles then, its members ranging from Thomas Mann to Bertolt Brecht: writers, artists, musicians, movie people, scriptwriters, intellectuals of every kind. There was even a salon of sorts in Beverly Hills where they regularly gathered, with plenty of Central European argle-bargle, most of it in German, some in English. He felt out of place there. The relentless sunshine of southern California blinded him and darkened his inner eye. In 1942 he met a Czechoslovakian girl who left him in 1944. (But then women never played the most important roles in his life.) He was lonelier in California than in that wretched pension in Zurich with its soupy smells, than in the dank provincial hotels in Nancy or Dijon with their horrid wallpapers, than in the furnished room on West Ninety-Sixth Street in New York. He had no friends, only acquaintances. He knew a few Americans and liked some of them; most of his fellow Central Europeans he did not like. They were bombinating in the sunshine, resounding with ideas of and about the world. The war was ending in Europe. Good things had come to them in America, and now they were ready to tell the Germans what they deserved. He thought about the devastation of Germany. In his notebook were the addresses of his remnant relatives and a few remnant friends. Would he now write them, would he now contact them, would he return to them? He turned his mind away from that. Then he became ill. He read Stefan Zweig's *World of Yesterday — Die Welt von Gestern —* written shortly before Zweig's suicide in Brazil in January 1942. He kept thinking and thinking about that. Zweig also could not face the world of tomorrow; Zweig, who had been healthy and safe and respected in Brazil, chose to die. He, B., is very ill and about to die. So . . . ?

In the city treasurer's room in Leipzig, an ugly clock in its dark oak Wilhelminian cabinet on the wall goes on ticking; it is ticking at two o'clock when the American army photographers come through the door. I doubt that the *Schatzmeister* took a last glance at the clock, for, if he had, he might have walked across the room (stepping over the legs of his daughter?) in order to stop it. On the white and shiny walls of the hospital in Los Angeles, an electric clock is relentlessly moving and humming. Our man looked at it before the last minutes of his life. There it was, the American world of Today adding up to Tomorrow, the New World forever, with enormous and growing hospitals and airports, all electrically humming. Immutable Progress.

"I know what you're after: Hollywood was as bad as the Third Reich in 1945. That won't get you very far, and it will be misunderstood by many people. There is no equivalence there, and hardly any connection. Besides, your two men are very different."

Of course. And of course I have more sympathy for B. than for A. I am sorry for B., and perhaps sorry for Frau A. and for Fräulein A., but I think that A. was a very stupid man. Stupidity, of course, is not a sin, except when it is willful, and in this German civil servant it *was* willful. All I can say is, God have mercy on their souls—on all of them. But there is one more thing I want to say.

"You have already said enough—or, rather, too little."

Yes, you are right,—though this is not a short story or a novel. But what I want to say is that both of them were foolish, and so was Stefan Zweig in 1942. Well, foolishness is not a sin, but suicide is. And because it is a sin, it is not really practical.

"Sin is not practical?"

It is often practical but only in the short run. Pleasurable, yes.

Practical, no. Consider old Zweig. A little less despair and he would have survived, comfortably, in Brazil. He would have survived not only the war but The World of Yesterday. Soon after the end of the war he would have been welcomed in Austria and Germany, been greeted with flowers offered by some who had betrayed him and by many others who had denied him, but what does that matter? In 1945 and thereafter there was a good deal of appetite for The World of Yesterday and for people who claimed it and belonged to it—many would have been ready to receive and adorn the famous exile writer, returning without much remorse. In sum, he spared himself a good lot of old-age happiness.

"Would Zweig have been at home in that ruined Vienna after the war?"

Perhaps not in Vienna but in Salzburg. He would have complained that things and people were not what they had been, but then this was true of everyone else, too. But let us not talk about Zweig. That stupid A.! All right, he would have lost his job, a city position, and would have had to go through a difficult year or two of de-Nazification, but nothing much else would have happened to him. Four or five years after the war he would live in a small modern apartment somewhere in Württemberg or Baden, perhaps even with a federal government pension, his daughter married to an American captain with whom he in the evenings could discuss the evil threat of Communism.

"And B. could have met a warm-hearted American nurse, Miss Tender Loving Care, and eventually gotten rid of the colostomy bag and perhaps even played cello again, if not in a great orchestra then in a well-paying television one."

You are not a cynic, and you ought not talk this way. I do not know what would have happened to him, and I doubt whether he would have lived long with that cancer of his. What I am certain of is that he would have had moments, perhaps long moments, of comfort and maybe even of happiness. Not only is our existence God's greatest gift to us, but His other gift to us is that life is unpredictable. I am not saying that death is not a change of state; what I am saying is that life is a long chapter of consciousness that is not for us to terminate.

"What you say is what French telephone operators kept saying to callers before France-Telecom became fully automated."

What was that?

" 'Ne quittez pas.' And you, too—go ahead. But watch out. You are always taken by coincidences. I suppose you chose the end of April 1945 because it was then that the Reich was cut in two, when the first Americans coming from the West were to meet the first Russians coming from the East."

Yes, that was really the end of an age and the beginning of a new one, even though it happened five days before Hitler killed himself and almost a fortnight before the Germans laid down their arms—the end of an age even more than the end of a war. Year Zero, 1945. What has stuck in my mind for a long time is the surrealism of 1945—the surrealism, for example, of the fantastic contrast between, say, life in Berlin and life in Hollywood, 1945. People dying and crawling in the ruins of Berlin, people sunning themselves in California. There was this connection: Goebbels admired Hollywood, and not only the technology but some of the scriptwriters' creations, which he wanted to emulate— even as in Hollywood a goodly number of the scriptwriters and composers in 1945 were refugees from Berlin.

"Well, wasn't there a difference between life at the court of Versailles and life at the court of Peking, say, in 1789 or 1689?"

Yes, but there was no connection there then. Now let me go out on a limb: there is something surrealistic in these very figures, *1945,* which pull in different directions. The *19* marks the twentieth century, of course; the *4* is a German number, a marching number; and now it is followed by the jaunty, bow-legged American *5,* a colt number, an American figure, a cowboy cipher, a Far Western year. And not far from California, under a brazed and burnished sky, in the American West—yes, that was a Far Western year—men put together a new kind of fire, as the Indians had once done in the unrecorded and unhistoric past, in the desert. They constructed a bomb from the electric particles of matter. Most of the scientists had also come from Germany; they grew up in gray *Mietkasernen,* dark Wilhelminian apartment houses in the gloomy streets of Central European cities. And now they were in the western American desert, in baggy suits pinned with badges marking their persons, chattering and excited under the complicated eyes of their American military masters, alternately wringing and clapping their hands as the hour of the sorcerer's apprentice drew near. And in 1945 there were fluorescences on the shining pages of *Life:* photographers with odd names like Ivan Dmitri or Gjon Mili, strange names that foreshadowed the names of the shadowless, dead-white, poisonous coral isles of the atomic age: Rongelap, Etorofu, Eniwetok . . .

"You stopped short of Bikini."

That was in 1946.

"You began this with a sentence: 'In 1945 the wind carries centuries in its mane.' Good, it is all right for a historian to employ poetry — once in a great while — but is it your job to bag the wind?"

The Ribbon

Y **1915** men and women of English, Welsh, Scottish, and Scotch-Irish origins in America were already a minority. An ever smaller minority, but they still composed the ruling class in American society, and they were still the people ruling American institutions and corporations and professions and businesses and even opinion making, which was something that Germans and other Europeans failed to understand. And by **1916** the sons of this Anglo-Saxon and Protestant American upper- and upper-middle class, believers in their kind of an athletic Christianity, were coming into accord with many other Americans eager to demonstrate their manhood and their Americanism in a Good War that would also be the end of all wars. And by **1917** this great and inchoate American nationalism — for that was what it was, inextricably mixed with an American type of idealism — swept the United States into the war. Inchoate and split-minded: because Americanism and globalism, nationalism and internationalism, isolationism and imperialism, coexisted, often in the same minds. And in **1918** came the end of the war, together with the end of monarchies, not only of the German imperial one but also of the Austro-Hungarian and the Turkish and of course the Russian ones, meaning Russia's withdrawal from Europe (for that was really what the Bolshevik Revolution had meant, all its vaunted Communist internationalism notwithstanding). And the really revolutionary idea was not the international Communism propagated by the Tartar-skulled fanatic Lenin but the doctrine of national self-determination, its prophet the pale puritanical professor Wilson, and now there were Englishmen and Welshmen and Scotsmen who thought that to be useful—a different breed of public men, to whom the older, more aristocratic managers of British foreign policy had given way. And by 1919 short-lived revolutions had flared and then burnt out in many places in Middle Europe, with its cities harboring political refugees who thought that the failure of *their* revolutions was only temporary, that they were still clever investors in the Wave of the Future—but that future would be something very different from what they thought or could even imagine. And by 1920 the chaos that bubbled in Europe after the war began to diminish. Paris (for a short time) was a *ville lumière* again, with new groups of Americans arriving at a time when *à l'américain* was a fashionable phrase because fashion began to be influenced by things American. And by 1921 New York was still the city of promise, though in that year mass immigration to the United States was closed by a new strict law, one of the great milestones in American history. And by 1922 "the fiddles tuning up all across America" (as John Butler Yeats, the poet's father, put it circa 1912) could be heard, here and there, across the Republic—yes, America may have had its large share of Babbitts, but that was the year when *Babbitt,* ironizing them, was a best-seller. And this was because the twenties were probably the only *modern* decade.

By 1923 something more important and more lasting than the many political revolutions of the previous years, including the Russian one, was happening: a drastic breakaway from the past, on so many levels and fields of life, ranging from automobilization through architecture and art and music to verse and speech and behavior, from new mental clothes tried on to clothes worn or not worn—a lasting trademark of this transitional twentieth century (a movement whose reappearance in the sixties would be raucous but feeble-minded). And one thing that the proponents and addicts of "modern" did not comprehend was that by 1924 something new had arisen in sunny Italy and something more ominous was growing in a dark-paneled Germany: new movements for a new order that was both nationalist and modern. *Modern,* because Mussolini's Italy was more modern than Ramsay MacDonald's or Stanley Baldwin's Britain or in some ways Calvin Coolidge's United States. And by 1925 the recognition that Britannia had become gray-haired and that her ancient manners and hypocrisies had ceased to be venerable saturated the minds of its bright and not so bright young men and women: the British social contract still held (as the failure of the great national strike the following year would demonstrate), but the old ways of thinking were becoming hollow, including the idea of empire. And by 1926 it was evident—or, again, it should have been evident for those American expatriates milling in cafés of Paris—that the cultural center, the intellectual, artistic, cerebrating capital of Europe, was no longer Paris, with its waiters and ancient corrupt politicians in their rusty black coats, but the Berlin of the Weimar Republic. And by 1927 more things were stirring under the German surface in the provinces, a new kind of cohabitation of the old and the new, while in Coolidge's America, including New York, the German element in the American democracy was coming up, ranging from the Broadway moguls through Alfred A. Knopf and H. L. Mencken. Yes, the German element was rising, as a perceptive American wrote two years later: "the German with which, I regret to say, we Americans have more in common than we have with the English." He wrote this when Grant Wood created his famous painted asseveration in which the faces, the glasses, the stances, the countenances of the grim American couple are German, not Anglo-Saxon (consider but the faded blonde Gretchen hairdo of the farmer's wife). The title of his painting is *American Gothic:* but *American* mattered more than *Gothic,* even as in 1928 America, with its masses of automobiles and skyscrapers and Hollywood movies, was ahead and yet not ahead of Europe, because of the still prevailing half-puritan materialism and the institutions and ideology of its people, with its nineteenth-century capitalism that had broken up in Europe in and after the war but that lasted, sort of, in America until 1929. But then, too, what crashed was Wall Street, not America. Amazing, in retrospect, was the endurance of the political and, yes, even of the social institutions of the United States during the Depression— the Depression during which evidences of a revolutionary spirit were few and which often brought families closer together and which hardly touched certain portions of society, even after 1930, when the waves of the Wall Street quake had reached the walls of many an American house.

But in Europe, especially in the center of Europe, things were different. By 1931 there were signs and symptoms—even in England—that the tide of dissatisfaction with the bourgeois and capitalist and parliamentary and liberal order, with its evident corruptibility and lassitude, was rising. It was or, rather, it should have been obvious that across the world there was now a new triangular configuration: Communism, represented and incarnated by Soviet Russia; democracy, or at least constitutional and parliamentary democracy, represented and incarnated by some of the states of western and northern Europe and primarily by the English-speaking nations of the world; and a third force, wrongly called Fascism (it was in reality nationalist socialism), soon to be represented and incarnated principally by Germany. And this triangular constellation of political and ideological forces would then be repeated across the globe, even in the Far East, and within almost every country and nation. And by 1932 in Germany Hitler was the leading political figure, preparing for his assumption and waiting for his installation of power. By 1933 he was the chancellor and soon thereafter the leader of a new German Reich; few people, perhaps especially in England and America, recognized what that meant. There were Englishmen and Englishwomen who, in 1934, distantly but at least in part favorably viewed what the new order in Germany was accomplishing. (And that, because of the slow momentum of opinions, contributed to the appeasement policy of Chamberlain and his ilk during the crucial years later.) But not in the United States, where, by 1935, President Roosevelt had the trust of the majority in whose everyday lives and in whose everyday thinking there were no revolutionary changes. But the superpatriotic flood of enthusiasm that had propelled America into the European war twenty years before by 1936 was succeeded by another great surge of American exceptionalism: the determination not to get involved in Europe's conflicts ever again. Because of the slowness of the movement of public opinion, the popularity of an American isolationism (an imprecise term) reached its peaks in 1937, at the very time when Mussolini and Hitler had begun to transform the political map of Europe (and the Japanese that of Asia). The British, closer to Europe, were forced to react, though quite reluctantly; in 1938 they and their government were still willing to acquiesce in a German domination of Central and of much of Eastern Europe; but by 1939 they felt compelled to realize that this might eventually mean Hitler's domination of much of the entire continent. And so they tried to deter Hitler by a definite British commitment to Poland. But this failed, and they went to war, still reluctantly, and at a time when the minds of most Americans were still divided. Those Americans who did not wish to go to war against Germany were not really pacifists, and those who wished to fight Hitler were not militarists: remnant elements of American innocence and other American inclinations to split-mindedness existed still. And then in 1940 Hitler came close to winning his war. Only Britain, led by Churchill, stood in his way. But the British alone could not subdue him or even defend themselves successfully without the full support of the United States. They represented old freedoms and perhaps the entire cause of civilization, but there were not enough of them. And they had an American president on their side who by 1941 was able to marshal the beliefs and the energies of most Americans for the construction of a vast arsenal of democracy, engaged more or less on the side of Britain, though it had to be the Japanese who finally pushed the United States wholly into the war. And by 1942 America and Russia mattered more in the ultimate balance of the world than Britain and Germany and Japan. And by 1943 most Americans accepted their alliance with Russia unquestioningly, wishing to leave their minds undisturbed by what it might mean if (or when) Stalin's domination would replace Hitler's, at least in the eastern portion of Europe. And by 1944 the first signs of a future American-Russian division of Europe began to appear, and Hitler and the Germans knew this, as did their now dwindling but committed and bitter collaborators across Europe. And by 1945 the war was over, in a year that was to be called Year Zero in Germany, while from the United States the floodlights of Hollywood and mirages of California still shone across much of the world, and through whose skies now burst the atomic bomb, first flaring in the western American desert not far from Las Vegas, whose creation began in the same year.

1946

ON A MILD SUNDAY EVENING in late August 1946, much of Chester County, in Pennsylvania, is verdant, undulant, radiant. Radiant because of the remnant blessing of an auriferous sun, which has begun to set in the west, but radiant in an intangible way, too, through the evening benison that the cooling air and the view of the soft countryside breathes into the souls of those fortunate enough to contemplate it. The men and the women dining on a terrace feel this, if only as a relief after a sequence of damp, hot days and nights that had made the sky a dirty gray canvas overall, with a broiling sun pressing the heat downward; and now there is a cool peacefulness all around.

It is also 1946, the American interval between the Second World War and the Cold War, but they don't know that. That is not of central importance for this vignette, where I want to describe the people, yes, but first a word about the arcadian character of this county where, unlike in the American West, the land has been made into a landscape. It has been so for a fairly long time, in part because of the placid grace of its undulating hills, in part because of the cultivation of its rich fields, in part because of the houses scattered along the country roads or tucked away in the green bowers of Pennsylvanian vegetation. In 1946 the mass suburban movement from Philadelphia has not yet begun, and Chester County is rural and private rather than fashionable. The few

occasional foreign visitors in this part of eastern America are sometimes amazed to find themselves gazing with envy and admiration at
isolated country houses suddenly visible at the end of unexpected lanes
between overarching trees, with their gardens and fieldstone walls—
and their rooms inside with a goodly share of old Philadelphia furniture, tall-case clocks, sideboards, girandoles, and small gilded mirrors,
the whole overlaid with the potpourri scent of freshly brushed rugs
and lemon-oil polish and flowers in ironstone pots everywhere. American domesticity at its best, prevailing during the rising tides of mass
democracy. And untouched by the world war that has roared across
Europe and England, leaving nothing unaltered.

On this terrace of a house near the hamlet of Chester Springs,
eight people are sitting down to dine. Below the darkening emerald of
a lawn, the last orange streaks of the sun are retreating from the burnished surface of a large pond, its smoothness disturbed only by the
slow, silent wake of two beautiful and malevolent swans. All the other
birds have quieted down; the only noise comes from the kitchen, where
the cook is clattering and clashing her tins. A pair of geese waddle lei-
surely across another lawn, behind which rises a rich green cornfield.

But this is not a typical Chester County house. It is modern, or
at least largely so. Its architect (one of the diners) added to the original small fieldstone farmhouse, enlarging it for its present owners and
adding white, curved concrete walls and large expanses of glass, including sliding doors opening to a terrace that is paved not with stone
or brick but with slate (the same slate repeated around the hearth of
the fireplace), with the purpose, willingly agreed to by the owners,
of making living room and terrace "organically" one, an "all-weather
living room." (This does not always work, since few things are less
cozy than a glass-walled modern room when it is raining outside, no
matter how the logs blaze in the fireplace.) The setting of the house is
not compromised, however, and the view remains beautiful. There are
a few modern chairs and tables inside, because of their owners' wish
for modernity—they are people who cannot deal with an idea unless
it is tied up in a package of sorts. That condition affects their conver-

sation, too. But I will be neither hard on them nor sarcastic at their expense. They are Philadelphians, and they are therefore behind their times, which should be an asset, though they do not think so.

Two of their guests this evening are K. and his wife, Anne, neighbors from a few miles away, connected to their hosts by background and upbringing and also other things (one of K.'s watercolors, for example, hangs in the hall). Connected, too, by reciprocal respect: the hosts respect artists, while K. respects their interest (as well as their large chunks of liberal opinions, made palatable by the sauce of their traditional, meaning good, manners). Our self-conscious K. is now forty-six years old and has less money than his hosts, whom he has known for many years. Perhaps especially this evening he enjoys a feeling that he is comfortably at home here with them. So is Anne, who enjoys it every bit as much but with not a trace of self-consciousness, perhaps because rather than in spite of her indifference to the politics of the general conversation. Unlike at other such dinner parties of Philadelphians in 1946, here the women do not depart from the table and go upstairs for half an hour, leaving the men to themselves. She is content talking mostly to her friend the hostess about feminine matters, domestic affairs and gardening and slightly gossipy subjects, while they enjoy the soft coming of the night.

And now, quickly, something about the other people, including the hosts. Within the pale mosaic of what goes under "society" in Philadelphia (it is a mosaic rather than a kaleidoscope because it changes not much, surely not in 1946, and when it changes, it does so slowly), they are a liberal, intellectual, Democratic subgroup in the country, and "Philadelphia" socially includes places even forty miles out. They take some self-conscious comfort from having opinions that are more liberal, more progressive, and more generous than those of other people. This is true of the hostess, too, a handsome woman with much inherited money, one or two of her striking features still very evident, who is less talkative than her New England counterparts, though that is her family's provenance. Her husband, a lawyer, also has inherited wealth, and he has given up his law practice, serving instead on the boards of a number of institutions with interests ranging from Archaeology to Planned Parenthood, among which his trusteeship of the University Museum keeps him especially busy. And there is a celebrated Philadelphia city planner who only a few years before advocated the razing of City Hall for a supermodern parking garage, though he no longer advocates such things; in 1946 the revival of Victorianism is around the corner (perhaps he knows that, perhaps he doesn't). And the architect of this renovated house, a squat Russian European in an ice cream–colored suit, who has chosen a public career in which he would earn the reputation of being a Philadelphia counterpart to Oscar Niemeyer, Marcel Breuer, Richard Neutra, Walter Gropius, Mies van der Rohe, Le Corbusier, and the rest—advantageously so, because in mid-twentieth-century Philadelphia, as Arthur Young once wrote about mid-eighteenth-century England, "people often alternate between a supercilious neglect of genius and a rhapsodical pursuit of quacks." (Substitute "acceptance" for "pursuit," and there you have Philadelphians to a tee.) The last couple are new neighbors whom the hostess, generous as she is and open-hearted, thought it would be nice to invite. They are the sort of young marrieds who flourished in Eastern America between, say, 1946 and 1956, who collected books and art with somewhat less enthusiasm than they would, on occasion, collect and refinish old farming implements and who might choose family names for the first names of their children. They are well mannered, well dressed, and rather quiet as they listen to the progressive opinions with which some of the conversation is liberally sprinkled. They are readers of the *Philadelphia Inquirer* and not of the *New York Times,* the large, torpid Sunday remnants of which still lie on some of the steel-and-chrome chairs of the living room. All in all, they think, without much of an inclination to emulate them, that they are in the company of very smart, sophisticated people.

What they do not know is something that Jakob Burckhardt wrote about seventy or eighty years before: the danger of all kinds of things becoming possible "mainly because there are everywhere good, liberal people who do not really know the boundaries of right and wrong and it is there that the duty of resistance and defense begins." But then patricians of Basel in 1866 were not like patricians of Philadelphia in 1946.

✳   ✳   ✳

"I think I know what you're after, in which case you might have included someone like Alger Hiss at this dinner party."

It was Hiss's wife, Priscilla, who was a Philadelphian, not he. But you are not entirely off the mark, because Hiss was close to the kind of eastern seaboard Quaker type who inclined to Communism—a period type, say, 1936 to 1946. And yes, Hiss, who was still *in floribus* in 1946, could have been a very welcome guest in this house and among these people at that time; they would have recognized his provenance, with his smooth mannerisms (note that I say *mannerisms* rather than *manners*), and his reputation and situation in Washington, so wonderfully close to the great wheels turning in the evolution of the world. You are, however, off the mark, because none of these people have really strong political inclinations—and, I believe, neither had Hiss. He was an ambitious bureaucrat, self-serving, a one-time homosexual, a quintessential Progressive: a man with a very weak character, which is why he was toying with Communism, in which he thought he saw but another means to eventually becoming an important member of a professional and intellectual and governmental elite. And about these people on that pleasant terrace, too: their political ideas are only the consequences of their self-conscious intellectual elitism: they are not radicals, they are progressives. When that rumpled and unattractive Whittaker Chambers appears on the national scene, they are inclined to believe Hiss rather than Chambers, though not forever. The case of Hiss will be but one of their minor and ephemeral disillusionments.

"All right. Now let's have some fun with names. Priscilla is a quintessentially Philadelphia Quaker name. And given the New England provenance of your hostess, isn't her name Libby?"

No, you're missing again. Yes, Libby is quite New England, but all the Libbys are intellectual, and this woman is determinedly not that. Which is in her favor, and may even help in preserving her good looks.

"And the young marrieds, with your attribution of their avocation, collecting old farm machinery. Don't tell me that they do not christen their children Ken and Gail."

No, they are not Young Republicans, though she will do a stint with the Junior League. I don't know their childrens' names; I know only that while they may be a little pretentious, they will not be absurd, like the Tiffanys and the Brittanys of the 1980s.

"Or Italians and Greeks giving their children names such as Drew or Kyle. I now read in the papers about Drew Mangiacavallos and Kyle Di Ciccos. But back to your vignette. You know that you have a duality about these people, or about some of them. Or, worse, a split mind and conflicting inclinations. You love this part of the country, and you like most of the people who live here, while at the same time you dislike some things about them, including some of their ideas and their occasional cant."

It isn't cant. It is at worst a substitution for faith and at best a kind of existential — existential, rather than social — dissimulation. The host, for example, has been brought up never to say anything bad about anyone.

"No matter what he thinks?"

Ah, that is a difficult question. I don't know. There is my conviction, contrary to Freud and perhaps also to Joyce, that speech is not merely the result of thought but that it often goes the other way, with habits of speech affecting and even forming habits of thought. If someone believes that he ought never to say anything bad about other people, he will — well, at least in some cases — *try* not to think anything bad about them, either.

"Does this mean that this man, the host, is not really a radical, though he may be a fool?"

No, he is not a fool, except perhaps in the unstinting rigidity with which he believes in Science, including Darwinism, Carbon Dating,

Progressive (including Sex) Education, Pre-Columbian Art, Mayan Architecture, and so on. He and his friends, including couples, join the University Museum people on archaeological expeditions, or what they call "digs," to Guatemala. In the 1940s these excursions are as social as they are scientific; some of the Best People fly down there, braving (if that is the word) the mud, the bad smells, and ceaseless cloudbursts of mosquitoes. And now, risking a bad metaphor, here is a proof that he is a good liberal rather than a good radical: once he was trying to break a tough, rotting Indian root with his shovel, but it wouldn't give, and some of the others laughed as the shovel kept jumping and ringing in his hands.

"You mean that he tried to get at the roots and couldn't. Isn't that true of almost all radicals?"

No, because he then gave up and laughed with the others, being a gentle man that he was and is.

1947

IN THE PENNSYLVANIA RAILROAD'S *The Senator* sits L. P. Applebach, the Edgar Fahs Smith Professor of History in the University of Pennsylvania, on his way to Washington. He was thinking of traveling on the Baltimore & Ohio, whose station at Twenty-Fourth and Chestnut is closer to his home than the Thirtieth Street station of the Pennsylvania. But he would have had to walk fast to catch the B&O train, and there was a Pennsylvania train forty minutes later, this on a pleasant late September morning on which he allowed himself a comfortable walk to the station and a comfortable club car ticket (knowing that his expenses will be reimbursed). Having descended through the bowels of the station to a dark and chilly platform, he was pleased to see Thomas Royal Baker, the chairman of the board of trustees of the university, waiting for the train on the same platform.

Presently they sit in adjoining chairs in the club car. Baker is crossing and uncrossing his bony legs; Applebach is rotund, with enough of a civic paunch to keep him from crossing his short legs too often. Baker is not a particularly pleasant man; he speaks not much, and listens only when he thinks he must. He is very conscious of his Philadelphian status. He calls Applebach "L. P." (for about a decade now; before that it was "Doctor," and before that "Applebach"), who is conscious of his position, too, for instance now, comfortable with his situation in this club car together with Baker, the two of them representative of the Areopagus of the university, aware of their classifiable appearance as two influential gents, Baker in his dark gray, he in his dark blue suit and with a thin gold chain and the PBK key across his midriff.

After having read his paper and putting it away, Baker swivels his chair a little, and they talk about university politics, but now when the train roars across the flat scrublands of Delaware, their talk turns to national affairs. They are Republicans, though they are not isolationists (having converted to Aid to Britain some time around October 1940). Now, in September 1947, they exchange their commiserating remarks about the state of the world, with Communism advancing across Europe and Asia because of the breezy irresponsibility of Franklin Roosevelt and the motley crowd that he had brought to Washington, most of whom are still around now, when the Republic is saddled with Truman, this prototype of a common man—vulgar, petty, and ignorant.

But things are about to change. Applebach does not know, and knows better than to ask, what brings his trustee to Washington. He himself is on his way to a meeting of the board of the Social Science Research Council, in his capacity as the delegate of the American Philosophical Society; he is one of the *augusti* among the American academic establishment, and he knows that. Now a new man appears in the swaying and rocketing club car. For a moment he hesitates, but then he waves to Applebach. As he walks by they talk for a minute or so, Munroe Whitman telling Applebach not to get up; then Baker turns his chair around a whit and without saying a word offers his hand, desultorily, gruffly. They shake hands, too, and Whitman saunters on, whereupon Applebach finds it politic and proper to discuss Whitman with Baker. Well, Whitman was one of those who made a career in Washington during the war; professor of political science and international relations at the university, he joined the OSS in 1943 and stayed in Washington after the war, first in some adjunct position at the State Department and now with the European Recovery Program or whatnot. Applebach tells all this to Baker, who grunts.

Things are about to change because the Roosevelt era is past, with its damaging illusions about many things, primarily about Communism and Russia. There is a turn in the course of the great American ship of state, and there will be replacements among its officers. Applebach knows this; Baker doesn't. When Baker says something to the effect that the Marshall Plan is just more bureaucracy, more money going down the drain, Applebach does not say much — a combination of silence and discretion is a smart thing to observe — perhaps because he does not take such a statement from Baker at its face value. At the same time, Applebach knows that Whitman, circa 1943, was a member of the American-Soviet Friendship Council and that Whitman had cut loose of whatever leftist associations he may have had — information that Applebach does not impart to Baker (given that he himself had given his name to support the establishment of a Philadelphia chapter of the council at the time), while he finds it proper to make a few derogatory remarks about some of the people who worked for the oss during the war. In sum, Applebach is comfortable with the knowledge that he is somewhere in the middle between Baker and Whitman, though fortunately situated closer to the first; between directors of the Pennsylvania Railroad and assistant secretaries of state; between the political ideas of, say, Senator Robert A. Taft and Secretary of State General Marshall.

And then the train rolls into Union Station, and after he has marched through its cavernous halls there is broad sunlight, an ocean of a big, blue and white sky; and driven in a taxi through the wide avenues of Washington, Applebach knows that things are and will be different now: these impressive vistas have changed, they have become ever more impressive, they have become great, shining and spacious, for this is now The Capitol Of The World.

Yes, in 1947 Washington has become The Capitol Of The World. There is nothing contrary in the prospects of these three people. They will see the world in much the same way; they probably already do. Containment, Marshall Plan, NATO—they will all accept it, some sooner, some later, which is the American way. And they will profit from it, now and then, though not as much as Dwight David Eisenhower, who will have Baker's and Applebach's and Whitman's vote in 1952. There is only one unpleasant element in all this: their snide remarks about the recent political history of the Republic—in Whitman's but also in Applebach's case—with a slight, though unacknowledged, feeling of discomfort. For not so long ago, they were among those who saw America as being properly in the middle between old imperialist Britain and rough pioneer Soviet Russia. That was their idea of the proper American course through the war and the coming peace—and also of America's progressive destiny through the ages. Now they are inclined to think and feel that that Rooseveltian view of the world was of course wrong, that giving Stalin and the Soviets the benefit of the doubt was an episode in the history of the Republic that must be rejected or at least forgotten. Its proponents will now be tried in the court of public opinion, and Applebach and Whitman will have nothing to do with them. Their disassociation with that view of the world—and with its former proponents, including some of their acquaintances and associates—has already begun.

"I have two objections. First, you have said and argued often that the United States should have geared itself up to oppose Stalin much earlier than in 1947. You have had no sympathy for some of those Rooseveltian illusions. But now you suggest that they were better than what came afterward?"

Not at all. I just said that there was nothing very wrong with The Capitol Of The World in 1947. (It was more than the Capitol Of The Free World—a somewhat silly and inaccurate phase.) I still prefer Whittaker Chambers to Alger Hiss, even as I know that there was plenty that was wrong with Chambers, because of his dogmatic and self-indulgent view of the world. I mean what he wrote in *Witness,* that the greatest struggle in the history of the world since the birth of Christ was the one between Communism and America, and that he was the focus at the center of that global drama—both of these obsessions being wrong, wrong, wrong. But these three gents on the train were devoid of the private spiritual tortures of old Chambers.

"Well, then, let's proceed to our old favorite, Samuel Johnson: 'Intentions must be gathered from acts.' Your Baker is an old Republican stiff, Applebach is a chortling academic philistine, Whitman is an intellectual operator—but they will not oppose the American commitment to stand up against Stalin. After all is said, they will be on the same side in 1947, and isn't that enough?"

In many ways it is. But then, each in his own way, they will be responsible for the rise of Dulles and of McCarthy and of untold others, and for the damages they will cause. Allow me to repeat once more, however: there was something majestic in Washington having become The Capitol Of The World in 1947 . . .

"Acheson wrote that book of his, *Present at the Creation*."

That was both pompous and untrue. Acheson was not present at the creation, but he was present at its packaging. But, whether creation or packaging, there was something not uninspiring about American might in 1947, as benevolent a might as could be expected from the greatest power at the pinnacle of the world, at any time.

"One more thing. You have it in for the Applebachs and the Whitmans, but how about Baker? Does he really belong in this picture? Or did you set him up for the straight man in your scene?"

No. Baker may belong in this scene to set up Applebach, but there is something else, too: he and his type are already outdated in 1947—though neither the Applebach nor the Whitman types know that. Remember what I wrote about that rocketing club car. The roadbed of the Pennsylvania Railroad in 1947 is none too smooth, because the directors of the Pennsy—Baker is one of them—had already chosen to invest as little as possible in maintaining and upgrading their passenger services and their tracks, for passenger traffic has ceased to be profitable, while freight still is. Fifteen years later they will switch their investments into hotels and suburbs and radio and plumbing equipment and will merge with the New York Central, and that will be the wreck and the demise of the Pennsy.

1948

AT THREE O'CLOCK on a beautiful September afternoon in the principal city of Transylvania, it is very warm, but the air is dry; there is a soft, steady little breeze flowing valleyward from the mountains, so that it is cool in the shadows of the great plane trees. The clock in the nearby church tower is broken, but a church bell is striking somewhere. Outside the main hotel and its restaurant, a father says good-bye, wistfully, to his ten-year old daughter. In her blue school uniform, prim and innocent, wearing her blue apron and white blouse, the little girl is going back to her school. She had received permission to take the lunch hour (more: in this instance, two hours) off, to be with her father, who has just given her a last kiss and then a somewhat unsure pat on her thin little back. He is a middle-aged man, getting a little corpulent, and with prematurely accumulating bags under his eyes. Otherwise he is different from other fathers in his town. He is older than them, and his clothes are better (he wears an American-made summer suit and a silk bow tie), and he has his large Buick automobile at the curb a few steps away; he looks at it, hesitates for a moment, and then chooses to go back to his nearby lodgings on foot. As he starts walking away, his back is slightly bent: for he is weighed down by a terrible presentiment that is more than a premonition, by a sudden awareness of a now unavoidable tragedy of his life.

Here is the story of that life. It is a twentieth-century life, because he was born in 1900, because his life was circumscribed and governed by the two world wars, and because it was circumscribed by the ideas and governed by the mentality of a twentieth-century Central European intellectual. But these categories are too imprecise, a more adequate description is necessary: "Central European" covers multitudes, and he is Hungarian, born and brought up, moreover, in Transylvania, which belongs to Romania now; and though he is Hungarian, he is an American citizen. "Intellectual" covers multitudes, too; again, it is perhaps only in America that he would be recognized thus, since he is not an academic, not a professional intellectual, but a man who has been an artist and an art critic and a scriptwriter and a novelist at various times in his life. There are many such men, all recognizable characters in certain coffeehouses in Berlin, Paris, London, New York, Rio, men with quick minds, rapidly darting eyes, some wit (superficial rather than shallow), many languages, much (though not always well-digested) memory. At best, the Koestler and not the Conrad type, if you know what I mean, and at worst — well, you know . . . This man is not among the worst: his judgments have often been wanting, but then they are compounded by the sentimental inclinations of his heart.

At eighteen he was a radical, a modernist, an atheist, in what was still old Hungary within the Dual Monarchy. When he was nineteen, the radical and the Communist regimes had collapsed, and official Hungary became conservative and counterrevolutionary. At twenty he discovered that he could paint. At twenty-two he could no longer depend on his mother (I don't know what had happened to his father, and he was not so unscrupulous as to be like the man about whom Shaw once wrote that while he did not throw himself into the struggle of life, he threw his mother into it). At twenty-three he was an art critic, and not too bad at it; but that was no way to make a living, and he had developed a few tastes for the better things in life. At twenty-five he was in Paris, actually painting and selling some of his paintings — uncategorizable, like certain Hungarian straw-colored wines, with elements of French post-impressionism and German expressionism but also with a Hungarian overlay of bold colors and daring proportions, more than pastiches. He was twenty-six when he met an American in Paris and impressed him, to the extent that the American once lent him money, which he partially (but only partially) repaid. At twenty-eight he was in Berlin, sitting at the Romanisches Café, finding himself at home in the talk-talk of all kinds of Central and Eastern European and German intellectuals, painters, photographers, critics, musicians, filmmakers. At thirty he was a stage designer for UFA films, which impressed an American representative of Paramount or MGM sufficiently to help him migrate to the United States soon after Hitler came to power. By that time he knew English well enough to write it. But he did not particularly like Hollywood. And he was not taken up by any of the important New York galleries, while life *à la bohème,* in a garret in Greenwich Village, did not attract him. Yet he was found to be attractive enough by a temporary inhabitant of Greenwich Village, a handsome American girl fleeing from Boston and with some money of her own. They married. They had a daughter. That marriage improved his lot: with his wife's help he met a few well-situated editors and publishers; he resumed his former career as an art critic, now writing in English, where his occasional grammatical and syntactical errors were easily corrected and amply compensated for by the impressive cultural references to names and places and works which he would stuff into his columns. He was, however, enough of a Central European intellectual to be inspired by political ideologies. He wrote about politics, too, in the *Nation* and the *New Republic,* articles against the prevalence of Feudalism and Reaction and Fascism in Hungary and in Central Europe; though not a Communist, he was something of a fellow traveler. But he was not altogether a fraud. He volunteered in the army at the age of forty-two and got some kind of a counterintelligence assignment. He was never in combat, but in 1945 he was able to make a short visit to Hungary and Transylvania in his American uniform. He found some of his friends there still, but most of his family was gone.

By that time he and his American wife had been divorced. He had ceased loving her, she did not love him either (mostly, though not exclusively, because of his infidelities). Yet he was a good and devoted father, insisting in the divorce settlement that if his former wife were to remarry he would get custody of the daughter. That happened in 1945. Returning to New York, he thought that ahead of him stretched the prospects of a successful career, that writing would allow him to establish a safe and good upbringing for his child. His mentality, you see, was split. On one side of his persona was the European Intellectual, the Artist, the Writer, the Radical, contemptuous of American capitalism and of conformism and of the coagulation of popular and political anti-Communist ideology soon after the war. The other side was his rejection of how Americans brought up, or did not bring up, their adolescent children. There was something within him (perhaps a nostalgia, or a desire for something that he himself had not experienced), a wish to be a dependable and protective, caring and respected father. But his designs did not come about. His great (or, I should rather say, large) novel was published in 1946, with no éclat and little financial success. Critics on whom he had counted for praise instead criticized the political and ideological machinery clanking through his bumpy prose, that is, when they did not ignore his book altogether.

Late in 1946 he met the cultural attaché of the Romanian legation in Washington. This man, a fellow traveler, a Francophile and a former poet, suggested that there would be a place for him in the new Transylvania, that he could write there and live there very well on American money, including the small trust fund that his wife had set up for their daughter's education; he could take all of his belongings with him, including his car. He was fool enough to consider that prospect. He intoxicated his imagination with potent and dangerous draughts of self-generated memories, self-colored reminiscences from those two or three weeks in 1945: of that Transylvanian town undamaged by the war, of the respect and the adulation with which he had been treated by virtue of his Americanness, of the offers and the availability of spacious apartments and of good spicy food, the plane trees and the one-story houses breathing the old country air—all of these things overlaid with what he thought were reasonable conditions extant in the institutions of the new regime: democratic, progressive, socialist. In his youth he had been an indifferent and rebellious student, but now he was impressed with the seriousness of schools in Transylvania, where Latin was still being taught and where he had seen a row of well-behaved young girls, yes, in their white blouses and blue aprons. "Ah, your pupils! It is like *le vieux monde*," he said once to their Romanian schoolteacher. "Vous pensez, monsieur?" she said—and he thought that he had complimented her.

He had made up his mind, he told his friends and informed his ex-wife, who was not easy to convince, anxious and worried as she was about her daughter, though not enough to exact more than a promise that the girl would never relinquish her American citizenship and would return to the United States for her college education. He sailed on a French ship with his little American daughter and his big American car in September 1947, driving across Europe with the necessary sheaf of papers and visas, staying for a week in Paris and then for another week in Budapest, all in all a three-week journey across a divided and dividing continent that was less pleasant and here and there more troublesome than he had anticipated. The cold war had begun to crystallize, the phrase *Iron Curtain* was already current, though the wire fences and the watchtowers were not yet erected; and there were some people in Paris and especially in Budapest who thought that he was moving in the wrong direction, that he had wrong ideas about what was happening and about what was going to happen, and on one or two occasions a few of them even said so. He thought that they were wrong, but he did not blame them for that. Once they arrived in his native town, almost everything went well, including finding an apartment with large, whitewashed rooms and high ceilings and large French windows, which he secured almost immediately, "for pennies," as he wrote in his first letters to his American friends.

And now it is mid-September in 1948, and he and his daughter have had a long lunch in the restaurant of the best—the only old and reputed and reliable—hotel of the city. But together with many other things in the town, it too has deteriorated, and I mean not only the many dishes penciled out of the menu but the entire atmosphere, which had become vacant and gloomy, in spite of the sun pouring through the plate-glass windows. And the regime in Bucharest has declared exchange regulations that are about to constrict his financial freedoms, meaning the easy and lucrative use of his American dollars, including the unvexed receipt of his monthly checks transmitted from New York, the availability and the value of which the Romanian Legation in Washington had guaranteed to be secure. And that poet-diplomat himself has been recalled from Washington and then disappeared. And a month ago he has received a certified letter from the central police office, telling him that he must re-register his Buick and pay a large fee, after which he has received a gasoline ration allotment that would allow him to drive hardly more than two hundred miles each month. And some of his new local friends, including the young woman who elected to be his mistress almost instantly upon his arrival the year before (when he and his car were wondrous appearances in the town, seen and known by everyone), were becoming warier and warier; some would on occasion evade him in public, on the streets. And one of his confidants, a Jew, also an American citizen, has told him only a week or so before that he could no longer handle the trading of his dollars on the black market and that he ought to go to the American Legation in Bucharest and register there, after which he should hide his American passport in a safe place. He did not go to Bucharest, but he did pay the required six-month call at the town's alien-registration bureau, where, for the first time, he was kept waiting, and for more than an hour; he was then called to a different office within the building, where behind the desk sat a new, youngish official with an unpleasant face, relentlessly smiling, malevolent, and full of a sense of his obvious power. "You are an American citizen," the man said, asking for the passport, which he then stamped, reducing the interval between registrations to every sixty days. "You were born here, I see." "Yes, here in Romania." That unceasing smile now broadened into a malignant grin. "Yes, but you are a Hungarian," the man said. "When this passport expires you need not go to Bucharest. You will get a new set of identity papers here." When he recounted this interview to his Jewish friend, the latter asked, "Did they take your passport away?"

"Oh, no," he said. "Watch out. They might."

So in September 1948 our man senses that ominous things are happening, closing in around him; that his American suit, the shroud of his Americanness, the security due to his American citizenship, were thinning and shredding fast; that he had made a great and tragic mistake. But now, on the sun-baked sidewalk in front of the hotel, he thinks only of his daughter. A great wave of sadness, compounded by gratitude and guilt, overcomes him. She had not minded leaving her American friends, she had not minded going to live in a strange world, on a strange continent, in a strange country, with him. Because she loved, because she loves her father. And now: what will become of her? There stretches before him the emptiest afternoon of his entire life, awful and alone in his now so empty apartment, alone with his worries; but while they have weighed down on him all day and the previous night, they are not what fill his mind now. It is when he sees the little girl walking hurriedly across the street that he cannot keep back his tears; he weeps and he weeps.

❀   ❀   ❀

"Did you know such a man?"

No.

"But you can obviously imagine him. Did you know anyone in a similar situation?"

Not really, but I can imagine it.

"Well, with your imagination, I would have liked more description of this Central European intellectual — say, in New York, in 1939. After all, the vignette is about him, and not about his daughter. All right — about his illusions, and their miserable failure, but since you are not writing a treatise about the psychology of emigré fellow travelers, those descriptions are needed. About all those Central European intellectuals in Berlin you have one sentence."

But they have been described so often —

"Mostly by themselves and by their latter-day sympathizers. You dislike most of them, because you know something about their short-comings."

Yes, I have little sympathy for that Weimar Berlin intellectual climate, for those people who oddly resembled intellectuals in New York—who took satisfaction from thinking that they were the intellectual and artistic avant-garde, knowing something about the superficial pleasures of the world, very much at home in Berlin where there were books to be bandied about, cigarette smoke, French cognac, loud German women with big painted mouths and bobbed hair. They also congregated in New York, in an America which, unlike provincial Germany, was not at all hostile to them, while they disdained common people in America as much as, if not more than, they did in Germany.

"Yet you seem to have a definite sympathy for your man."

Not sympathy but compassion. He is alone, awfully alone, because he has condemned himself to be a prisoner; and sooner or later his little girl will be a prisoner of sorts, too—because of him. He knows that.

"I know that compassion and sympathy are not the same, but they do overlap, they cannot be separated entirely, can they? But what will happen to him and to his daughter after that terrible sunny afternoon?"

I don't know and I don't want to think about it. Still—and not because of compassion—I *can* assume that they will survive, of course after many troubles, and eventually return to the United States.

"Will your man then write a book in America, an exposé of the cruelties of Communism in Eastern Europe?"

No, because he is not enough of an opportunist and because he will have become much, much older. And I fear that he will not live long, perhaps because what had gripped his heart that afternoon went so deep and weakened his heart forever.

1949

IN NEW HOPE IN BUCKS COUNTY, around six in the May evening, the sun is still strong: it warms the streets enough for some of the men to shed their jackets and for some of the women, their cardigans; here and there the sun paints unexpected strokes of light on the darkly rolling Delaware. The summer season, including that of the New Hope Summer Theater, is not yet, but there are people looking at the antiques shops and knitting shops and the second-hand bookshop while going toward the restaurants and their gardens, including those on the river road or across the river in Lambertville. In 1949 New Hope is past its zenith of fashionableness and prosperity, though not by much. In the late 1930s New Hope and Bucks County had become, rather suddenly, the preferred summer place for some people from New York: theater people, art people, music people, writing people from the upper Bohemia of New York who had congregated during the New Deal years, people who found the attractions of bucolic country living for the first time in their ambitious lives. George Kaufman, Pearl Buck, S. J. Perelman bought impressive estates near New Hope. Rodgers and Hart wrote "There's a Small Hotel" circa 1936 in and about a small hotel in Stockton, a few miles up the Delaware from New Hope, on the Jersey side. Like Provincetown or Key West or Big Sur or East Hampton, New Hope had its crowded days in the sun, a mentionable place in a detailed cultural history of America, retaining (or, rather, self-consciously pre-serving) its character to this day. But by 1949 the determined crowds and the glamorous list of theater producers and actors and actresses has thinned — together with their social and political (yes, political) con-victions of only a few years before. There are now groups of young people aspiring to careers on stage or in art, hammering and painting and nailing away behind the clapboard walls of the New Hope Summer Theater, which is to open soon; but there is a sense of passing things in the air.

A woman stands, for a moment, on the narrow wooden porch of a New Hope antiques shop. She shades her eyes against the westering sun. She is leaning against one of the posts. Her stockingless legs are straight and brown. She wears a large peasant skirt and sandals. She must have been beautiful once. She is about fifty. Her life is trailing be-hind her. She has been living around here for a long time, having come from Lancaster perhaps twenty years or so before. She was studying painting then; she joined a Communist-directed arts league or an art-ists' cooperative. There she met her husband, an Armenian sculptor and painter, stocky, mustachioed, thick-legged, mahogany-eyed, exuding a strong odor of virility, a cad. Their cohabitation began in small rented rooms bereft of furniture, on mattresses on the floors, rooms smelling of mice and dampness. Their landlords were old men with the faces of old typewriters and their landladies old women with the faces of old trolley cars. Eventually they moved up to places with a kitchen of their own where she cooked casseroles and had occasional parties with gin and dago wine. They had a daughter. Her husband ran around New Hope and the countryside in leather sandals, from which protruded his hairy toes and dirty toenails. He slept with numberless women, forcing them to learn carnal twists. On occasion, when it was the easiest way, he would bring one of his women to their house. She had a few lovers of her own, including one or two shy young men whom she tried to love, and succeeded, to her eventual peril. She was still rather beau-tiful then. Her husband abandoned her, disappearing into the jungles of bohemian Chicago and then to those of New York. After that she knew some kind of comfort with her old friends and other people in the Communist circle, though the comradely sentiments and the cooperation among the cooperative were waning.

In 1949 she is working in that antiques shop. She is waiting on that porch for her daughter, who is twenty-four, living and working as a waitress in a restaurant in Upper Black Eddy. It is a Saturday; she had said that she would come over to see her mother, but that is now doubtful. She is habitually unreliable, never meaning what she promises and says—or, rather, meaning something when she says so, but forgetting it soon. That is the difference between the two generations: the mother does not always say what she means but she means what she says, whereas the daughter does not, though she is not a habitual liar; she is more selfish than her mother, not out of dishonesty but out of inattention.

So here is this brown crone of a woman at middle age; behind her thickening waist she is trailing memories of her life like that large peasant skirt bought on a sale at a small department store. Does she still believe in Communism, in Cubism, in Free Love? In Russia? Cooperatives? Abstract Art? In sandal wearing, at that? Only if these things are still comfortable—or, rather, if it is too much trouble to change them. I do not know. She has become older, and there are her moments of anguish when she looks at herself; she knows not only that much of her life but that much of what she had believed are becoming, have become, passé. Her heart has not become constricted, but it beats slower. That much she knows.

And now her memory is especially wistful, since not an hour or so ago she had met K., who was one of her lovers ten years before. That was the only time, the only occasion, when K. had cheated (if that is the word) his wife. He was the same age as this woman, but he was teaching her painting. He had come to New Hope to teach a weekly class in a summer art school. He said that she was beautiful. Which she was. One day, three or four sessions into the class—about ten people had signed up—the loft that served as his studio had emptied, the others having left. He screwed up his courage and said something that was silly, out of shyness: that he would love to paint her in the nude. (Rather than proposing that they go out for a drink together.) To his great and explosive surprise she said, "All right," because she liked him, perhaps especially because of his shyness. They became lovers — then, and on two or three other occasions, when they met elsewhere, but never in a public place, and never for more than a couple of hours or so. (Of course he did not paint her.) He felt very guilty, she much less so. They did not see each other again. And now, ten years later, K. had come to New Hope to help prepare a show for a friend; they met on the sidewalk in front of the antiques shop and recognized each other; they talked for a while, and then K. left, driving Philadelphiaward with much confusion in his mind.

That night, after a stiff drink, he screws up his courage (if courage it is, and not something else). He suddenly says to Anne, "Guess whom I ran into in New Hope." He even adds (and I condemn him for this), "She looked pretty old to me." Wise Anne (with an absolutely accurate tone and emphasis): "You don't say!" That is all. You see, she knew about the woman, since (again due to the kind of guilt that often mistakes relief for conscience) he had told Anne about that affair — on an autumn evening, also fortified by drink, months after the New Hope summer school sessions had been over. She was shocked and quite unhappy then, but she forgave him, rather easily: because she knew him, and because she was wise.

"This is a short story — or, rather, material for a short story — and not a vignette. So why include it? I think I know why. Not because of the fleeting encounter of the woman and K. but because of your wish to portray her as a type. A period type."

You may be right, though not quite. She belongs to a period, which means more — it marks her more — than being a bohemian or artsy-craftsy or intellectual or radical type. The period may be definite, but she is not.

"But period types, social types, personality types — they do overlap, don't they? What seems to interest you, again, is how a certain person thinks. And consequently what her ideas are, which is why you pressed your thumb down — rather thickly — on her association with Communists."

No — what interests me is how she behaves. And how she lives. And — perhaps — how she feels. Of course that has much to do with what she thinks. But *how* she thinks: that is more important than her ideas, perhaps especially because she is a woman. Her ideas are at most indefinite rationalizations or, more generally, *pièces justificatives* of her thinking. Which does not mean that her mind is weaker than the mind of a man. Just the opposite. You know my conviction, which is that ideas do not exist in the abstract, that they are incarnated in human beings, that what men and women do or don't do with their ideas is much more important than what ideas do to them —

"Let me interrupt. You just said *incarnate*. If she is a period type, so is New Hope a period place. Both represent a Zeitgeist."

Perhaps. I should have said not *incarnate* but *represent*. I say *perhaps* because I am not always sure about the difference between those two, but that is a complicated philosophical problem that we now must let go. But a Zeitgeist is often not much more than a fashion. And fashions are, of course, important, in the intellectual as well as in the physical sense. Someone said that women are often torn between the desire to dress and to undress. What he did not say is that the first is as important as the second. Those stupid books about *The Authoritarian Personality* or whatnot are largely nonsense, especially when it comes to women. Whatever her existing ideas, when a woman falls in love, really in love, with a Communist or with a Fascist or with a capitalist, with a radical or with a conservative, then her ideas will change in one way or another — and not because she is blinded by her passion, not because she is passive or compliant, not because she is feminine or superficial, but because for her ideas do not matter much. That is something more than superficiality. She knows that for the new man in her life ideas do matter, and she respects him for that, and that may even be an element in her love for him, but not a decisive one, save in the negative instance: once she realizes that he does not really mean what he says about his ideas, her love, including her physical passion for him, may begin to fade.

But let me come back to what you try to define as the New Hope Zeitgeist. I disliked it and I dislike it still. You know that. Not simply because of the people who represented it, though most of them *were* unattractive. I dislike Communism, Abstract Art, Free Love—and ceramics classes, theater workshops, pottery galleries, and, yes, peasant skirts and men's sandals. But I can imagine myself listening to and arguing sympathetically with a young man or a young woman, an American radical, in the thirties, though not with the hangers-on of the sour liberal playwrights and Broadway directors in their country tweeds, since the only ideas that interested them were those that they had in common and repeated like incantations in the hope that they would make them feel good. But 1949 is not in the thirties, and by 1949 even the Communists no longer had the courage of *their* convictions—if they ever had. They too were cowards. And this woman had begun to see that, though it was but a very small portion of her burdens.

"Why this long diatribe against bohemian radicalism?"

Because it has caused plenty of harm to this country, though not the kind of harm that the anti-Communists and the so-called conservatives attributed to it. It has damaged the life of this woman who, when she was very young, saw that kind of life, those ideas, as an alternative attracting her away from where she was, or wherever she had come from. But she is not a pathetic person.

"No, she is not a weakling—which is perhaps the only good thing in your description. But you did say that her heart has become weaker."

Yes, but her mind has not. So let us then hope—and there is some reason to hope—that she will have a more placid and more comfortable old age.

"And what is the reason for that hope?"

The fact that by the time we meet her—in 1949, when she is fifty—she has learned how to live alone, with a sense of loss but not of emptiness in her heart.

1950

IN A NEW YORK hotel a middle-aged woman dines alone. It is her customary hour, half past six; since that is a little early for most people,
the dining room is almost empty. Hers is the only occupied table along
the wall. It is her usual one; she has been a resident of the hotel for a
year at least. Her waiter, too, is the usual one, bringing her dishes and
talking to her in irreverent New York tones but with a not unpleasant
compound of familiarity and deference. Her response to his phrases
and to his ministrations is pleasant, too, including a touch of apprecia-
tive gratitude. There is, of course, the unavoidable solitude between
courses, but that is not particular to her situation.

This hotel was built in the early twenties. It filled the need for a
first-class New York hotel near Gramercy Park, in a region of Manhattan where there were no such establishments except for the Brevoort
and the Fifth Avenue Hotel just above Washington Square Park. This
part of Manhattan, then and for some decades afterward, seemed a district still preferred by some descendants of Old Protestant New York,
including a generation already irrevocably removed from the circumstances and the sensitivities of *The Age of Innocence* or of *Washington
Square* but at the same time conscious of a need to identify themselves
apart from the monumental and sometimes blatant riches of upper Park
and Fifth Avenues and the rest, filled up by more and more success-

ful newcomers into the society of the city. There were a few out-of-towners who, visiting New York in the twenties and thirties, took pride in having "discovered" such a hotel in a part of the roaring city that was quieter and leafier than midtown Manhattan and also less expansive and expensive than the Saint Regis or the Plaza or the new Waldorf, those monuments of and to wealth. But there came the war, and the shortage of hotel rooms, and a transformation of New York. In 1950 the façade of this hotel still has the marks of the solid wealthy architecture of thirty years before, richly stuccoed by northern Italian plasterers, with a Beaux Arts touch at least on the lower portion of its elevation and on its canopy of wrought iron and glass. But now the window frames and sashes are thickened with many layers of slapped-on paint, and the lights in the public rooms are not as inviting as they once were, including the dining room with its peach-colored walls, after the wallpaper had been removed and the room repainted.

And the solitary woman at her dinner is peach-colored, too. But her external appearance (as the external appearance of the building) is not what concerns me. She may be nearing sixty. Her face is not ravaged by age or tragedy or despair. But her aloneness has a sadness about it, because it is loneliness rather than solitude. A year or so ago she was welcomed, rather effusively, by the hotel management, who made an arrangement for her as a resident. Afterward it became more and more evident to her that instead of having become a well-ensconced New York matron, she is a remnant. She is treated with respect, and yet with a circumspection implying that she is older than she is, which does not only mean her age. She had been divorced or widowed three years ago, she has no or only faraway children, but that is not the main condition of her loneliness. She has some money, and her hotel residence was supposed to furnish a refuge from the daily cares, the wear and tear of apartment life. Friends, theaters, music still exist for her in New York. (She is an intelligent woman who once had a modest position with a publisher, or an editing job at an arts-and-ballet magazine, or something like that.) But now she understands something that she may not yet be ready to admit: that her present way of life leads nowhere. She had elected that practical move into this hotel, of which she had had agreeable memories, for a restricted but easy and perhaps even smart way of life. But 1950 is not 1940, and not only has she become older and alone, but the entirety of New York and the world around her have changed, with marks of irrevocable decay. That much she is beginning to understand. She may have to escape, to move out to somewhere else, but whether she is still capable of gathering such a quantum of energy she does not yet know. For the sense of loneliness, unlike that of solitude, is wed to the sense of being abandoned—abandoned, or left behind—in a changed and changing world. That is what she and her kind feel in their bones, in 1950. Right now those peach-colored walls weigh on her spirit. But the distemper is not merely aesthetic; it is historical.

I think it is in his *Journals* that Arnold Bennett describes how the idea of *The Old Wives' Tale* occurred to him in a Paris restaurant, when his eye suddenly caught two older women sitting at a table. And it was more than an idea; the entire story suddenly crystallized in his mind. Their solitude clutched at this heart. But of course, I am not writing a novel—

"No, you aren't. You're not a storyteller. Besides, what Bennett saw was the end of a story, the long embroiderable past of the two sisters of *The Old Wives' Tale* arriving at its end, at that restaurant table. *His* mind was racing backward. Yours is not. So what is the significance of this vignette? The decline and decay of a New York hotel? Of New York? Your sketch is very thin."

I admit that I once saw such a woman at such a table in such a dining room in such a hotel, though not in 1950. And yet 1950 came to my mind . . .

"The historian, not a novelist. You are an imaginative historian but, please, keep in mind that imagination, too, depends on *some* kind of concrete evidence. Your argument is that 1950 was a sort of turning point or a marker in the history of the atmosphere of New York.

I presume this is what you mean. But doesn't that require more of an illustration?"

It does, though I'm not writing urban history. But I have often thought—and, yes, at that very time—that in or close around 1950 there was a sudden thrust of a rough uneasiness, an ugly little tremor beneath the surface that some people must have sensed, something different from the 1945 sense and idea of New York being at the top of the world and keeping on rising.

"I guess you're referring to that nostalgic—and, I think, imprecise—impression of New York in 1945, written about by all kinds of intellectuals and also Englishmen. Jan Morris wrote an entire book about that, *Manhattan '45*, decades later."

Yes, though Julien Green saw things differently when they drove him to a midnight Mass at the Manhattanville convent in December 1944: "the great freezing avenues in this part of New York, an unlovely night in a setting of sordid houses, shattered silence, blown to pieces by passing cars." How different that is from those mindless celebrations of New York at midcentury! The idea that in 1950 New York was the artistic center of the world—in part because of Abstract Expressionism, whatever that is—has hardened into a definition of cultural history by now. And yet the abandonment of New York had begun: in 1950 the city began to lose population, for the first time in its history. Fifty, forty, thirty, perhaps even ten or fifteen years before that, sensitive Americans, intellectuals if you wish, were fleeing from the dreadful lack of privacy, from the choking constrictions of life in American small towns, to what they hoped for, to the free anonymity of life in New York. But by 1950 that anonymity was constricting, not liberating; their privacy simply meant a dangerous kind of loneliness, and some of those people began to flee again, in the reverse direction.

However, I am concerned with one single woman. She was born in New York (to which I must add that she is of Anglo-Saxon Protestant birth—this not to categorize but to help describe her), and she was a certain kind of cultured and intellectual (in the broadest sense) of American woman who is now a period type, a Manhattan *Kulturträgerin* in the ways of the thirties and the forties. A reader and a small-scale patroness of the theatrical and musical arts, she had nothing phony or even superficial about her; she was a humane and liberal American woman at a time when such women were better, because their characters were often stronger, than intellectual men. When I say "liberal," I do not only refer to her political preferences, though she voted for Roosevelt four times; she was no isolationist, she was a Democrat. I mean that she possessed a liberality of mind close to what "liberal" had meant when Jane Austen was writing—a transatlantic twentieth-century woman whom Jane Austen may have recognized because this woman was conservative in a deeper sense, too: a believer in civilized standards of the past and in the necessity of their preservation. But, then, more and more things happened around her and to her (I repeat, I am not a novelist and will not spin out a story to invent and detail them), so that when this wave of loneliness rolled over her with full force, she suddenly understood, if only for a moment, that this wave threatening to drown her soul involved something greater than her own solitary situation, that is, the condition of a New York woman, nearly sixty, condemned to live alone. She was, for a fragment of a moment, conscious of history, of the history of New York, perhaps of America, perhaps of the world. That shock of cognition passed in an instant, but something from it remained within her.

"Well, you *ought* to write a novel once in your life, perhaps about a woman. Your picture is inexcusably incomplete and imperfect, despite that nice softness in the sentimentalizing of your imagination. However: softness does not art make."

Nor history. Of course it would be interesting to put together fragments of evidences from people who foresaw, or at least sensed, the decay of New York as early as 1950 or thereabouts. But let me return to my woman. She is not a monument of strength, and she is not confident enough to rely on her insights. Her peach-colored face is not a strong face; it is soft, with few wrinkles, and these aren't strong wrinkles either. But she is not yet beaten down, and she will cut her losses. There will be women like her who, even at her age and in her solitary condition, will be capable of wrenching themselves away from New York, going to live in a small seaside town in Maine. That will happen not in 1950 but twenty or more years later. I think and hope that she too will move out of her hotel, without much regret, and choose to live elsewhere, perhaps in a small town in northern New Jersey, taking one or two summer trips to Europe later in the fifties and growing through the autumn of her life without being weighed down by a hardly bearable burden of loneliness. What interests me is that moment of recognition on an October evening in 1950 that was something else than autumnal, and the meaning of that may just have stayed within her for a long time.

1951

K., WHO LIKES SPAIN, is not among the guests at a reception given by the consul of Spain in Philadelphia. K. and his wife are hardly aware that there is a Spanish consulate in Philadelphia; when they next travel to Spain, their travel agent will tell them that Americans need no visas there. Also, events involving the consul of Spain rarely receive mention in the social columns of the *Philadelphia Inquirer* and the *Evening Bulletin* (in 1951 there are five such columns in the Sunday *Inquirer* alone), and K. and Anne seldom peruse these columns — though the frequency of their mention will now increase. This reception (*un coctel,* as the Spaniards say among themselves) is small, because the guest list of the consulate is small and also because the consulate consists of but two rooms on the fifteenth floor of an office building in downtown Philadelphia. So it takes place in the small suburban house where the consul and his attractive wife live with their two small children and a maid.

It is a Saturday afternoon in late April 1951, when American-Spanish relations are on the mend; the five-year-old boycotting of Franco Spain, declared by the United Nations, is not only over, but Dean Acheson has offered the benefits of an American military alliance with Spain, including the building of American air bases on Spanish soil. Beyond diplomatic or strategic movements, across the United States Hispanophilia is rising. Even before these negotiations are concluded, a Spanish training ship has been paying courtesy visits to American ports, including Philadelphia, and such a visit is the occasion of the consul's reception. Next day, Sunday, the young Spanish cadets and their officers will attend High Mass in the cathedral on Logan Circle, where the mass of Mass-goers will be impressed by their splendid white uniforms and by their serried rows marching up to the communion rail (and will be startled by the crack of a brassy blast when the cornet will, in the Spanish military tradition, lift and blow his trumpet at the moment of the elevation of the Host). Now in the living room of this modest house stands a Spanish rear admiral, the commander of the *Don Juan Sebastián de Elcano,* a large and somewhat corpulent Spaniard (really a Basque) in his whites, amiable, with a certain largesse in his gestures that are perhaps Iberian compensations for his very limited knowledge of English.

Receiving the guests and interpreting for the commander are the consul and his wife. The consul is modest and well mannered; though he is relatively young, he represents the traditions of a monarchical and hierarchical Spain older than the Franco regime and the rule of the Falangists; he entered the Servicio Diplomático y Consular during the foreign ministry of Jordana, not under Serrano Suñer, who had Germanophile and Naziphile inclinations. The consul's wife is a daughter of Aragonese gentry from Madrid and Salamanca and was brought up in convent schools. She is feminine and motherly, knowledgeable and self-effacing at the same time. Being a Spanish lady, she does not and does not wish to play any part in political life; she fears Communism but she is not attracted to Falangists, either, because of their occasional vulgarities; and while she respects and is unquestionably loyal to the caudillo Francisco Franco de Bahamonde, she has heard enough about his calculating pettinesses at some of the Madrid *tertulias;* but, then, Franco is a *gallego,* a Galician, people known for the stinginess of their emotions.

All of this is unknown to their American guests and friends. They admire Franco. They admire Spain. They admire Spain because of Franco, even more than they admire Franco because of Spain. Franco fought against the Communists and won. Franco defended the Church.

Franco was right, and now, finally, the time has come when Americans recognize that, in the midst of the world struggle against atheistic Communism: too late, but never mind. To speak up for Franco's Spain is no longer controversial. The United States owes a debt to Spain; its government should never have gone along with those who boycotted and tried to subvert Franco's Spain. That was part and parcel of the insidious influence of radicals and liberals and Communists and fellow travelers and anti-Catholics, the kind of people who had brought us into an alliance with Soviet Russia, but their day is gone now, and most Americans know that to regard and to treat Spain as our ally is right.

Most Americans—and they may be correct. Yet this group of people, crowding around their host and hostess and the rear admiral, filling the living room of this small house, are a minority, a subgroup among Americans. For, with the exception of one couple, all of the American guests at this Spanish *coctel* are Catholics. About thirty people: Irish businessmen; a doctor and his wife; a professor from one of the Catholic colleges of Philadelphia; two intellectual priests, one of them a writer for the *Catholic World* (no *Commonweal* types here); the smartest-looking woman, the daughter of the only old Irish banker's family in Philadelphia, with her Cuban husband; and the most interesting man, a thin, ascetic old Philadelphia lawyer, a convert to the church, the gentlest of men with the strongest of opinions. A large old Spanish mirror, its corners full of silver sores (one of the few pieces brought from Madrid by the consul and his wife before they knew that, by necessity, their habitat in Philadelphia would be small), reflects the slow milling of the entire party, including the prelatical gestures of one of the Irish contractors who says that Generals MacArthur and Franco are two of the great living heroes in the world.

Now you must understand that these people are decent Americans, that none of them are Fascists (that silly term) or whatnot, only that they are Early Conservatives, people from whose ranks the Bill Buckleys will spring, and that most of them are Republicans now, in 1951, which is only worth remarking upon because most of them, being Irish, were Democrats as late as one or two years ago (most of them still voted for Truman in 1948). And, being Catholics, they have ties among them, with a freemasonry of phrases, references, allusions, and even a few jokes that they instantly understand. And that is one of the reasons why the only non-Catholic couple, a fortyish lawyer and his wife, find themselves to be somewhat extraneous. He is a Republican and a convinced anti-Communist, he knows some of the other people, but somehow the Catholic talk and the Spanish sherry is too much for his custom. Driving home, he and his wife suddenly feel a small surge of comfort as they stop at a red light in Bryn Mawr. On the left, in the leafy twilight, stands their familiar Episcopal church, a solid gray edifice with its proportionate tower under the soughing boughs of great trees and with its door painted in Chinese red (attractive not only because of its contrast with the graystone but because that scarlet suggestion of social self-assurance is germane to certain Episcopal church doors in eastern America). The freshly mowed grass around the church is softly streaked by light streaming from one of the mullioned windows, where a wedding rehearsal might be going on; or is it the rector reading in that walnut-paneled sanctuary that is so well stocked with his books? In any event, the scene is inviting; it is their church, their rector, and for a moment the lawyer is tempted to turn left into the church driveway to pay a quick call on Father X. ("You must drop in any time, *any* time.") But once the green light comes on they drive on toward their home, which is not far away. Both he and his wife feel a post–cocktail party and a late-spring tiredness. "Very nice people," he says, "the consul and his wife." "Charming people," she says. But among all the other people they did not quite feel at home.

"Across the Republic Hispanophilism is rising, Episcopalianism is declining. That is some juxtaposition. Entirely different things. Besides, one is ephemeral, the other protracted: that particular wave of Hispanophilia was a phenomenon of the 1950s, while the decline of Anglicanism goes on. You have this talent for connecting things but then stretching them out absurdly, attributing significance to them. I know: you are going to say that historically speaking or, rather, thinking, there are things that are significant and other things that are important. Granted. But not everything that is significant is or even becomes important."

Granted. I also admit that in this instance it was my literary — or, rather, pictorial — imagination that inspired me (seeing, for one thing, that scarlet door of the Episcopal church). But please consider that this is a vignette and not a historical essay. A fleeting vignette, but one anchored to history — in this case to April 1951. Let me remind you of two elements at work here. One is that Truman's sacking of MacArthur and the immediately consequent national hysteria were happening then. The other is that 1951 corresponded to a national turning point: for the first time in American history, American Catholics could feel that they were truly first-class citizens, that they were indeed more reliable patriots than were many, many others. In certain positions and occupations in 1951, being a Catholic (and perhaps especially an Irish American Catholic) was no longer a handicap but an advantage.

"That is another story: another outcome of anti-Communism and of the McCarthy period."

And McCarthy was already rising in 1951. But the clue to McCarthy was the feebleness of his opponents, and I do not only mean the cowardly Communists and some frightened liberals but Eisenhower's secretary of the army, that hapless Stevens, quaking in his boots (and, I think, an Episcopalian). Some of that had enduring consequences. Pat Buchanan, for example, wrote nearly forty years later in his autobiography that his and his father's two heroes were Franco and MacArthur. (And of course McCarthy.)

"But you seem to have some sympathy for the thirst of the Irish at that Castilian spring — "

Castalian spring, you mean. A *very* bad pun. But you're right, most of them are good people, and more individual than others might think. Not all of them will be or will remain McCarthyites. Not all of them will subscribe to Buckley, either. And I do not only mean what used to be called the lace-curtain Irish; remember my short reference to that rather elegant woman, the one with her Cuban husband. In 1951 she is still full of unsatisfied social ambitions; while she is intelligent and worldly, her house is full of chintz and toile-de-Jouy settees — no lace curtains there.

"Since she is so worldly, she seems like a skeptical sort. Does she go to Mass regularly?"

I don't know that, but I think so, even though she is often contemptuous of the populist and folksy sermons of some priests. There is, however, something classy about her missal — you know how, before 1965 or so, most people carried and read their own missals in church. It was the kind of small but thick leatherbound missal stuffed with holy cards tucked between its pages, its thickness held together by a wide black grosgrain elasticized band with a thin round gold clasp engraved with her monogram. Now *that* was a period piece. I haven't seen any of those missals for decades now.

"All right. But back to Hispanophilism now. You are not restricting it to politics?"

No, but I am interested in it only as an American phenomenon. It goes back at least to Washington Irving, and it is wide enough to encompass most of the American West, which is suffused with Spanish habits and, yes, even Spanish postures and gestures. (Or Hispanic American ones: Ronald Reagan's leathery face has often seemed to me to be that of a North American Perón.) Anyhow, what happens in 1951 is the discovery and the sudden fashionableness of Spain among all kinds of Americans, including movie people, fashion people, and second-rate writers. You know how after the Second World War it was no longer Paris that attracted them but Rome, and then in the 1950s came a Spanish phase. Think of Hemingway in Franco Spain, which he claimed to have fought against a dozen years earlier, in the company of Soviet journalists then, but now in the best boxes of the corridas and in the rich bars and hotels of Madrid, in the company of the most celebrated matadors and of dubious aristocrats from Andalusia.

"I know that you dislike Hemingway, but how about Spain?"

I dislike Hemingway, not in the least because he was faking; there is an excellent Spanish writer, Arturo Barea, who showed that *For*

Whom the Bell Tolls is stuffed with Spanish phrases, Hemingway show-ing off by including entire Spanish dialogues that no Spaniard would ever utter. But let's forget him. I like Spain very much — the country, the people, the music, the literature. The only exceptions are Spanish Vic-torian architecture and that execrable Gaudí — and, sometimes, Span-ish rhetoric, which, like Hungarian rhetoric, is often exaggeratedly de-clarative, with some unfortunate political or even moral consequences. There are even a few — very few — Spanish words that I do not like —

"Examples, please."

Jefe, for example. Or *eje.* Or even *embajada,* which has none of the stately tone of *ambassade.* Which brings me back to the 1950s, when the slow liberalization and even Americanization of the Franco regime was already occurring (and you know how, at the risk of misunder-standings, I have often defended the Franco regime, insisting that it was not typically Fascist) —

"Interruption. Your criticism of Franco is that he was, for a long time at least, opposed to the monarchy, that Franco was not sufficiently reactionary, whence, among other things, some of his and his party's pro-German inclinations."

And some of their lamentable rhetoric during the war. But much of that continued into the 1950s, when Franco Spain was the refuge for all kinds of former Nazified crooks, including some who at the end of the war had set out for Madrid, accompanied by a portion of their national treasuries. Of course, much of the same thing was happening in Argentina. But I am not thinking of the big Nazi fugitives, the so-called war criminals. I am thinking of those Argentinian or Spanish *em-bajadores* (oh, not of the Duke of Alba in London or of my modest and engaging consul in Philadelphia), with their broad smiles and ravenous white teeth under their brilliantined black moustaches, receiving dubi-ous Romanians or Croats at the *embajada,* exclaiming (falsely), "My house is your house," and so on. There was — at least in the 1950s — something crude and oily about some of these people. And, yes, there was a Spanish Olive Oil Institute that worked with the CIA and financed dubious "conservative" conferences in Madrid and at the Escorial. But, then, the Spanish are *honestly* a conservative people (unlike, say, the Argentinians), and these were only ephemeral excrescences. All I want to say is that the American Hispanophilia of the 1950s was a mixed bag.

"And isn't that true of all Hispanophilia? Or Francophilia, or Anglophilia, for that matter?"

Yes. You win.

1952

ON A MAY EVENING in 1952 K. and Anne are dining at the Philadelphia Museum of Art. They know the museum well, and they have lunched or cocktailed or taken tea there at times, but this is something of a special occasion. In black-tie and evening dress, they are a nice-looking middle-aged couple, and they enjoy the long drive from Chester County on a mild May evening, especially the last three miles along the East River Drive, where the traffic is now light and there are still a few racing shells with their crews on the Schuylkill, their varnished planks lit up by the setting sun against the darkening green of the jungly island clumps; the single small measure of discomfort being that their car is warm, Anne having asked K. to keep the windows closed in order to protect her hairdo. But about the evening ahead of them she is less self-conscious than K. He thinks of the splendiferous invitation in his pocket, printed on ecru bristol paper in eighteenth-century French lettering (and even spelling) and bordered by a rich cartouche, including two putti holding up a scroll:

M———

prie de faire l'honneur
à Monsieur le docteur Bornstein
et Madame Bornstein

au

SOUPER AUX CHANDELLES

au

Musée d'Art
de Philadelphie
Mardy, le 19 mai
à 8 heures

RSVP

"Extremely elegant," K. had said as he passed it to Anne after opening the envelope. "*Extremely* is the word," Anne said.

It *is* an elegant dinner, tendered by the director of the museum in the Louis XV room, newly furnished with two gilded eighteenth-century gueridons, a Versailles cornice, and a glistening dado the director bought from Carlhian, all of these out of Dr. Bornstein's recent donation. The table is bedecked with a gold cloth and set with Sèvres and porcelain-handled tableware. Champagne is served instead of cocktails, and the dinner, of course, has four courses, calligraphed in French from *potage* to *café*. The gueridons hold the candelabra; there are more candles in the sconces and of course on the table. It is all very splendid.

It is all very splendid except perhaps for the conversation. That is subdued—acoustically, too, since the ceiling is coffered and very high, and at the end of the room a trio with violin, viola, and cello plays Lully and Méhul and a little Mozart, but that eventually becomes too much. K. is subdued, too, a little overwhelmed by the opulence of the occasion. Anne is not; she enjoys the occasion and the setting, but she has her opinion of the director. The director is a terrible snob, the kind who knows how to treat people whom he thinks are important and does not know how to treat people whom he thinks are not important, by which I mean that he snubs or ignores them, which is a shortcoming not only of manners but also of judgment—the occupational handicap of snobs, since sometimes the unimportant turn out to be not so unimportant after all. He has snubbed K. in the past and shortchanged him. Three of K.'s watercolors were about to be bought by the museum and hung in the twentieth-century American collection, as recommended by the curator, but the director amputated the recommendation and bought only one, and the director had the curator represent him at the customary small luncheon honoring artists whose work was being acquisitioned by the museum.

But the K.'s had to be invited to this dinner, since K. had painted a portrait of Mrs. Bornstein last year. Whether she had asked the K.'s to be included at this dinner or the director thought he had to include them, Anne does not know and doesn't much care. She likes Mrs. Bornstein, who is a motherly, perhaps a bit overdressed woman who enjoys her husband's fame and riches, but a woman without pretensions. K. told Anne that she was an excellent sitter and funny, too; he brought back a few very good Jewish jokes, and when the portrait was finished she had asked them for dinner at the Bornsteins' Delancey Street town house, handing to K. his fee in an envelope and to Anne a silk-ribboned box containing a beautiful set of a Waterford decanter and six cut-glass liqueur glasses. Now, at the end of the *Souper Louis Quinze,* liqueurs appear together with the same kind of Waterford decanter and the same glasses, which amuses Anne, though not at the expense of Mrs. Bornstein.

It is not Mrs. Bornstein but her husband, the cardiac surgeon, who is fretful with a sense of self-conscious importance, interrupting the conversation often, determined as he is to impress those present with items of his worldly knowledge: for large chunks of the conversation consist, alas, of such things as restaurants in Paris and the financial legerdemains (including tax advantages) involved in the expansion of the Arensberg collection. About the collection there is plenty of name-dropping, at which excels the only other artist among the guests, a Philadelphia painter of German ancestry but with very determined English tailoring and connections (and a social anti-Semitism which of course is not apparent and is indeed hidden by many a smile in the direction of Dr. Bornstein). But the main stream of flattery aimed at the prominent cardiologist flows from the director, with his hopes for more Bornstein endowments to come, whence the arrangements tonight.

There are twelve men and women around the goldened table, and since this is Philadelphia, everybody knows everybody. This includes the two Old Philadelphian couples whom the K.'s know and who know them. At the end of the evening one of the men, a long-established patron of arts in Philadelphia and one of those responsible for the establishment of the museum thirty years before, says to Anne that K. is a good painter and that his work wears well. That speaks well of him, even though he had also been responsible for bringing the director to the museum a dozen years ago, when that roundhead from Virginia (originally from upstate New York) had impressed him unduly not only with the record of his acquisitions in Charlottesville but with his modernist views of art, with his careful mentioning of certain names, and with the general impression of his social acceptability. Since that time the director achieved what the phrase *cum laude* literally means: the knowledge of how to laud and flatter his patrons, subtly but advantageously, some of them understanding that there are now other patrons, other times.

"Well, it was a nice evening," K. says, as they start driving home. And later: "Mrs. Bornstein said that I should paint her sister." "I'm glad that you painted her," Anne says.

"This is a thin vignette about a rich dinner. And permit me to say that you yourself are very snobbish here. What is this, an acid little sally against nouveaux riches?"

Permit me to defend myself. On three levels. First—in order, though not in importance—my bête noire, the museum director, is not a nouveau riche but a parvenu. Second—

"Permit me to interrupt. That is a hairline difference, the kind of distinction that you like to make. All right, I accept it. But why has he snubbed K. in the past?"

Because K. was a Philadelphia gentleman, which he was not. But it is not quite that simple. He classifies K. as a Philadelphian who is genteel but is decidedly of a lower rank than those who matter—to him. The K.'s have not much money (though their money was inherited); they live far out in the country, but not on a horsey estate, and are in every sense far from the apogee of Philadelphia social and cultural life (though they are listed in the Social Register). He attributes the limits of their social—and K.'s artistic—aspirations to mediocrity, whereas their real source is modesty. I say "artistic," because K. had and has no aspirations to being either an avant-garde or a socially (rather than financially) successful painter. That was why this director of the Philadelphia Museum of Art chose to curtail the recommendations of his curator. In that case his social inclinations governed what should have been his professional judgment. Snobs classify, you know, and often wrongly. A man who is both (or, I should say, still) a Philadelphia gentleman and an amateur painter—that bothers *monsieur le directeur.* Of course K. is not an amateur.

"Well, I presume that the director failed to overhear what his patron said about K., which was a pity. But he may have felt, too, that Anne did not care much about him, which was not a pity."

Yes, and now let me proceed to my second point. The Bornsteins are nouveaux riches all right, but that's not what I have been writing about; what I am writing about is how the director is sucking up to them. (On other discreet occasions he may even make bad jokes at their expense.) Trying to impress them and the grand patrons of the museum with this overdone Louis Quinze *bombé* sumptuosity of a dinner. There is nothing very new in that. But in 1952 Balzac and Proust are dead. We face, or ought to face, a new phenomenon, which is that of the nouveaux nouveaux riches.

"Explain, please."

You understand that lately, decades after 1952, I have had a nostalgia for the nouveaux riches. I know their faults, and not from Balzac or Proust either. Their histories are perhaps *the* basic material for the novel of manners, but it seems to me that their day is gone, and in 1952 in Philadelphia we are at the cusp of that transition. Whatever their motives or, rather, purposes, the nouveaux riches, whether in Paris or in Philadelphia, did plenty of good things for culture. They did the right things, even when for the wrong reasons, and so what? They flourished at a time when culture and, yes, civilization required (or their wives required, though this seems not to have been the case with Mrs. Bornstein) that they buy fine furniture, books, and paintings and become patrons of operas, orchestras, theaters, and museums. *L'argent pour l'art,* yes, but *pour l'art.* And this was still the case with Dr. Bornstein, who was not a very pleasant man but who did give the money to the museum to buy all those things. More than that he did not do, because the museum was the place in Philadelphia that mattered to him, socially that was — and, soon after 1952, he realized that social Philadelphia did not really matter, or that it no longer mattered very much. Of course. The director had done his best to fortify Bornstein's perspective of Philadelphia society in 1952 or thereabouts. That perspective had come from the heart, Bornstein's cardiac element. The surgical element was there, too: there was a tax deduction involved with The Donation Of Bornstein. But that was secondary, and soon after 1952 the nouveaux nouveaux riches are here, and when they support (if that is the word) the arts, tax considerations are foremost. And worse is to come, because "art" is falling apart, and "society" is falling apart, and the Museum is no longer what it was, and for the nouveaux nouveaux riches the support of culture is no longer a requirement; whatever social aspirations they may have, they are different. The bourgeois chapter of history had closed, in Philadelphia as elsewhere.

"A chapter, or a period?"

An age.

1953

VITALITY ANIMATES the crowd entering for the eleven-o'clock Mass at Saint Boniface's, which is a parish in North Philadelphia, somewhere between the large parish of Saint Martin of Tours at Oxford Circle and other smaller ones in Logan, Olney, and Kensington. In 1953 it is still predominantly Irish, with a considerable number of German American parishioners. To begin with: the church is full, its pews packed tightly with people, row after row, including many young men among the faithful, who seem not too uncomfortable in the warm church (it is mid-June, with the temperature rising to ninety degrees or more, and Saint Boniface is not yet air-conditioned in 1953, though large fans in steel cages keep whirring steadily during Mass). This is a time in the history of America and of the Roman Catholic Church when church attendance is very high, for all kinds of reasons known only to God, though one may discern a possible source: a communal sense of the rise of prosperity and of confidence among the parishioners. Prosperity: because for some years now, and certainly since the end of the war, the oceanic tides of American growth, rising waves of democracy and of its wages and other benefits, have been spilling over and above the rising waves of costs and prices. Almost all of these parishioners' families own their automobiles now, most of them bought during the postwar years. Many of the young men in the pews are first-generation college students at La Salle, Villanova, Saint Joseph's, and their fathers and mothers are proud of them. At the recessional they sing "Faith of Our Fathers," a hymn reminiscent of an older time when the Irish were an oppressed people, perhaps bound together even more by the bitter memories of a faithful atavism than by the power of the Church, but that is long gone now, as is the Depression. Hence their confidence. No longer do they see themselves and, perhaps more important, no longer are they seen by others as second-class Americans. They are first-class Americans now, the most proven and most patriotic ones, because about so many things, including Communism, they have been proved right when many other people were wrong.

The church is prosperous, too: the two collections are enormous, the white parish envelopes fluttering into the ushers' baskets like so many flat little doves (this is a time when the parish bulletins print the amounts given by each family). While the church is getting hotter and the Mass (still in Latin, of course) is longer than usual, with a long Benediction added to its end, there is little stirring and shuffling, even during the (expectably) rambling sermon of the pastor who (to some) seems to half think as he speaks, especially when he raises his gravelly voice to smother the dubiety of what he thinks he says or what he ought to say or think. But I wrote "some." Does this bother the great majority of the people in this church? I think not. They are used to it, as they are used to the Philadelphia accent of the pastor ("gahspel"; "ahrgganization"; and "blessed by Gahd" throughout the Benediction).

Nearly everyone is going to the rail for Communion, including the entire crowd of the young, some of the boys, I presume, after some heavy petting and wrestling with girls, having fondled them at Ocean City the night or two nights before; but, then, the virtues of frequent Communion have been impressed upon them ever since second grade, and whether that kind of wrestling is a mortal sin (having a hot dog before midnight on Friday definitely is) hardly enters their minds. They are both reverent and irreverent: sometimes, between themselves, though in the presence of Catholic girls, too, they will refer to the wafers as "Communion cookies." However, that, too, may be a period expression, part of the irreverent American reverence for the faith, the way in which so many Americans speak of "Saint Joe's" or "Saint Pete's" when referring to a parish and a church. This is the *American* Roman Catholic Church, and don't think that the idea of putting the Mass into American English started with the liberal theologians infesting the Second Vatican Council in the 1960s; American priests proposed that in articles published in the *Catholic World* in the 1950s. The *Catholic World* was a very McCarthyite magazine then. In the late 1960s it turned liberal, as had many of the priests and nuns (the latter then shedding their habits). In the 1980s many of them turned in the Reagan direction. But how much do these things matter? Only God knows.

"I am glad for those last three words of yours. You are not saying that these people are not good Catholics? But then why are you writing—why are you concerned—about their politics or social life? You and I know very little about the quality of their faith. All we know is that when a man goes to Mass, that says something about him and something about his religion. And if we are concerned mainly with his religion, isn't that the place to stop?"

What I am writing about are *American* Catholics circa 1953, in the age of mass democracy, when religious history can no longer be church history, when it must, at least to a great extent, comprise the histories of parishes and the religious habits and, yes, the inclinations of people, not only what they do but what they think, in and out of Mass-going. Yes, there are Mafia members in Sicily and IRA terrorists in Ireland who are, and there were members of the Waffen-SS, including officers, who were, regular Mass-goers. The American situation is different. And perhaps more complicated. That is why I took the presumptuous liberty—I know that it is a very presumptuous liberty—of saying something about those crowds of young people going up to Communion without having gone to confession before, that is, without (again, I know that I only presume) having made their Act of Contrition. Of course I know that the virtue of frequent Communion was impressed on them by the nuns and priests who taught them early in life. And who am I to question the condition of their state of grace? But I know something of their behavior, which includes not only what they did or didn't do on Saturday nights but what I sometimes found to be a sense of deafness (or perhaps dumbness) to the Catholic doctrine of original sin, which they rather easily suppressed or forgot while satisfying their religious duty by attending Mass on a holy day of obligation. Are they listening?

"But they are *attending*, for God's sake. *Attending*, in English, also means listening. It means *to be there*. What a Jansenist you are!"

Ah, but attending, in America, does not necessarily mean listening. Also, you know very well that you're not insulting me by saying that—perhaps especially because of the stupid cliché current in the early twentieth century, according to which Irish-American Catholics were Jansenists because of the training of the Irish clergy. Total nonsense, considering that the essence of Jansenism was an excessive intellectual scrupulosity. And it is not intellectual scrupulosity that made me write this, save perhaps for the impulse to correct another entirely false notion that is now current, especially among conservatives: the idea that the 1950s was the last golden age of the church and of the faith.

"Entirely false?"

Not entirely—and that had something to do with the then still current dominance of the Irish in the American Church, who had more than one reason to feel secure in their faith, while they had become more than secure in their Americanism, again for more than one reason. The trouble was only that so many of them saw their Catholicism and their Americanism as identical. Not merely reconcilable or complementary; identical. That belonged to a certain period, to those brummagem "values" of the 1950s. But that would pass, not least because of the many saving graces in the Irish character, one being that they seldom take themselves too seriously. How wrong Howells was one hundred years ago! He welcomed immigrant Italians ("a race that is immemorially civilized") and hated the immigrant Irish (who "have lately emerged from barbarism"). "Scratch the mask of a modern Ital-

ian," he said, "and you will find a polite pagan, . . . but if one of these
Yankeefied Celts were scraped," you would find a barbarian. Well, less
than one hundred years later, a Boston Irishman becomes president of
the United States, cheered on and welcomed by the remnants of a desiccated Boston aristocracy. And who are the quintessential Americans
and who the barbarians now? There is many a Moynihan among the
Irish and, alas, many a Stallone among the Italians. Of course, not all
of them. But American life and the entertainment and communications
industries barbarized many young Sicilians (and by the 1980s made
many of them "conservatives"), whereas the Irish became bourgeois
and even liberal. Of course, language has had much to do with that.

"How about those German Catholics around Fifth and Olney?"

There, too — in 1953 many of them felt that some great injustice,
abetted by vast conspiracies, had been done to Germans and Germany,
including to the Third Reich. But no longer. They, too, have become
quintessential Americans.

"And the last two archbishops of Philadelphia have been a Polish
American and an Italian American."

With all respect due to them — and some respect is due — neither
is an improvement over even the most rigid of his Irish predecessors.

1954

See 1961.

1955

IT IS NEW ENGLAND, Indian summer, perhaps windier and cooler than usual on this October afternoon, so that the majestic spectacle of the trees loses something of its calm: the scarlet, brown, and gold leaves are blowing across the commons of the college. Otherwise the scene is familiar and recognizable. The wind does not prevail against the buildings and the white steeples, though it is chilly enough to hasten the trudging of the students across the campus. This is a women's college, one of the three most reputable and most prosperous New England ones, and this is 1955, still a few years before the customs of book bags, knapsacks, and ragged clothing. So there is the peculiar posture and walk of American girl students carrying their books against their chests and stomachs, holding them against their bodies. At half past six it is darkening, and the libe (that is what the library is often called) is filling up with students after their dinner in the high-vaulted neo-Gothic dining hall.

One of them will be helping out with the dishes at the buffet dinner given by the most eminent personage of the faculty, an often celebrated and nationally known poet who, besides being the occupant of a very easy Chair, is also a permanent scholar in residence and the beneficiary of other emoluments, including his rent-free white clapboard house on a pretty little street, portions of whose sidewalks are still laid out in old cobblestones. The lights are now on. Everything is pleasant on this street (except perhaps for the loud music pulsating from one of the houses).

Meanwhile the poet and his wife are a bit anxious about the previously unexpected arrival of two very different guests who in different ways announced themselves earlier that day. One is a very rich young man, an admirer of the poet and his frequent host (a) on his father's yacht, (b) in one of the two most expensive French restaurants in New York, (c) in Tuscan or Provençal villas, or (d) in other luxurious places not to be neglected or gainsaid. He had rung up from Cape Cod this morning, and the poet's wife said, after a moment of hesitation, "Come, have pot luck with us tonight," after which, somewhat foolishly, she made a *combinazione:* another guest is coming from Cape Cod, too, and would he give her a ride? "But of course." This other guest is a German Jewish social philosopher, a saturnine woman with a face like a crumpled ashtray, with a heavy load of Weimar German categorical thinking and talking, not the kind of artistic intellectual whom the youngish Maecenas of the arts customarily receives in Montetrufone or Les Baux or aboard that yacht—*summa summarum,* a non-Berensonian sort. She had announced her coming on the basis of a standing invitation proffered by the poet on the sands of Provincetown one night, a phrase that she now repeated on the telephone, though adding three times, "but maybe it is not gonvenient now for you," mistaking these repetitions for good manners. The poet-husband was not pleased with this arrangement ("why didn't you tell her that we might not be able to get her here tonight?"), but there she comes.

The Maecenas's Jaguar arrives promptly at seven, and out of it issues not only a surprising amount of luggage, including a small hamper of lobsters and white Burgundy and the philosopher-woman's tote bags exuding periodicals and books, but a third person, too, the Maecenas's recently acquired friend, a young fashion designer whom he calls "a modern priest of Venus, a genius at measurement." "Measurement?" "Yes, he will tell you how many pins can stand on the head of an angel." They will not spend the night, however, which is a relief; they will drive back to Boston. So it is only the philosophic woman who has to be shown to her room, with her thick ankles protruding from below her long skirt as she wheezily climbs the stairs.

But altogether the evening is a success. There are three other intellectuals, who know a Maecenas when they see one; the Frankfurt woman is less voluble than usual; there is enough food and drink, though perhaps the host places undue stress on the two bottles of Orvieto and on the emphatic salad, of which his wife says, "I have its recipe from Le Pavillon." A fire has been prematurely lit, and the poet must get up from his Danish chair three times to relight it, but now and then it blazes with a pleasant orange flare, lighting the handsome old sideboard, at home in this house but perhaps lonely in the company of all of those glass tables and Scandinavian rugs. The conversation fills the rich young man with satisfaction. Once in a while he looks at his fashion designer friend as if to tell him that these are interesting people to whom he has been brought tonight. They talk about many things, including two McCarthys, Mary and Joseph, the intellectual star of the first still rising in 1955, and the political star of the second setting. About Joseph: "a reactionary to the right of Louis the Fourteenth." No, the German Jewish woman insists: "a Fascist." About Mary: gossip, which the two nonintellectual guests greatly enjoy. About culture at large, wholesale and detail, with everyone agreeing that without culture there can be no civilization. About the Lonely Crowd and the contemptible aridity of suburbs. Yet, with all of the Orvieto and the Sangiovese, and the one funny dirty joke well told by the poet, there is a fatal and sometimes uncomfortable thinness in the air, the thinness of the sense of a comradeship that is ephemeral, consisting only of the self-conscious, occasional satisfaction of being a group of people whose cultural tastes and opinions differentiate them from other people, from all kinds of people, from the people.

At half past ten the Jaguarians leave. Afterward the host and his wife praise their friend, telling a few interesting details about his eccentric luxuries in which they have sometimes partaken. The philosopher-woman retires. There are now five of them, and the host puts on a record of Hindemith. The youngest of the three guest intellectuals, camp follower of the poet, writes in his diary next morning: "While we listened to that Hindemith record, I found myself feeling that if there's another war this is the kind of civilization I'd want to remember. Or want to try to save." Poor booby! What he and the others do not know is that in 1955 Indian summer in New England exists only in its meteorological and botanical sense: for while "culture" in New England is still there, civilization has been departing fast.

"You are rather nasty about these people, and of course I know why. Your impatience with intellectuals, especially with New England ones —"

It is not impatience. It is a trickle of irritation, gathering into a small pond of dislike. Alas, that pond is not stagnant, it is churning. My fault, I know.

"Can't do much about that, can you? But while 'churning' may suggest vitality, it surely obscures things, doesn't it? So I think that impatience *is* the proper diagnosis of your troubles — especially in this case, where you dismiss all of those people without describing them. They may be clear in your mind, but they're surely not clear on paper. You dismiss them (with that flick of your wrist that I know only too well) because they're not worth bothering with. Well, if so, why write about them at all?"

I'm afraid that you are right. So here I go. The poet, I think, speaks just enough for himself. His wife (a second or third one), a Connecticut woman, with money —

"A Libby?"

No, not a Libby; Libbys have intellectual inclinations but not determined ones. She is also — at least at this time — fairly subservient to her husband, which Libbys are not, though the two do quarrel a lot. In the depth of her soul a small new anxiety is roiling: the fear that her famous husband might soon think about bedding a pretty young admirer among his handful of graduate students. Besides, a Libby will not wear her hair brushed back in a knot.

Now to the Weimarwoman, whose hair is frizzy. In 1955 she is more than a refugee intellectual; among the New York intellectuals she has achieved a higher status, that of a European sage. The iridescent puddle of her reputation is such that the poet and man of letters cannot ignore it altogether, even as he is not too comfortable in her presence; hence his attitude to her is a combination of (New England) patronizing and (intellectual) uncertainty, with a modicum of respect that he thinks is courtesy. Because of that uncertainty he fails to recognize (as most other intellectuals fail to recognize, too) that the woman is a fraud. Coming now to the young patron of the poet's circle: does he descend from an old Boston family? Yes and no. He is the grandson of a moneyed class that had risen in Boston only after the Civil War. About them there is a splendid sentence by Howells—I admit that this is where that figure of the iridescent puddle came to my mind. Here it is, Howells about them circa 1870: the new rich in Boston float "over the turbid waters of common life like the iridescent film you may have seen spreading over the water about our wharves—very splendid, though its origin may have been tar, tallow, train-oil, or other such commodities." At least on one side the Maecenas's ancestors bore such names as Dow or Gow. Two generations later their blood has thinned. He is refined and homosexual. The kind of homosexual about whom that mad genial Edward Dahlberg wrote, "A great deal of sodomy is just a dithering male who is too nervous and too unsure of himself to take what is becoming the worst hazard today, entering a woman."

"Wham. That 'worst hazard' is arguable, though the 'dithering' is good."

Yes, and it is that dithering that keeps him from being happy. Robert Louis Stevenson once wrote that finding a way to be happy is "the whole of culture, and perhaps two-thirds of morality." It is more difficult to be happy than to be unhappy. And I am thinking not only of the poor little rich boy but of intellectuals who tend to take some comfort from their idea that their unhappiness is of a superior kind when compared to the unhappiness of other people. But I have been quoting too much to help me along.

"But not far enough. You cannot state your main thesis—yes, in this vignette it *is* a thesis—in a throwaway phrase, which is the persistence of culture when civilization has largely departed."

Well, "culture" between quotation marks. The bloody stupidity about which the woman from Frankfurt and the man of letters who has sprung from respectable New England ancestors see eye to eye is that "culture" is infinitely superior to civilization. A German idea, you know. But then this has long been the bane of the New England mind. It is all there in Emerson, who never saw the contradiction between his democratic declaration in "The American Scholar," in 1837, I think, and in what he wrote thirty years later, when he proclaimed that the progress of culture depended on small "minorities," on the "few superior and attractive men, . . . a knighthood of learning and virtue." (*Virtue* is good.) That that was not much of a progress toward refinement should be obvious to those of us who recognize that life in an ivory tower may be as unsanitary as it is stifling.

"I have heard that before, but is that your point?"

No, not really. It is not only that well before 1955 the alienation of intellectuals from what remained of civilization was almost complete—all their leftist or liberal ideologies notwithstanding. It is also that during the Eisenhower decade, the 1950s, civilized life in America began to come apart; the surface and morals were cracking, even though the wider public evidences of those cracks did not show until the sixties. Much of that started on the campuses, which was something new in American history, since what had happened on campuses mattered little before. There was, of course, more to it, but intellectuals and academics bore and still bear their responsibility—the positing of culture (and the positing of themselves as the representatives of culture) as something not only higher but more important than civilization, at the very time when civilization is breaking down. They didn't see this, and they don't see it even now. So what has been so good about their powers of perception? So let me insist on one thing only: the midfifties were a turning point.

"You know very well that this vignette, including this discussion, is not enough to sustain that. It calls for a book. Perhaps a short book, but a book nonetheless."

I know that. All I want you to admit is that this vignette is more than a diatribe against intellectuals, forced into a chapterette with the title *1955*.

"If I admit that, will it do you much good?"

Probably not, but I must leave it at that. For now.

1956

THERE IS AN UNUSUAL COMMOTION, a combination of discomfort and expectation in a large crowd, at an Air Force base in New Jersey on this late November afternoon. Photographers jostle and push with their equipment, while people clutch their coats and collars against the arrogant gusts of wind blowing across the tarmac from a torn sky. Hence the discomfort. The expectation concerns the arrival of the first refugees from the Hungarian Revolution in the United States, their patron and their hope.

There are about sixty of them. The big Air Force plane roars in, the propellers rattle and then clank to a stop. The door of the plane opens, but before the first Hungarians come down the steps, some of their handlers issue: army men, Air Force officers, CIA and public-relations people. The refugees blink, red-eyed. Young and old men and women with sharply etched faces, they hold on to their parcels. They step out of the plane, and their first breath in America is cut by the cold; the wind tears at them; and they are stopped by their herders when they clamber down. The shelter of a building is close, but they are told to line up and to bare their heads. Slowly, rather than reluctantly, they take off their hats (among them an old black homburg), their caps, and their berets. "The Star-Spangled Banner" and "The Stars and Stripes" crackle through a megaphone, its brassy sounds, too, torn by the wind.

They are ready to move but are told to stop now. The Secretary of the Army will address them first.

It is a long, awful speech, made longer by its interruptions, since it is translated by a woman into Hungarian—rather poorly, but that does not really matter. What matters is the discomfort of the people standing in the cold. Besides, what the American says hardly matters to them at all. But it should matter to us. "I want you to know what freedom is all about," Wilbur M. Brucker says. "First, I want you to applaud the American flag." Then he asks them to applaud the man standing beside him, who has been responsible for bringing them to the United States, for "the top-level handling of this great enterprise." *Tessék tapsolni!* "Please applaud!" the woman cries out to them, holding her microphone nervously. Then the Secretary: "You will have every kind of freedom in this great country, provided you conduct yourselves as honorable and upright people." He contrasts American freedom with Soviet tyranny. They know about that.

Two American women in the crowd are appalled. They will compose a short letter to the editor of the *New York Times,* ending with these two sentences: "One wonders whether the admonishments and the blatant demand for gratitude did not stir a familiar echo in their hearts of the voices of regimentation from which they have just fled. This reception of suffering people sounds more like a public-relations stunt than the hand of friendship freely held out." Of course they are right. It is a public-relations stunt.

"You're using this book—again!—to insert something about history that you know about and that has been bothering you for some time but that you haven't written about. Is that a good practice?"

You are right. It is not. I did not invent anything in this vignette because—

"I admit that Wilbur M. Brucker was a perfect name for a Republican secretary of the army in 1956. You could not have invented a better one. But you wrote, in reference to his speech, 'it should matter to us.' Why?"

Please keep in mind that, gripped as I was then with the Hungarian Rising of 1956, I was — and am — exercised about what it meant in America, to Americans, and that is why I am writing about it. It says something about 1956, and isn't this book about history, after all? For once, this vignette describes exactly what happened, the quotes are exact, and the letter from those women *was* printed in the *New York Times*. I know that this book must not consist of snatches of documents to which I want to bring attention, being a historian. My excuse is that all I have used for this vignette is one snatch. Somewhere in my files I have many other evidences, collected here and there, about the dishonesties of the Eisenhower and Dulles people in 1956.

"That with all of their propaganda about 'liberation' they did nothing for Hungary in 1956?"

You know very well that that isn't it. During the fever of those revolutionary days (and nights), I did not for a moment think that because of Hungary the United States should go to war or even threaten a war with Russia. But I thought then, and found plenty of evidence later, that Eisenhower and Dulles were not merely hypocrites but dishonest. First: through their agents and others, they had been very well informed of what was going on — which Eisenhower found it necessary to deny in his memoirs. Second, in order though not in importance: they did not want to tamper with the division of Europe or to suggest to the Russians that if they really withdrew from Hungary, there would be a corresponding American withdrawal of some of our forces or from some of our bases in another part of Europe. It may or may not have worked, but the fact that it was not even suggested to them says much. Third, and this is the worst: Eisenhower and Dulles were actually relieved when the Russians came back and squelched the Hungarian Rising. While it did not affect the division of Europe, it was a wonderful propaganda advantage to America; for public relations it was inestimable. Some of the Eisenhower people made revolting (and self-revealing) statements about that. All right, here is one of them, from a slimy book I read later, entitled *Escape from Fear,* by a Martin A. Bursten. The man standing next to Wilbur M. Brucker, whom the weary Hungarians were told to applaud, was Tracy S. Voorhees, a "prominent New York attorney, appointed by Eisenhower as his personal representative. He hired . . . a private public relations firm to 'sell' [Bursten's word, not mine] the Hungarian refugees to the people of the United States. The firm, Communications Counselors, a Division of McCann-Erickson Advertising Agency, [the] second largest organization of its kind in the world, did a spectacular publicity job. There was hardly a magazine, newspaper, radio program, or TV show which was not blanketed with effective and compelling material of the Hungarian project. The firm made available the former mayor of Budapest, the president of the Petofi Club, Freedom fighters of every age, size, weight and complexion, and artists and entertainers. . . . Nobody minimized the job done by Mr. Voorhees' public relations firm, for it was the first time that a government operation was using Madison Avenue to put its program across in the proper light, and with the time-tested techniques and expedients of the profession."

"And now you must stop."

Of course I stop; but I must say something about Americans at that time. You see, the reactions of the American people were different from those of their government (which was otherwise so popular and was overwhelmingly reelected, and during the fighting in Hungary, at that). The people were more generous and more sincere. They treated the Hungarian refugees exceptionally well. Of course there were some exceptions, including unsavory people cashing in on the situation when it was chic to be Hungarian. One example: my wife and I saw *My Fair Lady* in New York that December. There is a Shavian line in one of its ditties about "Zoltan Karpathy, that dreadful Hungarian." In November 1956 the Broadway people had changed that to "dreadful Romanian." Another example: there were (and are) some people of Hungarian origin in this country who had never identified themselves with their native land before 1956, but then and there they began to declare their concern with "my poor oppressed country." But what I think — and feel — is that I must record the reaction of the native Americans I knew. Their sympathy for Hungary and Hungarians was genuine. For many of them, I admit, Hungary was A Faraway Country About Which They Knew Nothing, and the entire tragic episode fitted only into their ingrained American view of the world: tyrannies abroad come and go, and so does American sympathy for some of their victims. But I remember a party in our neighborhood in December 1956, I think, where I, probably wrongly, spouted off about the Republicans' culpability, with all their fake "liberation" propaganda. There were some suburban types who did not like that, although by that time most people's interest in Hungary had faded. But there was a couple at that party whom I now remember, even though I have not thought about them, perhaps not even once, for more than thirty years. About a fortnight ago, for some mysterious reason, their images swam into my mind. I tried to recall their names, but I couldn't; but a few days later that too reappeared in my mind. The H.'s were a quiet couple. About forty, I think. She was dark-haired, and there was a kind of restrained fineness in her face, something like La Fontaine's "un sombre plaisir d'un coeur mélancolique." And she said to me: "You must feel very strongly about your country. But this is your country now. You will tell us" — she meant herself and her husband, who was listening — "how we can help." I think I babbled something about there being nothing I could think of right then but that I would —

I know very little about the H.'s. I cannot even recall their first names. I did not know exactly where they lived; I do not know whether they had children or not, though I think they had. I remember that once, when I was cajoling my wife (whose quiet reserve was not unlike that of Mrs. H.) to give a party for some people we then knew, I mentioned the H.'s, but nothing happened (my wife became ill that winter, and we did not owe the H.'s). Not much later they dropped out of my sight. But there had been a quietness in them that often impressed me when I saw them at others' parties, that made them different from many others. So something about them — and I do not only mean what she said to me that night — must have lived on at the bottom of my mind or, perhaps, heart. There was something about that reserved couple, a deep vein of private integrity of which they were probably unaware but that must have governed their lives. And there was something sad about them, too — because of their quietness. I have a sense of some kind of a tragedy approaching them. What happened to them? What happened to their children? In those sixties? Were the H.'s among the last representatives — not that they would ever think of themselves as representatives — of the accumulated decency of their race, of something that has accumulated through centuries? Oh, good and bad people will come and go, but I fear we won't see their likes for another thousand years.

"Did they reoccur in your mind when you were beginning to think about a 1956 chapter?"

No.

1957

THE RUSSIAN SPUTNIK had gone up, and there is some trouble with the launching of the first American satellite. Wernher von Braun is quoted in the press: "Instead of wasting time and energy in ponderous reappraisals and reexamination, we ought to pitch in to get the show on the road and get it into space."

These are his words, and how American they are.

Very American, too, are the words of the mechanics working on the rockets. A priest has blessed a Saint Christopher medal that will be inserted in the nose cone of the first American space missile. Often there is something going wrong with the engines in the last moment. People speak of gremlins. "Another gremlin," the mechanics say. The Catholic chaplain of the base fingers his rosary and says a prayer for the gremlins to disappear. Eventually they do.

Twenty-six years before, in 1931, when von Braun was a very young man, officers of the Reichswehr stood in their long gray greatcoats at Berlin-Lichterfelde. Small, stubby rockets were set up on the sandy field. Then they whooshed into the air. The first step for space travel, *Raumfahrt*, had begun. This great German achievement will have new, secret purposes in war, too. Some of the officers talk of this as they are driven back to their garrison headquarters in the thin Berlin rain.

In 1931 there were no army chaplains at Berlin-Lichterfelde. In 1957 a new age of faith is beginning.

"A little more research and reading, and you could have given us a detailed picture of that interesting scene, with those stiff German officers watching the first rockets go off on a November day, chilly on the edge of an unknowing and feverish Berlin, a year and a half before Hitler becomes their leader. But you didn't do that. Instead you go on to the new age of faith. At any rate, it turned out to be the American century, not the German one, and shouldn't we be grateful for that?"

Yes. I recently reread that once famous article by Henry Luce, "The American Century," which he published in *Life* in February 1941. It is rather engaging, you know—less arrogant and shortsighted and presumptuous than I had once thought. It is altogether in accord with the view of the world held by what at that time was still the Anglo-Saxon upper class in the American East. Then, a decade later, Luce helped to put his star candidate Eisenhower in the presidency, with foreign policy being run by the Germanophile Dulles and the American space race by von Braun—to whom, incidentally, American students at a large midwestern university chose to award their prize Patriot of the Year in 1958. (Engineer of the Year, perhaps. "Patriot"?) But, for once, it is not this peculiar American-German relationship that interests me. It is this American neomedievalism, which was evident in the 1950s and in so many ways.

"The Saint Christopher medal placed in the rocket?"

Exactly. Saint Christopher is the patron saint of travelers, of human beings in need of protection. That rocket is an unmanned rocket; it carries no human beings into space. And Superman and Batman are supermodern versions of medieval archangels, not to speak of the figures and the language of Star Wars. In 1957 we are less than a quarter-century away from a president, Reagan, who believes in astrology, Star Wars, Evil Empires. He speaks of those things and says that "the Force is with us," a phrase invoking some kind of a deity (what deity?) from the movie *Star Wars*. Since the 1950s we have been moving in that direction.

"Of a populist medievalism?"

Yes. Where else in the world could one read, as I read circa 1957, in a yearbook of a Catholic school, a photo caption that described a basketball player stepping into the chapel on his way to a big game as "saying a reverent hello to Jesus"?

"I have seen priests blessing basketballs and footballs, too, but what is uniquely American about that? Think of Neapolitans or Brazilians. It is the popularization of the sacred. Does that apply to those gremlins and the rosaries?"

It does, because of an American split-mindedness. The superstitious Neapolitan or the voodoo Brazilian is not split-minded, he is a committed materialist, with more than a touch of the pagan to boot. But there has been a kind of unrestrained spiritualism at the base of the American mind from the beginning. This does not mean that the colonists "remained" medieval—though there was much of that among the Puritans, who had fled from the dangerous liberties of Baroque and Renaissance Europe. What it means is that peculiar coexistence of fideism and materialism in the modern American mind, reminiscent of what Huizinga wrote about in *The Waning of the Middle Ages:* "A too systematic idealism gives a certain rigidity to the conception of the world. . . . Men disregarded the individual qualities and the fine distinctions of things, deliberately and on purpose, in order to always bring them under some general principle. . . . What is important is the impersonal. The mind is not in search of individual realities, but of models, examples, norms. . . . There is in the Middle Ages a tendency to ascribe a sort of substantiality to abstract concepts." All of this was as true for the Puritan minister as it is for the professor of sociology, for Superman as for the public-relations man, for the American Marxist as for the American anti-Communist, for the rocket mechanics as for the space priest.

Much of American literature is now suffused with that, too—I am not even thinking of the absurdities of science fiction. There may be no German novelists such as Pynchon, with his gravities and rainbows and gremlins, his literary fascination with occult junk. I read *Gravity's Rainbow* after I had been driving through New London, Connecticut, on an empty Sunday morning. It was a dreadful, soulless place—a city of emptiness, frozen skeletons of cranes, high wire fences behind which were piles of metallic trash. This mystagogue Pynchon was trying to write about London and Berlin during the last war, but he is strictly from New London. Anyhow, he should not have called his book *Gravity's Rainbow,* which is, when you think of it, not only a silly but a very hobbling title.

"He should have called it 'A Moveable Feast,' but of course Hemingway beat him to that. You must admit that 'Moveable Feast' was a very good title."

Admitted, though he applied it to Paris. Don't you think that there is something very American about a moveable feast?

1958

K. AND ANNE are chilled and uncomfortable in the Barcelona airport while waiting for the announcement of their plane, since it is suddenly and unseasonably cold in late September and they have but their summer clothes. They are returning home, after five months on one of the Balearic islands where they had rented a house. Because of their luggage they chose not to fly to Barcelona but to take the night boat to Valencia; K. had been too late to reserve their places on the Barcelona one, so they had to take the slower night boat to Valencia, where they arrived on a bright and hostile morning, with a day of long empty hours to kill. Around noon a big wind got up, wafting blossoms over the cars and dispersing the scent of the flowers garlanded in waves over the private walls, only the everlasting Spanish smell of cheap olive oil and anís hung in the air. Then they took the night train and a sleeper, *coches-camas,* to Barcelona, a wide old mahogany Spanish sleeping car swaying and racketing north slowly on the ancient roadbed. The wind rose ever more, and the night boomed without; the few forlorn stars shivered above the train. When they got to Barcelona, clouds were racing, and the cold was intense and treacherous, penetrating even the musty closeness of the taxi that took them to the airport. Checking in was easy despite the large heap of their luggage, because of the courtesy and ability of the porters; but in the end there was not much relief for them even in that Americanized atmosphere of a modern airport: their TWA flight was delayed for at least two hours, and they had to wait for at least four, having arrived very early because of the night train.

They sit on the plastic benches, very tired, almost too tired to doze off. Anne is trying to read, deedily occupied with her glasses. They are affected by the kind of nervous, red-eyed energy that rises from a combination of sleep missed and the anxious anticipation of starting to move again.

By about eleven it gets warm, almost uncomfortably so, with a resistless sun burning through the plate-glass windows of the terminal; and soon other Americans begin to arrive, in dribs and drabs, settling down on the benches, among them a very large woman in toreador pants, who asks Anne a list of senseless questions about where and when and how they can change their pesetas back into dollars. Her husband has the face of a Senate clerk. Then they move away. There now comes another American man, younger, better looking, who starts to chat with Anne and K., very determined to suggest that he and they are of a different sort from the toreador lady, whose silly stream of talk he had overheard. After about thirty minutes comes the first moment of promise and relief, the first announcement of their flight, so they may now go through customs and to the assigned gate—where they will sit and wait for another hour at least, but they do not yet know that. (It is like those modern doctors' offices, says Anne: when they finally call you, false relief that is, with the nurse taking you to a windowless cubicle where you wait and wait again for the doctor to appear.)

They will not see their recent fellow passenger again, except from a distance. He is on the other side of the waiting room, talking to another American with a rough face who is wearing fashionable canvassy traveling togs. The former had sat with them for more than half an hour, and they had talked long enough. He lives in Princeton, but neither Anne nor K. knows his occupation. He is, however, a new American type. He is very knowledgable: about restaurants in Madrid, about hotels in Barcelona, about duty-free prices in Amsterdam (the best in Europe, he says), about the famous American novelist living in

Ibiza, about the way to handle the surly and impolite French. His name-dropping begins to tire K. and Anne, especially after his inclusion of a few Philadelphian names. He has an expensive camera.

In the droning airplane Anne dozes off. In her half-awake state, impressions of their earlier travels in Europe swim up, cobwebbed, to her consciousness: young Americans abroad, snapping pictures with their Kodak box cameras, very different from this know-it-all. She is now vaguely aware of the great transformation from American innocence to global expertise, which has led to such appearances as this man taking good care to impress other Americans with his know-how of the world. When she wakes, she shakes her head, trying to disperse the cobwebs from her brain, and she suddenly understands that these New Americans know much less than they think they know.

"Well, it all started with the American century, didn't it? Can you—can a people—have it both ways?"

No, you're wrong—there *was* something innocent about Henry Luce, I mean, that *pronunciamento* of his in 1941. Though not about his wife. Her hard and selfish knowledge of the world was part and parcel of her sophisticated progress from Bernard Baruch to Fulton Sheen—

"From Condé Nast to Cardinal Spellman works better."

At any rate, the idea—or, rather, the pretension—that some Americans know not only how best to shoot or fish or fly but also how best to bed beautiful women and how best to outwit or beat their opponents throughout the world. An early example was that *Casablanca* movie celebrating the supremacy of the American male because of his wonderfully American know-how: Humphrey Bogart, the virile owner of the Bar Américain, who knows everything about Frenchmen, Germans, Arabs, black markets, false papers, roulette tricks, vintages, champagnes, and guns. Since that time, in the airplanes and the airports on both sides of the Atlantic one can see these new American types, with their displays of worldly-wise cynicism.

"Now, now. If this book is any good, you must not repeat your-self as you do. No more tirades about *Casablanca*! All right—there was a time when the CIA man was replacing the cowboy as a symbol of American male prowess in the popular imagination. But that didn't last long, did it?"

From about 1951 to 1963, I think—though it had a faint revival during the Reagan decade. George Bush and Bill Buckley were both CIA men, though no symbols of American male prowess, but the hero of the latter's spy novels has been that.

"And how about American innocence? Has it become extinct?"

No, though it may be fading among the young, which is bad news. But the great danger to innocence is of course not worldliness, it is sentimentalism; the sentimentalist is often a cynic at heart. And there is that other syndrome, that of an older type of philistine, perhaps even a wearied skeptic, who becomes tired of adjustments and accord-ingly sinks to accepting all kinds of new dismal things. There are many people like that.

"But not K., who is still an innocent and not a philistine."

Of course not. Rather, I am thinking of someone like Henry Cabot Lodge, who may have snubbed the eager traveler from Prince-ton in whatever airport they would have found themselves together. But then Lodge turned out to be a big oaf. It was in 1957 or 1958, at the opening of Frank Lloyd Wright's god-awful Guggenheim Museum in New York, that he felt it proper to compare the event to whatever was going on in the Soviet Union: "This kind of building can only exist in a democracy," he said. Of course.

"One last question. Was Frank Lloyd Wright a New American?"

Not really, though he liked to think so. He was the kind of village atheist who becomes celebrated and successful, the kind who does not guard his privacy from the pursuit of his neighbors but who pursues publicity with a shamelessly calculated determination.

1959

MELTON ABBAS, in Wiltshire (or Gloucestershire), rests in the afternoon sun; it is an "Oh, to be in England!" day, not in April but in June, with the Grantchester clock at ten to three, as if Rupert Brooke were still around, which of course he is not. Too many cars in Portland Street, which is a narrow one, the main thoroughfare of Melton Abbas, a village of no more than fifteen hundred souls. But behind the brick walls of private gardens the finely mown grass is emerald, and Mrs. Cartwright's (Philippa? Fiona? no, she is not young enough for those newly fashionable fifties' or sixties' names; Melissa, say, or perhaps even Stella) roses and peonies, her elegant white clusters of iris and her white poppies and her herbaceous borders, are beautiful, which is all to her credit, since she does not have a gardener, except for three days each May and two days at the end of the summer. Now her husband is busy with putting away things into the gardening shed and helping to put out things for the tea party to come. The sun is strong, but he is told not to bother with the lawn umbrella, since the McCalls are not due until about half past four, and by that time the afternoon shadows will have marched far enough up on the lawn to make sitting there comfortable and cool.

The McCalls are Americans, old acquaintances of the Cartwrights (well, for about a decade). I do not know where they met first, but there have been Christmas cards and some correspondence and even one or two small packages exchanged between them, and a year or so ago the four of them spent a quite pleasant evening in London, dining together in high style, at the McCalls' invitation. Hospitality in England is no longer—it cannot be—what it once was: the fact that their American friends treat them to dinner when in London is quite acceptable in 1959. But now the time has come to reciprocate, with the McCalls motoring through the West Country; Phil McCall's exact itinerary came in a letter months before June and then was confirmed by telephone from London. They spent the night in Salisbury, and they have a reservation in a newly refurbished and enticingly recommended inn near Frome (with cuisine prepared by a young English couple trained in France), so Melissa is off the hook—sort of. The idea now is to have high tea in Melton Abbas, to which her American guests enthusiastically rally and which she can do rather well.

There is more to the McCalls than to the standard American Anglophile's moving through the West Country in search of thatched-roof villages and so on. He knows something of this countryside, and not only because he served in England during the war (that was in foggy gray Norfolk, in the fenland of East Anglia, at an American air base). He is interested in English history and also in his own genealogy. He is an American stockbroker of Scotch (or Scotch Irish) parentage, as his name suggests; but his great-grandmother was English, indeed she had come from the West Country, and he found her name in a ship's manifest on a microfilmed roll at the Historical Society of Pennsylvania and then also on an old parish register in a village only five miles from Melton Abbas. That was some years ago, on his first visit to England after the war, at a time when he and his wife had not yet met their present hosts; but Phil McCall knows something about Melton Abbas, and he may be looking forward to knowing more.

His host knows this, which is why he told George to come for tea when they met earlier on High Street, Cartwright doing errands (mostly for his wife and for the high tea), George coming out from the booksellers', as usual. George said that he would like to come; he had found an interesting book in Salisbury the other day, *The Traditional*

Herbarium, and asked if Melissa would like to have it. Philip Cartwright said of course, and come for tea at around half past four; we are having some American friends, Melissa will be only too glad to see you. When Philip got home, his legs gimpy up the high stone steps leading to the kitchen, his hands full of small parcels, and told Melissa this, she did not seem to be exceedingly pleased, but that was that.

George is a Hungarian. He is more than a Hungarian or, perhaps, less of a Hungarian than he once was — meaning that he is more than an Anglophile Hungarian, he is an anglicized Hungarian. He came to England with his family as a young boy, in 1937, and he stayed. He is a bachelor and an amateur scholar, not only interested in but very knowledgeable about local history and especially architecture, sufficiently so that he is among the amateur experts of National Trust, having written scholarly articles and even a book or two about some of the old mansions in the west, though his most esteemed one is about an enormous pile of Jacobean brick and stone in the East Riding of Yorkshire, where he discovered documents relating to its original structure and the actual stonework bricked up in a small wing, both of which his more nonchalant and less enthusiastic English colleagues had missed. He lives in the small gate lodge of Fairbourne House, the only famous great house near Melton Abbas, and he knows and loves Melton Abbas and its history. Besides possessing the elementary social consciousness of a National Trust adjunct, of an amateur scholar of English architecture, and of course of an anglicized Hungarian, George is hardly a snob, though he does try to combine Toryism and bookishness. He does not ride; he walks.

And now it is half past four, and the two Philips, the American and the Englishman, are in the midst of a slow and deliberate conversation on the lawn (yes, the first peaks of the afternoon shadows are moving across the table, though not entirely: the chair that Philip McCall occupies still shines hot under the sun, but he does not mind that at all, he likes the sun). George arrives, with *The Traditional Herbarium,* which he gives to Melissa. She thanks him, with a carefully calibrated low grade of enthusiasm, rather apparent too from the nervous haste with which she puts that handsome volume down on the little hall table, as if she were momentarily beset with the suddenly accumulated duties of a solitary hostess, which she really isn't. Her donor doesn't notice this (though it will flash through his mind later), but he will not be able to avoid feeling that, somehow, his presence at the Cartwrights this afternoon is not unreservedly welcome. Sooner rather than later, there is a thin filament of tension in the air, a gossamer aura of irritation emanating from Melissa Cartwright's head, from somewhere under that handsome brow and hair, the latter freshly done up by the Melton Abbas coiffeur that morning.

She does not now much like George. She does not usually mind his being around, but she does mind when they are in the company of certain people. Then he monopolizes the conversation. Not that he is entirely devoid of English manners, for he has acquired here a goodly dose of restraint; but he knows a lot, and when people talk or ask him about something he knows, his interest bubbles forth and up, his talk is full of details, and the others gather their interests around his, whereby her carefully proportioned and planned symmetries of her party are compromised. Which is what she expects to happen now, and she is right. Her American guest knows much about the history of the county, perhaps more than she does but less than does George. The consequences are predictable. Phil McCall and George talk a lot, for a long time, about many things. Melissa's husband does not mind this, but she does. She feels restricted talking mostly to Jane McCall about teas, gardens, and London, which she knows well, but she does not play those strong suits of hers; she prefers to talk about America. It is not the restriction of the topics that vexes Melissa; it is the restriction of her ability to preside at the occasion. She is rather rude to George, turning away from him, addressing hardly a word to him for two hours, barely civil enough not to exclude him from a second pouring of tea and from a second round of scones and strawberries and clotted cream and sandwiches, though he *is* offered the trays last. Later that afternoon she turns determinedly to Phil McCall with one question after another about American things, with the purpose of excluding George from the conversation. Indeed, she even suggests that, after all is said and in spite of the three thousand miles or more between them, people such as the Cartwrights and the McCalls are distant relatives, members of a far-flung family, from which this foreigner, no matter how English his speech and his clothes and his habits and no matter how great his knowledge of England may be, is necessarily excluded.

She does not do this well enough, or perhaps she overdid it. When they leave, not only do the McCalls and George exchange cards and addresses (and a promise by George to send them an article about Fairbourne House), but Phil McCall (after George has left) says: "What an interesting man! Thank you *so* much for having had us over to meet him." George does not hear this; he is already on the road, driving homeward in his little car. But he is uncomfortable with the knowledge that Melissa Cartwright was irritated with him. Only—he does not understand why.

❋   ❋   ❋

"Well, a very tiny vignette this is."

I know.

"Are these people whom you have known?"

No, not one of them, not even George.

"Then what is the purpose? The source of the Englishwoman's irritation is not clear. Is it because George is a Hungarian? An intrusive foreigner?"

No, not really. Madam Cartwright is not a narrow-minded Anglo-Saxon; she does not dislike foreigners for being foreigners. On occasion she is even attracted and charmed by them—

"Stop for a second. Did she once have a frisson for this resident Hungarian in Wiltshire? You did not describe him physically (which shows that you are not *really* an English writer), but at least you suggest that he is not repulsive. Did she spurn—or, worse, ignore—his emanations once, I mean, emanations surely different from those on the afternoon you describe?"

I do not think so, and it does not matter. You misunderstand their relationship. She is one of those people who do not mind foreigners, who even like them—as long as they can patronize them. Once the foreigners prove to be smarter or better situated, they become unbearable, at least for certain people. I do not know whether that is a universal syndrome, but it is prevalent among Anglo-Saxons on both sides of the Atlantic.

"Well, it is certainly not true of the American visitor, as you describe him."

No, since Americans are often, though of course not always, more generous than the English.

"Perhaps, but that brings me to the second question. Did she want the Hungarian scholar excluded because this was an Anglo-American occasion? What you suggest earlier—though much too faintly—is the presence of that hypocritical English opportunism vis-à-vis Americans in this century, a deference to the latter's wealth and power, and hence a conscious wish to emphasize their special relationship—and of course every special relationship is by its nature exclusive of others."

Yes, that is there, too. But the emphasis is not on George the Hungarian; it is, rather, on George the scholar. She is vexed by his intellectual accomplishments, even more than by his intellectual powers. If their Hungarian acquaintance in Melton Abbas were a frayed aristocrat in exile, sufficiently presentable, exotic and talking not much, she would not at all mind him at that high tea of hers. On the other hand, if the fifth wheel at her party were an English architectural scholar (of course of a fairly good family) who monopolizes the conversation or tears the American guests away for a fast run through Fairbourne House, she *would* mind that—though, I agree, perhaps less than in the case of George.

"Well, I still think that you should have described her attitude to Americans better. And here is my last criticism. Is this vignette a proper period piece? Could this not have happened, in the same way, in 1939 or 1929 or even 1919, not particularly in 1959?"

No, because by 1959 those Anglo-American contacts were no

longer what they had been before; they had become frayed and more complicated. Around 1959 Harold Macmillan said something about the relationship between the British and Americans being like that between Greeks and Romans when the Greek heritage was being passed on to Rome; and with all respect to his classical education, he was wrong, that was not true enough. You know the story about the old Irish biddy, the one whom the neighbor women asked whether what people were saying about the young widow up the street was true, and the old woman said, "It is not true, but it is true enough." And it behooves us historians to think and say the opposite sometimes: this or that is true, but it is not true enough.

1960

A DIALOGUE OF THE DEAF at the American embassy in an Eastern European capital. The Public Affairs Officer has an appointment with the Fulbright professor of American Studies. The professor is twenty minutes late, inadvertently so. He had—or he thought he had—figured out how to get to the embassy building, but then he transferred to the wrong trolley car, which he realized soon enough; peering at the crumpled city map extracted from his raincoat, he got off at the next stop and made his way on foot through a maze of streets and then along an unmarked wide boulevard, an agitated progress that took him longer than what he had estimated before abandoning the trolley car. Now he enters the portals of the American embassy, a large building on a large square. There are two Marines posted inside the steel-barred doors, and he has to wait another five minutes until his presence is announced to his host by someone in a soundproof glass cage. The Public Affairs Officer is not particularly surprised or perhaps even irritated; he has expected this professor to be, well, a professor.

His patronizing inclination is unwarranted. His disdain is more ideological than social: the disdain and distrust for a representative of a class of opinion rather than the disdain of a worldly-wise diplomat for a hapless academic. This is 1960, and the composition of the Foreign Service of the Department of State has changed. It has been inflated during the war and especially during the cold war, including the creation of positions for Public Affairs Officers and the invasion of the Foreign Service by other governmental bureaucracies, including the United States Information Service. One result of this is the presence of cold war bureaucrats such as this one, a graduate not of Princeton or Harvard but of Fordham or Georgetown, whose concept of American national security (*security* is the dominant word here) is not only inseparable from but identical to the global struggle against the danger of international Communism and who therefore sees his duties as ensuring that the United States is not imperiled by inadequate recognition of that danger. His present visitor is one of the first American academics sent as a visiting professor to an Eastern European Communist country, accepted by the local cultural and university officials, and liberal intellectuals such as this one must be informed, instructed, and warned about the conditions of their presence here.

Unwarranted, too, are the confused expectations of the tardy professor. He does not quite know what to expect at this meeting at the embassy. Why the curt and inelegant telephone message? ("It's like a summons," the professor mutters to his wife.) "Or is he one of those who are supposed to spy on us?" (He had been warned by one of the faculty members in Madison, Wisconsin, or in Ann Arbor, Michigan, about some of the embassy people. The biology professor had gone to England to march for Nuclear Disarmament and then was called to the embassy in London and queried about his fellow demonstrators.)

But their meeting is not what either of them imagined. It begins—this is the routine followed by the Public Affairs Officer—with a sympathetic query and a consequent long discussion about the Fulbright professor's health insurance, residence permit, about his registration with the police authorities, about the bookkeeping conditions of his stipend, about the acquisition of an eventual driving license in this country. (Only after the meeting does it occur to the professor that this man showed hardly any interest in their living quarters and domestic arrangements.) Only later does the Public Affairs Officer ask something about the university and about the Fulbright professor's students. "We would appreciate it," he says toward the end of their interview, "if you could give us a list of your more promising students some time. And also of anyone at the university who may be trying to interfere with your lectures." "I wouldn't put up with anything like that," the professor says. Does this man think that he's a dope?

Yes he does. He does not see much merit in sending American liberals to teach in a Communist country, but now that Washington had decided to go ahead with such an experiment, he has to go along with it. Only: people like this one are hopelessly naive. Or less than naive: they are unwilling to pay sufficient attention to the insidious nature of Communism and of Communists. This man says that when he talked to the Assistant Minister of Culture the other day, the latter assured him that he welcomed more cultural contacts with the United States, that he was an avid reader of Poe and Crane and Hemingway. What a dope.

The American scholar may be a dope, but not quite the kind of dope his interlocutor thinks. His incompetencies are practical rather than ideological. He does not know (and perhaps he doesn't want to know) how to exchange his dollars on the black market (which is the only financial market there is in this country); he lets himself be blackmailed by the owners of their rented apartment, who are advancing their demands month after month; he waits in line for permits that are not needed and forgets to renew permits that are constantly required. Their nutrition is unhealthful, and the black nights in their apartment are either overheated or cold. He does believe in the evils of Stalinism, but he also believes that there exist Marxists with whom a dialogue is not only possible but desirable and that these include his students and probably the Assistant Minister of Culture. What neither he nor the Public Affairs Officer realize is that the aforesaid minister does not believe a word of Marxism — not in 1960, to be sure. That is not due to the deficiency of their knowledge of local politics, but of their understanding of human nature. And of history — but let that now pass.

"Let that pass? This is all about history and politics, and rather cryptic, at that. Especially about the Public Affairs Officer or whatever he is. The Fulbright professor is a type, though you may have forced him into too much of a caricature. Chronologically, too, those professors abroad did not much change: 1950 or 1960 or 1970 or the present."

No, whatever the shortcomings of my sketch of him (and I admit that it is a very thin sketch), 1960 may be just about right, since at that time even liberal professors no longer had many illusions about Communism or the Soviet Union, whereas they still have had their illusions about foreign intellectuals, including some behind the Iron Curtain. Which is why he is perhaps unduly impressed with this Assistant Minister of Culture who keeps talking to him about *The Red Badge of Courage*. But allow me to defend my choice of the Public Affairs Officer. He is a new breed of American official abroad — incidentally, one misunderstood or, worse, miscast by writers in the 1950s, including Graham Greene and Louis Auchincloss.

"You mean *The Quiet American?*"

Exactly. In *The Quiet American* Greene describes him as a dangerous idealist, a Puritan ideologue, a Harvard man. Note that my Public Affairs Officer issued from Georgetown or Fordham. He may not even be Irish; possibly Slovak or something like that on his mother's side. He may or may not have been a McCarthyite in 1954 when he was still a graduate student, but he was an avid reader of Whittaker Chambers's memoirs and of James Burnham and of big tomes like *Oriental Despotism*. Which brings me to Auchincloss, who wrote a novel about a young naive midwesterner who becomes a lawyer on Wall Street and learns about American internationalism from his social contacts there, gradually shedding his strong isolationist convictions. Auchincloss, ensconced in and knowledgeable about Wall Street, ought to have known better than that. His young protagonist would not have been an isolationist at all, not circa 1955. To the contrary: he would have been an unabashed interventionist, believing that the United States must engage itself against the international Communist conspiracy everywhere.

"You're too didactic now."

I am, probably, and I must now be didactic once more, about that Assistant Minister of Culture. He is a high functionary of a Communist government, probably a long-standing member of the party, but here is the difference: by 1960 those people no longer believe in Communism and not even in Marxism. They are bureaucrats without scruples, protecting their high positions and perks and emoluments, one of their many instruments for achieving that protection being the asseveration of their loyalty to the party line and, indirectly at least, to the Soviet Union. But this man and hundreds of others of his kind already know that while they must keep pronouncing their belief in the power of Russia, no one really believes in Communism, probably not even in Russia. The only people who still believe in international Communism in 1960 are to be found among intellectuals in the West, revolutionaries in the Third World, and of course many people in the United States. Let's not dismiss that easily. Twenty years later Communism will be crumbling everywhere, and yet the great majority of the American people will elect and respect Reagan, who obviously does believe in the real presence of the Evil Empire. Of course, one of the reasons for his election was the crumbling not of Communism but of liberalism. But that is another story, and I've been didactic enough.

"I'll say. Now, quickly, to amuse ourselves: what will happen to your three protagonists?"

Perhaps you are right: a bit of amusement is in order. By 1964 the Public Affairs Officer may be a CIA *rezident* in an embassy and by 1970 (to be sure, during the Nixon administration) perhaps even an ambassador in some godforsaken African country. Another ten years later the professor will be emeritus, the trajectories of their careers having been plausible, imaginable, predictable. About the Eastern European Assistant Minister of Culture — well, I *can* imagine him becoming a dissident ambassador or at least a dissident intellectual in, say, 1968 and then, by 1970, after his quick slipping to the West, an Adjunct Professor of International (or Intercultural) Relations at a southern or western American university, writing letters to the *New York Review of Books* and sending op-ed pieces to the *New York Times* soon thereafter. Now please note that neither the *New York Review of Books* nor the op-ed page of the *New York Times* existed in 1960. Had they existed then, this man would have been reading them — of course with the permission of his superiors, but avidly. Ten years later he might run across in the *National Review* a letter written by the former public affairs officer and in the *New Republic* another letter (not about politics; about Theodore Dreiser? or Thorstein Veblen?) written by the professor. He will recall their names, I think.

1961

In 1954 Jack O'Donnell was a college junior. Let me describe him briefly. That is easy: he had some of the features of John Kennedy and of a very young Tyrone Power, which is quite a cliché, except that he did not have a cliché face, with his exceptionally large eyes for an Irish American. He was handsome and temperamental, cultivating his Feckless Irish Charm together with a dark, spoiling kind of pugnacity. At Saint Athanasius College he was one of the few straight-A students, with a 3.97 average. At the same time he was the terror of some of the instructors, for at Saint Athanasius — a Catholic college almost always a year or two behind the circulation of new ideological currencies — Jack was the first person who had the gall (as one of his instructors put it) to call himself a conservative. During that hot and climactic year, for example, he was the head of a college group collecting 1 million signatures against the impending congressional censure of Senator Joe McCarthy. He was a McCarthyite, like some of the students (especially the budding Catholic Republicans in the business school) and unlike most of the faculty. But his political interests were not superficial. He had read at least one biography of Edmund Burke; he bought his own copy of Russell Kirk's *The Conservative Mind;* he took elective courses in Eastern European history and in the Soviet System; he wrote his honors' paper on the Roberts congressional committee's investigation of

Pearl Harbor, which he considered to have been a whitewash job. With
his agile mind he would needle his liberal professors about Yalta and the
unredeemed promises made by Franklin Roosevelt to Poland. When a
sociology professor said that a young Bantu child taken from Africa
and brought up in the United States would become a typical American,
Jack ventured to say that the selfsame child remaining in Africa would
become an even more typical Bantu. He was, however, always polite to
the handful of black students; indeed, unlike some of the other students,
including tribal Democrats who would rarely engage in a conversation
with a black, Jack would argue with the black students for hours, often
unaware of the sometimes insulting character of his arguments.

He was not a barbarian, this compound of shining goodwill and
black prejudices, this young Irishman who differed from the Irish
youths described by James Farrell or by Edwin O'Connor: *Irish* Americans, whereas Jack O'Donnell was an Irish *American,* the youngest son
of a North Philadelphia contractor. And though it was there, in that
Olney Avenue atmosphere, that he inhaled his early prejudices for isolationism and anti-Semitism and Anglophobia, he was not wholly part
of it. He admired, for example, Churchill's prose style. Such things set
him apart from the beer-and-bowling tastes of his neighborhood. He
was part of that, too, of course, including their summers at the Jersey Shore; including the athletic Catholic-college lifeguards with their
splendid torsos and short legs and their uncles' powerboats; including the enormous barns of bars where women play electric organs on
platforms, the newly installed pine paneling exhaling an acrid odor of
soap and sweat. When on those hot and damp Saturday nights, during
the last half hour before closing, the organist and the customers would
belt out the Notre Dame football song, Jack would mumble along. But
Irish-American patriot though he was, he was also aware of some of the
fossilizing manifestations of neo-Gaelic folkishness: he found it ridiculous, for instance, when he saw a picture in a newspaper of the John
Barry parade led by a dishevelled group in kilts calling themselves the
Lafferty Highlanders.

A Mick Tory, an Irish Fascist, some people called him: wrongly so. They assumed a connection between Jack's religion and his right-wing politics. Because Jack was a strong Irish Catholic (he spoke disparagingly of one of his liberal professors who had one offspring and no more), his critics assumed that he was a conformist who was simply smart enough to make a virtue out of what for him was an atavistic necessity. But it was not as simple as that. There was, for example, his trouble with his last religion exam. He had, as I wrote before, a perfect A average; but now he was about to spoil it because of one course, Religion 405, Sacramental Theology. He disliked Father Braun, who taught it ("a squarehead," he would mutter); he certainly did not like the spirit and content of the final examination. Part 1 was the true-false test. (Directions: If a statement agrees with the teaching of the Church, print T in the appropriate place; if not, print F.) "What," Jack said, armed with a mimeographed copy of the previous year's examination, "are answers to questions like these?" (Statement 6: "The body of Christ is present in heaven by its quantity and local extension." Statement 9: "The Eucharistic accidents inherent in the Blood of Christ are incarnated by the wine made from nothing else except pure grapes which are the valid matter for the Eucharist.") Or to the rest of the test? (Question 21: "The physical and chemical properties of the consecrated bread and wine involve which of the following theological realities: impanation; concomitance; consubstantiation; multilocation." Question 40: "Name six specific effects of Holy Communion." Question 41: "Write out five Acts of Faith in the Real Presence.") In the end Jack O'Donnell's common sense carried him over this cataract of conscience. He graduated with his 3.97 record, including a B-plus in Sacramental Theology. He had five offers of graduate scholarships, ranging from an assistantship at Marquette to a graduate scholarship at Colgate at $1,500 per annum, a fellowship at Georgetown at $2,000, and a research fellowship at Penn State at $1,750.

He took the last. He breezed through his master's program in two semesters. His professors thought well of him. Some of this information filtered downstate to Saint Athanasius, reaching Jim Devlin, one of O'Donnell's erstwhile professors, who shook his head in disbelief:

Devlin was a Franklin D. Roosevelt Democrat who thought he knew a Coughlinite or an Irish Fascist when he saw one. A year or so later Devlin found himself involved in an irritating argument with a group of students. This was in the fall of 1959, when Nikita Khrushchev was touring the United States and when the local Catholic press was whipping up protests against his visit. These students said that Khrushchev's presence in this country was soiling the soil of liberty and that not only was he justly forbidden from visiting Disneyland but he should not have been received by the president of the United States at all. Devlin had begun to explain to them some of the routine necessities of international courtesy. That quickly degenerated into an argument about the metaphysics of a world composed of different governments of different ideological systems. "Damn it," Devlin said, "the Russians have their own country and their own government. We have the right to dislike their form of government, but we don't have the right to foist our form of government on them." And: "You've got to grow up; you've got to learn to live with people who are different from you and me." After the class a sophomore sidled up to him. "Dr. Devlin," he said, "you know Jack O'Donnell at Penn State? A former student of yours." Devlin said that he did; with a distasteful expression he turned toward the steps. "You and he surely sound the same," this political science major from North Philadelphia said. "Dr. Devlin has the same ideas as Jack O'Donnell," he turned to a pal, "who is a liberal, a friend of my older brother, a really bright guy." There was a wince of pain on Devlin's face, convinced as he was that he had just met yet another example of the utter confusion of the sophomoric mind.

But less than a year later came a letter from O'Donnell to Devlin, who was now the chairman of the history department. O'Donnell had heard that there was an opening for an instructor in history at Saint Athanasius; he had finished all of his coursework *and* his dissertation, which was already accepted by the department at Penn State; he would receive his Ph.D. next January. He also wrote that he was about to get married and that he would like to come back to Philadelphia. In a separate package he sent Devlin a copy of his dissertation, the title of which was "The Persistence of the Jeffersonian Element in Democratic Party Platforms." As he read the dissertation, Devlin was surprised. To his credit, he was not unimpressed with it. Even more to his credit, he recommended O'Donnell's appointment for a three-year trial period. "We'll see how he does," he said.

And now it is 1961, and O'Donnell is cutting a fast figure on the Saint Athanasius campus. He announces that he voted Democratic in the last election; he coaches the debating team in an argument favoring the United Nations; he writes in the college paper that a strong civil rights bill is a necessity; he throws a hard question at William F. Buckley, Jr., during the latter's archangelic appearance at the Saint Athanasius Lecture Forum. At one of the tables of the faculty dining room there is now a buzz as people discuss O'Donnell's conversion. The consensus seems to be that Jack is an opportunist. Consider his mimeographed reading list for the standard American history course. At the top is Schlesinger's *The Age of Jackson* (required for everyone), and at the bottom is a notation: "History majors are advised to read at least one article from the *American Historical Review* or from the *Mississippi Valley Historical Review*. A regular perusal of the *Reporter* or of the *New Republic* is strongly recommended." Jack is an opportunist, Jack figured that he has to play up to Devlin. No, Jack is not an opportunist, someone interjects, though with a smirk: "He could have gone into his father's business, making thirty thousand a year." (The father, a contractor, is a big fellow, a Knights of Columbus potentate who knows how to throw his weight around.) "It's about time that O'Donnell moves into the twentieth century," someone else says.

No. Jack is moving out of the Irish Puritan seventeenth century. He is still picking his way cautiously over the slippery marble paving of the eighteenth, groping his way out from certain homegrown darknesses of the seventeenth toward the brighter lights of the Enlightenment. His conversion is sincere. It accords with his intellectual prospect of the world. Liberalism is ahead of him, not behind him; it is a step up, a phase in the evolution of the world and in his own evolution as an intellectual. Being a college professor is a step up from being a contractor, but there is more to that than opportunism: Jack not only thinks that a professional intellectual must *become* a liberal but has concluded that he must *be* liberal. Convictions, not hypocrisy, are at work here: intellectual convictions, true, but then so many American convictions really are intellectual ones. Jack's father, the heavy-duty contractor, was no intellectual, and now Jack is the first intellectual in the long history of an Irish-American family. They left the old island of Ireland because of the institutionalized prejudices from which they had been suffering; they carried some of their own prejudices with them, holding on to them for a long time until now, here in America, some of their offspring are becoming intellectuals. There is logic in that historical development. It is historical rather than social. It is not the Kennedy syndrome. It is the O'Donnell syndrome.

So now, in 1961, Jack carries his liberal devices on his aluminum intellectual armor, shining and bright. He quarrels with some of the Republicans in the business school; he appears on the college forum, speaking in favor of the nuclear test ban; and Devlin's suspicions about O'Donnell are melting away, even though a small, stubborn, Irish core of unmeltable skepticism remains. At the same time Jack is becoming, I fear, a bit of a bore on occasion. It is not only that his opinions have lost some of their earlier sharpness; his conversation, too, has lost some of its spark. He is putting on some weight, in more ways than one. He may not have become, as some people had put it, "positively sanctimonious"; he is, rather, negatively sanctimonious. He makes judiciously anticlerical statements with increasing frequency. Is he trimming the faith? Is he falling away from the Church? No: his pretty, strong-willed wife will take care of *that*. One day he sits in the library lounge, with Father Murphy and Witold, a young Polish Catholic exchange student who has come to Saint Athanasius for a year of bewilderment. Father Murphy has taken the teaching place of Father Braun, O'Donnell's former *prêtre noir*. Witold is an existentialist of great volubility, with decidedly radical Catholic convictions. He keeps asking Father Murphy what he thinks of Bernanos, of Dorothy Day, of the Catholic Worker movement, of the reactionaries in the Curia; he expostulates against the envelope system of donations, the football colleges, and Cardinal McIntyre; he says that the best thing for the church in the United States would be to lose its wealth and become *very* poor. Father Murphy is uncomfortable, feeling like an involuntary and somewhat costive Saint Sebastian pierced by all kinds of unwelcome intellectual arrows of a foreign manufacture. The back of his neck gets redder, when Jack O'Donnell walks in and sits down with them; now Father Murphy feels that he is surrounded by inimical forces. But it does not turn out to be that way. As Witold goes on and on, Jack's liberalism, his progressivism, his Americanism, rise geyserlike. In stumbling English, Witold, jumping from crag to crag, reaches the high point of his argument about a vast and desolate spiritual landscape: the Mass cards sent out by an IBM machine in a certain suburban parish, the Lenten hot dogs made out of tuna, and Bingo. "It is a Skandal," he says. "What is a scandal?" Jack says, irritated to a flush. "Come on, Witold, lay off." He sails into the flustered Pole, telling him that European Catholics are not really Catholics and that they had it coming to them. "They sold out to Hitler," Jack growls to Witold, "they sold out to Stalin, and before that they toadied before their kings and princes and their corrupt rotten aristocracies of landlords." "We toddied before Stalin?" says Witold, choking with rage; then he is speechless. Father Murphy breathes long draughts of relief.

And Jack's friends, too: the family friends, the North Philadelphia friends, the Jersey Shore friends. In a way, liberal Jack, the college teacher, is now closer to them than conservative Jack, the North Philadelphia Tory. They admire him in a way, as they admire John Kennedy, and not only when Kennedy is shown playing touch football or laying it on the Russians but also when he has the Nobel Prize winners at the White House for dinner or at a concert in white tails with his pretty wife. And anyone who doesn't understand this doesn't understand the United States at all: that all of American anti-intellectualism, including even the kind that raged during the McCarthy era, is a backhanded compliment to intellectualism, to the power of the brain. To be intellectual in the United States means to be on the way up—in 1961 certainly.

John Kennedy and Jack O'Donnell are *real* intellectuals, American intellectuals, not those Communist or pink pseudo-intellectuals, and these people are proud of them, in their way. They will occasionally drop a remark to Jack when they see him in June, early, with his wife and his babies at the shore: "Jack's a college teacher; he's got a lazy man's job," they will say. But they invite him to go deep-sea fishing on their powerboats, and when on Saturday nights, just before closing time, the electric organ trembles with the Notre Dame football song, they will slap Jack on his shoulders and he will sing with them one stanza, loud and clear. One evening at the bar, they introduce him to a local radio personage with the characteristic South Jersey first name of Vince. He tells Jack that he would like to put him on a radio discussion program with the characteristic title *The South Jersey Gabfest*. "I need a good liberal who can speak," Vince says. It is in the papers; it is a success; Jack appears four times; five alumni write in to the college; he is a credit to Saint Athanasius. He is Irish, democratic, liberal: an American Catholic intellectual, the salt of the American earth, the condiment of the concrete.

"Please explain that seventeenth- and eighteenth-century stuff. Not clear to me."

Let me illustrate it with the Tennessee monkey trial —

"What that has to do with the O'Donnell syndrome I cannot imagine. But go ahead."

People have seen that trial — in 1925, in 1961 (since then there was a successful bad play about it, *Inherit the Wind* or some such title), and today, too — as the classic American drama, the test case, the clash between the nineteenth and the twentieth centuries, between religion and science, between reaction and progress, between conservatism and liberalism, between William Jennings Bryan (the preacher-politician with his big sirloin face, representing the former categories) and Clarence Darrow (the progressive lawyer with his beetling brows, representing the latter). But what Darrow's Darwinism and Huxleianism represented in 1925 was not the twentieth but the nineteenth century, with its faith in science; and what Bryan represented were not the ideas of the nineteenth century but the religious sentiments of the seventeenth century, the atavistic biblical fundamentalism of a Gothic and, yes, often Celtic puritanism that was still alive in America.

"Is this what you mean when you say that in, say, 1960, liberalism is ahead of and not behind O'Donnell? But will he not realize, sooner or later, that while Darwin was ahead of, say, Cotton Mather, so much of Darwinism and Spencerism and Marxism are outdated in the twentieth century?"

Yes, but that would appear to him not in 1961 but later. It *will* appear, because he is an honest fellow. But I am writing about 1961, not 1981 or 1991.

"All right. 1961 is the Kennedy year. The Kennedy era opens. But you are saying that O'Donnell's conversion to liberalism was not quite the same thing as that of the Kennedys."

The Kennedys were more opportunistic, though in their cases, too, there may have been a few other things at work. I distrusted them in the 1950s, when I did not really believe that they had ceased to be McCarthyites deep down; but I was wrong, because the deep down did not really count, because the Kennedys were Kennedys and America was America. They too became liberals of a sort, because of the American idea of progress, which meant acquiring a more intellectual, rational, liberal, modern view of the world—in this country which at that time was conservative at home and revolutionary abroad, where young people were conservative to the bone and older people liberal in their minds, where workingmen were conservative and patricians liberal, where moving up in society meant becoming more liberal . . . well, at least to some extent. But in O'Donnell's case, there were no social ambitions involved, practically speaking.

"Well, you are only partly right. Much of this is arguable. But let's make a fast forward to the 1980s. How will O'Donnell stand then about political correctness, gay rights, pornography, feminism, and so on? Will he still be a liberal? Won't he be disillusioned enough to become a conservative again?"

Only partly so; and only with a lowercase *c*. As a matter of fact — you can see that I like him — his ideas will be a compound (a compound, not a mix) of what remains best in both liberalism and conservatism (if there is such an ism, but let that question go), because of what is best in his Irishness.

"One last question. That anticlericalism of his, which you suggested."

No, that doesn't go too far, either. He will cheer on some of the "reforms" of Vatican II but regret some of them later; he will be a good Catholic father and send his children to Catholic schools. Now here comes to mind something from 1961, involving Kennedy (whom he does not admire unreservedly) and the Church. O'Donnell's is an imaginary, or at least a composite, picture in my mind, but this picture and caption I saw and kept. Here it is: a photograph in the *Catholic Standard and Times*, the Philadelphia diocesan newspaper. There is a smiling priest and three smirking junior high school students. They hold up a giant envelope and a card addressed to President John F. Kennedy, The White House, Washington, D.C. The card has drawings of the Capitol and of Mary Immaculate and the phrases, written in large letters, "God's Blessing" and "Mary's Guidance." The caption notes that Saint John Chrysostom's School "conceived the idea of sending a Spiritual Bouquet to President John F. Kennedy as he took up his executive duties. . . . The card informs the President that the school's students and teachers will offer 2,285 Masses, 2,176 Holy Communions, 1,892 Rosaries, 93,201 ejaculatory prayers, and 15,488 other prayers for the success of his patriotic labors." They must be good at counting, Jack O'Donnell will say. That kind of anticlericalism I did not and do not mind.

"Well, those numbers *are* very American, aren't they?"

Yes, and I hope that battery-operated rosaries are not yet around the corner — though I did recently see a photo of the cardinal of New York on the front steps of Saint Patrick's, holding a cellular telephone to his big ear.

1962

In October 1962 Travis, the Anglo-Irish writer, is in New York. He finds his visit pleasant, despite the mixed bag of his anticipations and then his experiences in the first few hours. He had been in Manhattan ten or twelve years before; much of what he had heard in London about New York and some things that he had read about it prepared him for a less amusing stay now. And then the flight was tiring, and there were the idling wild crowds at Idlewild, and the depressing sight of an interminable urban, or nonurban, wasteland along the expressway, and the diabolical howl of an incessant stream of automobiles echoing from the tiled walls of the underwater tunnel from Long Island to Manhattan, and the monstrous impersonality of the skyscrapers in the darkening afternoon and the screaming avenue traffic, all so different from his eye-opening coming into Manhattan on shipboard in 1952 or thereabout. There was not a single note from his publisher or from anyone else upon his arrival at his hotel. But a change comes soon enough. Flowers and a fine bottle of whiskey arrive in his room, sent with a nice note from his publisher. Then he finds a small Italian restaurant nearby, where he dines alone and well and not at all expensively. Next morning the telephone rings and rings. After that he is seldom alone. His three weeks in New York will fly by in an agreeable whirl.

He is at or at any rate near the peak of his literary reputation, a writer of well-crafted, astringent short stories, whose subjects are less and less frequently Irish people and more and more the London middle classes, but then he has been living in London since the war. He is nearing sixty, a tall gangly man with a seamed face, not very voluble, especially when in the company of people he does not know well—a habit of reserve that he cultivates and that absolutely charms the New York Upper Bohemia hostesses. He is a prize at their parties in their hot-house apartments coruscating with mirrors and glass. And when one evening he rides in a taxi to one of those parties, the rich, electric glittering of Park Avenue impressing him anew, he thinks for a moment that this well-planned scintillation, even if ephemeral, may after all be a triumph of urbanity. He thinks he is strong enough not to see and judge and treat people simply in response to how they treat him, which in this place is certainly sufficient. He is impervious to the emphatic flirtations of certain women, including those of a lovely and intelligent Cuban girl with long black hair shining with the sparks and spangles of starry nights, more real than the spangles and sparkles of her sequined jacket. He is responsive and kind to her, perhaps especially to her verbal ministrations, but lets her go. He does have varicose veins.

He had asked his American publisher (for British tax reasons) to keep his last two royalty payments until he gets to New York. There comes a disappointment: the total amount is about half of what he had expected (and he is a careful and experienced estimator of his royalties); and his pragmatic questions on that first bright noon in the publisher's cluttered office about the mythical and confusing figures on the royalty sheets are of no avail. The subsequent excellent lunch with his publisher and an obsequious young editor in a sumptuous little restaurant does not much lift his spirits. But there are compensations accruing during the three weeks. The *New Yorker* prints and pays generously for three of his stories; one Sunday the *New York Times Book Review* prints a review of a collection of his critical essays on its front page; he enjoys, unexpectedly, his two-day excursion to New Haven, where he answers questions from respectful and intelligent students in a contemporary English writing seminar (there, too, he is pleasantly surprised by the amount of his honorarium, since it includes an unexpectedly large sum for his traveling expenses). And on his last day, during lunch at the same sumptuous little restaurant, when his American publisher suggests that he write a brief text for a photographic picture book about Manhattan, proposing a considerable sum for an advance, Travis says (and thinks), "I could do that"—and the little music of a few sentences forms in his mind as he rides back to his hotel.

Such are things in 1962, when the prestige of a writer from England is still high enough to be translatable into considerable financial advantages in America. Saturnine thoughts about New York in 1962 take final shape in his mind only when he has returned to London and is talking to his (second) wife. "Americans are less practical than they think," he tells her. "All that intellectual argle-bargle." He recounts how people reacted and talked about the Cuban missile crisis, which came and went during his stay. "All that argle-bargle," he repeats. "It did not occur to any of them that the Russians would never risk a world war because of Cuba." One of his American acquaintances called him up one day, asking, "How will you get back to England if there is a war?" Travis remembered that evening; it was getting dark, the telephone shone like a black cat with a round white face. He also recounts to his wife the two phrases (or, rather, definitions) that he learned while in New York: John Kennedy is surrounded by an Irish mafia, and literary life in New York is ruled by a Jewish mafia (the latter told to him late one night in a Third Avenue bar by an Irish writer who kept drinking nothing but pints of Irish lager, one after another).

There end, by and large, the New York recollections of Travis. They are not quite right; but, then, he is a writer, not a philosopher. A social observer, yes; but his comprehension of America and of Americans and, yes, even of New York and of New Yorkers has stopped within certain limits—and not only because, as Wilde once said, America and England are separated by a common language.

"This is not interesting enough. Not even for a period sketch."
Probably.

"Travis is not interesting enough. What makes him different from Jan Morris? Or Pritchett? An Englishman — all right, an Anglo-Irish-man — cossetted in New York."

But Morris did see the decline of New York. When she reminisced and wrote *Manhattan '45,* forty or more years later, she wrote that she chose that title "because it sounded partly like a gun, and partly like champagne, and thus matched the victorious and celebratory theme of my book. But like bubbles and victories, that moment of release, pride and happiness was not to last."

"And she was wrong. She wrote that Manhattan in 1945 'does not seem to have been an envious city.' It was that then and it was that in 1962 and it is that now. She may not have read her Tocqueville, includ-ing his great and grave maxim that whereas the dominant sin of aristo-cratic ages was pride, the dominant sin of democratic ages is envy. But she was good about details."

Travis will be good about details, when he writes his text for that New York picture book. Isn't that enough?

"For his book, yes, but not for this vignette. *You* should have done some of those details. Your job was to write about New York in 1962, which was a moment in its history, after all. Instead you go off again on your visionary track."

But only at the end. And, well, didn't I at least suggest that, when Travis is riding along a brilliant Park Avenue at night, he knows that the urbanity of New York cannot last? Still, you may be right. But I have a subtle, probably too subtle, reason for having sketched this. In 1962 Travis and New York are not what they were in 1952. His sense of won-der is largely gone. So is much of that electric, tingling exhilaration that New York produced for all foreigners, not only Englishmen. In 1962 New York is nervous and fretful, rather than exhilarating, though some of that still remains. And the most interesting matter may be that of the common language, because on one level at least American English and English English *have* become more alike, the second more and more influenced and even suffused by the first. Consider not only vulgar English writers like Roald Dahl, Kingsley Amis, and Anthony Burgess or the invasion of the New York magazine scene by very coiffed and very execrable Englishmen and Englishwomen beginning circa 1962, but also consider the spread of the transatlantic accent, even among the speakers on the BBC. On the other hand, the difference in the purposes of American and English speech remains.

"Now enough of these vignettes about English people in America. You know something about them, but at least I think that not enough. For God's sake, you must write about people and things that you know best."

All right. Now go on and read the next vignette.

1963

"INDIAN SUMMER THIS IS."

"Oh, no. It's not October yet."

"You're right, but for me it is Indian summer."

Words spoken by an elegant and still handsome woman in her late fifties, in a language — Hungarian — where the phrase *Indian summer* is more telling and startling than in English: it is old women's summer, *vénasszonyok nyara*.

"For all of us," another woman says, and around the table everyone laughs, a little.

They sit in beautiful afternoon sunshine. Six of them — two married couples, a widow, a single man — on the terrace of a hotel: a gravel ellipse under summer umbrellas now gathered in, on top of a stony rampart above a lake. The lake, the Wörthersee in Austria, in the province of Carinthia, is an old and famous summer resort in central Europe. This is mid-September, and half of the summer visitors and tourists are gone. On the narrow sandy beach on both sides of the terrace there are still a few bathers and swimmers. The wavelets of the lake keep lapping against the stones with a chilly monotony. But the sun is strong enough and the breeze from the lake gentle enough for some of the women to take off their cashmere cardigans and fold them or drape them on the backs of their chairs. The brightness of the air is almost supernatu-

ral: the mountains across look closer than they actually are. The lake is
dotted with the white flecks of a dozen sailboats and there comes, momentarily, the roar of a motorboat and a water-skier racing in its wake.
On a nearby promontory stands a large villa, its gardens descending
in terraces lined with laurels, roses, yews. The air is so clear that those
flowers, too, look closer than they are.

Some of the villas are postwar, and the waterskiing is postwar,
but otherwise the scenery is much the same as it was before the war,
thirty years ago, or perhaps even earlier. This group of six people know
that, and it is one of the reasons why they are here. They have been
here before, though perhaps not on the same terrace — they have come
over here from another hotel for the pastries and iced coffee, with
whipped cream for some of them. That afternoon custom is also as
it was before. They are survivors. One of the couples fled from Hungary, where Communism was about to be imposed, in 1947, the other
couple and the widow in 1949, the single man in 1956. They had lived
through the war and the German occupation and the siege of Budapest and the Russian conquest of Hungary. Now one couple lives in
New York, the other couple in Milan, the widow in Vienna, the single
gent in Munich. All of them had known each other in Budapest (two
of the women were classmates there), and now they are old friends. At
least three of them take vacations together each year; the others come
every two or three years, having spent weeks and months beforehand
writing letters and telephoning each other about when and where to
go (to a customary hotel of theirs or to another one?). All of them are
between fifty-five and sixty-five. The women are well dressed, two of
them rather smart in their imprimé dresses, silk scarves, and fine shoes,
their hair freshly done; the men are heavier and well dressed, too, in a
somewhat old-fashioned way, in their linen suits or sweaters with ascots tucked in around their necks. A foreigner would find it difficult
to classify them, even without hearing their strangely uncategorizable
language. Only the Austrians, the hotel personnel, and the older ones
among the waiters know that they are Hungarians, but not Hungarians
from Hungary: Hungarian emigrés.

They look well heeled, and so they are. Well they have survived everything, or almost everything, but they do have their memories of the people and the lives they lost: the widow's husband, beaten by the Communist police and dying ten years later in Vienna because of his hopelessly damaged kidneys; the brother of one of the men, killed in a death camp in Poland (two of the group are half-Jewish); the parents of another, deported by the political police and then permitted to return to Budapest, where they now live in two cramped rooms. But they have another set of memories, of other people and other lives too, and so their talk is the old high talk of old fashionable Budapest, with its inestimable knowledgeability of human matters. This lends another dimension to the music that murmurs beneath their talk, for each of them hears the sea of the past murmuring close, as if his left hand held a seashell against his ear, day and night.

"Must I tell you," one of the women says, "that one of the pleasures of friendship is talking about our own infirmities?" About a common acquaintance: "He is so selfish, and not only in the way he lives; he is always pushing others to arrange their lives as he wishes them to live." About another acquaintance's divorced daughter, who is pregnant again but not married: "She reminds me of Germany." "How?" "After expanding, she can't retain her conquests." About New York and one of the gentlemen's adventure there after he suddenly collapsed: in an ambulance, he was transported to a big hospital; no one knew whether he had a stroke or a serious heart attack; he was unconscious. "And guess what was the first thing the nurse said when I came to." "What?" "Man, you sure got cloudy urine."

But their conversation gathers speed and seriousness when they turn to the handsome widow. Gossip is thickening into advice. They know that she is being courted by another Hungarian emigré who lives in Switzerland and who keeps inviting her to Leysin or Davos in the summer and to Menton or Madeira in the winter and that a month ago he was in Vienna on business, setting up in the Sacher and asking her to dine with him, which she did. They know him; he is stocky, with a gravelly voice, rich, perhaps a *bit* vulgar, but he has, after all, placed himself in the very midst of rich life, in all those rich hotels and resorts and restaurants, where he makes sure that he is known, and in that rich apartment of his in Geneva. "Quite overdone, *üppig*," the widow says, in German. "He showed me his collection of emeralds. Stunning, but I think he collects them for investments, 'business,' *g'schäft*," she says, again with a slightly contemptuous Viennese pronunciation. "Vera!" her best friend stops her. "He talked about you to us in Milan all the time. *He* took us out to dinner, and to the Savini—" "Yes, because you had got him a ticket to the Scala." "Stop it. He is all *Feuer und Flamme* about you." *Feuer und Flamme*, fire and flame—they throw a few German phrases into their talk, not because they find themselves in Austria, but because that too was another old Budapestian custom. Vera smiles, quite contented, but she also shrugs her shoulders a little. They know her and love her and are convinced that marrying that man is what she ought to do, what she must do now, on the cusp of the autumn of her life. They know all about her, her virtues and her missteps (if that is what they were), including the fact that for two years she had a sad and rather hopeless love affair with a younger man, who had fled from Budapest to Vienna after the 1956 Rising, and also that many years ago one of the married men in the group had been in love with her, though they are sure (especially the women) that she has got no one now (but, as the men say among themselves while walking back to the hotel, one never knows).

However, what they know about her, what she did do, and what she will do, does not belong in this vignette. What belongs here is their survivorship. Great chunks of their lives had been amputated, all of them are maimed, in one way or another—but are they maimed any worse than are unhappy women or men of a corresponding class of people in, say, England or America? More, yes; worse, no. Their wounds are deeper but they heal better. The Muses are the daughters of Memory, but these people know how to govern their memories; they are the orphaned children but also the orphaned fathers and mothers of their memories. And they know where they are. In the midst of Indian summer, that is. Like all Hungarians, they are congenital pessimists;

but here they sit, in the still, warm September sun, having *Eiskaffee mit Schlag* on the Wörthersee, talking to each other in 1963 à la 1936. They all live a little beyond their means ("if I could only afford to live the way I live," one of them says), which is very Hungarian, too, and the six of them have a total of four children, which is very bourgeois, and they know that they will not live much longer and will then rest (if that is the word) in alien cemeteries; but now their flesh and their souls are warmed by this Indian summer, and perhaps they know that not only is this *their* Indian summer, it is the Indian summer of Europe or, more, the Indian summer of Western civilization, of the only civilization that they know—and that we know.

"I know that you know those people very well and that you are fond of some of them, but we are concerned with history, aren't we? I fear that you are overdoing that Indian summer bit. The Indian summer of Europe—or, at that, of Western civilization—were the years before 1914."

Of course. But this is something else: it is the Indian summer of Indian summer, the sun having come out for a few years, that's all. They are in the midst of the recovery of their lives, including some of their comforts and standards. That of course can happen anywhere, any time. But they are also in the midst of the recovery of Western Europe after the war—as a matter of fact, near its ephemeral peak. Incidentally, they know that. On that particular afternoon they do not talk much about politics, but they all agree—wrongly—that a United Europe is coming; as one of the men says, "That can no longer be reversed," and of course they are all in favor of a union of Europe. It did not happen that way, and perhaps it will never happen, but that is something we know now, after most of them would have died. But there is one thing I want to say. Having been cosmopolitan Hungarians, they have had bred into them the desire and love for Europeanness. And, unlike some

Western Europeans, they are also very pro-American. Because of many reasons: America the leader, the hope of the free world, et cetera, et cetera. They, including the couple who live in New York, understand little about American politics and American tendencies. Perhaps they like America for the wrong reasons. But they know that this recovery of Europe after the war, this restoration, was largely due to American generosity and to the American example. And so it was.

"Very nice; but that prosperity includes things that they do not and cannot like very much. All those crowds of tourists. The rise of the proletariat. Giving credit to the masses—that was the American achievement. After the war the Europeans have thought it best to emulate it: the welfare state, installment buying, and soon credit cards. The lower classes first merging into and submerging the middle classes. All polls and popularity contests and television. Well, it is usually you, not I, who keeps worrying about where this will lead, where it has already led, whether it has been any good."

Let's not think about the results. What I was trying to suggest was that there was this little Indian summer after the big Indian summer in Western Europe for about ten years, say, from 1958 to 1968, and that these people, not Western Europeans by birth but refugees and survivors, knew it perhaps better than any other people. And they are blessed thus, but perhaps they do not know that.

"Spare me your apocalyptics and tell me just one more thing. What happened to Vera and to fire and flame?"

Reader, she did *not* marry him.

"It's 'Reader, I married him.' You have your *Jane Eyre* wrong."

Well, she did not marry him, but not because he wouldn't have read *Jane Eyre* or wouldn't know Strindberg from Schnitzler. He was not civilized enough.

"But I feel, and perhaps you suggest, that she had slept with him once, maybe in Vienna, or how would she know about his apartment in Geneva?"

I am afraid that this must have been so, and I will admit that this would not have been taken so lightly either by her or by her kind of people fifty years before, which is why I insist that this was an Indian summer after the real Indian summer.

"There is, however, one good thing to say for this century, and you know what it is. In 1963 this woman, in her late fifties, is attractive; indeed, she is still sexually desirable. Wouldn't have happened in 1893."

Good point, but it doesn't belong here.

1964

AURORA, BAREFOOT, sits on a big, cracked leather beanbag on the floor of her newly acquired apartment in New York. She is thirty-three, a very attractive young woman, though now somewhat unkempt (she would not like that description and would even prefer "somewhat uncouth") à la mode of the sixties, except that she does not let her nice hair grow long but cuts it short. She is conscious of her looks and of her situation: Upper Bohemia, New York, 1964. I don't know whether she would recognize these terms as such, but the *upper* is there, jostling for place with her *Bohemia*. By "there" I mean the apartment, too, which is not in Greenwich Village or SoHo but on the top floor of a brownstone town house on the East Side in the Forties: it is not a loft but a studio; the windows need cleaning but are tall and airy; there are canvas-backed directors' chairs and track lights and in the other room a large Scandinavian slab of a bed, but the portière separating the rooms is Scalamandré, one of the rugs is a large knotted-silk Serebend, there are a Philadelphia Chippendale sideboard, a fine cherrywood lowboy, and four good Gostelowe chairs around a modern Italian dining table of marble, glass, brass. She holds one of those thick, half-opaque glasses in her hands; her nails are painted pale white; her thin wrists are beautiful. She talks with K., who is her older cousin once removed and who has come up to New York for a visit.

Yes, she is a Philadelphian who has rebelled à la mode. Her self-explanation is simple: she had to break away from a place where everyone acts and thinks in the same way, wearing the same clothes, holding the same ideas, reading the same papers and the same (few) books, incurious and ignorant of other people, other interests, other ideas, other preferences, other inclinations, other realities. Yet there was, and is, nothing very philistine about her Philadelphian father (her mother died young), a Democrat and a liberal who was in Rome after the war and then stayed there, where he met and married a half-Italian American divorcée, not at all a Philadelphian and, perhaps because of that, much more socially conscious than her husband. He is a soft and kind and gentle man, liberal in his view of the world and perhaps excessively trustful of Adlai Stevenson, the United Nations, Planned Parenthood, and modern art. Aurora was brought up partly in Italy, went on to Radcliffe or Wellesley, and married a very rich young man whose family had risen to the Social Register in Philadelphia but a few years before, mostly because of their large and visible public donations. The young couple had a very large house in the country, with a magnificent old stone barn, a large stable, and at least two horses, a hunter and a hacker for each of them. But they had less and less to do and to talk about together, and she left him. She has money of her own, including a settlement from her husband and the cash from a large diamond bracelet (rather un-Philadelphian in 1960) that he had given her for a wedding present and that she sold, not for what it was worth but for enough to buy her present apartment. And she is very busy now, being a young patroness and assistant stage manager of a ballet company, besides going to a sculpture class and smoking innumerable cigarettes, including one or two marijuana joints at night. Her nights are busy, she has come to know many young people in New York, of all kinds. On her left upper arm she had a daisy tattooed. Her bed is unmade but she has pulled that portière closed, and there are books and magazines strewn around the main room, including of course the *New York Review of Books.*

Whether she has a resident lover I don't know, and neither does K. She calls him Uncle K., which I find somehow endearing, but my main interest is him, not her. For he is perplexed—perplexed, rather than worried—which is the main theme of this vignette. He likes her, he thinks she is beautiful, and he is not particularly disconcerted by the bohemian accoutrements of her setting or by her bohemian clothing. (He does not see the tattooed daisy, because she wears a long-sleeved blouse with her blue jeans.) He does not feel particularly uneasy, perhaps especially after she pours him one or two strong gin and tonics in those thick glasses. She asks about Anne and about some of their common, rather distant relatives, and she shows him her unfinished, abstract wire sculpture, and it is only then, with the second strong drink in her hand, that she feels compelled to tell him a little about why she has chosen to live here, and she is relieved that he asks hardly anything about her circumstances (or about her divorce) and that he seems to be quite pleased with her. There is only a faint touch of anxiety on his part when he says good-bye and pecks her on her cheek: "Rorie, you must take good care of yourself here," with a very slight stress on the word *here*. And then comes the *esprit de l'escalier* when, in the elevator, he thinks that he ought to have asked more about the circumstances of her life, because he perhaps ought to have shown more concern and because, among other things, Anne would be interested in that.

He is not a stiff old gent—you know that. Or, rather, he is a bit stiff and a bit old, and he knows that, and that is what perplexes him. He is set back—a little—by the bohemian climate of her place and its evident air of some disorder, and he is inclined to think that she might be sailing too close to trouble, but at the same time he has a sense of nostalgic longing for her youthful independence. I am now over sixty, he thinks; and perhaps what she has chosen to do, something like this present chapter of her life, should have been a chapter of my life, too, but I missed that. And about this he is quite wrong.

He is wrong because he thinks—and says to people at home— that Rorie is a free spirit, which she is not.

"I know what you're getting at. But you just said that your main interest involves him and not her."

It does. He is wrong not only because of the shortcoming of his view of her *bohémienne* life; there is a shortcoming in his own self-knowledge. That kind of Bohemia was not and would never have been the place for him, not even temporarily. He regrets this and sees it as a quondam missed opportunity, even as a fault of his own character. Which it is not. He is naive and innocent in a very American way, for he thinks life is either-or: either a conventional life or an unconventional one; either conformity or freedom; either restriction or experiment. He should know better, since he is a painter: freedom *is* restrictions—all right, call them limitations. Sitting on a beanbag is not very comfortable, you know; an armchair is much better, not because it is upholstered but because it has a stiff back to lean against. (And those restrictions of freedom not only make us more comfortable. They do not impoverish us; they enrich us.) He mistakes ideas for principles, which is perhaps *the* American predicament. He leads an honorable life in Pennsylvania—and I do not only mean the respect owed him by other people—and he is not confident enough about that. He knows that his life is not constrained by social tyrannies, but his occasional longing for a little anarchy is sentimental, not romantic.

"Whence his misconception of Aurora's dawn of freedom?"

Yes. But it is not a complete misconception. Remember that he is perplexed rather than charmed and that he is also worried about her, a little. With every reason, of course.

"With *every* reason? Don't exaggerate. Don't make Aurora into a caricature. Is she simply a fool?"

You have just made me change my tack. Must I write more about her? She is not a fool, and beanbag and bare feet notwithstanding, she is just intelligent and self-confident enough not to become a caricature of herself or a type. She has better taste than judgment, and people with good taste do not become caricatures of themselves, no matter how wrong their judgment may be. One crucial element: she is very well aware of her looks. There is another element, no less important: she is aware of where she comes from and does not reject it entirely, despite all that talk of escaping from Philadelphia. She has good manners, and with K. she talks about their relatives with genuine interest.

"Which reminds me of your story about another Philadelphian gentleman-painter of a generation before, who went to see Mary Cassatt in Paris and was disappointed because all she wanted to talk about was their relatives in West Philadelphia."

But that was circa 1900. You know the other Mary Cassatt story: when she had come back from Paris for a short visit to Philadelphia, the social column of the *Public Ledger* reported the arrival of "Miss Mary Cassatt, the daughter of Mr. Alexander Cassatt, president of the Pennsylvania Railroad, who has been studying art in Paris, and who owns one of the smallest Pekinese dogs in the world." Rorie is no Mary Cassatt, and this is New York 1964, not Paris 1900. She will not have a Degas for her lover, but she will get involved with all kinds of dreadful men and women, including many frauds and phonies, though she will be strong enough to detach herself from them when finally necessary, at the cost of a bruised soul and, later, two hard lines gradually forming around her mouth. There is, however, an excuse for her illusions. In that studio apartment she has a large, beautifully framed photograph of her mother, whom she hardly knew (she died when Rorie was five), even though she knows that her mother was a very conventional Philadelphian lady and that the marriage of her parents was not a particularly happy one. She has no picture of her stepmother, whom she dislikes, not out of some Freudian jealousy but because of the stepmother's social ambitions and pretensions. It would be not much of an exaggeration to say that they hate each other, which is at least one of the reasons for her departure from life in Philadelphia to life in New York. Still, her illusions, Aurora's Illusions, of arriving at a life of a beautiful young patroness of the arts, of being accepted by all kinds of interesting and artistic people: she will soon learn, and, alas, painfully, that *ça ne marche pas*. That's not how it is, and that's not how she is.

"And a little later will she meet an attractive young man, for once good-looking, very lean and very blond, tweed jacket and khakis almost always, both a gentleman and artistic, only to find out later that he is homosexual?"

Plausible, but this is not worthy of you. I said that she is not my main interest, and I will not speculate further about her career in New York.

"One more thing: did you have to get in a dig against the *New York Review of Books?*"

It was not a dig but a mention, one small illustration among the details of her surroundings. However, I must admit: in 1964 the *New York Review of Books* was an emblem, a symbol; it had a cachet for people like Aurora. It had started the year before and was already a success, because its founders had recognized a sure thing, which was that for some time reviews had become more important than books and that reviews are what academics and intellectuals most like to read, so there was an obvious place for such a big sheet, especially when reviews elsewhere had shrunk or were flat. They recognized another thing, too: those personal ads, heavily laden with the intellectual perspiration of musky sexual promises. In publishing those ads in its large, floppy pages, the *New York Review of Books* was a pioneer and was most successful, because by 1964 we had moved into a society where no longer men and women of the same "class" but men and women of the same "culture" seek each other out—an interesting and even intriguing development, which has little to do with civilization while it has much to do with sexuality. And while someone like Aurora would not deign to consider any of those personal ads and perhaps not even to read them (unless someone points out a particularly ludicrous one to her), the sexual attractions—yes, they are sexual—of communing with a man of a different culture played a definite, though unadmitted, part in her decision to find a new life for herself in New York. Intellectuals make better lovers—she thinks this, at least for a while. But her learning process does not interest me at all.

"One really last question. What is a Gostelowe chair?"

A chair made around 1800 by Gostelowe, a Philadelphia cabinet-maker who specialized in chairs.

"And you seem pleased to know that."

I am ashamed to admit, yes.

1965

Lunch at a new Italian restaurant in North Philadelphia. The restaurant is full, and the food is rich. At one of its tables sit four men, one priest and three laymen: the vice president of the nearby Catholic college; a member of its board of directors and his friend, a lawyer; and the treasurer of the college, the brother-in-law of the college's president and an owlish little man in demeanor as well as in the cold material wisdom his owlishness suggests. Above the lawyer's thick neck shines the big brown slab of his face, which except for its color resembles not at all the turtlelike face of certain old Philadelphia lawyers (like the eagle, the turtle is a very American animal); he rather resembles his friend and neighbor, the member of the board of directors, except for the latter's silvery hair. The vice president is the only thin man among the four, with his thin-rimmed glasses and with a birdlike neck in his clerical collar. He defers to the treasurer, for more reasons than one: he is a listener rather than a talker, especially on this occasion, when the talk is mostly about the college's financial future.

This is a heady time for restaurants in America. They have begun to multiply even in Philadelphia, with a new generation of people having arisen who know more and more about restaurants, though perhaps less and less about their mothers' cooking. The austerities of dining out in Philadelphia are melting away in the affluence of the easy manners and money of the 1960s; Italian restaurants, for example (and it is an obvious example) are no longer quartered in the Italian neighborhoods of South Philadelphia. This one is opulent, with a menu large enough for a cruise ship, bound together by a deep-red braided cord. There are Pompeian decorations on the walls, white plaster statues at the entrance, white tablecloths and red napkins; no red-and-white-checked tablecloths here. The vice president is a quiet man and seems to be impressed, almost uncomfortably so. The others at the table seem comfortable indeed.

This is a heady time for colleges and universities in America. The predictions, including those of the demographers, of a few years ago were wrong: the number of college-bound students is leaping upward, not sliding downward; there is a general sense of national prosperity, together with a large increase of government monies available to colleges. Perhaps Catholic colleges benefit from these conditions now, after the Kennedy years, when the last vestiges of uneasiness with Catholics and their institutions have by and large vanished. The Americanization of the Church (instead of the Catholicization of America — but let that go for a moment) has leaped forward, unexpectedly assisted by the recent outcomes of Vatican II and *aggiornamento:* now the Mass is in English, and the Epistles and the Gospels are in American English, suited to the television age; guitar Masses are around the corner; entire religious orders of nuns are abbreviating or even shedding their habits. And that is also what these four men are talking about. They do not call it the Americanization of the Church, of course, but both the lawyer and the eminent member of the board of directors say that they love the new Mass. "Father, certain things *had* to be done," one of them says, and the others nod. But that is only part of the small talk. The purpose of their lunch is to talk about the financial future of the college. For despite that rolling wave of new enrollments, despite the corporate and government grants, there is a large debt to be serviced, while the new Costello Science Building (named after a former member of the board of directors) is already built and the new $3 million student center is about to be finished; and though the auditors have been perfectly satisfied with the present administration of the college's finances, "those people never think more than six months ahead," the lawyer says. And now the member of the board of directors drops his bomb. "Father, you'll have to think of selling the Scholasticate," he says. "Joe and I have been talking about this," and he looks at the treasurer, who nods. "I brought Tom with me," he explains, indicating the lawyer, "because he knows more about real estate than any other lawyer I know, or perhaps more than any honest lawyer should know," and they all laugh. Even the priest, who suddenly realizes that this has been prepared by the treasurer in cahoots with these people and that he himself will have to open this matter up with the president, who is away on a trip but will be back in a day or so, whose brother-in-law the treasurer is, and to whom he is—perhaps unduly—inclined to defer.

I shall not go into the intricacies of the personal relationships of the treasurer and the president and the vice president, suggesting the tension (if tension it is) between the worldly and the spiritual inclinations of the American Roman Catholic Church—I am no J. F. Powers—but allow me to insist that what is at stake here is the priority, the unquestioned priority, of the Americanization of the Church, instead of the Catholicization of America. Let me tell you why. Because of the Scholasticate. Because of the history of the Scholasticate. Because of the past and the present and the future of the Scholasticate. You see, the Scholasticate, where the seminarians and the novices and some of the priests now live, was acquired by the order a dozen years ago for a most reasonable sum (including tax benefits for its erstwhile owners). Carmarthen Hall was the splendid estate of the ———s, a Philadelphia family up there with the Wideners and the Elkinses and the Wanamakers and the Stotesburys in the list of prominent Philadelphians, nouveaux riches in 1900 but certainly no longer nouveaux in 1950. Yes, Carmarthen Hall arose around 1900, when the new rich built their estates on the outskirts of the great cities of America, large mansions with turrets and Norman roofs and parterres and parks, erected on foundations twenty feet deep and four feet thick, impressive monuments to these founders of family fortunes for the glory of themselves and for that of their wives and children. Yet their glory lasted scarcely beyond one generation, and sometimes not even that. By 1950 most of these estates and magnificent houses were empty; they could no longer be kept up. The reasons for this were — perhaps — taxes and the high cost of servants. Their owners could no longer afford them: this is what they said; it seemed reasonable enough then, it seems reasonable enough now. Yet there was another reason, on a deeper, more personal level: for when people say they cannot afford something, this usually means that they don't really want to afford it. But then they and their parents had not had these houses for long.

And so, circa 1950, their mansions were sold to institutions, often to Catholic religious orders. There was something sadly telling in the aspect of these estates then, but there was also something in their prospect that was very American and perhaps even inspiring. Here were these palatial mansions, these merchants' castles erected at a time when Protestant financiers and men of business had gathered much wealth and began to live as if they were the American Borgias and Sforzas and Medicis of the rising twentieth century, the richest and most powerful representatives of American civilization in the world. Well, it did not quite happen that way. After thirty or at most forty years of opulent (and sometimes uneasy) living there, they sold their houses to the institutions or the companies of the grandchildren (and sometimes even the children) of their Irish gardeners and handymen and chauffeurs. And so, around 1950, their estates became the novitiates and the scholasticates and the convents, the training schools of nuns and brothers and priests, of the children of the Catholic common people of America, full of vitality. As in the case of the Saint Athanasius Scholasticate. In occupying these houses, the new residents would sometimes change things around with not the best of taste. Still, they brought a new life into these abandoned mansions and premises, tending gardens where elegant, thin-stemmed flowers had once leaned against the walls, growing thick-stemmed vegetables for their own plastic-covered tables, keeping the rose beds, and, with respect and with pride, pointing out to visitors the rich mullioned windows, the stained glass, the carved moldings, the large Renaissance mantel over the fireplace. There was, after all, a strange kind of historical justice in the fact that some of these objects of the old European civilization now reverted to the possession of a new, American, and Catholic people. That the mantel carved by a French *ébeniste* four hundred years before, that the old stained-glass window set by an Irish glazier sixty years before, that the stucco swirls and crenellations on a ceiling kneaded into place by an Italian immigrant plasterer fifty years before, now look down on a crowd of *their* descendants, who have come to occupy these buildings after the cold men and women who had ordered them to be built left them for good. The smell of hot dogs and sweet popcorn and the sound of television now waft across these baronial halls — and also the occasional scent of incense, the communal murmurs of the rosary plainchant, and lusty caroling during the month before Christmas.

Ah, but it will not last. The Scholasticate's present occupants do not know that, but the treasurer and the director and the lawyer, all splendid Catholic laymen, know that, now, in 1965. For in 1965 — with all of that prestige and prosperity and building and enrollment and a pope visiting America, with 100,000 American Catholics filling Yankee Stadium at the open-air Mass — the Americanization of the Church and the Catholicization of America are like the ends of an open scissor, pointing at opposite directions. Or, rather: it is not so much the Americanization of the Church as it is the Americanization of its people. For some years now there have been fewer and fewer vocations, fewer and fewer young Catholics who enter the Church having chosen to become novices, postulants, brothers, seminarians, future priests and nuns. The numbers have been dropping, precipitously so. The treasurer knows this, and the priests know it, too. This lunch is an occasion of its recognition. Soon the superiors of Saint Athanasius, like the superiors of many other orders, will close down the large houses of their scholasticates or novitiates. They too will think that they can no longer afford this kind of upkeep. To many of them *aggiornamento* means going out into the world and joining in with the business bureaucracy of America, which is penetrating and indeed forming their thinking, ready as they

are to listen not only to lawyers and financiers but also to a new ar-
ray of management experts and developers. And so, four or five years
after that exploratory lunch, Carmarthen Hall will be abandoned by its
occupants again. The grass will grow rank, the mansion will be shut
down, except perhaps for a gatehouse and a trailer-house refectory;
again the wrought-iron gates will be locked save for a few hours each
day. The Scholasticate will be another transitory chapter in the short —
very short — history of Carmarthen Hall, because Catholic Americans,
too, with all their demonstrable vitality, will not be impervious to that
strange atrophy of the will, to the fatalism and the nomadic imperma-
nence that may be the eternal Indian curse on the American land.

"Whew!"

I guess this is what you'd call my moments of monumental gloom.

"It is monumental, all right. You made that merchant's mansion
into a monumental symbol."

No, it is a small symbol, though a symbol nonetheless. At any
rate it is in the nature of symbols that their size is incidental; it is the
significance of their meaning that counts.

"You don't have to tell me that. You've been didactic enough
throughout this vignette. And now I have two serious objections. First,
this is a big country, and the Church is a big church, a house of many
mansions, as has been properly said, and so its edifice *and* its history
include many different people, its nooks and crannies accommodating
Trappists and bingo parishes, Dorothy Day and Bill Buckley. My second objection connects with the first. Is it your suggestion that in 1965
and afterward the decline and the ruination of American Catholicism
(and *is* that an ism?) will proceed apace with the abandonment of that
pile of a building and of some of its contents? You know as well as I that
this isn't so. In one way or another the Church will last till the end of
time. Yes, there are people — including, I admit, American Catholics —
who do not really believe that. But you and I do; and you, even in the

gloomiest of your moments, know as a matter of fact that the Church, probably including even the Order of Saint Athanasius, will easily last not only beyond the demise of that Carmarthen Hall but beyond many other things besides."

Let *me* now say "Whew!" My alter ego is right. This peroration of yours is a breath of fresh air, dispersing monuments of gloom.

"I am glad you said peroration, not pontification."

No, the pontificator is not you but I. But now in the literal sense of pontification — that is, bridge building, connecting — my excuse, my reason, for this vignette is 1965, no more and no less. Yes, for American Catholics, including priests and bishops, the dependence on and the deference to real-estate tycoons, golfing lawyers, and so on are not new in 1965. They had been going on for a long time. What is new is that in 1965 it accords, it is almost synchronized with, the new Mass, the new liturgy, the new language — yes, language. And that has imminent consequences. The language of the new Mass includes such things as *headwaiter* for the steward at the wedding at Cana. (Why not *maiterdee?*) Only a year or two before 1965, Dwight Macdonald compared the language of the New English Bible to a parking lot where once a great cathedral had stood. Only a few years after 1965, I read in a Philadelphia newspaper an advertisement for a Catholic church in Camden; the ad announced to the faithful the advantages of Saturday afternoon Mass, in big letters: "Our Church Is Comfortably Air-Conditioned"; "Ample Parking in Church Yard."

And there is another connection here. I may be a conservative Catholic, but I will not agree with those conservatives who blame Vatican II for everything, who say that all was solid, traditional, hunkydory for the Church in the fifties. It wasn't. Here is the title of an article in a very conservative American Catholic magazine in 1956: "Let's Put the Mass into American." Here is some of the text: "The Church must adapt itself to the needs of modern American life. The American Church must take a more active part in the world by adapting the Church to modern life." This was written not by a liberal Catholic but by a McCarthyite priest. The Kennedy phenomenon was yet to come.

You know, of course, that John Kennedy and C. S. Lewis died on the same day. Lewis had written about himself that he was "a converted pagan living among apostate Puritans." Kennedy lived the life of a paganized Catholic at the very time when many of the apostate American Puritans might have been ready for conversion, but that was not to be. But let us not exaggerate the Kennedy phenomenon—it was a flash in the American pan, shorter than any of the chapters in the short earthly life of Carmarthen Hall.

"And more, or less, meaningful than the latter?"

Less, I think.

"Well, don't think too much, because God alone knows."

1966

THIS VILLAIN, associate professor of history at a large state university of one of the southern mid-Atlantic states, is talking to his wife about something important at the dinner table. That is a somewhat unusual occasion, because he rarely talks to her about anything that is important, except for faculty gossip and academic politics when those seem to be important for him. His wife has taken a job as a cataloguer at the university library, and their working hours, and dining hours, seldom match. They have no children. Both of them are in their late thirties; their marriage went flat and stale rather soon after their wedding. It would be a waste to describe them or their house in detail. They are a not untypical university couple, in a typical suburban house (modern, split-level, yellow brick with white siding) on the edge of a spreading Southern town. She is the better half of this couple; he is an academic opportunist, and a dull fish at that. What he is telling her is that a department meeting is coming up next day, and he will propose that a program of African-American Studies be introduced.

"Will *you* teach it?" "Of course not." "So why propose it?" "You don't understand. I just explained that to you." "You don't need it for your promotion, do you? You've told me umpteen times that your promotion is a sure thing. Didn't those on the rank and tenure committee tell you that?" "I just said that you don't understand."

Reader, *I* understand. But it is not simple. He is a Johnson voter, a Democrat, an academic liberal in favor of civil rights; but he has no particular affection or even interest in blacks, and as a matter of fact he keeps repeating a few nasty jokes about them whenever he visits his brother in northern New Jersey, where they both derive from. He has no interest in the history of the American Negro. His field is the history of the trade policies of the early New Deal, a narrow field, which he has plowed over and over without seeding it, practicing academic monoculture with an acceptable yield. So what is his purpose now? It should be obvious: to gain additional recognition, to impress some people, to take another small step in the direction of his promotion and thus at least a five-thousand-dollar increase in his salary; as he has told his wife innumerable times, that will be the time for her second car (which really will then be his car) or for a swimming pool.

It *should* be obvious, but it is not obvious at all. He is a lanky, tall, young man with a sallow, horsey face, a first-class golfer, already a champion on his public high school team in the New Jersey suburb where he grew up. His father was a salesman and his mother a dental technician. Everything indicates that he is an American materialist. He is less interested in history than in historianship, but then so are many of his colleagues. Where he differs from most of them is in his confidence in his athletic self, including his athletic appearance, in his avid interest in cars, and in his desire to eventually become a member of an expensive and luxurious golf club in Georgia, where he could then spend long weekends and perhaps even entire weeks during an increasingly easy teaching schedule. These are the things he hopes to be able to afford, depending on the future increments of his salary.

It is all very simple, as is the case with all materialists; but it is not that simple at all. For he is sincere when he elects to appear as spokesman for African-American Studies. His is not the calculated move of an opportunist. He contemplates that opportunity with something of the same kind of anticipation with which he contemplates the prospect of an eighteen-hole round on a course that he knows well enough to be the top man of the foursome he will be playing with: the proper application of his physical prowess on the links, the proper application of his mental prowess at the faculty meeting, both at the proper time. He knows that programs for African-American Studies have now been introduced at Chicago and Harvard and Berkeley and Duke. Most of his colleagues know that, too. And now he will impress them because he will represent an idea whose time has come, an idea that is already "in." His career may profit from it, but that is not the principal thing in his mind. *He thinks that this is what his mind, the professional academic mind, is for.* I submit that this is something relatively new. It is not materialism, and it is not hypocrisy. This man is a new breed.

"He is a dull fish, and you're making way too much of him."

Probably, but don't you see that his kind is a new breed? In a way — in a terribly cheap but complex way — this man is an idealist, but not what we think of as an idealist. He is convinced that his job is to represent ideas. *Represent* them, rather than explain them or even believe in them. He sees no contradiction in that. Nor is he a sales representative (the current term for a salesman) of ideas. A salesman must sell; his income and success depend on how much he sells out there. This man is a new kind of salesman whose income and success depends on how he impresses the other salesmen at the home office.

"I'm not so sure. You say that he is not a materialist, but would he for a moment entertain such an idea as this new program if it could endanger his material interests in the slightest? As a matter of fact, he thinks that it might enhance them. You say that he is not a hypocrite, but you yourself said that he has no liking for Negroes."

He is all of that, but don't you see that there is something worse at work here? This man is fundamentally, hopelessly dishonest. And he is dishonest in a new kind of way, in the way he uses his mind — openly, within his profession, without much calculating at all.

"You describe him as a kind of automatic dummy, with a mental antenna that responds to junk in the air — more precisely, to junk in the air that is blowing around more and more obviously, getting more and more widely accepted — and who thinks that that antenna *is* the most important part of the radio of his brain, its function being receiver as well as transmitter. What is so new about that?"

He is not a dummy, and his mind is far from being simple.

"Yes, I know your argument: that simple people are not simple at all; that, as a matter of fact, they are very complex — "

And that people's minds are becoming more and more complex, which does not of course mean that they are becoming more intelligent.

"But we know all that. Intellectual dishonesty is all around us now; it is the dominant affliction of this century. But then, the sins of the spirit have always been not only worse than but inseparable from the sins of the flesh — one of your main convictions. In this case you are not too convincing. Your man *is* calculating. His purpose is to impress at least some of his colleagues, and he surely expects to see his proposal reported next day in the campus newspaper. He wants to be popular, doesn't he?"

Yes, he does — he has always been that way.

"So is he really a new breed? You gave a physical sketch of him, and he reminds me of those second-line football coaches one sees on television: lanky, tall, very carefully got up and dressed, with their hair cut just before the game, walking around fiercely, chewing gum furiously, with an expression of a hardly disguised sense of superiority over the spectators and a hardly disguised contempt for the world around them — but that contemptuous look is incomplete, since they are very much aware of their image, with which they are principally concerned. The trouble with you is that you are too much concerned with ideas — all right, with the relation of men to ideas, with their management of them. You think that intellectual dishonesty is the worst kind of dishonesty — indeed, that there are really no other dishonesties — and that is to your credit. But consider, please, what difference does it make? In this case, I mean. You are, you always have been, skeptical and critical of ideas whose time has come, but sooner or later African-American Studies will appear in the curriculum of that university, whether this creep is the first to propose them or not. So do not build your case by insisting that this man has no material interests, that he is a new kind of dangerous succubus. Besides, once in a while there *are* ideas whose time has come that are actually good."

And is the recognition of the increasing prevalence of intellectual dishonesty not one of them? It suggests the increasing intrusion of mind into matter, a kind of spiritualization of matter that is full of unseen dangers.

"Going too far, again. Unseen? Perhaps. Unrecognized and unrecognizable? No."

1967

In the Episcopal Church of Saint Luke there is a christening. It will take place during the 11:00 A.M. service, not after it, which is an innovation among other innovations of the liturgy that the present rector has chosen to introduce and perhaps even to favor. Communion, for example, no longer consists of wafers but of crumbs from a large brown loaf of whole-wheat bread baked by Mrs. A., a parishioner living around the corner from Saint Luke, who brings it over to the church every Sunday morning, for which the rector solemnly thanks her, enjoying for a moment the pleasant warmth of the loaf in his hands; by the time of Communion, of course, the bread has cooled, and he crumbles it on a large silver plate, making sure that none of the crumbs falls on the floor. There is also an assistant, another parishioner, a large woman rather stately in her white alblike gown, gray-haired, with an interesting face, including a mouth not devoid of sensuality. However, Saint Luke is still much of a traditional middle-high American Episcopalian church in 1967. It was founded and built eighty years before in an already well-contained suburb of Philadelphia (in reality, a village within the unusually drawn large boundaries of the city), on land generously donated by what already was the second generation of an upper-class family and carefully, though perhaps no less generously, endowed by families of former Republican ironmasters one generation removed from their former Presbyterian or even Methodist parentage — families no longer considered parvenus in 1887 except by some. The Episcopal Church of Saint Luke is brownstone, resembling Anglican churches in England and Wales, except for the Romanesque arcade connecting it with the rectory and the fact that the churchyard is small, with no lych-gate and no more than a few tombstones. The woodwork, with carvings of the high stall of the choir, is very fine, and there are excellent stained-glass windows donated by successive parishioners, most of them between 1900 and 1925. There is, too, an impressive reredos (or is it the stone pulpit? or the baptismal font?) that a wealthy member of the congregation, an eminent Philadelphia lawyer, bought somewhere in France in the twenties and donated to Saint Luke circa 1928.

In 1967 the congregation has, of course, thinned. This is the standard Sunday 11:00 A.M. service, but the pews are less than half full. The population of the suburb in the middle of which Saint Luke stands has not thinned; as a matter of fact, its racial and social composition has remained fairly stable, even in 1967, as has the membership and the student population of its immediate neighbors, the Cricket Club and the Academy School, though there are now a few Italian-American members at the club (and Mexican waitresses) and a few Jewish boys at the academy (and Irish Catholics among their teachers). And the rector's substitute at Saint Luke is a Pakistani. (He also happens to be an assiduous member of the Philadelphia chapter of the English-Speaking Union.) And the father who brings the child to be christened is Cuban, and his wife is Nicaraguan.

The two ushers are white Anglo-Saxon Protestants still. They each have — well, at least one of them has — a rather severe Republican face, with steel-rimmed fiduciary spectacles and tight, bitten lips, unsmiling throughout. But the rest of the congregation smiles widely, for a baby is a baby; and when the impressive rector moves away from the baptismal font and his younger red-bearded curate holds up the baby, saying something jocular, the congregation breaks out in applause, and two older women in the front pew help by holding and handling the infant while its mother pittypats back and hauls out a crocheted blanket. The father beams, he is thankful for the kindness of the people of Saint Luke's, who have taken in him and his wife. During his six years in this suburb he was never snubbed by them, indeed, by hardly any one in this village of a suburb, except for one tweedy shopkeeper and an old Cuban-American woman who had lived here for decades and whose grandchildren were now at Yale and Vassar. But Saint Luke is now half-empty, and the rector knows it, and so does the curate, who next year will decide to abandon the ministry and enter law school. And, yes, there will be a few more Cubans and Nicaraguans and Mexicans and Pakistani in the pews, but not enough to fill them, and at some future time the brass plates with the family names of the erstwhile pew donors will tarnish when there will be no one to polish them.

In the Episcopal Church of Saint Anselm there is a funeral. This takes place on a Monday, the day after that christening at Saint Luke's, and everything (well, almost everything) is different. This is late March, but Sunday was still a day of drooping winter weather, with nothing but a wet blustery wind suggesting a cruel coming of spring; and now, twenty-four hours later, it is nearly seventy degrees—Philadelphia weather, as some of the people say to each other. The brownstone walls of Saint Luke's exhaled a damp cold; the white plaster walls of Saint Anselm's exude a damp warmth. The burn of the sun coats the doors and the windows of Saint Anselm, they glisten and shine; some of the yellow forsythia bushes along the brick walk from the parking lot have begun to bud, and the high-backed white boxes of the pews of Saint Anselm are full.

Saint Anselm is in Chester County, a good thirty-five miles from Saint Luke, and a much smaller church it is, a white clapboard building with honest lines, American and not English in style, with a Southern touch. Having fallen into disuse near the end of the past century, it was rebuilt around 1925, financed by a family of rich horse-estate people, foxhunting Episcopalians. In the 1920s and 1930s the minister, brought from Virginia, hunted, too; his successor did not, but he was game enough to be part of the annual Thanksgiving service at Saint Matthew's (a larger church five miles away) for the Blessing of the

Hounds and then to say the blessing before the brunch after the hunt in the big house of his principal patrons, descendants of the founding family and still famous for their horses. In 1967 the custom no longer exists, though the Blessing of the Hounds still prevails and indeed draws a larger crowd than ever before, because something like the suburbanization of Chester County has begun, and there are more and more parishioners around. The present rector is a modest young man, liturgically rather than socially ambitious, though aware of the obvious advantages that the annual herb garden show and sale offers the parish, whose congregation now contains a new variety of Episcopalians, including advertising executives recently moved farther out from the Main Line and "the kind of Montgomery County people," one older woman sneers, "who collect antique cars and were enthusiasts for Goldwater." There are, however, few of these new people at this funeral of old Doctor B., who was the medico administering to ailments physical and sometimes psychic of many of the people of the neighborhood who now fill the pews, uncomfortably warm in their winter clothes but comfortable with the hymns and psalms, which they know, and with the brevity of the service, which includes a eulogy. There are handsome women and men in the mourning crowds; their faces shine as they move out from the church into the great spring sunlight.

K. and Anne are among them. K. says to Anne, "Wasn't the church full?" Anne: "At funerals it's full." And that is what Saint Luke and Saint Anselm have in common.

And that is what K. knows, too, since they themselves last set foot in a church several months ago, at another funeral. He did come with me to a Catholic church once. K. and Anne spent Christmas Eve with us in 1966; and when they said they were ready to leave, I said that I was, too. I was on my way to Midnight Mass—early, because of the crowd. K. said that he would come with me, if I did not mind, and I was more than pleased. Everything was pretty: a thin expanse of snow lay on the ground, and Saint Mary's Church glowed at the end of the silent churchyard. We had come early, as I was aware that many people were going to Midnight Mass; but as we arrived at the doors, a good twenty minutes before midnight, the pastor and his grim lay helpers shut them in our faces. "I have to be careful about the insurance," the priest announced. "There are too many inside." I was embarrassed and angry. K. was not. But then in my church, as in almost all the churches of the archdiocese of Philadelphia, Midnight Mass on Christmas was soon abolished, as was the Mass in Latin, Confession before Communion, and many other things besides. However, my church is often full, and not only at funerals, and I think that K. knows that, too.

"Now wait a minute. The Latin Mass was abolished — I mean, in this country — in 1964 and 1965, not in 1967. That is only one thing. And what are 'the many other things besides'?"

Many things, including the awful television language of the Mass and those awful guitar Masses with those bleating nuns in civvies —

"Well, those are gone now, even though the music is still very, very bad. The music and the liturgy in the Episcopal churches are often good, but you're not going to tell me that that is reason enough to prefer Episcopalianism to Catholicism. Or — and this may be the main fault of this churchy vignette of yours — that the latter is preferable to the former because most Catholic churches are still full on Sundays."

You know me better than that. But back to 1967. There was a sea change then, some of it palpable, some of it not, which I think affected Episcopalians as much as the liturgical changes affected Catholics.

"That will be — it should be — difficult for a historian to illustrate, let alone prove through evidences, and you know that. However, a more important thing: how much does it matter whether churches are half-empty or full?"

I do not know, and no one knows, except God; but it remains true that we may find *some* evidence in the behavior of people. That tells us something (though not much) of what they think. And something (though surely less) of what and how they believe.

"I think that you should have stuck to that woman's throwaway remark about the Montgomery County Republicans with their collections of antique cars and their far from classy enthusiasm for Goldwater. She was probably an old-fashioned Democrat. Anyhow, I see the picture; I fear, though, that your readers, perhaps especially the younger ones, won't. She is referring to those country-club and county-seat Republican women who in 1968 will crowd around Spiro Agnew and be photographed with him in the parking lots of shopping plazas. Sketching these vignettes may be your forte, you know, not describing what Anglicans think when they sing their psalms."

Perhaps. But that is not what I'm writing about — or what I want to be writing about.

1968

A MAN STANDS ON A SMALL ISLAND in an estuary, hesitant whether to wave once more to his friends. Their boats have moved off the landing, in different directions; one has already turned away in the middle of the bay and the light is fading fast. This is the central portion of the Maine coast, Muscongus Bay, and there is more than a touch of autumn in the air, since it is almost mid-September, the Saturday after Labor Day. This has been the last party of the season; tomorrow there will be nothing but packing, and either that afternoon or Monday morning these people will start the long haul of their driving southward, to the suburbs of New York and Boston and Philadelphia and Baltimore and Pittsburgh. Here in the bay (or "in the river," as some of them say, a habit taken from the Maine mainlanders) they have their island properties, acquired many years ago or inherited from their parents or grandparents in the early years of the century, when these ancestors had elected to advance from the humid torpors of the mid-Atlantic summers to the coastal cools of Maine, establishing their modest summer seats in the rustic austerities of these islands, each with a white wooden or gray shingled house of its own. A little below, both geographically and socially, of the enclave of Northeast Harbor, perhaps even as comfort goes, since these houses are not mansionlike, and some of their owners even now pride themselves on not having electricity; but they are well built, comfortable enough, with bottled gas and plenty of fireplaces drawing well. These owners do not have yachts or large sailboats, but their outboard motorboats (at least two are a must for each island house) are broad-beamed and substantial. Each year they arrive in June and leave after Labor Day, their arrivals less synchronized than their departures, which occur, habitually, on the same weekend or two. They are either retired or well-off enough to spend three months of the year away from their suburban or country homes and offices and occupations, save for the occasional necessities of quick midweek forays south via Portland, by air. Some of them take regular winter vacations or even own houses in the Caribbean. An agreeable annual rhythm of life for these American couples in or just beyond middle-age, as agreeable as the rhythm of their daily life up here in Maine, which includes frequent parties on one island or another, the hosts signaling across the water with a rigged-up flag at one house or with the bang of a small brass cannon cemented down on the front lawn of another but more usually going out on their boats, sailing in a circle, and shouting across: "Drinks at five!" And now, I repeat, this is the last party of the year, a little later than usual, which is due not to the weather or to the calendar in 1968 but to the consideration that their friends feel they owe to their host and his wife: for these two will not be leaving now, they will stay on, during the entire fall and perhaps even the whole winter, here and later upriver in the village of Bremen, Maine.

There is always a touch of melancholy about these last parties, partly because of the ever swifter coming of the darkness in the evening. But, while *partir, c'est mourir un peu,* the melancholy is not unpleasant; it is washed away by plenty of drinks ("did you think we're leaving all those bottles of gin for the scavengers?") and by the anticipations of their houses and families at home. But this evening is somewhat different. Now their host turns back from the small dock and walks up on his lawn, getting smaller and smaller when seen from this distance; he wears white shoes, white duck pants, and a white sweater, but soon he diminishes into a white wisp and then disappears. I must not overdo the melancholy because that would be incorrect. He and his wife chose to discount it some time ago. They had talked long enough about their decision to stay here. Self-discipline, including a stiff reluctance to gnaw over anxieties, has long been bred into their bones. Now that they have cleared up the glasses and the plates and brought the dishes into the kitchen, there is a very determined blaze in the fireplace and the prospect of an easy supper with the many leftovers. Their talk is all about practical matters, about the new man in charge of the winter storage of one of the boats, about letting the mainland chandler know that they will need another two bottles of cooking and heating gas, about the house in Bremen, about their daughter's wedding reception. There is even a touch of adventure knowing that they have now cast off from New York, facing the chances and the conditions of the coming tide of autumn and of winter by themselves, here, alone.

Then he sleeps badly. At dawn it is as if the cold Maine morning has been invading the house, as if its gray light hangs over all the furniture like a cobweb, coming relentlessly closer, depriving him of further rest. This is rare for him, for he usually sleeps well; he is in good physical shape, trim, still athletic in the sixty-sixth year of his life, little to worry about when it comes to his health or to the tasks he has set ahead of him, for he is a good amateur carpenter and handyman and sailor. But a new chapter of his life has now opened, which is like stepping over a threshold and entering a new room, closing the door behind. Yes, there is a sense of adventure in this, in the plans ahead of him, some features of which he indeed anticipates; but he knows, too (and so does his wife, even more acutely), that the purpose of leaving their life in New York for Maine was the seeking of a refuge there, and when either of them says, "We've escaped from New York," they say so because in people's minds escape and adventure are often the same things, whereas refuge is not.

He is now sixty-five. His great-grandfather had moved from Massachusetts to Ohio, his grandfather from Ohio to New York, his father from New York to Montclair, New Jersey, where he was born, and now he is back in New England again. His grandfather made welding equipment, and after he had become a successful manufacturer, he died young, in a tuberculosis sanatorium in the Adirondacks. His son went to the best schools money could buy, became a stockbroker, entered the middle-upper-class ranks of New York, and settled in Montclair, which became an upper-class suburb around 1900. The present son's schooling and occupation resembled his father's, but their personalities were different: the father was a secret drinker, he an open one, sometimes slipping over into the no-man's-land of alcoholism. But he got cured of that around sixty, indeed to the extent that now, a few years later, he allows himself to drink again moderately and keeps to that without difficulty. He is a very disciplined man, insistent and precise in his business, used to taking tiny draughts of pride in his old-fashioned standards with his clients and with his firm. But the composition of his firm has changed, and their practices have changed, and life with his wife in New York has changed. It was different from the way he had envisaged it, and he decided one day this spring that he had to leave New York, a decision that — perhaps surprisingly — met with no opposition either from his wife or from his children, though no doubt for reasons of their own; in his wife's case, her agreement was in exchange for his promise to spend their money and the two worst of Maine months, February and March, in a rented villa known to them in the British Antilles. Their son lives in California, their late-born daughter (this is 1968) is a college dropout, has caused many a worry for her father, and lives with the son of another retiree (an artist) in Maine: he is a lobsterman in the summer and a sign painter in the winter. At this moment they are up-river, in Bremen, in the small house that her father bought some years ago, one of those thousands of gaunt and New England Gothic square wooden buildings whose windows have a cold stare of their own, but in this case they have enough modern heating and plumbing and good pieces of furniture to be liveable.

The imperfect sleep did not discombobulate her father. It is a squally morning now, and his mind and hands are full with plenty to do. But when in the afternoon he takes his first drink, he knows only too well that this is now the middle of the autumn of his life, as it is autumn in Maine, and winter will come soon, with its beauties and difficulties arriving together. Outside everything is flat and gray, with the green tufts of the islands getting pale in the melting fog. In a few days he will be alone. His wife will be going down to Boston for two weeks, after which he will close and nail and pad and shut the house down, and they will go to Bremen, where their daughter will be married on a late October day marred by sheets of rain, though the reception at the inn will be bright and smart, arranged to a tee by his still mahogany-tanned, rich-voiced, alcoholic wife; in one of her three new dresses, she will be a beacon of elegance in that plain little church, as if it were a wedding in Montclair or Chestnut Hill. He will be there, with his trimmed white moustache, with his blue-eyed smile, and with God knows what anxious sentiments swelling in his breast. There will be quarrels and then loneliness. The price of refuge, but he hopes to have his hands full. There is work to be done on both houses, he says to people, to her, and to himself.

But there will be coziness in the yellow lights of the little houses of the village of Bremen, and the evening will have swallowed up the afternoon, and the fog the rain. As they walk into their house, now vacated by the bride and groom, who are on their way to Quebec in her parents' station wagon, his wife says to him, "Well, that's what she wanted. We always gave her what she wanted. I only hope that it works for her." What she doesn't say is "This is what you wanted, and I only hope that it works for you." But that is what she thinks, even as she knows that "for you" does not quite mean "for us."

"I fear that your crucial word is wrong. This couple does not seek *refuge;* they *retreat* from New York."

Perhaps the wife, but not the man with whom I am concerned. Retreat suggests the possibility and the potential desirability of returning, which is not what he wants. He does not want to return to New York.

"Well, he does retreat into the wilderness, which is a very American thing to do—"

You know very well that this is not the case. He may—I am not sure of that—be aware that he belongs to the last generation of family that has risen in the world (occupationally, financially, socially) and that this is no longer happening or even possible for what remains of his family. What he wants to do is to save what he still can, and I don't mean money: his remaining chance for a few reasonably safe—and healthy—years.

"The American dream turning into a nightmare in New York. You suggest this, but too faintly. What has happened to him in New York? There was this *bon mot* (I'd call it a *mot mauvais*) surfacing around 1968, that a conservative (of course meaning a neoconservative) is a liberal mugged by reality. Your man is not a liberal and not an intellectual, he is a not untypical though creditable WASP (forgive this silly term), and was he ever mugged?"

No, he was not mugged, though he witnessed something like a mugging. It happened in broad daylight, at a shining noon hour in midtown Manhattan, on Forty-Fifth Street, between Madison and Park. A black deliveryman and a white deliveryman were fighting on the pavement while shouting obscenities. People watched. Another black climbed down from a truck. Together they kicked and pummeled the white one; in the end they pushed him down to the pavement, laughed and spat at him, and then jumped into the truck and drove away. No one stopped them. He wanted to stop them (he had been in the Navy), but his wife screamed and held him back. What upset him was not the brutality and the ugliness of the scene. He suddenly realized that whites were now afraid of blacks. That hit him in the craw—

"That this was racism in the reverse, because in the past blacks used to be afraid of whites?"

This was something new. Blacks are a minority, just as Jews were a minority in Germany, but were there any Nazis afraid of Jews? And there was this in his mind too: that somehow these white people in New York were hopeless because they were responsible for what was happening, though not only because of the former mistreatment of blacks by white Americans. They were responsible because of their own acceptance of the cult of brutality and of ugliness. The law of the jungle had broken to the surface here, in midtown Manhattan, and the people there were not up to it.

"One street scene in New York, and he is off to Maine. You're going too far again."

No, there was more to it. Don't forget that it was you who asked whether he had been mugged or saw a mugging. It came together with other things: for instance, he was not an Old New Yorker, meaning that he was more keenly aware of what he saw as the decay of the city than some of the Old New Yorkers who thought (thought, rather than felt) that New York has always meant change and that they must stay reconciled to that. He saw, more keenly than others, the quick decay of all those monumental buildings only a few decades after their and his youth, when they had been the wonders of the world, not only because of their majestic presence but because of the opulence of their decorations, which had been made possible because of the abundance of an American civilization. His office was on Park Avenue South, and he saw the signs of that devolution every day. The crenellations and the machicolations of the bastions of American prosperity were crumbling. Not only did he see the stucco replaced by plastic inside those buildings, but he was dismayed by what was going on within his firm. The coming of new people and their doings, cutting corners, and I do not of course mean the physical rearrangement of the office but the novel practices of people that were distasteful to him. So he was ready to retire, in more than one way. He knew that he was more and more out of place and that these people knew that. And of course there was his place in Maine.

"But isn't that retreat — or, all right, refuge — in Maine an illusion, too?"

I hope not. But about New England . . . well, somewhere in my files there is a poem from the April 1945 *Atlantic*, "Indian Summer," by someone whose name is unknown to me, a Constance Carrier:

> New England is a savage still at heart,
> hiding in every empty cellar-hole,

in ambush at the edge of every field,
lurking behind each granite-ridden knoll.

The gaudy violence of an autumn day
prevails against white house and whiter steeple:
the scarlet leaves, like feathered arrows flying
blow in the wind above an alien people.

This is a land unconquered and aloof,
secret and harsh and ribbed with stubborn stone.
As watchful as an Indian warrior waiting,
it keeps an ancient silence of its own.

"All right, though not a great poem. And I don't know how pertinent it is for 1968. Let me remind you that I was in Brunswick, Maine, in 1968 and found that there were at least five barbershops on the main street. The land unconquered and aloof had been conquered by the tourist industry."

Conquered, or merely overrun? Well, at least partly so. But I am anxious not so much about this man's illusions of Maine, where he knows things and most of the people well enough. I am anxious about his old age, which, despite his excellent physical and existential condition, will now be coming fast. Yes, old age *may* bring some wisdom — but it brings more tiredness than wisdom. And that tiredness (whether it includes wisdom or not) is the soft deepening feeling and recognition of what one is, leaving behind the feeling and the recognition of what one wants to be. That may include wisdom — but not necessarily so.

1969

THE MORNING AFTER CHRISTMAS in 1969 K. suddenly died. They had had a Christmas family dinner the day before, somewhat later in the afternoon than was their custom. Anne was a bit harrassed and perhaps even irritated; K. was unusually quiet. He forgot, as he had often before, to put the white wine in the fridge (Anne yanked it from his hands and put it out in the cold against the garage wall), and later he forgot to open it in time; but the main source of her really very temporary displeasure was the weather: a day of icy rain. But the dinner went on nicely, and the grandchildren liked their presents and were funny at times. After dinner, when they moved to the living room, which was still strewn with the detritus of wrappings and packages, there was some talk about their son's kidney troubles and the prospect that one of them may have to be removed. K. said that he'd give him one of his kidneys; they do transplant them now, you know. "Dad, I don't think I'd need that," the son said, and that was that. He and his family left early, because of the icy roads. After about nine—the television was on, but they weren't watching it much—K. said to Anne that he had a sharp pain in his left side and could not move one of his legs and his arm. Anne was more than worried; she had an odd, dark premonition. Their doctor they could not raise that night. Given Christmas, almost an hour passed before the ambulance arrived. The emergency room and the corridors of the hospital rang with emptiness. They were antiseptic, overheated, and bereft of human presences. A lone Iranian intern had to decide whether to place K. in the cardiac section or in Intensive Care. K. smiled but he could not raise his arm. They put him in Intensive Care; he was alone in a large room. He pressed Anne's hand. "I'll be all right tomorrow," he said. Anne went home in a taxi, alone on the dark roads, with her mind racing fast and her heart clutched frozen. To her surprise, she went easily to sleep. She woke at half past six, put out the dog, and drove to the hospital on a bright morning; it was bright enough to be cruel. When she had closed the front door the telephone began to ring, but she chose not to go back for it. It was the hospital, calling to tell her that her husband was doing badly. When she walked into the hospital, through the Emergency entrance, she knew that there was something awful behind that morning brightness. As she left the elevator on the second floor, the head nurse looked up from her desk, stood up, and took her hand. "Your husband just died," she said. The two other nurses looked at her with the sincere custom of awe.

"Near morning [he] slipped as gently out of life as he had passed through." That is a sentence from a short story by John McGahern, an Irish writer, a sentence on which I cannot improve.

I wrote that he died "suddenly," but perhaps that is not quite right. In that very moment Anne knew something that I think most of us experience at some time in our lives. When something bad unexpectedly happens to us — whether a physical or mental blow — we are shocked rather than surprised, because somehow we know that, yes, we should have thought of this, in part because we have been foolish enough not to pay attention to the signs foretelling this, and in part because of the feeling that, yes, of course we have deserved this. (The mixture of this sudden sense varies from person to person, but some measure of that compound is always there — perhaps because of the presence of divinity in every human heart?) Enough of this, however. There *were* obvious signs of which Anne had been quite aware: K.'s blood pressure, his growing quietness during the past few months, including his unspoken worry and reaction to his son's illness. And that incident two months before. Stephanie and I were in their car with them; K. drove. It was a Sunday afternoon, we were returning from having cocktails with friends; it was a golden Chester County October twilight. "Well, at least they [meaning the developers] haven't destroyed much around here," S. said to Anne. "It hasn't really changed much in the last twenty years." I was in exuberant high spirits, lifted by drinks and by the sights of a landscape that has meant more to me than to K. the painter, to whom it naturally came as part of his heritage. "I'm glad *John* isn't driving," S. said. K. was a cautious driver, but he knew these roads all around, turning left and right at stop signs on short stretches until we came out on the three-lane highway. A minute later came the crash. Three boys on an overpass threw a big rock at the car. It shattered the windshield. It did not quite break through the windshield; there was a starburst of glass but no one was hurt; the ugly gray chunk of concrete rolled off the hood. We didn't pull over; Anne shouted, "Go on!" A mile or so away there was a parking lot, with a supermarket that smelled of soap. I never saw K. so shocked. His hands were trembling for long minutes afterward. "I don't understand." "I can't understand," he kept saying for a long time. For a fraction of a moment he had seen those boys laughing.

That memory stayed with him, I fear, until his death, for the perception (and the idea) of purposeless evil, of youthful evil, was so alien to him. Barbarism, to him, was a passing phenomenon of youth in the history of a person or of a country or of a civilization, a stage to be rapidly outgrown. He did not know history enough.

I know enough history, and perhaps too much (too much: all knowledge being a question of quality, not of quantity). Now I am in an Episcopal church, at K.'s funeral service, the day before New Year's Eve. For some reason the service is in the late afternoon, not in the morning. The church is full of families and of our friends. Contradictory impressions float in my mind. The service is like the old Catholic Mass, and the English language of it is good, and the music is good. And I know that all of this belongs to the Modern Age, and now to the end of the Modern Age, because the Anglican Church was, after all, one product of that age, and God save its remnants: but there is no sacred mystery left. At some future — and, for me, irrevocably distant — time, will there be a barbarian Catholic Mass with one or two touches of unearthly and mysterious beauty? Perhaps. I won't live to see it.

The lights of the brass chandeliers of the church reflect in its large windows. It is dark now. My eyes are drawn to the red and gold lights in those windows. It is as if I were seeing tall red apartment houses built early in this century, with their Queen Anne gables, with some of their windows alit, glistening at nighttime — as if this church were not in a southern Pennsylvania field, on the verges of the American Southland, but somewhere in a northern bourgeois setting, in a secluded park in the midst of a great wintry city, separated by only a few hundred feet from those apartment houses from where a few old people, old women in their old fur coats, some with smart silk scarves over their heads, can walk to this surviving urban and urbane church even in rain, wind, or snow. I imagine this and see it, sight and imagination being simultaneous; neither can exist without the other. Well, my imagination is still vitalized by scenes of the Bourgeois Age, which is what the Modern Age will be called one day.

I miss and I will miss K. very much.

"Well, I am shocked and surprised. You said that your book will end in 1991. You killed him off twenty-two years early. Why?"

Very simple. Self-indulgence, I fear. I found — some time ago during this writing — that I would run out of vignettes after the sixties. The 1970s and the 1980s — they do not inspire me enough.

" 'Inspire'? Or 'interest'?"

Both. And I've become older. But there is another, connected reason for stopping at the end of 1969. It was over then — for Anglo-Saxon America, I mean.

"Will you tell me what you mean? This is too much."

What I mean is that the mutations of the sixties — beneath them, of course, in the great, slow earth slides of behavior and belief — have remained with us till this day, and their consequences will remain for a long time to come. I am not thinking of the stupidities of the radicalism and of the young of the sixties: that did not matter, because they were as conformist as young people always are; they were not revolutionaries, they were only playing at being revolutionaries. I am not thinking of politics, either, for what the sixties led to was the collapse of more and more illusions, from which the so-called conservatives were to profit, though only for a while. What I have in mind is the erosion of beliefs and of institutions and of manners and morals and habits that can no longer be restored. The pendulum never swings *back*. History is not a mechanical clock.

"Well, here is another subject of a difficult book which you won't ever write. Come clean now. You have been writing about the decline not of the West but of the Anglo-American upper class. But did they not deserve their fate?"

I cannot answer that. But perhaps *fate* is not the operative word. Their troubles began to rise when they began to abandon their belief in their destiny—and the substitution for that was their belief in fate. When they—and it came naturally, alas, to most of them—found it necessary to believe Science, Darwin, et cetera as the incontrovertible kind of reality in the world (including popular sovereignty, of course), once they believed that the world and human nature, including their own, was determined, their minds were no longer muscular enough to resist that. Yes, already a hundred years before the 1960s, it had to be a Disraeli to ask whether man "is an ape or an angel. Now I am on the side of the angels." That was a quip, and whether Disraeli believed it or not I cannot tell, but at least he said it.

"Well, they had a good run—about two hundred years."

Yes. For those two hundred years they were, you know, the most respected and admired men in the world. Think only of the English word *gentleman*. The other day I read the memoirs of an old Hungarian diplomat, an old-fashioned conservative after my heart. He writes a beautiful eulogy about Franz Joseph, enumerating all the qualities of this last emperor of the oldest royal family in Europe, and the best thing he can add about Franz Joseph is that he was a gentleman. The history of the gentleman ideal has yet to be written.

"The trouble with you, among other things, is that you know many things and, I admit, you have flashes of understanding, but do you have to tell—I mean, write—everything? Isn't it enough to tell *some* things that you really know you know?"

You're absolutely right. But that has been the excuse for this book, including its odd—perhaps crazy—form, or call it genre. That is secondary, of course. You may remember that I was—once—mentioned in the *Times Literary Supplement* as "a conservative polymath." Quite wrong: I am a reactionary impressionist. But this book is not about me, except in my inevitable capacity as a participant observer of some people and some things. However: its theme includes us, too. We are all of us more conscious of what is happening, of where we find ourselves in history, than were any other people at any other time. The expression *find oneself* is right. Or it should be. The Romans near their end, the medieval people near their end, knew something was happening to them, but they did not know where they were—at the end of an entire age in history, I mean. On the other hand, listen to the voice of the Hungarian Catholic poet János Pilinszky: "The God exiled from behind the facts bleeds through the tissue of history from time to time. The traces left on it are so endlessly undemanding that it is questionable whether we can ever get at it."

"Well, you have tried—even though your focus was never clear enough. You know, your protagonist may not even be K. Your heroine is Anne."

You know very well that there is no protagonist in this book. There is only a thread, and I fear that a thin thread it is.

"All right. But what happens to Anne?"

She is still alive, a triumph of character—evident, too, from her love of and loyalty to her husband. There is a sentence by Robert Musil about that. "There are, in the relationships to those one loves, a great many problems that become buried under the edifice of the shared life before they can be fully worked out; and later the sheer weight of things as they have actually turned out leave one no strength even to imagine it all differently." That is all quite well put, but with too strong a touch of Viennese despair. There was—and is—nothing very wrong with Anne's imagination.

"Agree. And now let's have a drink. It's all over."

It's all over for this work, for this book, and probably for most of the world that I (and you, my alter ego) cherish and stick to, but God is infinitely good, since it is He and not Voltaire who allows and even prods us to cultivate our garden. And what a beautiful afternoon it is! Look at the color of the water. And at Stephanie's yellow and blue flowers. That heap of pots there is her job, but there are my heads of asparagus appearing and the raspberries are coming out. Let's try to coax her out of the kitchen and busy ourselves there. What a beautiful afternoon this is!

The Ribbon

N 1945 in the United States, a new era was beginning, for the effects of the Second World War were to prove greater and more enduring than those of the Depression. By 1946 many Americans began to be uneasy about the new world order, or disorder, including the specter of Communism (and what a minority saw as the domestic specter of a super-patriotic anti-Communism). And by 1947 the American government and the majority of its people took up the challenge of a new, superimperial commitment, not only to contain Russia but to fight Communism almost everywhere on the globe, whereby many things changed, and Washington became the political capitol of the world. And by 1948 the Iron Curtain was finally clanging down across the continent of Europe. And by 1949 the American presence in Western and southern Europe and the overall commitment to combat Communism were established and accepted by most Americans, while remnant leftists and Communists became a small, endangered species among them. And by 1950 (when the Korean War erupted) not only had Washington become the capitol of the world but New York had become the capitol of the artistic and even of the intellectual commerce of the Western world, the center of wheelers and dealers and of Abstract Expressionism — but what did that really matter? When the crumbling of its buildings had begun and thick paint was not enough to mask decay, and when the old American liberal optimism was waning in the rooms and on the faces of men and women in Manhattan apartments. And by 1951 the North Atlantic Treaty Organization included Spain and Greece and Turkey, none of them bordering the North

Atlantic. And by 1952 the endless churning of American social life brought ever newer people to its surface, representing new combinations of power and prestige, a condition to which the beneficiaries of a still extant older social order were adjusting themselves with little resentment and with little thought. And on the American political scene by 1953 the most important presences were President Eisenhower and Senator McCarthy. The latter was only half-Irish but his powerful following corresponded with the rise of the Irish in America (not that all Irish were McCarthyites!), who, because of the national ideology of anti-Communism and because of the national respect for organized religion, were for the first time regarded not only as first-class citizens but as more reliable patriots than were many others; being a Catholic was now an asset, no longer a handicap. And by 1954 the transformation of the United States into a "military-industrial" state (against which President Eisenhower made a single cautionary reference in his farewell address six years later, an address prepared by one of his more liberal speechwriters, but to which transformation his reign had contributed so much) was in full swing. Some of this was probably unavoidable, given the circumstances of the world at that time, but of course not all of it was. More significant was the great change in American political mentalities beginning at that time, the portents of which almost no one recognized. In 1955 a "conservative" (the quotation marks are intentional) movement in the United States was congealing. Less than thirty years later it propelled Ronald Reagan into the White House, and more Americans designated themselves as conservatives rather than liberals. Of this liberals and intellectuals were, and remained for a long time, ignorant. In 1956 the Hungarian anti-Russian and anti-Communist Rising meant the turning point in the historical development of the cold war, and the Eisenhower people were not honest about it. (They claimed that the Rising had surprised them, which it didn't; they did not even consider negotiating with the Russians about it, and the Russians' brutal crushing of the Rising did not really displease Eisenhower and Dulles, for it gave them yet another inestimable propaganda advantage.) And 1957 was the year of the rockets, the first a Russian one; but the Russians' supremacy over the Americans in the space race was very short-lived, and it was nothing compared to the pan-Americanization of much of the globe. By 1958 the British prime minister, Harold Macmillan, saw (and said) that Britain was something like Greece and America the new Rome, but that was too simplistic a view; not only was the Empire gone, but by 1959 the government and the people of Britain had finally accepted not only the end of Empire but also the unquestionable preeminence of the Americans. And that preeminence was represented by a new kind of American businessman or government operative abroad: a know-it-all American, Hemingwayesque or even Buckleyesque without any of the older American innocent abroad. Yet the self-assurance of this kind of a man was brittle. And brittle, too, was at least some of the scaffolding of the pan-American world empire in some places. By 1960 American airplanes were crisscrossing the stratosphere, flying back and forth with impunity across the Russian empire, until one of them was shot down and its mercenary pilot confessed (and the president prevaricated); and by that time De Gaulle and Castro and Pope John XXIII appeared on the world scene, none of them in American pay. And in 1961 John F. Kennedy was inaugurated as president, but that was really the end, not the beginning, of the great Irish surge to the front of the American scene.

And by 1962 the dissolution of what had been more or less traditional, or at least conformist, American ways of life had begun. And this would have happened even without the soon-developing "revolutionary" dissatisfaction with the Vietnam War—because the revolutionaries of the 1960s were only playing at being revolutionaries, and because the ideas of the 1960s, including "liberation" from this or that, were nothing but exaggerated and sometimes bizarre repetitions of the ideas and fashions of the twenties. And yet the effects of the sixties went on, involving not only fashions but all kinds of behavior and expression and of course what remained of family life and of the respect for marriage after it had been broken into shards after a decade of the false "togetherness" of the American fifties: suburban America split up along its black asphalted seams, while a national division about war in Vietnam was about to occur. And by 1963 conservative Europeans still nourished their illusions about America, while the illusions (and the lives) of American conservatives were no longer Gothic but supermodern. And by 1964 the rejection of almost everything that seemed—but often only seemed—to have been old-fashioned and authoritarian led to a short-lived new bohemianism, which, for the first time in the history of bohemianism, was also or pretended to be also chic. And this involved the emulation of the primitivism of the young, leading to national habits of puerility and the primitive emulation of proletarians, whether white or black, including fantasies about their power and brawn. And by 1965, together with the modernizing of this and that at the Vatican Council, this affected the religious rituals as well as the thoughts and the teachings of Catholics too. And by 1966 the transformation of educational institutions followed, as a matter of course, propelled by the opportunism typical of professional academics, whose ranks were now inflated, in part because of the massive monies on which the universities had come to depend. "Knowledge without integrity is a dreadful thing" (Dr. Johnson), but now not only the integrity but often knowledge itself was badly wanting among a new breed of ambitious academics and professionalized intellectuals. And even though this is a big country and in **1967** remnants of an older America and the presence of older Americans still existed—space being a blessing, difficult to destroy even when bulldozers and cement mixers are chewing away greedily and neverendingly at its edges—by **1968** Truman Capote, a talented American of Southern sensitivity and decadence who had become a malignant gnome with a sharp eye, thought he could do nothing better than to record the sexual itchings and the rash perversities of upper-upper-class women and men of New York—a New York whose stony streets were crumbling and wherefrom some of its oldest and established people had begun to flee. And in **1969** Americans were shot to the moon, not an everyday event, and yet something to which Americans reacted with much less fervor than when Lindbergh had returned from Paris, when many millions had cheered him along those great new stony avenues whirling with real ticker tape. Meanwhile, universities and foundations were establishing Institutes and Departments and Centers for Urban Studies at the very time when the great cities of America were shivering and deteriorating and when the urban and urbane bourgeois period of American history had come to its end. And the silly (and imprecise) acronym wasp had been coined and became current at the very time when the upper-class wasp predominance in what was left of society, of its mores and of its tone, was gone, too. The word *civilization*, according to the *Oxford English Dictionary*, first appeared in 1601: "to make civil; to bring out of a state of barbarism, to instruct in the arts of life; to enlighten and refine." *That* sense of civilization had come to an end. But it lived on in the gardens of America and in the minds of ever more scattered, but perhaps still numerous, men and women.